Business and Finance

Money Supply-Dec. (M1)

Annual percent change

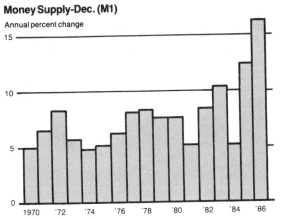

Interest Rates

Percent

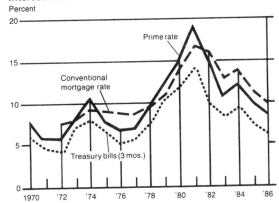

Common Stock Price Index (NYSE)

Index (Dec. 31, 1965 = 50)

Corporate Profits After Taxes

Annual percent change

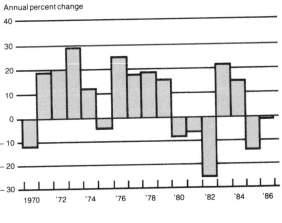

Business and Finance	1970	1980	1983	1985	1986	Average Annual Percent Change 1970-80	1980-86
M1 money supply, Dec. ($Bil.)	417	417	527	627	731	6.7	9.4
Prime rate charged by banks (%)	7.9	15.3	10.8	9.9	8.3	NS	NS
T-Bills, 3-month (%)	6.4	11.4	8.6	7.5	6.0	NS	NS
Commercial paper, 6-month (%)	NA	12.7	8.9	8.0	6.4	NA	NS
Home mortgages, conventional (%)	8.5	14.0	13.4	11.1	9.8	NS	NS
Mortgage debt outstanding ($Bil.)	474	1,475	1,828	2,267	2,566	12.0	10.6
NYSE common stock index, 12/31/65=50	45.7	68.1	92.6	108.0	136.0	4.1	13.2[1]
Dow Jones Industrial Average	753	891	1,190	1,328	1,793	1.7	15.2[1]
Pre-tax corporate profits ($Bil.)	75	237	208	224	232	12.0	0.9
After taxes ($Bil.)	41	152	130	128	127	13.8	-1.7
Gross private domestic investment ($Bil.)	44	37	502	642	671	10.8	7.4
Residential ($Bil.)	37	123	153	189	218	10.7	8.3
Nonresidential ($Bil.)	104	323	357	443	437	11.5	5.6

1. 1982-86.   NA Not Available.   NS Not Significant.

Source: Economic Indicators (July, 1987).

BASIC ECONOMICS

•

8TH EDITION

THOMAS J. HAILSTONES
D. J. O'Conor Professor of Economics
Xavier University, Cincinnati

•

FRANK V. MASTRIANNA
Dean of the College of Information Sciences
and Business Administration
Slippery Rock University of Pennsylvania

Published by

H39 **SOUTH-WESTERN PUBLISHING CO.**

CINCINNATI   WEST CHICAGO, IL   CARROLLTON, TX   LIVERMORE, CA

P R E F A C E

Each year seems to generate greater interest in economics. Our fast-paced lifestyle and world-wide political and economic events have generated more excitement about economics. In the past dozen years we have experienced double-digit inflation, food shortages and surpluses, tax cuts and tax increases, high and volatile interest rates, record federal deficits, a taxpayers' revolt, a flood of imports, and a host of other domestic and international events that have affected our daily lives.

The questions of why and how, the analysis of existing conditions, and solutions to economic problems are discussed in schools, homes, offices, workplaces, featured on television, and debated in the halls of Congress. To understand many of the social, political, military, and economic problems and issues of our society, it is necessary to know more about the nature and function of our economic system.

Basic Economics is intended to give the reader a basic understanding of the operation of our economic system; to explain the roles of demand and supply in determining prices, to compare the merits of competition vs. monopoly, and to explain the use of antitrust regulations; to demonstrate the role of money and its effects on our economy; to present a measurement of production, employment, and income; to show the current methods of economic analyses and the development of both demand-management and supply-side economic policies that are used to stabilize the growth of economic activity; and to relate international economics to our domestic economy. In short, the book endeavors to take the reader from scratch through a relatively high level of economic analysis in one term.

Basic Economics deals with both micro- and macroeconomics. For *microeconomics,* it treats the pricing mechanism, the role of demand and supply, elasticities of demand, competitive vs. monopolistic pricing, and the need and purpose of antitrust regulation. From the viewpoint of *macroeconomics,* the text deals with concepts of the economy as a whole, such as total production, employment, income, recession, and inflation, rather than with the problems of the individual or the firm.

The text is designed for a one-term course at the college level and primarily for those students, such as preprofessional, business, liberal arts, and agriculture, who will take only one course in economics. It may also be used for an introductory course for economics majors and is likewise suitable for a survey course for graduate students. In addition, the text has also been used successfully for teaching economics in management development programs.

Each chapter ends with a list of new terms used in the chapter and review questions that are also suitable for classroom discussion. In addition, there is a glossary, along with the index, at the end of the book for quick student reference.

A *Study Guide* is also available for student use. It contains such related materials as detailed economic data, economic problems, topical readings, and objective questions for each of the textbook chapters. The *Study Guide* is designed to enrich the student's understanding of economics and enhance achievement on examinations.

An *Instructor's Manual* accompanies the text. It contains more detail about the purpose, teaching suggestions, and discussion questions for each text chapter. In addition, it includes a bank of examination questions for each part of the text. These questions may be used, if desired, to test student achievement.

For the eighth edition of *Basic Economics*, all factual and statistical materials has been updated and/or expanded. New graphs have been inserted to illustrate scarcity, production possibilities, tariffs, and international exchange rate determination. In addition to the usual treatment of inflation, the eighth edition covers disinflation and deflation, and their effects on the economy. Other new topics include privatization, banking reform, monetarists vs. fiscalists, the role of nonbank banks, the decline of union membership, and the deficit reduction act.

Numerous comments have been received from professors and students who used earlier editions of *Basic Economics*. Many of these included suggestions for additional materials in the book. Although much has been added over the years, we have resisted enlarging the volume significantly through careful pruning of some topics and effective consolidation and integration of others.

We wish to thank not only those who assisted with the first seven editions, but also those who offered suggestions for improvement of the eighth edition of *Basic Economics*.

Thomas J. Hailstones

Frank V. Mastrianna

ABOUT THE AUTHORS

Thomas J. Hailstones is the D. J. O'Conor Professor of Economics and former Dean of the College of Business Administration at Xavier University in Cincinnati, Ohio. Before Xavier, he taught at the University of Detroit, Notre Dame, and for the U.S. Air Force. He received the Ph.D. in Economics from St. Louis University.

Dr. Hailstones has lectured throughout the United States and abroad. He is a member of the Board of Directors of the Clopay Corporation, Gradison Cash Reserves, Inc., The Ohio National Fund, and the Student Loan Funding Corp. He has been an economic consultant to many companies, both large and small. In addition to numerous articles for academic journals and trade periodicals, Dr. Hailstones has written or co-authored a number of college textbooks. His current texts include ones on introductory, managerial, and supply-side economics.

Frank V. Mastrianna is Professor of Economics and Dean of the College of Information Science and Business Administration at Slippery Rock University in Pennsylvania. Prior to this present position, he served in a similar capacity at Xavier University. He received the Ph.D. in Economics from the University of Cincinnati.

Dr. Mastrianna has been a visiting professor at a number of universities. In addition, he has conducted workshops and been a featured speaker for many government, business, professional, and civic groups. He currently serves on the Board of Directors of the Union Central Life Insurance Company as well as numerous other boards and councils. As founder of his own consulting firm, he has engaged an extensive work involving economic evaluations of businesses and human capital. Dr. Mastrianna has co-authored textbooks covering a wide range of economic topics. He has also served as consulting editor and reviewer of several others.

C O N T E N T S

23 The Balance of International Payments   440

PART 1

THE
ECONOMIC
SYSTEM

1 THE NATURE AND SCOPE
OF ECONOMICS

2 THE PROCESS
OF ECONOMIZING

3 OUR ECONOMIC SYSTEM

4 THE CIRCULAR FLOW
OF ECONOMIC ACTIVITY

1

THE NATURE AND SCOPE
OF ECONOMICS

■

Every day it becomes more apparent that economics plays a major role in our lives. Our decisions on what profession to enter, where to work, and where to live are based in large part on economic considerations. If we own a business, economic factors dictate whether or not we earn a profit and continue to operate or fail and go into bankruptcy. Economics applies directly to the earning of our incomes and to the spending of our money. Aside from the direct application of economics to our lives, we are also affected indirectly. Economic policies help determine the level of production and employment in our nation, the amount of taxes we pay, how much aid we give to developing nations, and how much of our resources we devote to preserving our natural environment. Economic measures influence the prices we pay, the purchasing power of our dollars, the availability of goods and services, and our standard of living.

ECONOMICS DEFINED

Economics means many things to many people. To some it means thriftiness, but to others it means the arranging of a large mortgage loan. To some it implies budgeting for household purchases or saving for an automobile, but to others it means the analysis of a multimillion dollar income statement. To the President of the United States it means the study of economic conditions of the nation, the presentation of a $1,000 billion plus federal budget, and the proposal of various economic measures that will maximize total production, employment, and income for the nation. The ubiquity of economics offers a challenge to the scholar in deciding where to begin the study of economics. As with any study, a logical place to begin is with a definition, since it serves as a point of departure for explaining, examining, and analyzing the various aspects of the subject at hand. For our purpose, we shall use the following definition: **Economics** is a science that is concerned with the production, distribution, and consumption of goods and services.

Economics Is a Science

We must keep in mind the fact that a **science** is an organized body of truth coordinated, arranged, and systematized with reference to general laws or principles. Frequently when one thinks of science, one thinks of the physical sciences, such as physics, chemistry, and biology. There are also, however, nonphysical sciences, which include philosophy, mathematics, psychology, politics, and economics. Economics is considered to be a science because it is an organized body of truth coordinated, arranged, and systematized with reference to certain general laws and principles.

Unfortunately the laws and principles of this science, economics, are not so universal or ironclad as the laws of the physical sciences. For example, physics gives us the law of gravity. From this law you know that if you hold this book 2 feet above the desk and then release your grip, the book will fall to the desk. You could try this experiment for hours on end and you would get the same result each time. The law of gravity is, therefore, a universal law that will hold in all similar circumstances.

In economics we do have a few universal laws, such as the law of diminishing returns. According to this law, if all factors used in production are held constant except one, and if this factor is increased a unit at a time, the size of the increments of output resulting therefrom will eventually diminish. Likewise, the laws of supply and demand state in part that when demand increases and supply remains constant, the price of a commodity will increase. Many other laws in economics are only general—not universal, for they apply in most instances but not in every case. For example, the law of consumption states that as the real income of a family or individual increases, the percentage of income spent on consumption will decrease. This is generally true. Most of us, as our real income increases, will save a larger percentage of our income and, as a result, the percentage of our real income spent on consumption will decrease. Every tenth individual, however, might spend more than is earned regardless of how much that person's salary increases.

In the physical sciences we know what reaction to expect when we apply a certain stimulus to a given set of conditions. In economics, where we are dealing with individuals, the circumstances may never be exactly the same because of differences in personality, environment, IQ, and other factors. Consequently, it is more difficult to develop hard and fast laws, and the study of economics becomes more difficult and complex.

Economics and Production

In economics we define **production** as the creation or addition of utility. **Utility** is our term for usefulness. It is the ability of a good or service to satisfy a want. We are producing whenever we make a product or render a service that is useful. The four most frequently recognized utilities are (1) form, (2) place, (3) time, and (4) possession. Form utility applies to products, which are tangible in nature, but not to services, which are intangible. The other three forms of utility apply to services as well as to products.

Form Utility.   **Form utility** occurs when we improve or increase the usefulness of a commodity by changing its form or shape. Undoubtedly we would all agree that metal in the form of a late-model Mustang is more useful than a heap of iron ore or a few steel ingots. Most of our factories add form utility in producing such items as furniture, toys, and computers.

Place Utility.   **Place utility** occurs when a good or service has more usefulness in one location than in another. The movement of the good to a more useful location creates place utility. For example, a Texas sports star buying a Cadillac will pay a certain price f.o.b. Detroit. However, as long as the car remains in Detroit, it will be of little value to the buyer in Texas. Consequently, the buyer will pay an additional sum of money to have the car transported to Texas.

Time Utility.   **Time utility** occurs when a commodity or service is more useful at one time than at another. Let us say that you are offered a position as the southern California representative for a Midwestern firm. In addition to the education and the ability to do the job, assume that you must provide your own car to call on company customers. If you do not have a car, you might ask your prospective employer to wait a few years until you can save enough money to buy a car. You would probably be told, however, that the position must be filled immediately. In this situation the car is more useful to you now than later, for without it this job opportunity may be lost. Rather than let the opportunity pass, you may go to an automobile dealer, select a car, and pay for it on the installment plan.

The person, company, or financial institution lending you the money relinquishes that money for a period of time to make a product available to you now. The lender is entitled to some remuneration, usually in the form of interest, for the service in creating this time utility. Production in the form of time utility is a big business in our economy. In 1986, about $560 billion in installment and other consumer credit loans was outstanding, and family home mortgages were approximately $1.5 trillion. Indeed, time utility is a potent force in our economy.

Possession Utility.   **Possession utility** results when the ownership of a good or service is transferred from one person to another. For example, a set of carpenter tools on display in a hardware store is of no value to the carpenter who may need them as long as they remain in that window. If the carpenter obtained possession of the tools, however, they could be useful to the carpenter in earning a living. In negotiating a transfer of the tools from the hands of the original owner or producer to the carpenter, a salesperson creates possession utility. That is true also of the transfer of the ownership of homes, food, clothing, and other items.

Economics and Distribution

At first glance many individuals may regard this part of our definition as referring to the physical distribution of goods and services from the producer to the consumer, or what is called *marketing distribution*. If that were the case, however, our definition would be redundant since we have indicated that such distribution is part of production because it creates place, time, and possession utilities. But in our definition of **distribution** we are referring to the allocation of the total product among the factors of production. In monetary terms it can be considered as the distribution of money incomes among the owners of the factors of production.

Factors of Production. Before a person or business can engage in the production of goods or services, certain prerequisites or corequisites are necessary. These are (1) labor, (2) land, (3) capital, and (4) entrepreneurship, known as the **factors of production.**

Labor. **Labor** refers to the time and effort of human beings involved in the productive process. Labor includes both physical and mental application by individuals and groups—both executives and blue-collar workers. It includes the application of human effort for the production of services as well as the production of goods.

Land. As used in economics, the term **land** is much broader than the concept of real estate. It includes not only real estate but all the resources of the land, sea, and air. Such items as coal, oil, lumber, chemicals, water, coral, air, and rain are illustrations of this factor of production.

Capital. Goods produced may be consumed directly or used in production. **Capital** includes those goods used to produce other goods. Capital also includes goods that produce services. Such items as blast furnaces, punch presses, buildings, bulldozers, computers, trucks, airplanes, and the like are considered capital. In a narrower sense of the term, capital is often applied to money. From an economic point of view this is correct insofar as money can be used to purchase the equipment, material, and labor necessary to produce other goods.

Entrepreneurship. **Entrepreneurship** is derived from a French word meaning "an undertaking." The **entrepreneur** organizes the business enterprise and assumes the risk. This function is distinguished from that of the laborer, the landlord, and the capitalist. It is the entrepreneur, or enterpriser, who combines the other factors of production—land, labor, and capital—to produce the final product.

Today a renewed emphasis is being placed on the concept of the entrepreneur. Many universities and state industrial development departments are teaching special courses and conducting workshops in entrepreneur-ship. Many individuals have taken on the role of entrepreneur. Both in the United States and abroad, particularly in developing countries, there is a growing need for the promotion of business and economic develop-ment by entrepreneurs who can put all the factors together.

The Problem of Distribution.   In a self-sufficing barter economy, individuals produced for their own needs, and if there were any excess, they may have traded with their neighbors. Under this type of system, individuals generally used their own labor or that of their family, their own land, their own tools, and their own entrepreneurship to produce the goods they needed. Assuming the right of private property existed, there was no question about the ownership of the goods they produced or about the share to which they were entitled.

In our modern, complex economy, the problem is more involved. An individual who wants to produce must still use the basic factors of produc-tion. In bringing together the factors of production, however, the entre-preneur may use the labor of one person, the land of another, and the capital of a third. By combining their activities, a product is produced that has a certain value. Now the big question arises: What will be the share or remuneration of each of the factors for its contribution to the total product? In our economy remuneration for the factors of production—labor, land, capital, and entrepreneurship—is made in the form of wages, rent, interest, and profits, respectively, as shown in Figure 1-1. This is called the functional distribution of income.

The problem of distribution has plagued economists for nearly two centuries, and we still do not have a simple solution. In earlier days, most economists and textbooks devoted a considerable amount of time to this problem. Consequently, we have had a whole parade of theories about functional distribution.

Theories of Distribution.   The theory of distribution is not a single integrated theory. Instead it is made up of numerous theories endeavoring to explain how the remuneration to one or more of the factors is determined.

Theories abound in the determination of wages, rent, interest, and profit. All add to the complexity of the issue. If one studies any economic system other than capitalism, one will find that the theory of distribution differs. Thus, in a way, the theory is a product of our economic environ-ment.

Allocation to Factors.   Although none of the theories can adequately ex-plain how the remuneration to a particular factor of production is deter-mined, each adds a modicum of understanding to the method or process of its determination. For example, profits may arise according to any one of several theories or a combination of several of the theories. Furthermore, in determining the remuneration to any one factor, the other factors cannot

Figure 1-1   Functional Distribution of Income

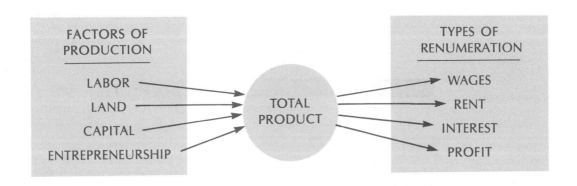

be ignored. Wages should not be so high that they leave an inadequate profit. Nor should wages be neglected in taking care of the other factors.

The problem of distribution or allocation is very much with us today. A labor union, for example, seeks a larger share of the total product when it requests a wage increase for its workers. Management may be seeking a larger profit and thus a greater share of the total product when it increases prices or reduces cost. Many of our current labor-management disputes arise from disagreement on this basic problem of allocation. Owners of capital may demand a higher rate of interest for the use of their funds, or landholders may raise the rent in an effort to increase their share of the total product.

Although it is impossible for every factor to increase its relative share of the total product, all can have a larger absolute return by contributing to an increase in the size of the total product. Thus, increases in productivity from various sources are the means of improving the return to all factors.

Today our national statistics reveal how much of our total production is being allocated to each of the factors of production. Approximately 74 percent of the national income goes for wages and salaries, less than 1 percent for rental income, about 9 percent for interest, 8 percent for proprietors' income, and the remaining 9 percent for corporate profit. However, this is not to say that this is what the allocation should be. To establish any criterion for this latter determination, it would be necessary to leave the realm of **positive economics,** dealing with what is, and delve into **normative economics,** what ought to be.

The attempts of the administration to impose voluntary presidential wage-price guideposts during the 1970s met with only limited success because, in large part, they froze the shares of the total product allocated to each of the factors of production. Labor unions particularly did not like this aspect of the wage-price guideposts. In this regard much objection was voiced against the compulsory wage and price controls imposed in the early 1970s and the voluntary wage-price guidelines implemented by the President in the late 1970s as a means of combating inflation.

Economics and Consumption

Consumption refers to the use of a good or service. After getting up this morning, you may have had cereal or eggs for breakfast. If you drove to school or to work, your car consumed gasoline. It is not necessary to absorb a good completely in order to have consumption. A good may be consumed little by little, day by day, such as your automobile tires, your home, or the soles of your shoes. Consumption may be regarded as the most important function in economics in the sense that it is the ultimate end of economic activity. Without consumption there would be little need for production and distribution.

Goods and Services

The last part of our definition deals with economic goods and services that satisfy wants. Economic goods may be in the form of wealth or income. Economic services are part of our income. This means little unless we elaborate on the meaning of an economic good and an economic service.

Characteristics of an Economic Good. To be an **economic good,** an object must be: (1) material, (2) useful, (3) scarce, and (4) transferable. Let us look at these characteristics.

Material. To be an economic good, an object generally must be material. Thus, your books, pencils, automobiles, shoes, and thousands of other commodities are economic goods. Certain immaterial things, such as ideas, are productive and can satisfy wants in the same way that economic goods and services do. They are not generally classified as economic goods, however, because they are immaterial.

Useful. To be an economic good, a commodity must have the ability to satisfy a want. Most commodities are useful. Examples of such commodities include typewriters, watches, homes, and thousands of other products. Since wheat is edible, it is an economic good. Ragweed, on the other hand, generally has no practical use and is not classified as an economic good. Oddly enough, it is possible that a good may be useful in one circumstance and not in another. For example, garbage in one community is collected and sold for feed or is processed into fertilizer. Therefore, it is an economic good. In another community it may be an absolute nuisance and may have to be incinerated. In such a case it is not an economic good. Frequently a use will be found for a previously useless commodity, and it may change from a noneconomic to an economic good. In fact, many industrial by-products have made such transitions.

Scarce. Scarcity is an essential characteristic of an economic good because it is this element, along with the usefulness of the item, that determines its value or price. If a useful material object exists in such abundance that anyone can readily obtain it without exerting much effort, it does not have an exchange or monetary value. Consequently, it is not an economic good. Such is the case of air, which is probably the most useful good in existence. However, who is going to pay for the air when all one must do is breathe it? You might object by saying that we pay for warm air in the wintertime and cool air in the summertime. That is true, but in such cases a particular type of air has become scarce and that is why we pay for it. In the winter we pay for fuel to heat our homes, offices, and factories or we buy an airline ticket to Florida to enjoy a few weeks in the warm sunshine. Generally, the scarcer the good, the greater its value or price.

Transferable. If an object is material, useful, and scarce, but not transferable, it loses its value as an economic good. For example, the gold in seawater is not an economic good because the cost of extracting it is prohibitive. Certain minerals and metals known to be present in the Antarctic region are noneconomic because at the present time there is no way of extracting and transferring them to a place where they can be of use.

Economic Services. Usefulness, scarcity, and transferability may be obtained from a source other than a material good. For example, a doctor administers to the sick, a lawyer defends clients, an entertainer keeps the audience amused, and an instructor helps you to obtain an education. Such activities are classified as economic services. **Economic services, then, are nonmaterial activities that are useful, scarce, and transferable.** Services are rendered by the laundry, the auto repair shop, the hairstylist, and hundreds of other businesses today. Presently, approximately 74 percent of our labor force is engaged in the production of services. It is estimated that by 1992, eight out of every ten workers will be employed in service occupations.

Types of Goods. In classifying goods in relation to one another, we can distinguish three principal types: economic goods, free goods, and public goods. As has been stated, an object that is material, useful, scarce, and transferable is classified as an economic good. A **free good** lacks the element of scarcity and, therefore, has no price. In this category we find air, sunshine, and, in some cases, water. A **public good** is an economic good to the supplier but a free good to the user. We often classify our public parks, our libraries, and the water from a public drinking fountain as public goods. In the final analysis, however, it may be said that since these goods are provided by tax money, which the user ultimately pays, they are economic goods. This same classification can also be applied to services.

Economic goods are also classified according to their use. **Consumer goods** are those that are directly utilized by the consuming public. Many items, such as books, tires, shelter, food, and clothing, fit into this category. **Capital goods**, or producer goods, are those used to produce other goods, either consumer or capital goods. Buildings, machinery, and equipment are capital goods.

Wealth.   **Wealth** may be defined as things of value owned. Wealth, then, consists of a multitude of goods. Estimates of the total wealth of the United States range from $9 trillion on up. The differences in the various estimates arise from three sources: (1) differences in opinion on what should be included in wealth, (2) the handling of intangibles, and (3) the valuation of the goods that constitute wealth.

As we have said, in general, wealth is the sum total of our current economic goods. Some experts measure wealth by totaling the assets of the individuals and the firms of the economy. Others add to this the property and the assets of the federal, state, and municipal governments. In counting resources, certain authorities want to include only those that have been extracted and are ready for use. Others want to include as wealth the total value of all resources whether extracted or still in their original state.

Many people think of money as wealth, but money, as such, is not wealth. It merely represents wealth or a command over goods and services. The more money the individual has, the greater the command over goods and services. Although money is not wealth, wealth can be measured in terms of money.

These questions concerning intangibles arise: Should stocks, bonds, and mortgages be included in our count of wealth? The answer is no. To include them, along with the physical assets they represent, would result in double accounting. What about education and training? It would seem logical to include these factors in our wealth since they are used to produce other goods and services. Many economists would like to see these included in the valuation of our wealth.

A question often arises about whether to use the original or the replacement costs of economic goods in determining their value. In the matter of intangibles, how do you measure the value of an engineering degree, the training of a doctor, the skill of a mechanic, or the knowledge of a schoolteacher? These problems multiply as the concept of wealth is analyzed, and it becomes difficult to obtain agreement on the exact value of our wealth.

Income.   Often there is confusion and misunderstanding between the concepts of wealth and income. Wealth is a stock concept; it is the total value of our economic goods at any given time. **Income,** on the other hand, is a flow concept; it is the total value of the goods and services produced over a period of time, usually a year. If we were to take a picture of the economy on the first day of a certain year, we might observe that the total wealth amounted to $9 trillion. Then, if we were to count the goods and services produced during that year, the total might be $4,500 billion. This would be our income. Does this mean that our total wealth at the end of the year has been increased by the total amount of production during that year? The answer is no, since not all income or production is counted as wealth. Most of our income is consumed as it is produced. Only that portion which is not consumed is added to our wealth. This consists of production in the form of machinery, equipment, and buildings that were not consumed or offset by depreciation during the year.

Although **real income** is the value of the goods and services produced, we frequently think of income in terms of money. **Money income** is derived from the production of goods and services, since the owners of the factors of production are compensated in dollars for their productive contribution. Thus, the money incomes received are equivalent to the total value of goods and services produced.

There is frequently a correlation between wealth and income. We use our wealth, that is, our building, machinery, equipment, and resources, to produce goods and services, or income. Usually the greater the wealth, the higher the income will be; for the more means we have at our disposal, the greater will be our productive capacity. The greater our production or income, the higher our standard of living. Consequently, it behooves a nation not to consume everything it produces but to channel a portion of its output into the form of machinery, equipment, and technology in an effort to increase production and to improve the standard of living for the future.

Thus, we see that our definition or concept of economics is very broad. It encompasses all our business activity as well as many of our social activities. Furthermore, such special fields as production, finance, marketing, transportation, and labor are related to and are a part of the study of economics. Economics arises in connection with the individual, the family, the firm, the industry, and the nation as a whole. It is evident that economics pervades our entire society and daily affects our lives.

ECONOMICS IS RELATED TO OTHER SCIENCES

As a science, economics is related to other sciences. Since some of its laws, such as the law of diminishing returns, are based on physical phenomena, economics is related to physics. Since it operates within a nation, it is related to the political structure of that nation and, therefore, to political science. Income determines the standard of living. A low standard leads to social problems. Thus, economics is related to sociology. Since it deals with human behavior, it shares this phase of its study with psychology. For example, the reasons why individuals spend or save are psychological as well as economic.

Economics is also related to philosophy. Economic acts are human acts, and human acts constitute a proper subject for ethics, a branch of philosophy. Occasionally someone advocates an economic doctrine that is in contradiction to a moral principle. In such a case, the moral principle should take precedence over the economic principle.

Economics, especially at the advanced level, is closely related to mathematics. Not only do economic theory and analysis today rely on the use of statistics, econometrics, calculus, linear programming, and other mathematical tools, but much progress has also been made through computer application to economic problems. In its relationships with both physical and nonphysical sciences and exact and nonexact sciences, economics is certainly related to logic, the science of sound thinking, just as any study should be. It is senseless to study any subject without adhering to the rules of logic, whether reasoning from a particular instance to a general principle or from a general principle to a particular application.

Prudential Judgment

But even in applying the rules of logic there may be many problems to which there is no one correct, definitive answer. There are many gray areas in economics. Economists may disagree on whether a firm should raise prices or cut costs in an effort to increase profit, or they may argue that it is better to advertise through television than through newspapers.

In many cases there may be no way of determining who is right or wrong regarding some of the conclusions. Much depends upon the prudential judgment of the individual involved. Since prudence is an intellectual virtue by which one selects the best means for the end intended, a **prudential judgment** is based to a large extent upon the knowledge and the experience of the individual. Some economists may prefer to engage the government in deficit spending by borrowing more and increasing spending. Others may think that it is better to hold spending constant and to decrease taxes, which in turn would require the government to increase its borrowing to maintain the same level of spending. Both are aiming at the same end, that is, to increase deficit spending, but both are trying to accomplish it by slightly different means.

An example of serious disagreement on economic issues occurred in 1986 when President Reagan sought to reform the U.S. federal tax structure. The President's objective was to reduce government spending, lower taxes, and narrow the federal deficit. Recommendations from business executives, labor leaders, members of Congress, key officials in the administration, and government and private economists were diverse. Although many supported the President's proposal, some wanted fewer federal spending cuts and smaller tax reductions. While some recommended continuation of tight money and high interest rates as a means of fighting inflation, others advocated easier money and lower interest rates to reduce unemployment. Situations like this often cause confusion in the mind of the average citizen. It is hoped that by the time you finish your study of economics, you will be better able to understand or reconcile such differences.

Economy—Only a Part of Society

Frequently when we study economics, we mentally extract the economic system from its total environment and analyze it in isolation. We find out what makes it "tick," what its functions are, and how it can serve us. We study the individual parts, relate them to one another, integrate them, and analyze the economy as a whole. After we have done this, we should put the economy back into its original place in society and study its relationship to the rest of society. We frequently neglect to do this, however, or we tend to ignore or de-emphasize the other aspects of our society.

Although we may analyze the economy as an isolated unit, we must keep in mind that it is a part of a larger unit, society. Consequently, after we have obtained our facts, established our principles, and drawn our conclusions, we must fit economics into its proper sphere and reevaluate our conclusions in relation to the cultural, social, political, and moral aspects of society. If we do not do this, we can be misled very easily. For example, economics may stress the improvement of our standard of living as a prime objective. To obtain such an economic objective at the expense of our political or moral welfare, however, could be highly dangerous.

ECONOMIC THEORY VERSUS ECONOMIC POLICY

In the study of economics we need to distinguish between **economic theory**, which develops the rules and principles of economics and which serves as a guide for action under a given set of circumstances, and **economic policy**, which is that action taken under the same set of circumstances. It would be fine if our economic policy always followed our economic theory. But economic problems or issues are often political, military, and/or social problems as well. Frequently, therefore, economic policy is modified by political, military, and social policy. For example, if economic theory dictates that we should maintain or increase taxes, we may find that during an election year the economic policy often yields to political policy and a tax cut is put into effect to woo the voters. In another case, in order to prevent, or reduce, a federal deficit it may be necessary to cut government spending in such a manner that it reduces social programs designed to help the poor people of society.

ECONOMIC DECISION MAKING

Once a decision has been made and an economic measure implemented, it cannot be undone. A physical scientist can experiment by applying a variable to a given set of constants to test and measure the reaction
of the variable. The experiment can be repeated by duplicating the constants, applying another variable, and measuring its effect. In this way
the scientist can experiment until the variable, or solution, that has the
most desirable effect on a given set of conditions is found. Unfortunately
the economist cannot keep all the economic factors constant. The economist
has very little, if any, control over them. In addition, once the effects of
a variable have been measured, the constants (economic conditions) cannot
be reconstructed exactly as they were before the application of the variable
to test a new variable.

The economist, or policymaker, therefore, has to make a judgment in
selecting the best variable (or means) to attain the desired objective. Full
employment, for example, is a widely accepted objective for the economy.
See Table 1-1. If the economy is not at full employment, as designated
by point *A*, there are several approaches to attaining full employment.
Although there may be widespread agreement on the objective, there
will be a variety of opinions regarding the best means of attaining full
employment, designated by point *B*. One group of economists may suggest
raising economic activity and employment through the private sector of
the economy. Within this group, some will propose that measures be
taken to increase consumption. Others will strongly advocate that it is
better to increase investment to stimulate employment. Those touting investment may differ in their approach. Some will claim that the best way
to stimulate investment is through the adoption of tax credits and/or accelerated depreciation. Others will vouch for increasing the money supply
and/or lowering interest rates to increase investment.

Another group of analysts, however, will stoutly maintain that it is
better to work through the public sector of the economy. This group may
also be split into two camps. Most will suggest working through the federal
government. But a few may point out that state and local governments
spend 50 percent more for goods and services than does the federal government, and therefore more may be accomplished by working at the state
and local levels. If those suggesting expansion of federal government activity prevail, still another question has to be answered. Is it better for the
federal government to increase government spending directly or to decrease taxes and let consumers and businesses do the spending? Once
this decision is made, someone has to determine whether the federal government is going to operate with a balanced budget or a deficit budget.
If the latter, one more question remains. Where is the government going
to get the money—from the public or from the banks? Each of these sources
of funds can have different effects on the economy.

You can see that to get from a position of nagging unemployment to

Table 1-1   Economic Decision Tree

Alternative Measures that Can Be Used to Increase
Economic Activity and Reduce Unemployment

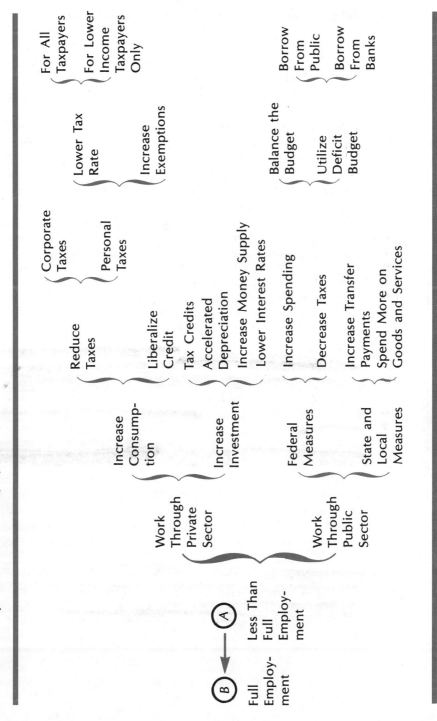

full employment there are several alternatives. There is no one best way. There is also no certain way, since all factors cannot be controlled. Each approach can have differing effects on the total economy and can affect some sectors of the economy more than others. But right or wrong, someone, after taking into consideration all the economic, political, social, and other factors involved, has to make a decision of what or what not to do.

In effect, the policymaker can design a decision tree similar to the one shown in Table 1-1, which shows some of the alternatives that could be selected in an attempt to solve the problem of unemployment. Some attempt could even be made to quantify these measures by assigning probabilities to them, which in itself leads to still more decisions and prudential judgments. Economic decision making becomes more complex when one realizes that the measures to expand the economy and reduce unemployment may aggravate inflation and make the attainment of stable prices, another of our economic goals, more difficult.

MICROECONOMICS AND MACROECONOMICS

The study of economics can be divided into two broad areas: microeconomics and macroeconomics. **Microeconomics** deals with the economic problems of the individual, the firm, and the industry. It endeavors to discover what motivates the individual to spend or to save. It treats the principle of supply and demand, the determination of price for the firm, and other similar factors. **Macroeconomics** deals with the aggregates of economics. It includes in its subject matter total production, total employment, and the general price level. It analyzes the problems of the economy as a whole rather than those of the individual, the firm, or the industry. It suggests ways and means of obtaining a high level of employment. It formulates ideas on monetary and fiscal policy as a means of stabilizing the economy.

Fifty or sixty years ago economists dealt primarily with microeconomics. Since the 1930s, however, a great deal of emphasis has been placed on macroeconomics. Today we study both areas; but since in this book we are mainly interested in the explanation of our economic system in general, the way it operates, the factors that affect output and employment, and the influences on our standard of living, we will concentrate primarily, though certainly not exclusively, on macroeconomics.

SUMMARY

Economics is a science that is concerned with the production, distribution, and con-

sumption of goods and services. It is a science because it is an organized body of truth coordinated, arranged, and systematized with reference to certain general laws and principles.

Production is a process that brings about the creation or addition of utility. Several types of utility exist, including form, place, time, and possession utility.

Distribution as used in economics generally refers to the allocation of the total product or income among the factors of production. The factors of production are labor, land, capital, and entrepreneurship. They are reimbursed in the form of wages, rent, interest, and profits, respectively, for their contribution toward the total product. Several theories exist that seek to explain distribution.

Consumption is the utilization of a good or a service. It is the ultimate end of all economic activity. Wealth is our total collection of economic goods. An economic good is one that is material, useful, scarce, and transferable. Any activity that is useful, scarce, transferable, but not material is an economic service.

Goods can be classified as economic goods, free goods, and public goods. Economic goods may be divided into two groups, consumer goods and capital goods. Income is equivalent to the total goods and services produced over a given period.

Economics is related to other sciences, such as physics, psychology, sociology, political science, and philosophy. Logic, a branch of philosophy, is essential for the development of sound economic reasoning. Prudential judgments frequently enter into the determination of economic goals and principles as well.

There is a distinction between economic theory and economic policy. The first deals with the rules and principles to be used under a given set of economic conditions. The latter deals with what we actually do under such conditions. Differences between the two frequently occur, since economic policy is often modified by political, social, and military policy. Economic problems and issues often can be presented in the form of a decision tree showing alternatives and choices. After proper analysis a prudential judgment can be made regarding alternative solutions.

The study of economics is divided into two broad areas: microeconomics, dealing with the actions of the individual, the firm, and the industry; and macroeconomics, dealing with aggregates such as total production, employment, and income.

NEW TERMS AND CONCEPTS

Economics	Land	Consumer goods
Science	Capital	Capital goods
Production	Entrepreneurship	Wealth
Utility	Entrepreneur	Income
Form utility	Positive economics	Real income
Place utility	Normative economics	Money income
Time utility	Consumption	Prudential judgment
Possession utility	Economic good	Economic theory
Distribution	Economic services	Economic policy
Factors of production	Free good	Microeconomics
Labor	Public good	Macroeconomics

DISCUSSION QUESTIONS

1. Do you think that economics will ever develop into an exact science? Why or why not?
2. In what manner does production include more than the manufacture and fabrication of goods?
3. Can you cite recent instances which tend to show that the problem of distribution is a continuing problem in our economy?
4. Can you name some commodities that were at one time free goods but are now economic goods?
5. How can the wealth of our nation be increased?
6. Do you think that an estimate of the value of education should be included in the measurement of our wealth? If so, how do you suggest that it be measured?
7. What is the relationship between economic theory and economic policy?
8. Explain why there are frequently different opinions or judgments among economists on matters of economic policy.

SUGGESTED READINGS

Boulding, Kenneth E. *Economics as a Science.* New York: McGraw-Hill Book Co., 1970.

Bowden, Elbert V. *Economics: The Science of Common Sense,* 5th ed. Cincinnati: South-Western Publishing Co., 1985.

Carson, Robert B. *Economic Issues Today.* New York: St. Martin's Press, 1983.

Friedman, Milton. *Essays on Positive Economics.* Madison: University of Wisconsin Press, 1985.

Friedman, Milton, and Rose Friedman. *Free to Choose.* New York: Harcourt Brace Jovanovich, 1980.

Fusfeld, Daniel R. *The Age of the Economist.* Glenview, IL: Scott, Foresman and Company, 1986.

Heilbroner, Robert L., and Arthur M. Ford. *Is Economics Relevant?* Pacific Palisades, CA: Goodyear Publishing Co., 1971.

McCloskey, Donald. *The Rhetoric of Economics.* Madison: University of Wisconsin Press, 1985.

Pearce, David W. *The Dictionary of Modern Economics.* Cambridge, MA: MIT Press, 1983.

Robbins, Lionel C. *The Nature and Significance of Economic Science.* London: Collier Macmillan Publishers, 1984.

Schultz, George P., and Kenneth W. Dam. *Economic Policy beyond the Headlines.* New York: W. W. Norton & Co., 1978.

Simon, William E. *A Time for Truth.* New York: McGraw-Hill Book Co., 1978.

Smith, James F. "The Business Economist at Work." *Business Economics,* 1985.

"What Good Are Economists?" *Newsweek,* April 1985.

2
THE PROCESS
OF ECONOMIZING

■

Our material wants are nearly insatiable. No matter how much in the way of material goods and services we obtain, there is generally something else we would like to have. On the other hand, the individual or family means (income or wealth) by which we obtain goods and services are usually limited. In other cases there may be an economy-wide shortage of the goods and services available. **Economizing** is the process of applying scarce means in an endeavor to satisfy unlimited wants, whether we are referring to individuals or to the total economy.

ECONOMIZING

Very few of us have all the means, or money, necessary to obtain all the goods and services we desire. Consequently, we buy first those things we need and then those we desire the most, and we do without the others. We consciously or unconsciously form a subjective scale of preference for goods and services and purchase accordingly.

As an individual, you are forced to economize daily. Perhaps you have deliberated about whether to buy a new car or to repair the old one. As a result of buying necessities, you frequently must give up such things as fine clothes, amusements, dates, and elaborate vacations. Even if you have a new car, mod clothes, and the like, you will realize that you had to give up other things to get these items. Thus, you are continually economizing when you apply scarce means, in this case money, to your unlimited wants.

Nations Must Economize

We economize not only on an individual basis but also on a national scale. No country has all the resources necessary to satisfy the wants of its people. It must use the available labor, land, and capital to produce the maximum amount of goods and services. The total output and standard of living of any nation are dependent upon the extent of and the use of the following: (1) population, (2) natural resources, (3) technological development, and (4) entrepreneurship, which are common terms for the factors of production when referring to them on a national scale.

Population.   Generally the larger the population of a given nation, the greater the total production of goods and services of that nation. Total output is influenced, however, by the age structure and educational level of the population, the size of the labor force, the skill and the mobility of workers, and the industriousness and psychological attitude of the people.

Natural Resources.   Since land, including natural resources, is an essential factor of production, it stands to reason that the greater the amount of such resources at the disposal of a nation, the greater that nation's productive potential. Natural resources consist of land space, raw materials, sources of energy, and atmospheric conditions.

The fertility of the soil affects the total output of crops. A nation with ample forests, coal, petroleum, iron ore, and other materials is in a better position economically than a nation that lacks these resources. Rivers, lakes, and coastal waters are important not only as means of transportation and for the development of power, but also as possible sources of food and minerals. The land also gives us our sources of energy. Heat, water, steam, electricity, and even nuclear energy are derived or developed from the use of land, raw materials, and atmospheric conditions.

Technological Development.   The degree of technological development has an important bearing on total production. People can produce more with the assistance of machinery, better technical processes, and the use of industrial energy than they can with manual labor alone.

The continuous increase in the standard of living in most countries over the past decades has resulted from the use of better machinery and equipment. The development of better fuels to operate new and powerful machines, the discovery of new chemical mixtures that result in new products, the processing of minerals in new ways which make them less costly, the use of computers, and other developments all tend to enhance the output of goods and services and to improve their quality.

Entrepreneurship.   Although people are able to make use of their labor, natural resources, and even capital equipment to produce goods and services, greater productivity can be obtained by a proper combination and direction of the use of these resources. Therefore, both the knowledge of how to utilize resources efficiently and the production and allocation of goods and services among the people are important. Leaders with foresight and organizational ability are required. There also must be a proper framework or economic system within which they can work. In this regard, the nature and types of business enterprises, the monetary system, the capital structure of various industries, and the extent of government regulation have an influence upon the entrepreneurial activities within a nation and, therefore, upon the total production and standard of living.

Scarcity and Choice

Even at full employment of labor and productive capacity, scarcity exists because we cannot produce all that society wants. Therefore, choices have to be made regarding what and how much of each item is to be produced. This relationship between scarcity and choice is often demonstrated through the use of a production-possibilities curve. Assuming full employment of labor and capacity, and the interchange of productive resources for different purposes, Figure 2-1 shows the production-possibilities curve (often called the production-possibilities frontier) for guns and butter.

It shows that at the extreme either 15,000 guns (shown at point *A*) or 5 million pounds of butter (shown at point *F*) can be produced. However, a combination of guns and butter can be produced, such as 9,000 guns

Figure 2-1 Production-Possibilities Curve

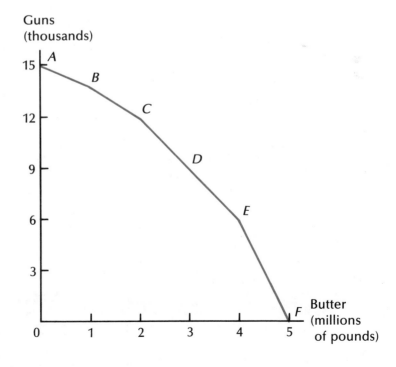

and 3 million pounds of butter (shown at point *D*). Moving along the production-possibilities frontier, it is easy to see that in order to produce more butter, guns have to be sacrificed and vice versa. In short, choices and substitutions have to be made.

It is also possible that a nation may not be producing to full capacity, as shown by point *U* within the production-possibilities frontier in Figure 2-2. This could result from idleness during a business recession or lack of maximum efficiency in the use of productive resources in a full-employment economy. It can be seen in Figure 2-2 that total production can be increased and better choices (for example, *C*, *D*, or *E*) can be made by employing idle resources and/or maximizing the economic efficiency of these resources.

On the other hand, even if the economy is maximizing the efficiency of its resources at the full-employment production-possibilities frontier level, it can increase its total production and improve choices by the use

Figure 2-2   The Expansion of Output from Both within and beyond the Current Production-Possibilities Frontier

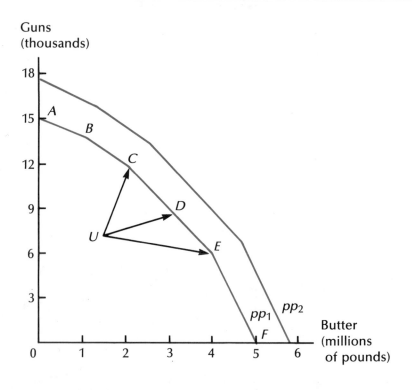

of technological development, innovations, and other measures that will increase productivity and expand its frontier, as shown by line pp_2 in Figure 2-2.

An analogy similar to the foregoing can be made for an individual or family by assuming that income is the limited resource available for the purchase of goods and services.

Economizing in the United States

In the United States we are blessed with an excellent combination of the four factors of production. First, we have a skilled, versatile, and mobile labor force of more than 120 million out of a total population of 242 million. Second, we have an abundant supply of natural resources. A study of economic geography will reveal that our resources are as good as, if not better than, those found in any other country of the world. Therefore, we have the raw materials from which we can produce an abundance of goods and services. Third, we have the highest degree of industrial technological development in the world. The average industrial worker has access to about $50,000 worth of machinery and equipment.

Today, machines and processes are also permitting us to make better use of brain power. For example, how long would it take you to do your math problems without a calculator? A computer in use at one of our large jet aircraft manufacturers can complete in a minute the calculations it would require a mathematician 7 years to do on a desk calculator. The more machinery and equipment at the disposal of the worker, the greater the productivity. Capital, as well as technological development, is truly responsible for much of our productivity.

The fourth factor of production with which the United States and other modern industrial countries are blessed is a high degree of entrepreneurial efficiency. We seem to have the technique and the ability for getting goods and services produced. We have developed a large body of managerial techniques, and we place considerable emphasis on the training of young people for positions in business. For example, nowhere else in the world can one find business schools at the university level to the extent that we have them in the United States. In recent years, however, a number of nations in Europe, Asia, and South America have been establishing graduate schools of business patterned after some of our outstanding schools.

The United States today has one of the highest per capita outputs, as well as the highest total output, of goods and services among the major countries of the world. In 1986 we produced $4,209 billion worth of goods and services. This was nearly double the output of the Soviet Union, which was second in total production.

On a per capita basis, we produced output worth over $17,000 for each person in the economy. Although the U.S. for decades had been

and in 1990s ?

the world leader in production and income, some nations have now surpassed or approached our level on a per capita basis. Output per capita in Switzerland, for example, is 111 percent of the U.S. level; Sweden, 76 percent; West Germany, 76 percent; and France, 67 percent. On the other hand, U.S. output per capita is still substantially above that of such major nations as Great Britain, the Soviet Union, Japan, and Italy.[1]

Our problems of economizing in the United States, choosing whether to use our resources to build highways or new homes, whether to buy a color TV set or to take a vacation, whether to go to college or to buy a car, are much more pleasant to deal with than the problem of economizing faced by many developing nations in which they must decide which crop will render the greatest yield from the land in order to alleviate hunger. But the United States and other industrial nations must start paying more attention to the process of economizing. With the accelerated depletion of world resources, the squeeze on energy, and the food shortages that have occurred throughout the world in recent years, there is a need to utilize resources and human energy more effectively to maximize output for the satisfaction of basic necessities and wants.

PROBLEMS OF SCARCITY

Unfortunately some areas of the world do not seem to have the proper ratio of population, resources, and technological development required for high-level production. In fact, we should consider ourselves very fortunate to live in a country that has all the requisites for a large output and a high standard of living. It is something to be really thankful for when we consider that one-half of the world population of 5 billion are living at the bare level of subsistence and go to bed hungry every night. Because of the lack of one or more of the essentials, productivity is insufficient to provide them with the basic requirements and necessities for a comfortable living.

Nature and Scope of Problems

Millions of people suffer from economic privation. Although mainland China, with its 1 billion people, is said to have ample resources, it lacks the capital investment needed for the utilization of its resources for the development of an adequate transportation system, and for the buildings, machinery, and equipment necessary to process the raw materials into finished products. The little that is produced must be shared by an exceptionally large number of people. Thus, the per capita output or income

---

1. Bureau of the Census, *Statistical Abstract of the United States: 1986* (Washington, DC: U.S. Government Printing Office, 1986).

India and Pakistan are in a similar situation with their combined populations of 770 million people, only moderate resources, and a shortage of capital.

Japan must economize very wisely to produce a sufficient amount to support 117 million people from the production of a land area that is about the size of Montana. Imagine what would happen if we were to crowd one-half of the people of the United States into the state of Montana and tell them to feed and clothe themselves directly or indirectly from the resources of that area alone.

Some areas are underdeveloped technologically, others lack natural resources, and some are plagued by a shortage of population. In colonial days, the United States had an inadequate labor supply for proper development. Thus, various schemes were adopted to help populate the country with workers.

Even today there is a shortage of workers in Canada, Australia, New Zealand, and some other countries of the world. In these countries there is also a need for capital. In fact, the Gordon Commission Report on the future economic development of Canada, issued several years ago, stressed the need for increased population and recommended liberalization of the immigration laws. As the result of ample resources plus technological development, Canada and New Zealand rate high in per capita income among the nations of the world. Thus, population may cause trouble either by being excessive compared to the land area or by being too sparse.

A Solution: Increased Productivity

Frequently when a country finds itself lacking the population and/or natural resources necessary for a high level of output, it can overcome the deficiency with ingenuity and fortitude. Japan, for example, has been offsetting its lack of resources in the past few decades with an exceptionally high degree of industrial efficiency. This permits Japan to import raw materials, process them into finished goods, and sell them in the domestic and foreign markets at a profit.

A shortage of resources or labor may be overcome by discovery of new sources, the development of new and better techniques, and the use of better machinery which produces greater yields from existing sources. During World War II, for example, there was much discussion about the adequacy of our oil reserves. Consequently, large oil companies, aided by government tax allowances, accelerated oil exploration activities. In addition, the oil companies, along with government agencies, began to experiment after World War II with the production of shale oil. Early attempts to extract oil from shale were hindered because the costs were prohibitive. With improved mechanization and the use of atomic energy, however, the production of shale oil became less expensive. Similarly, progress is being made in the production of gas from coal through a process of coal gasification.

Such examples of ways in which productivity has been increased can be multiplied thousands of times. Synthetic fibers for real fibers, plastics for metals, electric energy in place of water power, nuclear energy as a substitute for coal and gas, computers as a substitute for labor, and other similar developments have increased productivity. In the future we will witness more extensive use of geothermal and solar energy, commercial processing of seawater to extract its mineral contents, and new and better machines that will do things we now consider highly improbable. All such developments will ease the problem of economizing by obtaining more productivity from existing resources.

Aid to Developing Nations

Many nations, however, do not have the resources, the skilled labor force, or the technological ability to make offsetting changes for improvement in their standard of living. Furthermore, many of them are producing at the level of subsistence and are unable to devote resources to capital formation. Approximately one-third of the world's total countries have annual per capita output of $2,000 or less as compared with annual per capita output of more than $17,000 in the United States and $10,000 or more in most developed nations. Many developing nations, especially those in which the rate of productivity is increasing at a slower rate than the population growth, need outside help. To alleviate hunger, poverty, and sickness, they need short-term aid in the form of food, clothing, and medical assistance. To solve their basic economic problem, however, they need long-term assistance in the form of technical assistance and the infusion of capital. It is for this reason that a blue-ribbon committee of the World Bank has suggested that each developed nation contribute an amount equivalent to seven-tenths of one percent of its GNP in the form of aid to developing nations.

SPECIALIZATION AND EXCHANGE

Productivity determines income, and income determines our standard of living. Therefore, it behooves each individual or nation to increase its productivity. One way of achieving this goal is through the use of specialization and exchange.

Nature of Specialization and Exchange

Specialization is the process by which an individual, a firm, a geographic area, or a nation limits the scope of its productive efforts instead of trying to produce everything that is needed by that economic unit. In this way the unit can become very proficient in production. **Exchange** is the process of trading the excess of specialized commodities over and above the needs of the individuals who produce them to others for goods required or desired by the specialists. We can produce more in the aggregate through such cooperation than we can individually.

As we have said, in our economy individuals, firms, geographic areas, and the nation as a whole specialize. Individuals usually concentrate on a particular occupation or profession. Most firms engage in the production of a limited number of items. Many parts of the United States concentrate on the production of certain products, such as cotton in the South or cattle in the Southwest. From an international point of view, Brazil concentrates on coffee, Argentina on beef, Cuba on sugar, and England on industrial commodities.

An economy of specialization and exchange yields higher individual and total incomes than an economy characterized by self-sufficiency. Specialization gives an individual an opportunity to become more proficient in one particular field of endeavor. Therefore, the total production is greater than it would be if each person endeavored to produce all the goods and services that each needed or desired.

Consider what would happen if the members of your class were to pool their financial resources, buy a plot of land, and then subdivide it so that each class member could build a house. There no doubt would be some poorly constructed houses among the group because very few of us have the necessary ability, knowledge, or experience to build a good house. Think how much wiser it would be to check the class before starting. Among its members might be an architect, an electrician, a few carpenters, some bricklayers, a plumber, and other skilled laborers. Each person could work in his or her specialized field, using the rest of the class members as helpers to do the unskilled labor. If the architect designed all the houses, the electrician wired them, and the carpenters, the bricklayers, the plumber, and others did their respective work on each house, the job of building all the houses could be completed much sooner and you would end up with better houses.

Limits to Specialization and Exchange

The U.S. economy utilizes specialization and exchange to a high degree. This process has played an important role in raising our standard of living over the years. The degree of specialization and exchange is limited, however, by the size of the market. It is not profitable to engage in this process if the sale of the items produced is insufficient to provide the producer with a decent standard of living, or if one cannot produce enough to become any more efficient than others. Thus, we must look at the market. If it is adequate in size, then specialization and exchange have merit.

For example, a tremendous amount of specialization and exchange and a very fine **division of labor** (breakdown and simplification of jobs) exist in the automobile industry. A few decades ago, if you were to observe the workers on an auto assembly line, you could watch the semi-built cars pass by an individual worker's station at the rate of 5 or 6 per minute. During the few seconds the car was passing through a given station, a person could do only a limited amount of work on it. As a result of the division of labor and specialization, each worker became very efficient in the job and more autos could be turned out each day than would be possible if each individual started from scratch and built a complete auto. Today the functions are still performed, but many are now done by automation, especially with the use of robots. When a company produces hundreds of thousands of automobiles a year, the process of specialization and exchange is profitable. However, it would not be profitable if the total demand for autos amounted to only a few thousand a year.

The size of the market is determined not only by the size of the population but also by the income or the purchasing power of the population. People cannot buy goods and services if they do not have the means to do so. The size of the market is also affected by the transportation system of the economy. The better and cheaper the system of transportation, the more people can be reached.

LAW OF COMPARATIVE ADVANTAGE

An individual, a firm, an area, or a country may develop naturally into an area of specialization, but frequently the principle of economizing must be applied to determine what should be the nature of a producer's specialization.

Absolute Advantage

When a producer is endeavoring to specialize, it will pay to engage in the type of activity in which the producer has an absolute advantage. Let us assume that a woman can average $750 a week as an engineering consultant. If she works an 8-hour day and a 5-day week, this amounts to $150 a day, or $18.75 an hour. Suppose, however, she must take time out, 2 hours a day, to type her reports. That means that she can engage in her professional work only 6 hours a day, or 30 hours a week. As a result, her earnings are reduced to $562.50 a week, or $112.50 a day. She would be wiser to devote a full 8 hours a day to her consulting and to hire a typist, who probably would do a neater, more accurate, and faster typing job at less expense. If she were to pay the typist $7.50 an hour for typing 2 hours each day, the consultant's net earnings would be $135 a day ($150 minus a $15.00 payment to the typist) instead of the $112.50 she would make if she did her own typing. Thus, she would be better off to engage in her specialty and to let the typist do the typing, which is his or her specialty.

Similar situations occur when one section of the country is more proficient than another in the production of certain commodities. Texas can grow cotton better than Iowa. Thus, it specializes in cotton while Iowa concentrates in corn, and the two states exchange their products.

Comparative Advantage

When each of two parties has an absolute advantage over the other in the production of a particular commodity or service, it is easy enough to decide the respective areas of specialization. But what happens when one party can produce two commodities or services more efficiently than a second party? Should the individual or the country with the absolute advantage produce both commodities for itself? Although the one producer has the advantage in the production of either commodity, it is economically wise to specialize in the production of that commodity in which that producer has the greater comparative advantage and to let the other produce that commodity in which it has the lesser comparative disadvantage. This is the **principle of comparative advantage.**

Let us again consider the engineer. Suppose that, in addition to being a first-class engineer, she is more efficient in typing than anyone else whom she might hire. She might be able to type in 1 hour what it takes a regular typist 2 hours to do. Therefore, she reasons that instead of hiring a typist to do the work, she should do it herself. Is she right in doing her own typing as well as consulting? If she does her own typing, she still must take time out, say 1 hour each day, from her consulting to do so. This means that she would net $131.25 a day (7 hours times $18.75 an hour). But if she hired the typist, she could devote her full time to consulting. Her gross earnings would be $150 a day; and after she pays the typist, she would have a net income of $135 per day. Thus, the engineer would be better off to specialize in that service in which she has the greater comparative advantage, and let the typist perform that service in which she has the lesser comparative disadvantage, typing.

An Example of Comparative Advantage between Nations

This same principle of comparative advantage applies to firms, areas, or nations. We shall consider an example from a national point of view. Disregarding other factors (exchange rates, transportation charges, insurance payments, the law of diminishing returns, and national defense), let us compare two hypothetical countries. Suppose that each of the two countries has 5 production units and that a production unit is equal to a certain combination of labor, land, capital, and entrepreneurship. Assume that each country devotes 3 units to the production of cotton and the remaining 2 units to the production of wheat. Assume further that Country X produces 30 bales of cotton and 60 bushels of wheat, while Country Y produces only 15 bales of cotton and 40 bushels of wheat. Country X

Table 2-1 Production of Countries *X* and *Y* before Specialization

	Cotton		Wheat	
	Production		Production	
Country	Units Used	Bales	Units Used	Bushels
X	3	30	2	60
Y	3	15	2	40
Total	6	45	4	100

would be more proficient than Country *Y* in the production of both cotton and wheat, as demonstrated in Table 2-1.

Table 2-1 shows that 10 production units are being utilized in a manner that yields a total of 45 bales of cotton and 100 bushels of wheat. Furthermore, Country *X* has an absolute advantage over Country *Y* in the production of both wheat and cotton.

Now the problem is to decide whether *X* should produce both cotton and wheat and let *Y* shift for itself, or whether *X* should specialize in just one of the commodities. If it were to apply the law of comparative advantage, *X* would produce the commodity in which it has the greater comparative advantage. According to our example, *X* should specialize in the production of cotton, for it has a 2 to 1 advantage in the production of this item over Country *Y*, while it has only a 3 to 2 advantage in the production of wheat. If Country *X* were to devote all its units of production to cotton, it would produce 50 bales. If Country *Y* channeled all its production units into wheat, it could produce a total of 100 bushels of wheat. Thus, the new schedule of output can be seen in Table 2-2.

The two countries combined have a total gain of 5 bales of cotton. Now you may ask: Who gets what? That depends upon the exchange between the two countries, but it should work out favorably for both. In order to regain its former ratio of wheat to cotton, Country *Y* would demand 15 bales of cotton, the amount that it gave up in order to specialize, in exchange for 60 bushels of wheat. On the other hand, Country *X* could afford to give 20 bales of cotton, the amount it obtained through specialization, in exchange for 60 bushels of wheat and still lose nothing compared with what it originally had. It is easy to engage in trade when one country needs only 15 bales of cotton and the other can afford to give as much as 20 bales of cotton for 60 bushels of wheat.

The exchange ratio of wheat to cotton will be set by bargaining between the two countries, and final settlements will depend upon many economic circumstances. If we assume that the countries are of equal economic strength, they might split the difference and set the exchange ratio at

Table 2-2 Production of Countries X and Y after Specialization

| | Cotton | | Wheat | |
Country	Production Units Used	Bales	Production Units Used	Bushels
X	5	50	0	—
Y	0	—	5	100
Total	5	50	5	100

17.5 bales of cotton for 60 bushels of wheat. Trading on this basis, assume that Country X exports 17.5 bales of cotton, reducing its total used domestically to 32.5 bales. This means that each country would have 2.5 more bales of cotton than it had when each country produced both wheat and cotton. In exchange for the cotton, Country Y would have to send to Country X 60 bushels of wheat. The amount of wheat remaining in Country Y would be 40 bushels, which would be the same amount it had under the first plan. Country X would have 60 bushels of wheat, the same amount it had before any specialization and exchange took place. The final position after the specialization and exchange would show a total gain of 5 bales of cotton: 2.5 for Country X and 2.5 for Country Y. Both would have the same amount of wheat as they formerly produced. See Table 2-3. In this simple example both nations benefited by utilizing the principle of comparative advantage. In actual trade, however, many additional complex factors must be considered, such as shipping costs and exchange rates.

Table 2-3 Gains Resulting from Specialization

Country	Cotton (Bales)	Wheat (Bushels)
X	32.5	60
Y	17.5	40
Total	50.0	100

Comparative Advantage in Practice

Much can be gained by putting the principle of comparative advantage into practice. Individuals make use of it when they choose one occupation or profession in preference to another. Large firms increase their profits in this manner. For example, large automobile producers can make most of the parts that are necessary for the manufacture of cars. They buy most of the parts from independent suppliers, however, and devote most of their time, money, and effort to the actual assembly of the automobiles. Other companies build stores, sell them to a second party, and then lease them back. This permits them to use their money and time in their retail businesses instead of becoming part-time landlords.

A large portion of the sectional or regional trade within our nation is based on the law of comparative advantage. As a result we have a cotton belt, a wheat belt, a dairyland, a cattle-raising area, steel-producing centers, textile-producing areas, and an automobile region. Since much of our international trade is based on this principle, we have similar areas of concentration throughout the world. For example, we see a heavy concentration of coffee production in Brazil, sugar in Cuba, rubber in Malaya, ships in England, and computers in the United States.

Limitations to Comparative Advantage

Specialization and exchange can increase productivity and enhance the standard of living, but a region or nation must be careful not to overspecialize. An economy made up of specialists without anyone to direct its overall activity may not be able to accomplish its maximum potential. Furthermore, undue dependence upon one or a few products by a region or a nation can lead to difficulty if the demand for those products fluctuates or collapses. For example, Detroit is vulnerable to business recessions because of its heavy concentration of automobile production. When auto sales fall off to any considerable degree, widespread layoffs in Detroit occur. Likewise, the economy of Cuba is largely affected by the demand for sugar, just as the demand for coffee has a major influence on business activity in Brazil. It is economically wise to specialize, but it should not be overdone. Some diversification in production is beneficial.

Whether or not it is advantageous to specialize and to adhere to the principle of comparative advantage depends to a large degree on the demands of the market. Since consumption is the ultimate end of economic activity, we must channel our human energy, resources, and capital into the production of those commodities that are demanded by individuals in the economy.

Military consideration is another factor that limits the use of the principle of comparative advantage. Even though it may be more costly to produce certain goods domestically, it may be wiser in the long run to do so if those commodities are essential to military production. In the event that a war should occur, a country may be cut off from its source of supply. This occurred in World War II when the Japanese invasion of Southeast Asia cut off the United States from its rubber supply in Malaya. As a result, we encouraged and even subsidized the production of synthetic rubber in spite of its higher cost. Subsequent developments in the production of synthetic rubber have made it lower in price than natural rubber.

SUMMARY

Economizing is a process of applying scarce resources in an endeavor to satisfy unlimited wants. Both individuals and nations must economize. Nations have the problem of making the best use of population, natural resources, technological development, and entrepreneurial functions to obtain maximum production. Economizing involves the relationship between scarcity and choice. The relationship can be demonstrated by the use of a production-possibilities curve.

Total production will be affected by the composition and age structure of the population; the size, skill, and mobility of the labor force; and the industriousness and psychological attitude of the people. Production ability also depends upon the natural resources of a nation, including land space, raw materials, energy sources, and weather. Technological development, in the form of better machinery and equipment, finer technological processes, or greater energy, affects production. Even with ample population, resources, and technological efficiencies, a high degree of entrepreneurial skill is necessary to get the goods from the raw material stage to the market for the finished product.

Some nations, due to the presence of more or better factors of production, have a larger output and therefore larger income than other less fortunate nations. The United States is among the leading nations of the world in the production of goods and services and the level of income.

Total production can be enhanced by the use of specialization and exchange, but it has certain limits. Specialization and exchange operate in conjunction with the principle of comparative advantage. This principle states that a productive unit which has an absolute advantage over another in the production of two commodities should produce that commodity in which it has the greater comparative advantage, and the other produce the commodity in which it has the lesser comparative disadvantage.

Whether the government is socialistic, communistic, or capitalistic, the basic function of any economic system is to provide the framework for economizing. There must be some way of deciding what and how much is to be produced, the manner in which it will be produced, and the means by which goods and services will be distributed to the people in the economy.

NEW TERMS AND CONCEPTS

Economizing
Specialization

Exchange
Division of labor

Principle of comparative
 advantage

DISCUSSION QUESTIONS

1. To what extent do you engage in the process of economizing in your everyday activities?

2. Is it true that an increase in population in a given nation will result in a decrease in the standard of living? Why or why not?

3. How will increased use of nuclear energy or other new means of power affect the problem of economizing?

4. Should the nations with an abundance of resources share them in some way with nations that have inadequate resources for the attainment of a reasonable standard of living?

5. Should the United States and other developed countries contribute an amount equivalent to seven-tenths of one percent of GNP in the form of aid to underdeveloped nations? Discuss.

6. The European Coal and Steel Community, established in 1952, provides for the sharing by several nations of natural resources located within certain areas of Europe. What is the significance of such an operation in regard to the imbalance of resources throughout the world?

7. Indicate some ways in which you or your friends practice the law of comparative advantage.

8. Do you think a nation should try to become as economically independent as possible? Why or why not?

SUGGESTED READINGS

Casson, *The Entrepreneur: An Economic Theory.* Totowa, NJ: Rowman & Littlefield, 1982.

Galbraith, John K. *The Affluent Society*, rev. ed. New York: The New American Library, 1984. Chapters 8–10.

Heilbroner, Robert L. *The Making of Economic Society*, 7th ed. Englewood Cliffs, NJ: Prentice-Hall, Inc., 1985.

Leftwich, Richard H., and Ansel M. Sharp. *Economics of Social Issues*, 6th ed. Plano, TX: Business Publications, 1985.

McNamara, Robert S. *One Hundred Countries, Two Billion People: The Dimensions of Development.* New York: Praeger Publishers, Inc., 1973.

North, Douglas C., and Roger L. Miller. *The Economics of Public Issues*, 6th ed. New York: Harper & Row, 1983.

Root, Franklin R. *International Trade and Investment*, 7th ed. Cincinnati: South-Western Publishing Co., 1988.

Rostow, W. W. *Stages of Economic Growth.* New York: Cambridge University Press, 1971. Chapters 1 and 2.

3

OUR ECONOMIC SYSTEM

■

Basic economic questions apply to any type of economic system. Decisions on what to produce, how much to produce, and what methods to adopt in allocating goods and services are confronted by any society, but the questions are answered in different ways. We shall first consider fundamental principles and policies in terms of the United States economy.

FREE ENTERPRISE CAPITALISM

A **free enterprise capitalistic system**, or **market economy**, is distinguished from other types of economic systems by the fact that the decisions about what and how much to produce, and the manner in which goods and services are to be allocated, are made primarily by individuals and firms in the economy. Both socialism and communism, on the other hand, advocate a considerable degree of government direction and control of the production and distribution functions of their economies.

Under our capitalistic system, capital goods are owned and used mainly by individuals and firms rather than by governmental agencies. This capital may be in the form of land, equipment, and buildings, or it may be represented by money that can be used to purchase these capital goods. The institution of private property is essential to a capitalistic system. This implies more than the ownership of real estate. It means not only that individuals have the right to own, use, or sell land, equipment, and buildings, but that they also have the right to the ownership of the fruits of their productivity. Thus, when farmers grow cotton on their land with the use of their labor and capital, the cotton becomes their property and they can dispose of it as they see fit. In a similar fashion, a firm that produces shoes is entitled to the ownership of the shoes and can sell them as it desires. After compensating the owners of the other resources that have contributed to the production of the shoes, the firm is entitled to what is left of the total revenue. This residual return is called **profit**, and profit is the incentive for obtaining and using capital goods to produce goods and services that satisfy consumer needs.

The Profit Motive

Under the free enterprise system individuals may offer their services to someone else in exchange for a wage payment, let someone use their land in exchange for rent, or lend their money to another in exchange for an interest payment. On the other hand, instead of selling productive services to another, a person can combine several factors of production to produce goods and sell them at a profit. But to operate a business, one must produce goods or services that people want and must offer them at a price they are willing to pay. The farmers who grow cotton and sell it at a profit are benefiting not only themselves but also society by supplying a basic commodity that is needed or desired. Likewise, the shoe producer is satisfying people's wants for shoes in addition to making a profit. Since the cotton grower and shoe producer may use the labor, land, and capital of others, they provide jobs and income for other members of the community. Thus, in a model situation the producer, in the process of using property to make a profit, will increase the well-being of other people. To be successful, consumer demand must be satisfied. In some situations, however, the producer may suffer a loss or may exploit people by supplying them with an inferior product or by underpaying the factors of production that are utilized.

In the operation of our economic system, the ultimate use of our work force and resources and the allocation of goods and services are determined primarily by consumer demand. Individuals express their demand in the prices they are willing to pay. Usually the stronger the demand, other things being equal, the higher the price that consumers will pay for a particular good or service. Through these prices, businesses obtain the revenue necessary to purchase the human energy, resources, and capital goods necessary for producing the goods and services that are demanded. The opportunity to make profits serves as an incentive for businesses to produce these goods and services.

If the demand for a particular commodity is strong enough, it will be produced. Sometimes, however, there is such a large demand for total goods and services that we do not have sufficient labor, resources, and capital to produce all of them. What, then, is produced? Once again, in a model system it is the consumers who decide. The firms and industries with the strongest demand for their products will have the revenue necessary to bid relatively scarce productive agents away from other uses. If consumer demand for a particular commodity is weak and the price offer is so low that it does not yield a profit, few resources will be devoted to its production.

The Role of Competition

Free enterprise capitalism, resting as it does on the institution of private property and on the profit motive, relies upon **competition** to make the system function. Business firms compete for shares of the consumer's dollar. In the markets for productive resources firms compete for scarce materials and energy. In a command economy, production quotas are assigned to firms by a political leader or a planning committee. Similarly, resources are directed to employment in various industries. When allocation decisions are decentralized, as in a free enterprise economy, competition serves to regulate the volume of output and the allocation of resources.

If competition is effective, the economy functions efficiently without an overseer. Through competition, consumers are protected against the marketing of shoddy products and the charging of exorbitant prices. The prospect that rival firms will offer a better product at the same price or a comparable product at a lower price forces each firm to maintain quality and to restrict price increases. Resource owners and workers are protected against exploitation by the opportunity of alternative employment made available by competitive firms. The possibility open to the resource owner of selling resource services to the highest bidder prevents any one firm from keeping resources in its own employ at depressed prices. In this way effective competition regulates the power of business firms, preventing any one firm from dominating the market. Each firm is free to pursue its own profit without direct concern for the overall allocation of resources and products in the economy. Yet the impersonal force of competition assures the regulation of production and the flow of resources toward the most efficient firms that can afford to offer the highest prices for the factors of production.

Of course, competition is not always effective, and it is seldom perfect. Sometimes business firms may be able to exclude others from the industry and thereby exercise substantial control over price, industry output, and employment conditions. When this happens, it is deemed the responsibility of government to restore competitive conditions. Rather than taking control of the industry or assuming ownership of the means of production, the central political authority is expected to impose legal sanctions against restraint of competition or abuses that are defended in the name of competition.

The guiding principle of competitive capitalism is that privately owned firms should produce the goods and services wanted by consumers in the quantities they wish to consume. So that firms may satisfy consumer wants by pursuing the immediate goal of profit, competition is relied upon as a mechanism for regulating trade. Only where it is believed that competition cannot be made to work effectively—such as police and fire protection or public utilities—does the government operate to influence or control production. Otherwise the government is expected to create and enforce laws which assure that conditions of competition will prevail.

Price as a Rationing Mechanism

Although consumer demand is the primary determinant of what and how much is produced, the decisions are by no means made unilaterally by consumers. Supply also has an influence on the price of commodities and, therefore, on the determination of what and how much is to be produced. Because of a shortage in the supply of particular resources, consumers may have to pay a higher price than they desire in order to obtain a particular good or service. In such a case, they will have to pay the price or do without it. Thus, price serves as a rationing mechanism to decide which consumers will receive the particular good or service. It will be those who are willing and able to pay the highest price.

Prices Allocate Factors of Production. In determining what and how much to produce, our capitalistic system works in a democratic manner based upon dollar votes. Other things being equal, the use of resources and human energy is determined by the total number of dollars spent on particular goods and services. Thus, the more dollars an individual or group accumulates in some manner or other, the greater the potential influence for determining what is to be produced. Although this is a democratic process according to dollar votes, it is not necessarily democratic as to personal preferences.

Since those with the most dollars have the most votes, inequities may develop. If certain individuals or groups acquire an excessive number of dollars, it could be detrimental to the economy in general and to other individuals in particular. For example, large amounts of dollars hoarded rather than spent or invested could lead to a decrease in business activity and result in unemployment and loss of income for workers and lower profits for business. Even when all dollars are spent, one can envision a situation in which an economy might be producing a great number of palatial homes, high-priced cars, and yachts, while the community is deprived of much needed low-cost housing. There might be much spending on entertainment and on frivolities in the economy in general while some families are short of basic necessities and modern conveniences.

Prices Help Determine Incomes. Through consumer demand, not only do individuals determine what and how much is produced in the economy, but they also determine, in part, the incomes paid to the various factors of production in the form of wages, rent, interest, and profits. Revenue from the sale of goods and services provides businesses with the means by which they can obtain labor, land, and capital to produce the goods demanded. The payment of income to the owners of these factors or resources serves as their means to purchase a certain portion of the goods and services produced by the economy. Although many other things (such as the productivity of the factor of production, its supply, government regulations, the presence or absence of a labor union and other institutional forces) have a direct bearing on the payment of income to each of the various factors, the ultimate source of income payments to the factors of production is generally the revenue from consumer purchases.

In a model system each factor is remunerated according to its economic contribution toward the commodity or service being produced. In turn, its contribution is measured by the price that the firm was willing to pay for it, which in turn would be limited by consumer demand. Thus, our strong demand for automobiles is, in part, the reason why auto workers have historically been among the highest-paid workers in the world. The income of a factor of production is affected, on the other hand, by its productivity and scarcity. If the supply of a particular type of skilled labor is limited, such workers will be able to command a higher compensation for their services than will unskilled workers. For example, superstar athletes and entertainers have special skills that permit them to command higher compensation.

BUSINESS FIRMS

The process by which we determine the allocation of our factors of production, the flow of income, and the final distribution of goods and services is facilitated by our business organization. Production for the purpose of satisfying consumer demand in our capitalistic economy usually is undertaken by privately owned enterprises. Starting a business involves a risk, but the opportunity for profit induces hundreds of thousands of individuals annually to try to become successful entrepreneurs. Some knowledge of the structure of our various types of business firms, therefore, is beneficial for a better understanding of the operation of our economic system.

There are more than 14 million business enterprises in the United States, exclusive of our 2.3 million farms. Most of these enterprises have less than 4 employees. Less than 1 percent have more than 500 employees. These large firms, however, provide the majority of all jobs in the United States.

There are more enterprises in services, 37 percent, than in any other nonagricultural category, most of them single proprietorships. The second largest category, wholesalers and retailers, makes up about 25 percent of the firms. In a recent 4-year period, the number of wholesale and retail firms increased by 11 percent. An 18 percent increase came in services. There was a 10 percent increase in contract construction firms, and finance enterprises showed a 14 percent increase. On the other hand, manufacturing had a 12 percent increase in the number of firms, but its total production increased about 50 percent. This unusual phenomenon resulted because the average size of manufacturing firms increased during this period, partly as a result of mergers and consolidations.

Types of Business Firms

There are four basic types of business enterprises in the United States. They include (1) single proprietorships, (2) partnerships, (3) corporations, and (4) cooperatives. Each has certain advantages and disadvantages.

Single Proprietorships. The **single proprietorship,** or one-person owner-ship, was the earliest form of business enterprise. At present there are 12.2 million individually owned businesses and farms. In a single propri-etorship one individual owns and directs the business. This person risks individual property in the business. If successful, the individual receives all the profit; but if the business fails, that person must suffer all the losses.

Ease of entry is one of the major advantages of the single proprietor-ship. Practically anyone who can accumulate a small amount of savings or can borrow some money can go into business. Another advantage is the flexibility of management in a single proprietorship. The proprietor can make decisions without having to obtain the approval of a board of directors or convince other members of the firm.

One of the biggest disadvantages of the single proprietorship results from the lack of distinction between the business and the owner. If the owner fails, creditors, through court action, may take personal assets, such as the owner's house and automobile, as well as the assets of the business, to satisfy debts. Another disadvantage is the difficulty of raising sufficient funds for a large-scale operation. It is also difficult to sustain continuity of the business over an extended period of time, since the death of an owner automatically terminates the proprietorship. The busi-ness can, however, continue under a new proprietor.

Partnerships. A **partnership,** as defined by the Uniform Partnership Act, which has been adopted in most states, "is an association of two or more persons to carry on as co-owners a business for profit." The partnership is usually found in small businesses that require a limited amount of capital which can be contributed by the partners. It is also found in professional practices, such as law and accounting. There are at present slightly fewer than 1 million active partnerships in operation in our economy.

The partnership has an advantage over the single proprietorship in that it can usually raise more funds to operate the business, since it can obtain funds from the several partners. Another advantage is the diversity of management that it permits. Responsibility for various functions of the business can be divided among the different partners.

On the other hand, the partnership has most of the disadvantages of the single proprietorship, plus a few of its own. Its continuity is uncertain, since the withdrawal or death of a partner legally dissolves the partnership, although the business may be reorganized by the remaining or new part-ners. In many respects the action of any one partner can bind the partner-ship. Thus, poor decisions or unsound commitments made by any one partner bind them all. Furthermore, since a partnership, like a single pro-prietorship, is not a separate legal entity, the partners are legally respon-sible for the debts of the firm. This means that the personal assets of the partners may be seized if necessary to satisfy partnership debts. Furthermore, each partner is individually liable for all the debts of the partnership incurred while that partner is a member of the firm.

Corporations.   In the Dartmouth College case in 1819, Chief Justice Marshall described a **corporation** as "an artificial being, invisible, intangible, and existing only in contemplation of law." Thus, a corporation is a separate legal entity apart from its owners. It is a "legal person" in itself. Contracts can be made in the name of the corporation, it can own real estate and other assets, and it can sue and be sued.

The corporation has several advantages over other forms of business enterprise. It has continuity of life, since ownership in the form of shares of stock can be transferred without dissolving the corporation. Through the sale of stock it can raise large sums of money. Unlike a single proprietorship or partnership, the corporate owners have *limited* liability. They can lose only what they have invested in the business. Furthermore, owners can pledge their stock as collateral for personal or business loans, whereas partners cannot pledge easily their interest in their business for such loans. Since the owners elect a board of directors, who in turn select the management personnel to operate the business, it is possible to remove inefficient managers. Additional funds for expansion of the business can be obtained by issuing more stock or by floating bond issues.

Although it is a very attractive form of business enterprise, the corporation is not without its disadvantages. It is required to pay income taxes, and the stockholders must also pay income taxes on the dividends they receive out of corporate income. No such double taxation exists on single proprietorship or partnership income. The state requires a fee for incorporating a business, and it often charges an annual franchise tax. A corporation can engage only in the business for which it is authorized. Before entering other types of businesses, it must have its charter amended by the state. Numerous reports must be filed annually in the state in which the business is incorporated and often in other states in which the corporation may be doing business.

One of the salient features of the corporate form of business enterprise is the fact that business ownership can be spread over a large segment of the population. Any individual can be a capitalist simply by purchasing a few shares of stock. Since most stocks sell for a price of less than $100, it is relatively easy for many persons to become stockholders. In fact, more than 42 million citizens (individually or through pension plans) own stock in the 2.8 million corporations in our economy.

Cooperatives.   A **cooperative** is a type of business enterprise owned primarily by the people who use it or buy from it. A cooperative may be incorporated and pay dividends to its stockholders. But unlike in a corporation, each shareholder has only one vote in managerial affairs regardless of the amount of stock held by the individual. A major difference between a cooperative and other forms of business enterprise is that the net income, after payment of the nominal dividend to shareholders, is distributed among the customers of the cooperative on a pro rata basis according to their respective purchases from the cooperative.

Although the consumer cooperative has been in existence in the United States for more than 100 years, it has not achieved national significance. A major reason for its lack of acceptance or success is the fact that our large chain stores and discount stores, operating on a low-markup, large-volume basis, give us commodities at prices that are difficult for the cooperative to meet. Nevertheless, consumer cooperatives are of some significance in many European countries.

In the United States, marketing cooperatives are rather prevalent in agriculture. There are 6,125 cooperatives that market farm commodities and provide farm supplies. In addition there exist in our economy about 20,000 credit unions, through which members can save and borrow money.

COMPETITION IN THE ECONOMY

In a market economy, production and distribution are governed principally by a multitude of independent decisions made by individuals and businesses. Buyers express their demand for particular goods and services by their dollar votes. Some buyers with more dollars and a strong demand for particular commodities will outbid others to obtain the particular goods or services they desire.

Producers in a free market seek the business of individual buyers by underpricing other firms, by putting out a better product, or by giving better service. Competition among producers restricts one firm from charging an excessive price. Competition among consumers for products helps the company to receive a reasonable price for its product. Competition among firms often leads to more and better products for the consumers at lower and lower prices. Competition is responsible for new products, new techniques, and improved services. Thus, competition becomes the market regulator of the free enterprise economic system.

Competition also implies freedom, that is, freedom to enter or to go out of business. It provides the opportunity to make a profit, but it does not insure against losses. Under competition people are free to decide how they want to use their labor and whether they want to work for themselves or someone else. The right to choose the type of work they desire is limited only by their qualifications. Landowners are free to utilize their land or to rent it to others, and the capitalists are free to utilize their capital or to loan it to others in return for interest. Entrepreneurs are free under a competitive system to combine the labor, land, and capital of others, provided they can remunerate the holders of these factors of production for their use.

In a free enterprise system, workers compete against each other for jobs, and they frequently change jobs. Firms compete against each other. New firms continually come into existence, and old firms go out of business. New ideas, new products, and new services are continually appearing on the market, each competing for the consumer's dollar. In a free enterprise system, the consumer is sovereign. The consumer approves or disapproves of products by a decision to spend or not to spend and by a decision to buy this commodity or that commodity.

Competition and Monopoly

The degree of competition that exists in one economy compared with another varies greatly. Even within a particular economy, the degree of competition varies among different industries. Furthermore, not all markets fit the model of perfect, or free, competition described in our textbooks. Various qualifications, restrictions, hindrances, and regulations are imposed, voluntarily or involuntarily, on individuals and business firms in a market economy. Monopolies and oligopolies, as we shall see in subsequent chapters, exert pressure on prices and output; labor union activities modify the free operation of labor and wage markets; and the government regulates many industries directly or indirectly.

Government-Regulated Markets

Frequently a market for a good or service may be more orderly and may operate to the best interest of the consuming public if the firm that produces the good or renders the service is regulated to some degree by a governmental agency. Public utilities fall into this category. Experience has shown that it is better to grant one firm a monopoly to supply water, gas, electricity, telephone service, transportation, or other services for the community, rather than to permit free competition in these fields. In exchange for the **franchise** that gives a firm a monopoly to supply a particular type of service, the public service commission of the state or the community maintains regulatory powers over the monopoly to insure that it charges reasonable prices and provides adequate service.

Agricultural markets are regulated in large part by the Department of Agriculture. A firm cannot engage in interstate transportation without the approval and regulation of the Interstate Commerce Commission. Airlines are regulated for safety purposes by the Federal Aviation Administration. The sale of stocks and bonds and the banking business are closely regulated for the interest of all concerned.

In addition to regulating certain markets, the government occasionally enters a business directly, such as the printing business and the making of rope for nautical purposes. At times the government enters a business indirectly, as, for example, the production of electricity from multipurpose water projects (such as TVA, Shasta, and Hoover dams), which also provide flood control, irrigation, and improved navigation.

Mixed Economy

Although the determination of what to produce, the amount to be produced, the prices to be charged, and the compensation to the factors of production is generally based upon the free decisions of individuals and firms, our economy is often referred to as a **mixed economy.** This stems from the fact that, even though the market economy is characterized by competition and freedom, the competition is not perfect and the freedom is not unqualified.

Some decisions regarding production, such as the building of roads, schools, and municipal buildings, are made by federal, state, and local governments, and the use of labor in and outside of the armed services is determined in part by military authorities.

Regulated public utilities exist along with unregulated industries; monopolies stand side by side with highly competitive firms; giant corporations compete with small, single proprietorships; the government regulates some industries and not others; and government operations occasionally compete with private industry. Since we have many types of competition and the economy contains both free and regulated markets, it is appropriate to refer to it as a mixed economy.

ROLE OF THE GOVERNMENT IN THE ECONOMY

The concept of a mixed economy brings into focus an important question: What should be the role of the government in the economy? Should it be active or passive? Should it regulate or not regulate? Should it engage directly in business? Should it encourage business activity or not? Historically the role of the government in our nation's economy has been one of nonintervention. In the past several decades, however, there has been a tendency to move in the direction of increased government actions.

Economic Liberalism

Since economic liberalism was the prevailing economic philosophy in much of the 19th and early 20th centuries, our economy developed within its framework. Economic liberalism implied freedom of action for the individual and the business enterprise. The major tenets of economic liberalism were free trade, self-interest, private property, laissez-faire, and competition.

According to this philosophy, individuals were free to seek their own occupations, were free to enter any business, and were free to act as they saw fit to improve their economic welfare. Economic society was held together by mutual exchanges that were founded upon the division of labor and that were prompted by self-interest. Self-interest was the motivating force of the economy. For example, to increase his or her economic welfare, an individual might decide to produce goods and sell them for a profit. But in so doing, that individual automatically would benefit the community as well by purchasing raw materials, providing employment, and supplying goods or services. A laborer seeking to increase wages would do so by increasing productivity. This in turn would benefit the employer as well as the community in general. According to Adam Smith, often called the father of economics, the individual, in seeking personal gain, was led by an "invisible hand" to promote the welfare of the whole community.

Under economic liberalism individuals were free to engage in the trade, occupation, or business they desired. Workers were free to move from one job to another, and there was freedom to enter into or exit from any industry. Workers were free to work or not to work, and businesses were free to produce or not to produce.

Competition was the regulator of the economy under economic liberalism. Businesses were to compete with one another for consumer trade by developing new and better products and by selling existing products at lower prices. Free entry into the market assured ample competition, and prices were determined by the free forces of supply and demand. Competitive forces determined not only the prices of goods and services, but also wage rates.

Since self-interest was the motivating and driving force of the economy, because individuals, in promoting their own self-interest, would promote the welfare of the economy as a whole, and since competition was to serve as a regulator for the economy, a policy of **laissez-faire,** or non-government intervention, prevailed. This was a policy of government "hands off" regarding the economic activities of the individuals and businesses. From the economic point of view the government was merely to protect private property, to enforce contracts, and to act as an umpire in the case of economic disputes.

Weaknesses of Economic Liberalism

In this system we can picture, on the one hand, each individual and firm seeking their own self-interest, competing for jobs, sales, and markets with the weak falling by the wayside. On the other hand, we can see the government standing by, relying on competition to regulate the economy, not interfering unless absolutely necessary. For various reasons this system was to enhance the welfare of all. Truly it was a philosophy of "rugged individualism."

In theory, economic liberalism was a sound philosophy, and our economy prospered under it. It was not, however, without its weaknesses. The most pronounced weaknesses of economic liberalism were its extreme stress upon self-interest and its undue reliance on competition to regulate the economy and to promote the general welfare. Self-interest in many cases promoted greed, materialism, and the abuse of economic liberty;

and competition proved to be an inadequate regulator to prevent these abuses.

Economic liberalism left the door wide open for trouble. Certain individuals and firms began to interfere with the economic freedom of others. Under the aegis of economic liberalism and the guise of competition, large firms began to exploit small firms. Monopolies arose, and business integrations became prevalent. Markets were controlled and consumers exploited. Competition beat wages down, and the market wage paid by the employer was often less than the living wage required by the dignity of human labor. In stressing the individual aspect of private property, the social aspect was often ignored. Thus, one person's private property was frequently used to the detriment of another's property.

Government Intervention

Government intervention was and is necessary to remedy the inequities that developed under economic liberalism. Much of our railroad and subsequent interstate commerce regulation was designed to restrict the malpractices of carriers. The antitrust laws are necessary to prevent the restraint of competition by monopolies and large-scale business combinations. Labor laws are essential to protect the rights of laborers. Public utility regulation is necessary to prevent consumer exploitation, food and drug laws are designed to protect the health of our citizens, antipollution measures are enforced to preserve our environment, and safety regulations are enforced to protect workers.

In addition, government intervention in the form of socioeconomic legislation designed to promote the common good has been increasing. The Social Security Act, for example, provides aid to widows and orphans, pensions and medical care for the aged, and compensation for the disabled. Another part of that Act set up the system which provides for unemployment compensation. The minimum-wage laws help protect our standard of living, fair employment practices acts help prevent discrimination in regard to job opportunities, and the consumer product safety laws keep hazardous products off the market.

With increasing government intervention there is scarcely an area of importance in the economy today that is not affected by government legislation. There seems to be little doubt that the amount of government regulation, restriction, and intervention in our economy is substantial. Certainly we no longer have free enterprise to the extent advocated by 19th century liberalism. We have moved a long way from the laissez-faire aspect of the free enterprise system. Just how far we have moved is an interesting question.

Although much of the government intervention in our economy is necessary to correct abuses or to promote the general welfare, some of it might be considered unnecessary. Sometimes it is difficult to determine whether government action is needed. It is unfortunate that we cannot use a computer to measure the necessity of any particular piece of suggested government legislation. Whether the government should intervene in any particular case and to what extent frequently depends upon prudential judgment; and, as mentioned previously, prudential judgments of various individuals and groups differ widely.

Subsidiary Role of Government

What, then, can we use as a criterion to determine the need for government action in any area of the economy? In the absence of anything better, we can use the well-regarded law of social philosophy based upon the concept that the community and the state are subsidiary to the individual. Since "subsidiary" comes from the Latin word *subsidium*, meaning "help" or "assistance," the **principle of subsidiarity** implies that each higher unit in the economy exists to give assistance to, or to benefit, lower units. In the normal order of things, individuals should do what they can for themselves. What they cannot do for themselves, they can do through the community by cooperating with other people. What the communities cannot do can be done by the state. According to the principle of subsidiarity, it is wrong for a higher economic unit to take unto itself a function that can be performed adequately by a lower unit or by the individual.

The principle of subsidiarity helps to protect our free enterprise capitalistic system and to maintain some degree of laissez-faire. According to this principle, the federal government should encourage states, communities, subordinate groups, and individuals to handle all matters that they can handle adequately; higher economic or political units should intervene in the activities of the lower units only when necessary, and then in a subsidiary or helpful way and not in a manner that will destroy or absorb the lower unit. In short, it maintains that the higher unit be subsidiary or helpful to the lower unit or to the individual, but the higher unit should limit the amount of intervention.

Proper Role for Government.   In many cases it will easily be discernible whether government intervention violates this principle. For example, if the government were to decide which school you should attend, what subjects you should take, where you should work when you graduate, and what pay you should receive, it clearly would be a violation of the principle of subsidiarity. In most cases the main objective of working is to secure the income necessary to provide the goods and services necessary for your own livelihood and that of your family. In our present economic system the average individual is quite capable of earning a living through self-motivation and industry.

On the other hand, since the average individual is unable to protect life and property against invaders, vandals, fire, floods, and so forth, the maintenance of military, fire, and police protection by the states and communities does not violate the principle of subsidiarity. The use of broad-scale economic policies to stabilize the economy can be rendered effectively only by the federal government. The line of demarcation, however, sometimes becomes very nebulous. Take the concept of a federally guaranteed annual income for every U.S. citizen. Although experiments have been completed, arguments regarding its necessity are still being formulated. Likewise, legislation proposed in Congress for enactment of a national health insurance plan elicited heated debate.

Today we are interested in preserving our environment in order to have clean air, pure water, and noise abatement. But we are having difficulty determining who should pay for it: consumers, businesses, or the government. Furthermore, it is being debated whether local, state, or federal regulation should take precedence in the enforcement of antipollution measures. In many actual cases the government is performing services or producing goods that can be obtained through private enterprise. Presently the federal government operates about 20,000 business enterprises.

In determining whether government intervention is necessary or not, much depends upon the prudential judgment of the individuals and the groups in the economy. The principle of subsidiarity may be difficult to apply at times because of the inability to determine precisely whether a certain bit of suggested government action is necessary or to determine whether or not a lower economic unit can perform a particular function adequately. Yet the principle can be applied readily in many cases. Furthermore it can serve as an excellent and consistent guide in helping to prevent indiscriminate and contrary decisions regarding government intervention.

The New Federalism. Based on his belief that individuals and business firms were overtaxed and overregulated, that social welfare and entitlement programs had become too large and burdensome, and that government's 22 percent share of the GNP was excessive, President Reagan in 1982 launched his program of New Federalism. **New Federalism** is a program designed to transfer, or return, numerous social and economic functions from the federal level to the state and local government levels. When the program is fully effective, state and local governments, as well as individuals, will have to become more self-reliant. In his State of the Union message in January 1982, President Reagan made clear the direction he was going to pursue. At that time he made known plans to transfer 40 programs, such as food stamps, aid to families with dependent children, and job training, to the states coupled with a transfer of certain tax monies to the states and local governments to carry on their new responsibilities.

Privatization

In an attempt to rely more on market incentives to determine the production of goods and services, the U.S. government began in the latter part of the 1970s to remove government regulations from several industries. Since then we have seen much deregulation in the airline, trucking, railroad, natural gas, and banking and finance industries.

In addition, the federal government in the 1980s started to privatize certain of the economic services it was performing. Privatization refers to the shifting or returning of government economic functions or services to the private sector of the economy. Privatization is carried out primarily via competitive bidding by private companies to perform a service or by the outright sale of government assets.

The administration's 1987 budget contained several proposals for privatization. A partial list of possible privatization candidates includes mail service, energy generation, land management, housing development, printing, facilities maintenance, and data processing. Currently the federal government is considering the sale of some government-owned power dams and railways. Other countries such as Great Britain, France, and Japan have divested themselves of government services and assets in the past few years. The rationale behind the privatization is the belief that private enterprise can provide certain goods and services more efficiently and less expensively than the government.

GOALS FOR THE U.S. ECONOMY

In recent years a number of goals for our economy have been established by various private and government agencies that analyze our economic system. These goals are not a set of hard and fast objectives that must be accomplished, but rather suggested goals or ends toward which the economy should strive. The four primary economic goals that stand above all others are (1) full employment, (2) stable prices, (3) economic growth, and (4) equilibrium in our international balance of payments. These are supplemented by numerous other goals such as preservation of our environment, elimination of poverty, equal employment opportunity, and improvement in the quality of life.

Full Employment

Full employment means a condition in which 95 percent of our civilian labor force is employed. This allows for 5 percent frictional unemployment. There are always workers quitting, getting fired, in transit from one part of the country to another, and temporarily laid off. Furthermore, a number of persons want to work but have difficulty obtaining or holding a job because of physical or mental handicaps. Consequently, we can always expect some slack, or unemployment, in the labor force. For all practical purposes, we consider ourselves to be at full employment when unemployment is 5 percent or less. For a few decades the acceptable unemployment rate (at the full-employment level) was 4 percent, but as a result of the changes in the structure of the labor force that occurred with the passage of time, this figure was changed in the late 1970s to 5 percent.

Stable Prices

Stable prices are said to prevail when the Consumer Price Index, which measures changes in the cost of living for a typical family, moves 2 percent or less in either direction during the period of a year. Changes of more than this amount have substantial effects on the purchasing power of families and on the value of the dollar.

Economic Growth

The economy requires a healthy rate of economic growth. Total output must grow if we are to absorb the approximately 2 million new workers who enter the labor force annually, plus another 2 million or more workers who are displaced each year as a result of technological development and automation. If we merely produce the same level of output each year instead of increasing it, we will have fewer jobs, growing unemployment, and a decline in the per capita income of the nation. In order to maintain, or increase, our existing standard of living and to prevent unemployment from rising and recession from occurring, it is necessary to increase our gross national product continuously, unless, of course, workers are content to take the benefits of higher productivity in the form of shorter working hours instead of additional goods and services.

Past experience indicated that with a real growth rate of less than 3 percent, the U.S. economy suffers from growing unemployment and limited gains in per capita output and income. Unemployment at the end of 1981, for example, was 9.4 million, or 8.6 percent of the labor force. But by the end of 1982, unemployment exceeded 12.0 million, or 10.8 percent of the civilian labor force. Why? Simply because the real output of goods and services, instead of growing, declined in 1982. When recession occurred in 1982 and we failed to absorb all the new entrants into the labor force plus many of those displaced by technological change, unemployment rose. Furthermore, a sizable number of workers withdrew from the labor force because they were unable to find work.

Higher employment and substantial per capita gains, however, seem to occur when the economic growth rate exceeds 3 percent, as it did in 1983 and 1984. The current potential annual growth rate of the U.S. economy is 3.0 percent, reflecting a 2.5 percent annual growth in employment, a 0.5 percent decline in annual hours per worker, and a 1 percent per year growth in productivity.

Balance of Payments Equilibrium

Our economy has become more and more interdependent with other economies throughout the world, and events abroad can have a pronounced effect on the U.S. economy and vice versa. In the 1960s we became increasingly concerned, if not alarmed, about the growing deficits in our international balance of payments. Consequently, we added a fourth major economic goal—equilibrium in our balance of payments. It is desirable to have the value of our exports equal to our imports so that the inflow and outgo of currencies are in balance and the international value of the U.S. dollar remains stable.

COMMAND ECONOMIES

In our capitalistic system, decision making is exercised primarily by individuals and business firms in the economy. It must be remembered, however, that there are other economic systems throughout the world. Not all people, including some in the United States, are sold on the advantages of capitalism. Many feel that its disadvantages, such as recurring recessions, presence of unemployment and poverty, administered pricing by monopolies, wasteful use of resources in some respects, and unequal distribution of property and income, far exceed its advantages. As a consequence, in some nations there may exist a form of economy other than capitalism. In some nations leaders prefer a more centralized type of economy because it is easier to exercise dictatorial control. Thus, in many parts of the world various forms of socialism, fascism, and communism exist. In contrast to free market economies, these are called **command economies.**

SUMMARY

Our economy operates as a free enterprise capitalistic system. By capitalism we mean that capital, or producers' goods, is used for the production of additional goods and services. The right to private property is essential to the operation of this system.

Labor and resources are utilized and allocated in this system according to consumer demand. Consumers, through the prices they are willing to pay, provide the entrepreneurs with the means of obtaining the necessary labor and resources to produce the desired goods and services. Profit serves as an incentive to get the goods and services produced, and prices serve as a rationing mechanism

in the distribution of these goods and services.

About 12 million nonfarm business enterprises engage in production for the purpose of satisfying consumer demand in the United States. Four predominant types of business enterprises exist in the United States: the single proprietorship, the partnership, the corporation, and the cooperative. Each has advantages and disadvantages.

Competition is the regulator of the free enterprise system. Although competition is dominant in our economy, some of the markets are regulated for some reason, such as safety, economy, or protection. Occasionally the government enters a business directly or indirectly when it is essential for the good of the economy. Thus, because of the complex mixture of competition, regulated and unregulated markets, and private and government-operated businesses, it is said that we have a mixed economy.

Our mixed economy developed within the framework of economic liberalism. The main tenets of this philosophy were free trade, self-interest, private property, laissez-faire, and competition. The undue stress on self-interest, however, led to some abuses and inequities over the years, and competition proved to be an inadequate regulator. To correct these inequities, government legislation was required. In addition, much government intervention in the form of socioeconomic legislation has been enacted in the past few decades. As a result of this government intervention in the economy in the past 50 years, we have moved a considerable distance away from the laissez-faire aspect of economic liberalism.

Although much of our government intervention was and is necessary to prevent and remedy inequities in our economic system, and a good deal of it is in the form of socioeconomic measures designed to promote the common good, some of our government action may be considered as an infringement upon the economic freedom of both individuals and businesses.

Whether or not the government should intervene and to what extent it should intervene is a controversial question. In this regard the principle of subsidiarity serves as a good touchstone to determine the need for government intervention in any particular case. In recent years there has been considerable government deregulation of industry and privatization of some government services.

In its operation, there are four generally accepted primary goals for our national economy: full employment, stable prices, economic growth, and equilibrium in our international balance of payments. These are supplemented by numerous minor goals.

NEW TERMS AND CONCEPTS

Free enterprise capitalistic system (market economy)	Partnership	Laissez-faire
	Corporation	Principle of subsidiarity
Profit	Cooperative	New Federalism
Competition	Franchise	Command economies
Single proprietorship	Mixed economy	

DISCUSSION QUESTIONS

1. Discuss the importance of private property to the operation of a free enterprise capitalistic economy.
2. It is said that consumer demand influences the determination of individual income. Discuss how this can be so.
3. How does the price system serve as a rationing mechanism?
4. What is the role of profit in a capitalistic economic system?
5. Distinguish between a "market economy" and a "command economy."
6. What are some of the advantages of the corporate form of business enterprise?

7. It is often said that laissez-faire and free trade are incompatible. Explain.
8. Explain a situation in which a high degree of competition may not be beneficial to consumers and to the economy in general.

SUGGESTED READINGS

Bowden, Elbert V. *Economic Evolution*. Cincinnati: South-Western Publishing Co., 1985.

Economic Report of the President. Washington, DC: U.S. Government Printing Office, published annually.

Friedman, Milton. *Capitalism and Freedom*. Chicago: University of Chicago Press, 1981.

Galbraith, John K. *The New Industrial State*. Boston: Houghton Mifflin Co., 1985.

Hailstones, Thomas J., and Frank Mastrianna. *Contemporary Economic Problems and Issues*, 8th ed. Cincinnati: South-Western Publishing Co., 1988.

Heilbroner, Robert L. *The Nature and Logic of Capitalism*. New York: W. W. Norton & Co., 1985.

_____. *Between Capitalism and Socialism*. New York: Random House, Inc., 1983.

Kirzner, Israel. *Discovery and the Capitalistic Process*. Chicago: University of Chicago Press, 1985.

Schnitzer, Martin C. *Comparative Economic Systems*, 4th ed. Cincinnati: South-Western Publishing Co., 1987.

Simon, William E. *A Time for Truth*. New York: McGraw-Hill Book Co., 1978.

Walsh, Carl E. "Selling Government Assets." *FRBSF Weekly Letter*. Federal Reserve Bank of San Francisco (May 16, 1986).

4

THE CIRCULAR FLOW
OF ECONOMIC ACTIVITY

■

In producing the goods and the services to satisfy consumer demands and to make profits, business firms in our economy must utilize the factors of production: land, labor, capital, and entrepreneurship. Since the first three of these factors are generally owned by someone other than the entrepreneur, the business firm must remunerate the owners of these factors for the services they render. The payments by business firms for the productive factors naturally become income to the owners of these factors of production. This income in turn is used as purchasing power by which the owners of the factors of production can buy goods and services. Likewise, the profits of the entrepreneurs, or businesses, become purchasing power with which they can buy goods or secure additional factors of production.

The demand for goods and services by the income recipients leads to more production, which in turn brings about additional payments of income to the owners of the factors of production. This continuous operation of demand, production, income, and new demand sets up the **circular flow of economic activity** in our economy. Not only is it the mechanism by which we determine the use of our land, labor, capital, and entrepreneurship, but it is also the mechanism by which we determine the payments to the factors of production and by which we distribute income to various individuals and firms in our economy.

CIRCULAR FLOW DEMONSTRATED

Since we will be referring repeatedly to this concept, let us demonstrate it graphically. At this point we will divide the economy into two segments: businesses and individuals. Government will be added at a later point. In our modern economy, most individuals work for business firms or are in business for themselves. Individuals offer their productive services to business in exchange for remuneration in the form of wages, rent, and interest, and the owners of the business receive a profit for their contribution.

These income recipients use their money to buy the goods and services produced by businesses. If all the goods and services produced are sold—and they should be if people spend all the income they receive—businesses will be induced to produce a second round of goods and services, and the process will start over again. Continuation of this process keeps our economy producing, paying incomes, spending, and allocating goods and services to the individuals according to their demands. This process is shown in Figure 4-1.

In this model it can be seen that all income finds its way into the hands of the individuals represented at the right in Figure 4-1. Since the profit of a business becomes income to its owner, these individuals include the owners of businesses as well as the owners of the other factors of production. The value of the goods produced is determined by the cost of production—payments for labor, resources, and capital in the form of wages, rent, and interest, plus the profits for the entrepreneurs. We can say, therefore, that the total payment of income in the economy is equal to the value or cost (including profit) of the production. Individuals, including business owners who receive income in the form of profits, will have sufficient income to buy the goods and services produced by the economy.

A Stable Economy

If all the income is spent, businesses will move all the goods off the market and will be induced to produce the same amount again. But we know from our experience that individuals do not spend all the income they receive. Many people save some of their income. What happens to the circular flow in this case? Unless there is additional spending from some source to make up for the amount of saving in the economy, saving may have an adverse effect on the level of economic activity. Let us assume that businesses produce 500,000 units and distribute $500,000 income. If

Figure 4-1   Circular Flow—Simple Model

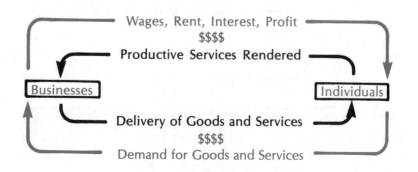

individuals spend the $500,000 to buy 500,000 units of consumer and capital goods, all production will be sold at an average price level of $1 per unit. However, if people spend only $400,000 on consumer goods and save $100,000, not all goods will be sold unless the savings are used directly to purchase capital goods or are borrowed by individuals other than savers to buy consumer or capital goods. Thus, we can maintain a given level of economic activity only if we have an amount of borrowing and/or non-consumer spending in the economy equal to the amount of savings, as shown in Figure 4-2.

Since spending on capital goods is referred to as **investment** in current economic analysis, we can conclude by saying that as long as planned investment (I) equals planned savings (S), we will have a stable flow of economic activity. In such a case total spending will equal total income. Since total spending is a measure of total demand and income is equivalent to total production (supply), the demand for goods and services will equal the supply.

At any given time, actual investment will equal actual savings. This is so because output equals income and by definition investment is the difference between total output and consumption. Savings is the difference between total income (output) and consumption. Therefore, investment, which could include the accumulation (inventories) of unsold consumer goods, has to equal savings.

There are times, however, when *planned* investment will differ from *planned* savings. When this happens there will be a change in economic activity until savings comes into balance with investment. When planned investment is greater than planned savings, the economy will expand,

Figure 4-2   Circular Flow—Stable Economy (Planned I = Planned S)

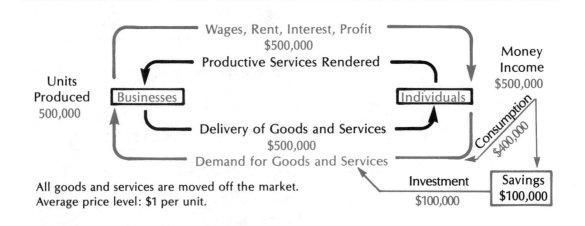

causing savings to increase until it comes into balance with investment. If planned investment is less than planned savings, the economy will contract, causing savings to decrease until it comes into balance with investment. As long as planned investment is equal to planned savings, of course, the economy will stay in equilibrium.

A Contracting Economy   *as a result of production > consumption*

Any time that planned *I* does not equal planned *S*, there will be a disruption in the circular flow of economic activity. For example, suppose that out of the $500,000 received by individuals, $400,000 is spent on consumption, and of the $100,000 saved only $50,000 is invested directly by the savers or indirectly by the borrowers. In this case, after producing 500,000 units valued at $500,000, producers would see only $450,000 returning to buy the goods produced. This would result in a decrease in the level of economic activity because one of two things or a combination of both would happen: (1) an accumulation of unsold goods or (2) a reduction in the prices of the goods.

Inventory Accumulation. If the price level is maintained at $1 per unit, the $450,000 that flows back will purchase only 450,000 units. This leaves 50,000 units unsold in inventories (unplanned investment), as shown in Figure 4-3. If the producers of 500,000 units sold only 450,000 units in

Figure 4-3 Contracting Economy—Inventory Accumulation
(Planned *I* < Planned *S*)

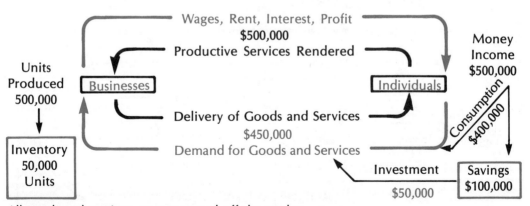

All goods and services are not moved off the market.
Average price level remains at $1 per unit.

one period, they might adjust their anticipated sales to 450,000 units for the subsequent period. Reduced production of 400,000 units plus an inventory stock of 50,000 units remaining from the previous period would yield the desired supply of 450,000 units. This move would cut back current production, and the producer would use less labor and fewer productive resources. As a result, there would be less income paid out, and spending would fall accordingly. The net result would be a decrease in economic activity in the subsequent period. Production, employment, and income would fall, and this could lead to further declines in business activity, resulting in more inventory adjustment. This is the incipient state of a *recession*, which occurs when there is a noticeable drop in the level of business activity.

Drop in Prices. Under certain circumstances, when $500,000 of income is paid out but only $450,000 returns to buy the goods produced, the market could be cleared; that is, all the goods could be sold by a reduction in the price level to 90 cents per unit. In that event $450,000 could buy 500,000 units. In fact, this is what frequently happens as competition forces prices down when total supply exceeds total demand. If prices begin to fall, however, certain high-cost producers may not be able to make a profit by selling at this lower price, and other producers will make less profit per unit. Consequently, the incentive to produce will be weakened, many firms will cut back production or go out of business, and total output in the subsequent period will be less. This means that fewer factors of production will be utilized, less income will be received, and total demand will fall. (See Figure 4-4).

Figure 4-4   Contracting Economy—Prices Decline
(Planned *I* < Planned *S*)

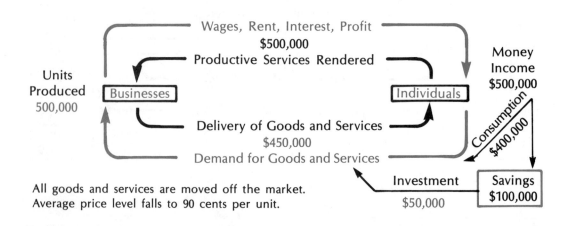

Whenever planned *I* is less than planned *S*, total spending will be less than total income and total demand will be less than total supply. This will lead to a decrease in production in subsequent periods because of inventory accumulation (goods not sold) or falling prices or a combination of both. As demand slackens and prices fall, the producer will cut production to get rid of accumulated inventory. As production is cut, incomes will fall, and this will reduce employment and income. Hence, we will have a decrease in the level of economic activity, which might precipitate a business depression. Inventory depletion was a contributing factor to the recessions of 1980 and 1982.

An Expanding Economy

If planned *I* were to exceed planned *S*, businesses and individuals would borrow more than they saved. This would cause spending to exceed total income and demand to exceed total production. Assume 500,000 units were produced and $500,000 was distributed in income. Assume also that individuals spent $400,000 on consumption and saved $100,000 that found its way directly or indirectly into investment. If businesses were to borrow an additional $50,000 from some source, such as a bank that can create money, for the purchase of machinery and equipment, total planned *I* would be $150,000, which when added to the $400,000 in consumer spending would make total spending $550,000. Such action might cause an increase in the level of economic activity or an increase in the price level, depending on the circumstances. (See Figure 4-5.)

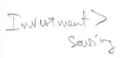

Figure 4-5 Expanding Economy—Output and/or Price Rise
(Planned *I* > Planned *S*)

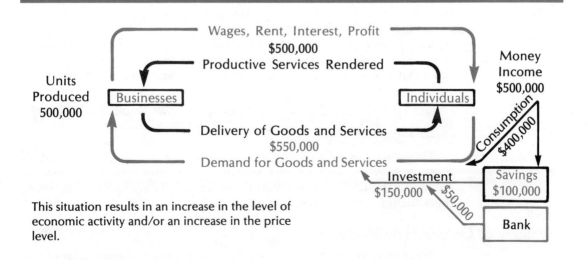

Wages, Rent, Interest, Profit
$500,000
Productive Services Rendered

Money Income
$500,000

Units Produced
500,000

Businesses

Individuals

Consumption $400,000

Delivery of Goods and Services
$550,000
Demand for Goods and Services

Investment
$150,000

Savings
$100,000

$50,000

Bank

This situation results in an increase in the level of economic activity and/or an increase in the price level.

More Goods and Services.   Naturally businesses will endeavor to increase production to satisfy the additional demand for goods and services. If the economy is in a state of less than full employment, that is, if labor, resources, capital, and capacity to increase production are available, additional goods and services will be forthcoming to satisfy the higher demand. Certainly if there is an additional $50,000 ready to buy goods, some enterprising businesses are going to produce the goods demanded. When they do, total production will be increased to 550,000 units. In addition, the price level will remain at $1 per unit, since the $550,000 in spending is exchanged for the 550,000 units produced. Businesses, which must pay for additional productive agents, will pay $550,000 instead of $500,000 as they did formerly, and income will increase accordingly. This in turn will increase spending and bring about more production. As a result, the economy will be operating at a higher level of production and employment. Therefore, whenever planned *I* exceeds planned *S*, total spending will exceed total income, demand will be greater than supply, and there will be an increase in the level of economic activity, provided that we are at less than full employment. This increase in economic activity will be necessary to meet and to satisfy demand.

Higher Prices.   If the same situation occurs in a period of full employment, the immediate result will be higher prices (inflation). Under full employment, businesses will be unable to obtain the necessary labor, resources, capital, and capacity to produce additional goods. It is true that some businesses will endeavor to increase production to satisfy the demand for the additional 50,000 units, but the only way that they will be able to obtain the necessary factors of production in the short run to increase output will be to bid the factors away from other producers.

This will force prices upward as entrepreneurs bid against each other for the relatively scarce factors of production. Furthermore, instead of having an increase in total production, the price level will rise to $1.10 per unit and the $550,000 of spending will be used to buy the 500,000 units of output as individuals bid against each other for the limited supply of goods available. Although the composition of production (the amount of capital goods compared with consumer goods) may be changed, the total amount of production will not be changed, at least in the short run. If after a while productivity can be increased through more efficient use of labor, better utilization of resources, and expanded capacity, the inflationary pressures will tend to be alleviated.

Thus, we can say that at any time planned *I* is greater than planned *S*, an increase in the level of economic activity will result, provided we are at less than full employment. If we are at full employment, however, this situation will merely cause prices to rise.

Summary of Circular Flow Model

We can sum up the foregoing discussion regarding the relationship of investment (*I*) to saving (*S*) and its effect on the economy. Whenever:

Planned I = Planned S, the result will be **equilibrium,** or a stable flow of economic activity. Prices will tend to remain stable.

Planned I < Planned S, the level of economic activity and/or prices will tend to decrease. Income will fall, and savings will decrease until it comes into balance with investment ($I = S$).

Planned I > Planned S, the level of economic activity will tend to increase if the economy is at less than full employment. However, if the economy is in a state of full employment, there will be no increase in the level of economic activity and prices will tend to rise. Income will rise, and savings will increase until it comes into balance with investment ($I = S$).

GOVERNMENT AND THE CIRCULAR FLOW

At one time the primary function and objective of federal financing was to raise sufficient funds through taxation to cover the cost of performing the necessary services expected of the federal government. Therefore, great emphasis was placed on balancing the budget, even though budget experts were not always able to balance the revenue and the expenditures. In recent decades, with the move away from laissez-faire, we have used government spending as a means of stabilizing the level of economic activity, and at times we have purposely operated at a deficit.

A Balanced Budget

Since government spending can affect the circular flow of economic activity and the price level, a closer inspection is in order. Actually, if the government balances the budget, it will in effect spend the same amount as it collects in taxes. What individuals and businesses give up in spendable funds to pay taxes, and consequently reduce their total spending, will be spent by the government; and as a result, the total spending in the economy will remain the same. Thus, a balanced budget *tends* to have a neutral effect on the economy. For example, in our circular flow, if individuals, as shown in Figure 4-6, were taxed $50,000 out of their total incomes of $500,000, they would have only $450,000 for spending on consumption and investment. The adverse effect of the government tax on the economy, however, would be offset if the government in turn spent the $50,000 it received in taxes. Under such circumstances, total spending would remain at $500,000 and the total goods and services that were produced would be moved off the market. There might be a change, however, in the composition of the goods and services produced, insofar as government spending would be substituted for some of the private spending on consumption and investment.

Notice that a balanced budget *tends* to have a neutral effect on the economy. This assumes that taxpayers will pay their taxes with monies

Figure 4-6   Balanced Budget—Stable Economy

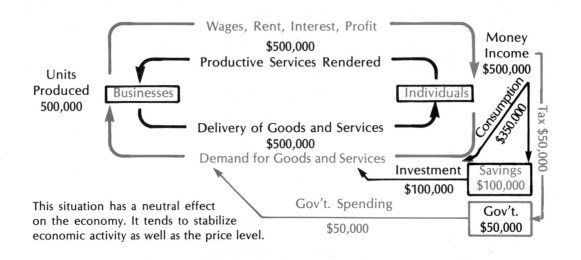

This situation has a neutral effect on the economy. It tends to stabilize economic activity as well as the price level.

that would otherwise be spent for consumption or investment purposes. However, this is not always the case. A balanced budget may have an effect other than a neutral one, depending on the source of taxation and the direction of government spending. An expansionary effect could result, for example, if the government, in its taxing process, absorbed idle funds that were not going to be used for consumption or investment.[1]

A Surplus Budget   *Causing slowing in economy*

If the government has a surplus budget, that is, if it spends less than it receives in taxes, this will tend to decrease the level of economic activity or cause a decline in prices. During a period when strong inflationary forces exist, a surplus budget is occasionally used as an anti-inflationary measure. Since the government spends less than it collects in taxes, this causes the total spending in the economy to decrease, which in turn will have a disinflationary effect on the economy. Assume in our circular flow that the government were to tax $50,000 but spend only $25,000. This would mean that total spending by consumers and investors would be reduced from $500,000 to $450,000 as a result of the tax payments. This would be offset, however, only to the extent of the $25,000 of government

------

1. For a more complete explanation of the balanced-budget multiplier effect, see page 336.

Figure 4-7   Surplus Budget—Contracting Economy and/or Declining
Price Level

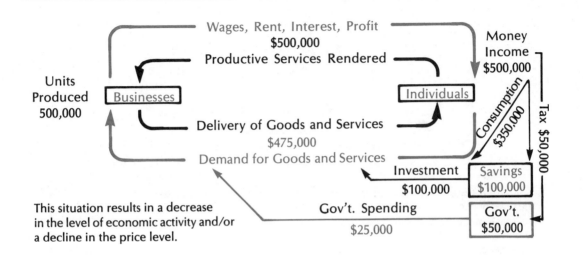

Wages, Rent, Interest, Profit
$500,000
Productive Services Rendered

Money
Income
$500,000

Units
Produced
500,000

Businesses

Individuals

Consumption
$350,000

Tax $50,000

Delivery of Goods and Services
$475,000
Demand for Goods and Services

Investment
$100,000

Savings
$100,000

This situation results in a decrease
in the level of economic activity and/or
a decline in the price level.

Gov't. Spending
$25,000

Gov't.
$50,000

spending. In effect, total spending would be reduced to $475,000 for the economy as a whole. Consequently, spending would be less than income, demand would be less than supply, and there would be a decrease in the level of business activity or a decline in the price level. This is demonstrated in Figure 4-7.

A Deficit Budget   ~Increase economic activities~

If the government operates a deficit budget, that is, if the government spends more than it collects in taxes, this will tend to bring about an increase in economic activity or raise prices, depending upon the circumstances. Since the government spends more than it collects in taxes, the expansionary effects of government spending will more than offset the contracting effects on consumption and investment resulting from the taxation. Referring once again to our circular flow concept, if individuals receive $500,000 in income for producing 500,000 units of goods and services and the government taxes $50,000, total spending by consumers and investors will be reduced to $450,000. If the government spends not only the $50,000 it collects in taxes but also an additional $25,000, which we will assume it borrows from the banks, total spending will rise to $525,000, as shown in Figure 4-8. Since total spending will exceed total income, demand will exceed the supply of goods and services available. Consequently, a deficit budget will tend to increase the level of economic activity

Figure 4-8   Deficit Budget—Expanding Economy and/or Rising Prices

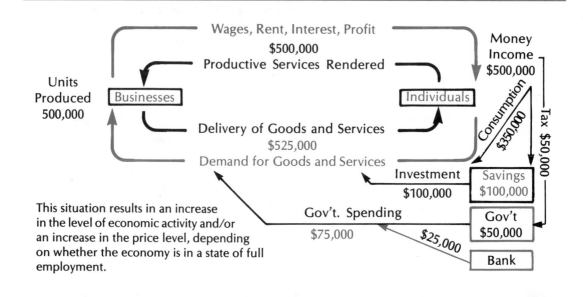

if we are at less than full employment. If the economy is at a state of full employment, however, it will merely cause a rise in the price level.

It must be realized that our examples were based on certain assumptions which may or may not be valid. We assumed that (1) individuals always pay taxes out of current incomes; (2) if individuals did not pay taxes, they would spend the money for consumption or investment; and (3) the government borrows from the banks instead of from individuals and firms in the economy. We will see later that if these assumptions do not apply, our analysis will be modified. The reactions will be the same but less intense. However, we can sum up the effects of government spending on the circular flow of economic activity at this point as follows: A balanced budget tends to have a neutral effect on economic activity and the price level. A surplus budget tends to decrease the level of economic activity and/or the price level. A deficit budget, on the other hand, tends to increase the level of economic activity or the price level, depending on the level of employment.

Complicating Factors

The circular flow—including changes in production, employment, and income—can be influenced by other factors as well. Modifying our basic model, for example, can be changes in the money supply, the use of credit, spending or investment abroad, and the purchase of foreign products. We will see how these affect economic activity in subsequent chapters.

INFLATION

In our foregoing analysis we assumed that inflation occurred only in a fully employed economy. It may occur, however, in an economy of less than full employment.

Definition and Types of Inflation

There are many definitions of inflation. In the simplest sense, **inflation** is merely a persistent increase in the price level. But inflation may be one of four types: (1) demand-pull inflation, (2) cost-push inflation, (3) structural inflation, or (4) social inflation.

Demand-Pull Inflation.   The type of inflation that we have discussed thus far is known as **demand-pull inflation.** Sometimes this is referred to as excess-demand inflation, and it occurs when the total demand for goods and services exceeds the available supply of goods and services in the short run. This is much more likely to occur in a fully employed economy because of the difficulty of producing additional goods and services to satisfy the demand. Competitive bidding for the relatively scarce goods and services forces prices upward. The excess spending may result from several causes. Consumers may decide to spend past savings, the government may operate at a deficit, consumer credit may be liberalized, commercial and bank credit may be extended, or the money supply may otherwise be increased. Generally when the money supply or other forms of purchasing power increase faster than the productivity of our economy, demand-pull inflation results.

Cost-Push Inflation.   The second type of inflation is known as **cost-push inflation**. This may occur in a fully employed or an underemployed economy. It is difficult to say whether it starts with increased wages, higher material costs, or increased prices of consumer goods. If wages or material costs do increase for some reason, however, producers are likely to increase the prices of their finished goods and services to protect their profit margins. Rising prices in effect will decrease the purchasing power of wages. As a result wage earners, especially through their unions, may apply pressure for further wage increases. This in turn may lead to further increases in the price of materials and finished products, which in turn leads to further wage increases and develops into what we generally call the **wage-price spiral.**

Cost-push inflation has become more pronounced in the past few decades with the growth and strengthening of labor unions. It also has been aggravated by the use of administered pricing by large and powerful producers. **Administered pricing** is simply a situation in which a seller can exert an undue influence on the price charged for a product because of the absence of competition. Although usually referred to as cost-push, price-pull inflation, labor unions call it price-pull, cost-push inflation to de-emphasize the role of wage increases as a cause of inflation.

Structural Inflation.   Another type of inflation that may occur with unemployment in the economy is **structural inflation.** This arises when there is a substantial shift in demand to the products of one industry away from those of other industries. It assumes that there is a certain amount of inflexibility and immobility among the factors of production, and specifically that wages and prices tend to have downward rigidity and upward flexibility as a result of administered pricing and labor union pressures. If there is a heavy shift in the demand to the products of Industry X and away from the products of Industry Y, for example, it could push production in Industry X to, or near, full capacity. Under such circumstances the increased demand could cause prices to rise in that industry as a result of demand-pull inflation. This will cause the general price level to rise, since it is assumed that prices in Industry Y will not decline because of inflexibility. In addition, because of the immobility of labor and resources, Industry X may have to pay higher wage and material costs as it endeavors to increase production. This whole situation is aggravated when the inflationary effects spill over into other industries. The increases in wages and prices in Industry X may actually cause wages and prices to rise in Industry Y. The general increase in the price level could instigate wage increases and subsequent price increases in Industry Y. Although production and employment may be lessened as a result of demand shifts away from Industry Y, employers within Industry Y may be forced to pay higher wages to offset the higher living costs in an effort to hold on to experienced and skilled workers. In effect, structural inflation, which can occur at full employment or with unemployment conditions, contains elements of both demand-pull and cost-push inflation.

Social Inflation.   In recent years economists have observed the growing occurrence of a fourth type of inflation known as **social inflation.** It results from the increasing demand for more government services in the form of Social Security payments, improved unemployment benefits, the distribution of more welfare, wider health care coverage, better rent subsidies, and a host of other social services. Social inflation is also encouraged by the rising costs to private enterprise originating from greater fringe benefits, such as longer vacations, more paid holidays, shorter hours, better pensions, and broader hospital and insurance coverage for employees. Moreover, the cost of helping to preserve the natural environment through the use of expensive antipollution and depollution equipment, either by the government or by private enterprise, exerts increased pressure on the price level. In addition to environmental protection standards, other governmental forces, such as equal employment opportunity measures and occupational safety and health regulations, add to price pressures. Social inflation may occur at full employment, adding to demand-pull inflationary pressures, or at other times it may augment cost-push or structural inflationary pressures.

One answer to each type of inflation is increased productivity. In demand-pull inflation, if productivity can be increased to provide the additional goods and services demanded, the inflationary pressure will be removed. On the other hand, the demand for goods and services can be decreased by reducing the money supply or by reducing spendable income. Cost-push and structural inflation can be modified if wage increases are kept in line with increases in productivity. If wage increases would accelerate in proportion to the increase in productivity, incomes would stay in balance with the amount of goods produced. Goods and services would be available when wage earners spent their higher incomes. Social inflation can be held in check, of course, by limiting government and private outlays for social services or by giving up spendable funds, through taxation and redirected expenditures, to cover the cost of socioeconomic measures.

Stagflation

With the slowdown in the economy and the decrease in demand associated with the recession of 1970, the price level continued to rise. By that time the demand-pull factors had been supplemented and eventually supplanted by pressures of cost-push, structural, and social inflation. Nevertheless, the decrease in investment in 1970 caused the real GNP to decline modestly and the rate of unemployment to exceed 5 percent. For the first time in recent history, we had the anomaly of recession and inflation simultaneously, which was labeled **stagflation.**

A slow recovery from the recession failed to improve the unemployment or inflationary situation by mid-1971. Wage and price controls helped hold the price level increases to 3.4 percent annually in both 1971 and 1972. With the removal of compulsory controls in January, 1973, however, inflation resumed at a faster pace. The price level, aggravated by fuel and energy shortages, food scarcities, world mineral shortages, and continued high demand, rose at a rate of 8.8 percent in 1973 and reached a double-digit inflation level of 12.2 percent in 1974. By that time we were in the midst of the 1974 recession and unemployment had risen to 6.0 percent. During 1975 the unemployment rate averaged 8 percent.

With the economic recovery after the 1974–1975 recession, the inflation rate declined to less than 5 percent by 1976. Subsequently, upward price pressures moved the inflation rate back to the double-digit level by 1979. It remained there even during the recession of 1980 in spite of President Carter's voluntary wage and price standards. Finally, with the recession of 1982, the annual inflation rate fell to 3.9 percent. It remained at 4 percent

Table 4-1 Production, Capacity, Prices, and Unemployment

Year	Production[1] (Billions)	% Capacity[2] Utilized	Price Level (1967 = 100)	% Change[3] in CPI	Unemployment (Millions)	Unemployment (% of Civilian Labor Force)
1960	1,665	80.2%	88.7	1.5%	3.9	5.5%
1965	2,088	89.6	94.5	1.9	3.4	4.5
1970	2,416	80.9	116.3	5.5	4.1	4.9
1971	2,485	79.0	121.3	3.4	5.0	5.9
1972	2,609	84.0	125.3	3.4	4.9	5.6
1973	2,744	87.9	133.1	8.8	4.4	4.9
1974	2,729	83.6	147.7	12.2	5.2	5.6
1975	2,695	74.1	161.2	7.0	7.9	8.5
1976	2,827	78.8	170.5	4.8	7.4	7.7
1977	2,957	82.4	181.5	6.8	7.0	7.1
1978	3,115	84.8	195.4	9.0	6.2	6.1
1979	3,192	85.2	217.4	13.3	6.1	5.8
1980	3,187	80.9	246.8	12.4	7.6	7.1
1981	3,249	79.9	272.4	8.9	8.3	7.6
1982	3,166	72.1	289.1	3.9	10.7	9.7
1983	3,279	74.7	298.4	3.8	10.7	9.6
1984	3,490	81.0	311.1	4.0	8.5	7.5
1985	3,585	80.4	322.2	3.8	8.3	7.2
1986	3,677	79.4	328.4	1.1	8.2	7.0

1. In 1982 constant dollars.
2. Output as a percentage of total industry capacity.
3. Annual changes from December to December.

Source: *Economic Report of the President* (Washington, DC: U.S. Government Printing Office, 1987).

or less through 1985 and 1986 in part because the economy was not operating at the full employment level. Table 4-1 summarizes the statistical data since 1960.

Regardless of the causes, inadequate economic growth, unemployment, and inflation are major problems of the economy. Although we have many techniques for measuring and alleviating unemployment, complexities make it more difficult to measure the impact of inflation. Furthermore, it is more difficult to impose anti-inflationary measures, such as higher taxes, tighter money, higher interest rates, and federal budget reductions, because they are politically and socially unpopular. Moreover, many of the measures designed to slow down inflation aggravate unemployment. On the other hand, measures designed to expand the economy and reduce unemployment often exert inflationary pressures on the price level.

SUMMARY

The decisions of what and how much to produce that are made by millions of consumers and business firms generate a circular flow of economic activity. According to this pattern, as consumers express their demands, the entrepreneurs utilize the factors of production to produce the desired goods and services. Incomes either are spent for consumer goods and services or are invested in capital goods. When any saving takes place in the economy, it disrupts the circular flow unless the saving is offset by an equivalent amount of borrowing and investment.

Whenever investment is equal to saving, total spending is equal to income, demand is equal to supply, and all the goods and services are moved off the market. This induces business to produce a like amount of goods and services in the subsequent period. Thus, whenever planned investment is equal to planned saving, equilibrium in the level of economic activity results and prices tend to remain stable. If planned investment is less than planned saving, however, a decrease in the level of economic activity and/or a decline in the price level results. On the other hand,

if planned investment is greater than planned saving, an increase in the level of economic activity results if the economy is in a state of less than full employment. Otherwise it leads to higher prices.

Government spending also can have an influence on the level of economic activity and the price level. A balanced government budget tends to have a neutral effect on economic activity and prices, whereas a surplus budget can lead to a decrease in business activity and/or lower prices. A deficit budget can lead to an increase in the level of economic activity or higher prices, depending on the employment status in the economy.

Higher prices, or inflation, result from several causes. Demand-pull inflation arises when the total demand for goods and services is greater than the available supply of goods and services. It usually occurs during periods of full employment when we are unable to increase the output of goods and services in the short run. Cost-push inflation results when businesses increase their prices to offset an increase in the cost of labor and materials or for some other reason. Price increases lead to further increases in wages and materials, which bring about further increases in prices. Structural inflation is a combination of demand-pull and cost-push. Cost-push, structural, and social inflation may occur in an economy at full employment or less. In the last few decades the U.S. economy has experienced unemployment, inflation, and stagflation resulting from a variety of causes.

NEW TERMS AND CONCEPTS

Circular flow of
  economic activity
Investment
Equilibrium

Inflation
Demand-pull inflation
Cost-push inflation
Wage-price spiral

Administered pricing
Structural inflation
Social inflation
Stagflation

DISCUSSION QUESTIONS

1. Describe the relationship of planned investment to planned saving and the effect of that relationship on the circular flow of economic activity.
2. How can the accumulation of large inventories adversely affect the circular flow of economic activity?
3. Why is it necessary to consider the government sector of the economy as part of the circular flow?
4. What effect will a surplus budget have on the circular flow of economic activity?

5. Will a deficit budget always increase the level of business activity? Why or why not?
6. Distinguish among the four types of inflation: demand-pull, cost-push, structural, and social.
7. What type(s) of inflation is (are) most likely to occur in a period of less than full employment?
8. How does stagflation compound the difficulty of applying measures to stabilize the level of production and employment?

SUGGESTED READINGS

Deficits: Their Impact on Inflation and Growth. A staff study for the Joint Economic Committee of the U.S. Congress. Washington, DC: U.S. Government Printing Office, 1981.

The Federal Budget: Its Impact on the Economy. New York: The Conference Board, Inc., 1982.

Fighting Inflation and Rebuilding a Sound Economy. New York: Committee for Economic Development, 1980.

Habeler, Gottfried. *Stagflation: An Analysis of Its Causes and Cures.* Washington, DC: American Enterprise Institute for Public Policy Research, 1977.

Hazeldine, Tim. *Full Employment without Inflation.* New York: St. Martin's Press, 1984.

Hein, Scott. "Deficits and Inflation." *Review.* Federal Reserve Bank of St. Louis (March, 1981).

Humphrey, Muriel, and Augustus F. Hawkins. *Goals for Full Employment and How to Achieve Them under the "Full Employment and Balanced Growth Act of 1978."* Washington, DC: Leon H. Keyserling, 1978.

"Production and Capacity Utilization." *Economic Trends.* Federal Reserve Bank of Cleveland (Monthly, 1987).

PART 2

THE MARKET
MECHANISM
AND COMPETITION

5

PRICE: THE ROLE
OF DEMAND AND SUPPLY

■

In a free enterprise system, the forces of supply and demand are relied upon to determine prices. Consumers express their demand in the prices they are willing to pay for various products. Business firms seeking profit cater to consumer demand by offering goods and services at various prices. Consequently, a market is established in which the final price of a good or service is determined on the basis of costs to the producer and usefulness to the buyer.

THE MARKET MECHANISM

Changes in either demand or supply bring about adjustments in the amount of goods sold, or price changes, or both. If consumers throughout the nation, for example, begin buying more lawn mowers, retail outlets will have to order inventory replacements and additional mowers from wholesalers. Manufacturers in turn begin to produce more mowers. Depending on the available supply and the cost of resources, these additional mowers may be supplied at the same or at a different price. At any rate, consumer demand is made known to the producers through the marketing structure. At other times, suppliers will endeavor to anticipate the demands of consumers and supply the goods before there is a strong reflection of demand. The system does not work perfectly; at times there are lags and leads in the market, gluts and shortages occur, and prices fluctuate. But considering the billions of items produced and sold each year, the system seems to do an excellent job of satisfying consumer demand.

The demand for producer goods can be traced to the demand for goods and services that directly satisfy human wants. For example, the desire of individuals for shelter gives rise to a demand for brick and lumber, which in turn gives rise to a demand for iron and steel with which to make tools and machines for production of brick and lumber, and so on. Therefore, we may say that the demand for a commodity that grows out of the desire to satisfy the demand for some other good or service is **derived demand.**

DEMAND

In studying the influence of demand on the price of any given commodity or service, we must recognize two levels of demand—individual or personal demand and market demand. Market demand is the aggregate of individual demand.

Individual Demand

Demand implies something more than need or desire. Of course, an individual must feel a need for the usefulness that a good can provide before considering ways and means of procuring the good. In addition, an individual must possess purchasing power if the need is to be satisfied. You may have a strong desire, for example, for a new Porsche; but unless you have the cash to pay for it, or the ability to buy on credit, your desire will have no influence on the market. Individual demand, therefore, implies a desire plus some purchasing power. It signifies the quantity of a good that an individual stands ready to buy at various prices at a particular time.

The usefulness of a good to an individual at a particular time depends upon the number of units that the individual has recently consumed or that may be available for use when desired. If the number of units that have been consumed or that are available is large, the utility of an additional unit is likely to be lower than it otherwise would be. The price of a commodity will usually affect the quantity that an individual will buy at a given time. For example, a shopper may buy 1 pound of cheese at the grocery at a given price, but would purchase less if the price were higher. On the other hand, the shopper might buy 2 pounds if the price were low enough. Again, merchants are aware of the relationship of the subjective prices of potential buyers—the prices that consumers will pay—to quantities that will be bought when they conduct sales or give quantity discounts.

Market Demand

Market demand (or simply demand) consists of the total quantity of a good that would be bought in the aggregate by individuals and firms at each of several prices at a given time. **Demand**, therefore, is defined as a schedule of the total quantities that purchasers will buy at different prices at a given time. An accurate schedule of this kind for a specific commodity is difficult to construct in advance because it requires that we know just how many units people would actually buy at various prices. We do know, however, that at a given time consumers will usually buy more units of a good at a low price than they will at a high price. The reasons, of course, are the three simple and general facts that (1) those who are willing to buy the commodity at a high price may purchase more of the product at a lower price; (2) some buyers in lower income groups may not be able to afford the product at a high price but will buy the product at a lower price; and (3) some persons who could afford to purchase the product at a high price, but may not do so because they do not think that it is worth the price, will buy the product at a lower price. A lower price for an article, therefore, nearly always results in the sale of a larger amount of that product. Conversely, a higher price, other things remaining the same, usually tends to curtail the amount that can be sold. Thus, we are justified in concluding that the quantity of a good that consumers will buy tends to vary inversely with the price.

The expression "tends to vary inversely," as used here, does not imply that the variation in the amount sold is always proportionate to the change in price. Indeed, in many instances a decrease of 50 percent in the price of a good probably would not result in a 50 percent increase in the number of units sold; nor would an increase of 25 percent in the price be likely to result in a corresponding decrease in the amount that would be purchased. In some cases the change in the quantity sold might be more than proportional to the change in price; in others, it might be less.

A Market Demand Schedule

Since the quantity of any good demanded ordinarily tends to vary inversely with its price, we can construct a hypothetical schedule of prices and quantities to illustrate this relationship. Let us assume that on Tuesday at noon the buyers at the Minneapolis market would buy at different prices the amount of oats shown in the second column, D (demand), in Table 5-1. Notice that larger amounts of oats would be bought at lower prices.

The relationship between price and the number of bushels that would be bought is represented graphically in Figure 5-1. The vertical axis indicates at regular intervals the price per bushel, and the horizontal axis shows the quantity in millions of bushels. Thus, to locate the point for the demand for 5,100,000 bushels at $1.25 a bushel, a horizontal line to the right is drawn from that price and a vertical line upward is drawn from that quantity. The point of intersection of the two lines is thus determined by reference to the two coordinates, price and quantity.

When all the points have been located in this way, they suggest a curve that slopes downward to the right. If the price and the quantity changes were infinitely small and if they varied according to the proportions indicated in the schedules, the result in the graph would really be such a curve. For our purposes, therefore, we may construct a curve to indicate demand. A **demand curve** indicates the number of units of a good or service that consumers will buy at a given time and at various prices. This curve is merely a graphic way of representing how the quantity of oats that would be bought varies inversely with price.

Table 5-1 Demand Schedule for Oats

If the Price Is:	Millions of Bushels of Oats That Will Be Bought		
	D	D₁	D₂
$1.50	2.0	3.0	1.0
1.45	2.3	3.4	1.3
1.40	2.8	4.3	1.6
1.35	3.5	4.8	2.1
1.30	4.2	5.6	2.7
1.25	5.1	6.6	3.4
1.20	6.1	7.7	4.4
1.15	7.3	9.0	5.4
1.10	8.5	10.4	6.7
1.05	10.0	12.0	8.0

Figure 5-1 Demand Curve for Oats

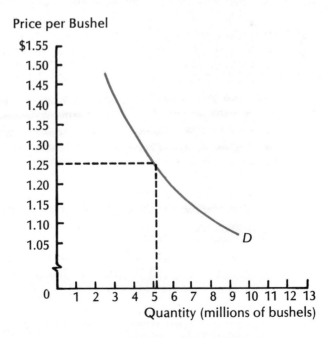

The demand schedule may be represented by a curve or by a straight line. The curve may have a slight or steep slope, it may be continuous or discontinuous, or it may be smooth or jagged, depending on the nature of the demand for the particular product and the ability to obtain sufficient information to plot the demand schedule. Consequently, there are all kinds and shapes of demand curves.

Although the normal or typical demand curve moves downward to the right, it is not uncommon to find a product for which the demand will move downward to the right over a given range of prices but then eventually curve backward to the left. This would indicate, of course, that in certain price ranges, less of the product would be purchased at lower prices. Prestige items are sometimes in this category. Mink coats, for example, are a status symbol to many consumers. As the price is lowered, more consumers will buy mink coats. But if the price became so low that almost anyone could afford to buy a mink coat, it would lose its prestige status, and it is possible that fewer consumers would want to buy one.

Changes in Demand

Remember that on a typical demand curve more will be sold at lower prices. Notice on the demand curve in Figure 5-1 that at a price of $1.25 a little over 5 million bushels of oats would be sold, but at a price of $1.20 more than 6 million bushels would be sold. Consequently, if a price of $1.20 were charged instead of $1.25, does this mean that there is an increase in demand? Absolutely not. Remember that we defined demand as a schedule of amounts that would be purchased at various prices at a given time. Even though we altered the price from $1.25 to $1.20 and sold more, this is not a change in demand. Nothing has happened to the demand schedule. We simply moved to a lower price to take advantage of larger sales at lower prices. This is known as a movement along the demand curve, sometimes referred to as a change in the quantity demanded, and should not be confused with a change in demand. To have a change in demand, or what is sometimes referred to as a shift in demand, a different amount of the product would necessarily be purchased at given prices, i.e., a new schedule.

An increase in demand means that a greater quantity will be bought at each price. Thus, in Table 5-1, D_1 is a schedule showing an increase in the amount that will be purchased at each of the prices as compared with that for D in the second column. If the demand curve for D_1 is plotted, it will lie to the right of that for D, as shown in Figure 5-2. It indicates, for example, that at a price of $1.25, 6.6 million bushels will be sold.

A decrease in demand means that a smaller quantity will be bought at each price. In Table 5-1, D_2 is a schedule showing a decrease in demand, as compared with that for D. The curve for D_2 will lie to the left of that

Figure 5-2   Demand Curves for Oats

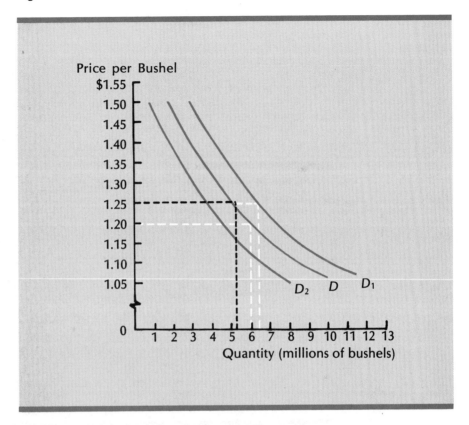

for D, as shown in Figure 5-2. A change in demand may result from a number of causes, such as a change in income, a change in population, new uses for a product, more advertising, and even a change in the prices of competing products.

Quantity Sold as a Function of Price

We usually think of the quantity of a good sold as dependent upon, or as a function of, price and express it as $q = f(p)$. However, it should be readily apparent now that many other factors besides price affect the quantity of a good sold. The quantity sold is also influenced by the level of disposable income, by the price of other goods (both complementary and substitute goods), by outlays for advertising, and by many other considerations. Thus, it is just as proper to write $q = f(DI)$, disposable income, or to combine all factors affecting quantity sold into one equation and express it as follows: $q = f(p, DI, px, a, . . .)$, where p is the price of the product itself, *DI* is the level of disposable income, *px* is the price of other commodities, and *a* is the advertising outlay.

SUPPLY

As in the case of the demand for goods, there are also two levels of the supply of goods: individual supply and market supply.

Individual Supply

The **individual supply** of a good that is offered on a market signifies the quantities of the good that an individual stands ready to sell at various prices. To determine the total supply that any individual might offer to sell, it would be necessary to know exactly how much would be sold at each possible price. For example, if water were very scarce and you possessed a limited supply, you might be induced to sell a few gallons at a certain price. If the price offered were higher, you might sell a larger quantity; and at a still higher price, you might be willing to sell even more. But if your life depended upon retaining a minimum supply for your own use, you would not part with all the remainder at any price. This example illustrates the point that individual supply, which is contributed to the total market supply, consists only of that portion of his or her stock that an individual can be induced to sell at various prices.

Market Supply

The **market supply** of a good consists of the total quantities of the good that sellers stand ready to sell at different prices at a given time. A schedule representing the market supply of a good would contain all the quantities of the good that all potential sellers would sell at various prices. As in the case of the demand for a good, it is essential to keep in mind that we are considering here the behavior of a great many individuals or firms. The market supply refers to the total quantities of a particular homogeneous product, one that is identical with all the sellers. Supply, like demand, is always specific. For example, it does little good to talk about the supply of automobiles in the market. To be meaningful as far as measurement is concerned, we must talk about the supply of Fords, Chevrolets, Toyotas, Cadillacs, Hondas, and various other makes and models. It is obvious that the supply of and the demand for Cadillacs constitutes a different market than that for Hondas.

A Market Supply Schedule

Just as with demand, it is convenient for purposes of analysis to construct a market supply schedule. Therefore, let us set up a hypothetical market supply schedule for oats on the Minneapolis market at noon on Tuesday, as shown in the first and second columns of Table 5-2.

The same method used in plotting the demand curve for oats can be used to plot the supply curve, which is shown by S in Figure 5-3. A **supply curve** is a line indicating the number of units of a good or service that will be offered for sale at different prices. The supply curve rises from left to right because as the price continues to rise, the intersection of lines drawn from prices and quantities climbs higher and higher to the right.

Changes in Supply

Market supply is the counterpart of market demand. In the case of reproducible goods, the quantity demanded usually tends to vary inversely with price. The supply offered, on the other hand, ordinarily tends to vary directly with price; that is, a higher price usually—but not always— results in a greater amount offered for sale. But remember, just as with demand, when price changes and a greater or lesser amount is offered for sale, that is not a change of supply. It is merely a movement along the supply curve.

A change in supply means that a different quantity will be offered for sale at each price. An increase in supply means that a larger amount will be offered; a decrease in supply means that a smaller amount will be offered at the same price, as shown in Table 5-2. If we plot the supply

Table 5-2   Supply Schedule for Oats

If the Price Is:	Millions of Bushels of Oats That Will Be Offered		
	S	S_1	S_2
$1.50	10.0	11.1	9.0
1.45	9.6	10.8	8.4
1.40	9.2	10.4	7.8
1.35	8.5	9.8	7.2
1.30	7.8	9.1	6.3
1.25	6.9	8.4	5.3
1.20	5.9	7.3	4.3
1.15	4.8	6.4	3.0
1.10	3.6	5.3	1.6
1.05	2.0	4.0	-0-

Figure 5-3 Supply Curves for Oats

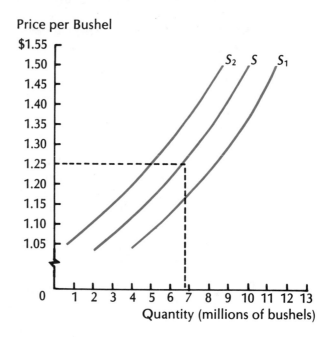

curve for S_1, showing an increase in supply, the curve will lie to the right of that for S. The curve for S_2, showing a decrease in supply, will lie to the left of that for S, as seen in Figure 5-3.

The total quantity that will be offered for sale is limited both by the quantity in existence at the time and by estimates of prospective sellers as to probable costs of producing future supplies of the good. In the long run, however, the supply of reproducible goods is conditioned by the availability of the factors of production and by the costs of production.

HOW DEMAND AND SUPPLY DETERMINE PRICE

Now let us assume that at noon on Tuesday the demand for and the supply of oats on the Minneapolis market are as shown in the D and S columns of Tables 5-1 and 5-2. Table 5-3 reproduces these schedules.

At what price will oats sell on the commodity exchange? The price will be determined by the interaction of demand and supply and will be at the point where "demand and supply are equal." More precisely, the price will be determined where the quantity demanded equals the quantity

Table 5-3 Demand and Supply Schedules for Oats
(Millions of Bushels)

Price per Bushel	Demand	Supply
$1.50	2.0	10.0
1.45	2.3	9.6
1.40	2.8	9.2
1.35	3.5	8.5
1.30	4.2	7.8
1.25	5.1	6.9
1.20	6.1	5.9
1.15	7.3	4.8
1.10	8.5	3.6
1.05	10.0	2.0

supplied. Since the market is cleared, this price is known as the **equilibrium price.**

To show the interactive relationships of demand and supply, we can reconstruct the demand and supply curves for the schedules in Figure 5-4. With reference to price and quantity, the curves intersect at a point that indicates a price of $1.21 and a quantity of 6 million bushels. What is the significance of this?

It simply means that at a price of $1.21, 6 million bushels will be bought and an equal amount will be offered for sale. According to our definition of competition, since no single transaction can affect the market price, any consumer who wants to buy oats at this price can buy as much as desired. Likewise, any seller can sell at the same price. No consumer whose subjective price is higher than $1.21 needs to pay more because at that price as much as is desired can be purchased. And no consumer unwilling to pay that price can buy.

On the other hand, sellers whose subjective prices are lower than $1.21 can sell at the higher price. And those who are unwilling to sell at $1.21 will have to keep their oats because consumers can obtain all they want at that price. Therefore, $1.21 is the equilibrium price and cannot change until there is a change in the relationships between demand and supply. This explains what we mean when we say that the forces of demand and supply are impersonal, and that under a condition of pure competition no one individual can influence the market price either by buying or refusing to buy or by selling or refusing to sell.

Under these conditions of demand and supply, if the price were anything other than $1.21, the quantities consumers would be willing to buy and the amount of oats offered for sale would be out of balance. In such

Figure 5-4   Demand, Supply and Market Price

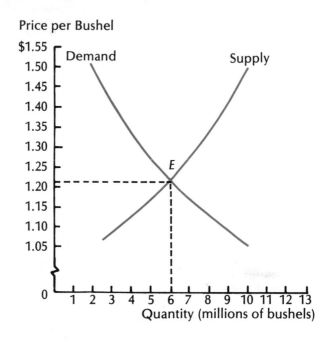

a situation, forces of the market would come into play to adjust the price to $1.21, or the equilibrium level. At the price of $1.25, for instance, the quantity that sellers would be willing to supply would exceed by approximately 2 million bushels the quantity demanded by consumers. Consequently, not all the oats would be sold. But notice that there are sellers who are willing to sell their oats at lower prices of $1.23, $1.22, and so forth. Rather than hold their oats, they will offer to sell at the lower prices. As the price is lowered, notice that certain consumers who would not pay $1.25 for oats will pay $1.24, $1.23, or less. Therefore, as the market conditions force the price of oats downward, the number of sellers decreases and the number of consumers increases until the amount of oats offered for sale and the quantity purchased come into balance at an equilibrium price of $1.21.

On the contrary, if a price of $1.15 exists in such a market, it cannot continue. At that price the quantity demanded exceeds the quantity supplied by more than 2 million bushels, and some potential consumers would have to go without. But observe that some of the consumers are willing to pay more than $1.15 for a bushel of oats. Rather than go without, they would offer higher prices of $1.17, $1.19, and upward. As they bid the price upward, a twofold action will take place in the market. The higher prices will deter some consumers from making purchases as well as induce more sellers to offer their products for sale. The resulting increase in the amount offered for sale and the decrease in the amount that will be purchased finally bring supply and demand into balance at the equilibrium price of $1.21. In a free market no other price can prevail. At any other price either a surplus or a shortage of the good will exist in the short run, as shown in Figure 5-5.

If someone wants to set the price at other than the market price established by the free forces of supply and demand, the market will have to be rigged or the forces of supply and demand changed. This is exactly what happens when the government sets a parity price for certain agricultural commodities that is higher than the market price, or establishes a

Figure 5-5 Surplus, Shortage, and Equilibrium

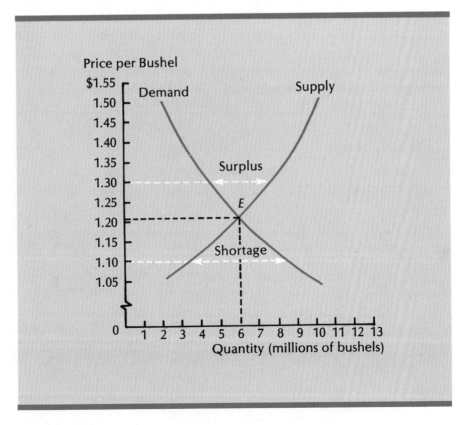

ceiling price lower than the market price during a wartime period. Business firms charged with price fixing are often guilty of collusion with other firms in an effort to interfere with the free market forces. This, likewise, was the rationale behind the oil export embargo when members of OPEC raised prices substantially above the market level in the 1970s.

Under free market conditions the number of possible relationships between demand and supply is practically infinite. For instance, demand may increase while supply remains constant, or vice versa. Again, demand may increase while supply decreases, or vice versa. Or both demand and supply may increase, but demand may increase more than supply.

In any case, however, we can rely on this simple principle: In any new relationship between demand and supply, an increase in demand relative to supply is sure to result in a higher price, and any decrease in demand relative to supply will result in a lower price. On the other hand, an increase in supply will lower the price, and a decrease in supply will raise the price, other things remaining unchanged, as can be seen in Figure 5-6. Based on these principles, it is easy to visualize why world oil prices skyrocketed in the mid-1970s when the Arabian oil nations imposed a petroleum export embargo. The decreased supply of oil coupled with an increasing demand led to substantially higher world oil prices.

Figure 5-6   Alternate Supply and Demand Positions

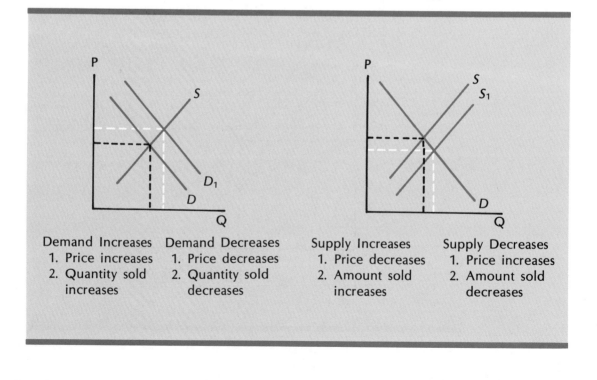

Demand Increases	Demand Decreases	Supply Increases	Supply Decreases
1. Price increases	1. Price decreases	1. Price decreases	1. Price increases
2. Quantity sold increases	2. Quantity sold decreases	2. Amount sold increases	2. Amount sold decreases

ELASTICITY OF DEMAND

The seller is often faced with a problem of determining at which price to offer goods for sale. It is true that a greater amount can be sold at lower prices. But will greater revenue from the larger sales offset the reduced revenue from the lower price? Since the change in sales is not always proportional to the change in price, this can present a real problem not only to sellers but also to consumers. Fortunately there is a way to measure the change in relationship between price and the amount sold. **Price elasticity of demand** is a measure of consumer responsiveness to a change in price. Whether a merchant will benefit by an increase or decrease in price will depend on the degree of price elasticity.

Measuring Price Elasticity of Demand

Let us illustrate price elasticity of demand by constructing three demand curves and measuring their elasticities. In Figure 5-7, observe that for the demand schedule D, 1,600 units are sold at the price of $10; but if the sale price were only $8, the number of units sold would then be 2,000. Elasticity may be measured in either of two ways: the formula method or the total revenue method.

Formula Method. The formula measures the relative change in amount sold compared with the relative change in price and may be stated thus:

$$\text{Price Elasticity} = \frac{\text{\% Change in Quantity}}{\text{\% Change in Price}}$$

A few minor problems arise in applying the formula method. The percentage changes can be computed by using the original price and quantity as bases. If this is done, however, the result will be a different measure of elasticity, depending on whether the price is being decreased or increased. Obviously this would lead to much confusion.

A method often used is to calculate the percentage change by using an average base.[1] The percentage change will be identical whether moving up or down on the price axis. In our example the absolute change in price of $2 would be divided by $9 (the average price between $10 and

---

1. When this method is used, the formula for price elasticity becomes:

$$\text{Price Elasticity} = \frac{\dfrac{Q_2 - Q_1}{\dfrac{Q_1 + Q_2}{2}}}{\dfrac{P_2 - P_1}{\dfrac{P_1 + P_2}{2}}}$$

Figure 5-7 Demand Curves Showing Different Elasticities

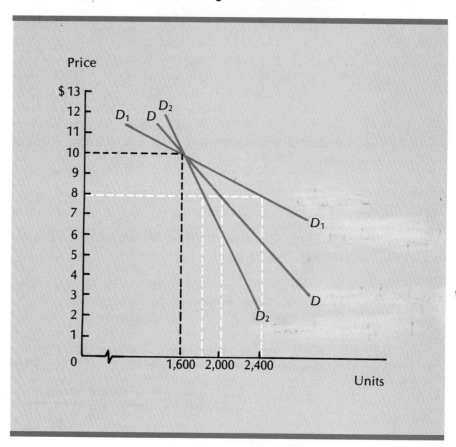

$8) and would be equal to 22 percent. The relative change in amount sold would likewise be 22 percent (400 ÷ 1,800 = 0.22). Consequently, the measure of price elasticity of demand would be 1.0 (0.22 ÷ 0.22 = 1.0). This means that a given change in price will bring about a proportional change in the quantity sold. A 1 percent decrease in price results in a 1 percent increase in the quantity sold. A 3 percent increase in price results in a 3 percent decrease in quantity, and so forth. A coefficient of elasticity of 1.0 is known as **unitary elasticity,** and it is the point of demarcation between an elastic and an inelastic demand. Any value greater than 1.0 is known as an **elastic demand,** and anything less than 1.0 is referred to as an **inelastic demand.**

Now let us measure the elasticity for the demand schedule D_1 in Figure 5-7. Observe that when the price is changed from $10 to $8, a 22 percent change when using the average price as a base of the change, the quantity demanded increases from 1,600 to 2,400 units, an increase of 40 percent

(800 ÷ 2,000 = 0.40). In this case the measure of elasticity is 1.8 (0.40 ÷ 0.22 = 1.8). This means that a 2 percent change in price, for example, will result in a 3.6 percent change in the quantity demanded. In short, consumer demand is elastic, and the quantity demanded will change in greater proportion than the change in price.

Demand schedule D_2 shows less consumer responsiveness to a change in price. Notice that a 22 percent decrease in price from $10 to $8 results in a mere 11 percent increase in quantity sold. This gives an elasticity of demand of 0.5, which indicates that the demand is inelastic and that a change in price will bring about a less than proportional change in the amount sold. A 1 percent increase in price will result in a 0.5 percent change in the quantity sold.

Total Revenue Method.   Of what importance is this information about elasticity, inelasticity, and measures of 1.8, 0.5, and 1.0? To the seller it is extremely important, since it indicates what is going to happen to total revenue received from the sale of products as prices increase or decrease. Likewise, it is important to the consumer. After all, total revenue received by sellers from the sale of the product is nothing other than total expenditures for the product by consumers. From a given consumer income, more spent on one commodity, of course, means that there will be less to spend on others.

The total revenue method of measuring elasticity is less exact, but it tells more directly what happens to total revenue. Furthermore, it shows more clearly the important significance of a coefficient of elasticity. This method can be summarized by remembering:

1. If price changes and total revenue remains constant, unitary elasticity of demand exists. In this case, the decrease in revenue resulting from a lower price will be offset by the increased revenue resulting from an increase in sales. If elasticity is 1.0, sales will increase in proportion to a price decrease.

2. If price changes and total revenue moves in the opposite direction from the price change, demand is elastic. In this case, the decrease in revenue from a lower price is more than offset by the increased revenue from an increase in sales. When elasticity is more than 1.0, sales change in greater proportion than price changes.

3. If price changes and total revenue moves in the same direction as the price change, demand is inelastic. In this case, owing to an elasticity of less than 1.0, the increased revenue from higher sales will not be sufficient to make up for the loss in revenue resulting from a lower price.

The measure of elasticity can be applied to supply also. If a given percentage change in the price of a good results in a greater percentage change in the quantity supplied, the supply is elastic. If the percentage change in price results in a lesser percentage change in the quantity offered, the supply is inelastic. And if the percentage change in price results in a proportionate change in the quantity offered for sale, unitary elasticity exists.

Characteristics and Range of Price Elasticity

It is not easy to construct an empirical demand curve, let alone calculate the elasticity of demand for a product. In the first place, it may be difficult to gather sufficient statistical information to determine how much of a good consumers will buy at each of a series of prices. But it can be done and is being done more and more by firms. Secondly, if a price change is made in an effort to observe the change in quantity demanded, the analyst must be certain that no other changes are taking place, such as an increase in income or greater advertising expenditures, that also will have an influence on the demand.

The degree of price elasticity will depend on the nature of the product or service, such as whether it is a necessity or a luxury; whether it is a small or large budget expenditure for the consumer; whether it is a durable or perishable item; whether it is a complementary or substitute item; and the number of uses to which the item can be put, as summarized in Table 5-4.

The degree of elasticity may range from perfect elasticity, which indicates that an infinite amount of the product could be sold without a change in price (depicted as a straight horizontal line in Figure 5-8a), to perfect inelasticity of demand, which indicates that the same amount would be purchased regardless of price (represented by the straight vertical line in Figure 5-8b). Most goods and services, of course, have a price elasticity lying somewhere between the two extremes. Perfectly unitary elasticity is shown in Figure 5-8c.

Although we tend to say that the more horizontal the demand curve, the more it tends to be elastic, this is not always true. Anytime you have a straight-line, slanted demand schedule, there will be certain areas of

Table 5-4 Characteristics Affecting Elasticity

Tend toward Elastic Demand		Tend toward Inelastic Demand	
Luxuries	Substitute goods	Necessities	Complementary goods
Large expenditures	Multiple uses	Small expenditures	Limited uses
Durable goods		Perishable goods	

Figure 5-8 Three Demand Curves Showing Different Elasticities

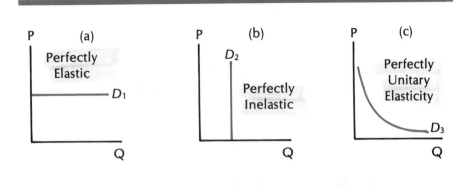

the schedule that are elastic, there will be others that are inelastic, and at some spot it may measure unitary elasticity. This can be clarified by referring to Figure 5-9. Notice on the demand line that a change in price from $9 to $8, a price change of less than 12 percent, brings about a change in quantity demanded from 10 to 20 units, an increase of 67 percent. At the lower end of the vertical axis a price change from $2 to $1, which represents a 67 percent change in price, results in an increase in quantity demanded from 80 to 90 units, or a quantity change of less than 12 percent.

At one end of the scale we have a price elasticity of demand of more than 5.0 and at the other end a highly inelastic measure of less than 0.2. Any change in price through the range of $10 to $5 is elastic, but any change in price between $5 and $1 is inelastic. Observe further that a point of unitary elasticity exists at $5. In fact, on the given demand schedule the point of maximum revenue for the seller would be at $5, since a higher price would result in a decrease in revenue, as would a lower price. For a demand schedule to possess unitary elasticity throughout, it would have to be represented by a rectangular hyperbola as shown in Figure 5-8c. In such a situation, changes in price and quantity demanded are proportional throughout the curve.

The quantity demanded of a particular good is affected not only by its price but also by the price of other goods. A change in the price of commodity *A*, which may be a substitute or complementary product, can affect the sale of product *B*. This is usually referred to as **cross elasticity of demand.**

In addition, the quantity demanded for a given good is affected by the level of income of potential consumers. As the level of income rises, the total demand for goods likewise will rise. But the demand for each good does not necessarily rise proportionally with a rise in income. The demand for some goods may rise in greater proportion than the increase

Figure 5-9   Demand Curve Showing Differing Degrees of Elasticity

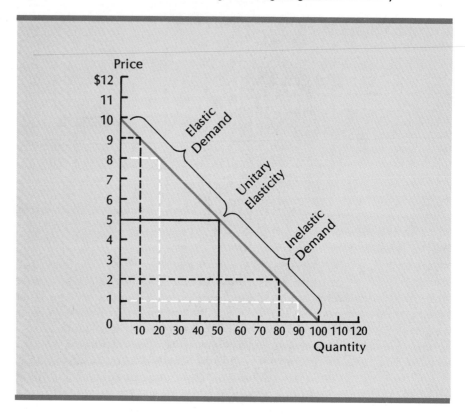

in income and the demand for others less than proportionally. The relation-ship between changing income and changes in demand for a particular good or service is known as **income elasticity of demand.**

In previous chapters we learned that prices serve as rationing mecha-nisms allocating final goods and services, that prices help allocate the various factors of production to their respective uses, and that prices in large part help determine incomes. The reliability of prices in performing these functions greatly depends on the extent to which competition pre-vails within the economy. The presence of monopoly, strong labor unions, government regulations, and other institutional factors, as we shall soon see, can modify the operation of the price system.

SUMMARY

In a free enterprise system the forces of demand and supply determine prices. Indi-

vidual demand signifies the quantities of a good that an individual stands ready to buy at different prices. Due to the operation of the principle of diminishing utility and to limitations of purchasing power, an individual will usually buy more units of a good or service at a lower price than at a higher price. Market demand is the total quantity of a good that will be bought in the market at a given time. It may be represented by a schedule or graph indicating the quantities of a good that would be purchased at different prices at a given time. An increase in demand implies that more of a good will be purchased at each price; a decrease in demand means that fewer units will be purchased at each price.

The supply of a good or service at a given time is the quantity that sellers will offer for sale at different prices. The term may refer to individual or market supply. Supply may be represented by a schedule or graph showing the quantities that will be offered for sale at different prices at a given time. An increase in supply implies that more of a good will be made available at each price; a decrease in supply means that fewer goods will be made available at each price. Under free market conditions, price is fixed at that point where demand and supply are in equilibrium, and it cannot change unless there is a change in demand or supply or both.

Elasticity of demand is a measure of the responsiveness of consumer purchases of a good to a change in its price. Price elasticity of demand can be measured by either the formula method or the total revenue method. There are various degrees of elasticity of demand. An elasticity coefficient of 1.0 designates unitary elasticity. Anything above 1.0 is said to be elastic, while any measure below 1.0 is inelastic. According to the total revenue method, if total revenue moves in the opposite direction from a price change, demand is said to be elastic. If it moves in the same direction, demand is inelastic; and if total revenue remains constant, unitary elasticity exists.

Among the factors that affect price elasticity of demand are the nature of the product, its price in relation to total expenditures, its durability, the availability of a substitute, and the number of uses. Elasticity of demand may range from perfectly elastic at one extreme to perfectly inelastic at the other. It is also possible to calculate cross elasticity of demand and income elasticity of demand.

NEW TERMS AND CONCEPTS

Derived demand
Market demand
Demand
Demand curve
Individual supply
Market supply

Supply curve
Equilibrium price
Price elasticity of
  demand
Unitary elasticity
Elastic demand

Inelastic demand
Cross elasticity of
  demand
Income elasticity of
  demand

DISCUSSION QUESTIONS

1. The impersonal forces of demand and supply in the market determine prices under most competitive conditions. Explain.
2. Define demand. What are the three basic elements in the definition?

3. Why does a normal demand curve slope downward to the right?
4. Distinguish between a movement along a demand curve and a change in demand.

5. Why does the supply curve slope upward to the right?
6. Explain why under competitive conditions market price cannot be higher or lower than that established by the free forces of demand and supply.
7. If both demand and supply increased, but demand increased more than supply, what would happen to price?
8. Define price elasticity of demand. If 46,000 units of a good could be sold at a price of $22, but 54,000 units could be sold at a price of $18, would the demand for the good be elastic or inelastic? What would be the elasticity coefficient?

SUGGESTED READINGS

Friedman, David D. *Price Theory*. Cincinnati: South-Western Publishing Co., 1986.

Hirshleifer, Jack. *Price, Theory and Applications*. Englewood Cliffs, NJ: Prentice-Hall, Inc., 1984.

Koch, James V. *Industrial Organization and Prices*. Englewood Cliffs, NJ: Prentice-Hall, Inc., 1980.

Leftwich, Richard H. *The Price System and Resource Allocation*, 8th ed. Hinsdale, IL: Dryden Press, 1982.

Schumpeter, Joseph A. *The Nature and Necessity of a Price System*. New York: Columbia University Press, 1934.

Thomas, Robert P. *Microeconomic Applications: Understanding the American Economy*. Belmont, CA: Wadsworth Publishing Company, 1981.

Watson, Donald S., and Malcolm Getz. *Price Theory and Its Uses*, 5th ed. Boston: Houghton Mifflin Co., 1981.

6
PRODUCTION, COST, AND PROFIT

■

Under highly competitive conditions there is nothing a firm can do to control its cost per unit of input because that cost is the price of a factor of production determined by supply and demand in the factor market. Nevertheless, the firm can alter its cost per unit of output by using better production techniques, by obtaining more efficient use of labor, by spreading fixed cost over a greater range of output, and by employing other methods. Since a firm's cost of production largely determines the supply of goods that it offers on the market and affects its profit position, a further insight into cost concepts is in order at this point.

THE PRODUCTION FUNCTION

The quantity of goods or services offered for sale will be affected by costs of production. Production cost, however, will in turn be affected by certain physical relationships between factor inputs and product output. The relationship between factor inputs and product output is called the **production function** of the firm. This production function exhibits certain properties that determine the way in which cost varies with output.

Law of Diminishing Returns

The essential function of management in providing a supply of goods is to organize land, capital, and labor so that the best combination of these factors will be used. There should not be too much of one factor and too little of another. The farmer, for example, realizes that a given amount of land requires a certain amount of labor and a specific number of machines. Likewise, the office manager knows that the most efficient operation of a certain number of machines requires a definite number of employees. In either case, if the factors engaged in production are not in the proper proportion, the unit cost will be higher than it otherwise would be and the farmer or the manager will not realize the maximum returns from their efforts.

In every instance where goods are being produced, there is an optimum proportion of the factors of production. This optimum or "best" proportion of the factors is determined in part by the **law of diminishing returns,** or the **law of diminishing productivity** as it is sometimes called.

To illustrate the law of diminishing returns and its effect on cost of production, let us assume that an entrepreneur owns a tool shop with four machines, adequate space, and an ample supply of raw material. If only one worker is hired, the net result will be a limited amount of production, since it will be difficult for one worker to attend to all four of the machines, keep the supply of raw material flowing smoothly, remove and package the finished product, maintain the premises, and do other jobs connected directly or indirectly with the operation of the machines. In fact, some of the machines may be idle a good part of the time. If a second worker of equal ability were hired, total production would increase. It no doubt would more than double, since production would not only benefit from the physical labor of the second worker, but also from the machines operating more of the time. Consequently, total output might rise from 10 units to 22 units.

A similar increase might take place when the entrepreneur hires a third worker, with production rising to 36 units. In fact, if a fourth worker were hired, one person could attend each machine and production might rise still further to 52 units. In each case the increase in production per additional worker exceeds that of the previous worker. This increase in output per additional worker is known as the marginal product of labor.

Marginal Product. The **marginal product** (*MP*) of any input is the increase in total output resulting from an additional unit of that input. In this case our input is labor. But how long can this *MP* continue to increase? Provided all other factors—space, machines, materials—remain fixed, a point will soon be reached at which the fixed factors will become overtaxed or reach their maximum use compared with their previous underutilization. Upon hiring a fifth worker, for example, production still rises. The fifth worker may run stock, package material, and do other jobs that permit the machine tenders to devote more time to their machines. But the increase in production may be less than it was with the addition of the fourth worker. Let us say production expands by 15 units, as shown in Table 6-1.

If additional workers are hired, the *MP* will diminish further. As the hiring continues, you can visualize a situation being reached in which the fixed factors are used to full capacity and there will be absolutely no increase in output. In fact, a stage might even be reached where workers begin getting in each other's way and a decrease in total production could result.

Although it is possible to have increasing marginal productivity, especially in the early stages of production, and even constant marginal pro-

Table 6-1 Input, Output, Marginal Product, and Average Product

Units of Labor	Total Output	Marginal Product	Average Product
1	10	—	10
2	22	12	11
3	36	14	12
4	52	16	13
5	67	15	13.4
6	78	11	13
7	84	6	12
8	88	4	11
9	90	2	10
10	90	0	9

ductivity over a certain range of output, diminishing marginal productivity is more prevalent. Consequently, we hear much about the **law of diminishing marginal productivity,** or **diminishing returns.** This law may be stated as follows: As additional units of a factor of production are combined with fixed quantities of other factors, a point will be reached where the increase in output resulting from the use of an additional unit of that factor will not be as large as was the increase in output due to the addition of the preceding unit.

Average Product.   In dealing with the cost of production, we are also interested in the average product because it too affects the per unit cost. **Average product** (*AP*) can be defined simply as the output per unit of input. Thus, in Table 6-1, when 3 units of labor are used and the resulting total production is 36 units, the *AP* is 12 units (36 ÷ 3 = 12). Observe also that the *AP*, like the *MP*, increases, reaches a maximum, and then declines. This follows from the fact that additions to total product (*MP*) influence the average product. Any time the *MP* is greater than the *AP*, it pulls up the *AP*. When the *MP* is less than the *AP*, it reduces the *AP*. This relationship is shown in Figure 6-1.

Remember that to pull the average product down, the *MP* must be less than the *AP*, not merely declining. Notice in Table 6-1 that *MP* with the addition of the fifth unit of labor declined from 16 to 15 units, but that *AP* rose from 13 to 13.4 units. This is because the *MP* of 15, although diminishing, is still larger than the *AP* of 13. But, again, a point is actually reached where the *AP*, like the *MP*, begins to decline.

Figure 6-1   Relationship of Marginal Product to Average Product

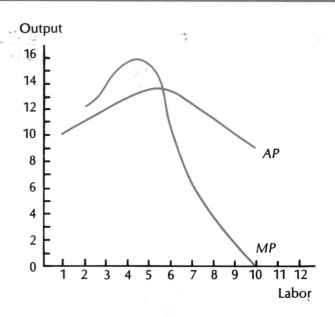

Returns to Scale

The law of diminishing returns applies when one or a few productive agents in the input mix are varied and the remainder are held constant. But what happens if all productive agents are varied proportionately? Suppose, for example, that all factors in the input mix were doubled. Would output double, increase by 50 percent, or perhaps even increase 150 percent?

If output changes in a given proportion to the change in inputs, **constant returns to scale** exist. A doubling of all inputs, for example, will double output. On the other hand, when output increases in smaller proportion than the expansion of inputs, it is an indication of **decreasing returns to scale.** That is, if the entrepreneur were to double all inputs, then output would not double. In contrast, **increasing returns to scale** imply that a doubling of all inputs would more than double output.

COSTS OF PRODUCTION

For all practical purposes the measure of production cost is money, and the cost is figured in terms of payments for labor, capital, materials, and other items directly or indirectly related to production. In addition, in a capitalistic economy an imputed cost allowance is made for the services of the entrepreneur, since it is the opportunity for profit that induces the entrepreneur to assume the risks and to undertake the production. Once in operation, a certain minimum profit is essential if the entrepreneur is to continue producing a good or service. This amount of profit, therefore, is considered to be a cost of production.

Alternative Uses and Opportunity Costs

Under a system of private enterprise, a factor of production is usually employed for production of a specific good only if it is worth more when used for production of that good than it would be if used to produce something else. For example, if there is competition for labor, the automobile manufacturer bids for the labor of mechanics by offering to pay at least as much for their labor as do other employers of mechanics. Other employers likewise compete for the labor of workers of all types.

The same principle operates to determine the cost of materials used by a producer. The automobile manufacturer and all other users of steel must pay a price for steel that is at least equal to the value of that material if used for some other purpose. Likewise, the cost of capital goods and borrowed funds in the form of bank loans is largely determined by the value of such goods or funds if devoted to some other use.

The amount of payment necessary to attract a given factor of production away from the next best opportunity for employment is referred to as **opportunity cost.** This cost exists whether payment is made in the form of cash expenditures or not. For example, suppose you are a farmer and you have a farm on which corn would be the most profitable crop to produce and wheat would be the next most profitable. If you decide to grow corn, the opportunity cost of producing a corn crop will be the value of your land and labor if they were used to produce a wheat crop.

Explicit and Imputed Costs

Expenditures for production that result from agreements or contracts are **explicit costs.** Such costs are always recognized because they are stated in objective terms, usually in terms of money, and are a matter of record. Expenditures that are attributable to the use of one's own factor of production, such as the use of one's own land, are **implicit** or **imputed costs.** In normal accounting procedure, imputed costs often ignored. Nevertheless, in determining the true profit, imputed costs must be recognized as a part of the real cost of production.

Classifications of Costs

Now that we have seen how the physical factors of production can affect the supply of goods and the general cost of production, we can explain and analyze the various costs used by the economist to study business firms.

The costs of production in an individual plant may be classified broadly into fixed costs and variable costs. **Fixed costs** are those costs that remain constant as output varies. Unless the plant capacity is changed, the amount of total fixed cost *(TFC)* in a firm does not vary with the volume of production. *TFC* is frequently referred to as **overhead** and includes interest incurred for construction or the purchase of equipment, depreciation costs, property taxes, and insurance. In addition, a portion of salaries paid for executive and supervisory services may properly be regarded as fixed expenses because a minimum managerial staff must be maintained even when the firm is operating at a limited capacity.

Although the *TFC* remains constant, fixed costs per unit of production decrease with an increase in output. **Average fixed cost** *(AFC)* is calculated by dividing the total fixed costs by the number of units produced. For example, if the *TFC* in a given plant is $1 million and 100,000 units are produced, the amount of fixed costs incurred in producing any one unit is $10. If production is increased to 1 million units, *AFC* falls to $1. The *AFC* continues to decrease as the *TFC* is spread over a larger number of units, but it never disappears entirely. Column 8 of Table 6-2, for example, shows what happens to a $50 total fixed cost when it is converted to average fixed cost.

Variable costs are costs of production other than fixed costs, such as labor and materials. **Average variable cost** *(AVC)* is found by dividing the total variable cost by the number of units produced. As long as the prices of the variable factors remain constant, *AVC* decreases as production increases until the point of diminishing returns is reached.

An Example.   In column 6 of Table 6-2, we can see that if the cost of a variable input is $10, the *TVC* will increase by $10 each time an additional unit of input is added. Consequently, *TVC* increases from $10 to $100 as the inputs increase from 1 to 10. *AVC* can be found by dividing the *TVC* shown in column 6 by the total output shown in column 2. Notice that the *AVC* starts out at $1 per unit of output, drops to $0.75 in line 5, and rises thereafter, reaching $1.11 on line 10. Notice also that the point of lowest *AVC* corresponds with the point of diminishing average productivity, or the point of highest average product.

Total cost *(TC)* is the sum of total fixed and total variable costs at a particular level of production. **Average total cost** *(ATC)* is found by dividing total cost by the number of units produced or by adding the *AFC* and *AVC*. *TC* increases as production increases, but not proportionately. *ATC* decreases, as a rule, until a certain number of units has been produced. Soon after the point of diminishing returns is reached, the *ATC* increases as production increases. This is shown in column 10 of Table 6-2, which indicates that the lowest *ATC* is $1.41 on line 6.

An exceptionally important concept to the economist is marginal cost.

Table 6-2 Hypothetical Productivity, Cost, and Revenue

(1) Input	(2) Total Output	(3) MP	(4) AP	(5) TFC	(6) TVC	(7) TC	(8) AFC	(9) AVC	(10) ATC $	(11) MC	(12) AR	(13) TR	(14) MR	(15) Profit
1	10	—	10	50	10	60	5.00	1.00	6.00	—	2	20	2	−40
2	22	12	11	50	20	70	2.27	0.91	3.18	0.83	2	44	2	−26
3	36	14	12	50	30	80	1.39	0.83	2.22	0.71	2	72	2	− 8
4	52	16	13	50	40	90	0.96	0.77	1.73	0.63	2	104	2	14
5	67	15	13.4	50	50	100	0.75	0.75	1.49	0.67	2	134	2	34
6	78	11	13	50	60	110	0.64	0.77	1.41	0.91	2	156	2	46
7	84	6	12	50	70	120	0.60	0.83	1.43	1.67	2	168	2	48
8	88	4	11	50	80	130	0.57	0.91	1.48	2.50	2	176	2	46
9	90	2	10	50	90	140	0.56	1.00	1.56	5.00	2	180	2	40
10	90	0	9	50	100	150	0.56	1.11	1.67	—	2	180	2	30

UNITS

COST

REVENUE

$$\frac{\Delta TR}{\Delta TO}$$

average per unit

$$\frac{\Delta TC}{\Delta Total\ output}$$

PROFIT MAXIMIZE

WHEN   MR = MC

99

Marginal cost (MC) is the increase in the total cost resulting from the production of one more unit of output. MC is strongly influenced by the law of diminishing returns, and the shape of any MC curve will depend on the shape of the marginal product, MP, curve. Column 3 of Table 6-2 shows the MP schedule and column 11 shows the MC for our hypothetical firm.

Notice that the values of MC decrease, reach a minimum, and then rise thereafter. Observe further that as the MP rises, the MC declines. Then, when the MP starts to decrease, the MC begins to increase. The

Figure 6-2   Relationship of Average Fixed Cost, Average Variable Cost, Average Total Cost, and Marginal Cost

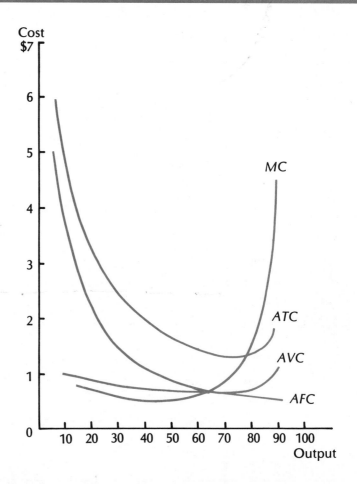

Marginal Product ∝ $\dfrac{1}{Marginal\ Cost}$

point of lowest *MC*, $0.63 as shown on line 4, corresponds with the point of highest *MP*, also shown on line 4. This reveals the close, but inverse, relationship between *MP* and *MC*.

In computing the marginal cost, remember that it refers to the increase in total cost per additional unit of output, not input. Since the second unit of input cost $10 more but resulted in an increase in total output of 12 units, the marginal cost, or increased cost per unit of output, will be equal to $0.83, as shown on line 2 in column 11. Similarly, if the successive increments of total cost are divided by the respective marginal products, the marginal cost for each line will be found.

The Example in Graphic Form.   The relationship of these cost values can be seen much more clearly if they are presented in graphic form, as shown in Figure 6-2. In this case *AFC* will be represented by a curve continuously decreasing in value as total fixed costs are spread over a wider and wider range of output. *AVC* will be a curve decreasing, reaching a minimum, and then rising in value because of the law of diminishing marginal productivity. *ATC*, which is a combination of the *AFC* and the *AVC*, likewise will drop and then rise again. Notice that when both the *AFC* and *AVC* are falling, the *ATC* will be falling. A point is reached at which the *AVC* starts to rise while the *AFC* is still declining. What happens to the *ATC* at this point will depend on the relative strength of the two curves.

In Figure 6-2 notice that initially the downward pull of the *AFC* is stronger than the upward pull of the *AVC* so that the *ATC* continues to drop for a while. But eventually the upward pull of the *AVC* overcomes the downward pull of the *AFC*, and the *ATC* rises thereafter. Graphically, *MC* will decrease, reach a minimum, and then rise owing to its close relationship with the marginal product curve. Anytime *MC* is less than the *AVC* or the *ATC*, it will effect a reduction in the *AVC* and/or *ATC*, in much the same manner that the marginal product affects the average product. Whenever *MC* is greater than the *AVC* or *ATC*, it will cause them to increase. Furthermore, by its very nature *MC* will intersect the *AVC* and the *ATC* lines at their lowest points.

REVENUE AND PROFIT

In the preceding chapter we saw that the demand schedule indicates the quantities of a good or service that will be purchased at various prices. It was pointed out, too, that under competitive conditions the price would be determined by the free forces of supply and demand. Although conditions are not always competitive, we will accept for the present the supposition that the market price becomes the price at which an individual firm can sell its product. This will permit us to look at some revenue concepts and relate them to the cost concepts to analyze the profit situation for an individual firm.

Revenues

Average revenue *(AR)*, as used by the economist, is the revenue per unit sold. It is the market price from the viewpoint of the seller, and it may be computed by dividing the total revenue by the number of units sold. **Total revenue** *(TR)*, of course, is the amount of revenue or income received from the sale of a given quantity of goods or services. It can be calculated readily by multiplying the *AR*, or price, by the number of units sold.

An extremely important and more complex concept used by the economist is marginal revenue, which parallels the marginal cost concept explained earlier. **Marginal revenue** *(MR)* is the increase in total revenue that results from the sale of one more unit of output. This can be calculated by dividing the increase in total revenue resulting from the use of an additional unit of input by the increase in total product.

In our example in Table 6-2, the values of the *MR* and the *AR* are identical. This will not always be the case. Anytime you are dealing with other than perfectly competitive conditions, the values of the *MR* and the *AR* will differ. With a constant price, however, whenever the firm sells an additional unit at the market price of $2, it will add $2 to its *TR* and the *MR* will equal the *AR*, or price.

Constant Price

$MR = AR$

Profit

Total profit is the difference between total revenue and total cost. Whether a firm makes a profit, and how much profit, depends on the relationship of its revenue to its costs. Even when a firm is not making a profit, the decision of whether to continue to operate or shut down will depend, again, on its cost-revenue relationships. A firm can analyze its profit situation in many ways. For instance, it may compare its total revenue with its total cost by using a break-even chart, or it may engage in marginal analysis by dealing with marginal revenue and marginal cost concepts.

Total Revenue Versus Total Cost

By comparing total revenue with total cost over a given range of output, a firm can determine at which levels it makes a profit and at what levels it suffers losses. Furthermore, it can determine at what point its losses cease and profits begin. This, of course, is known as the **break-even point.** It may be given in terms of the total output, or it may be analyzed in terms of total inputs. Other firms construct their break-even charts in terms of capacity to indicate at what level they must operate their plant to avoid losses and make profits. Naturally a firm will endeavor not only to reach the break-even output or capacity but also to go beyond it as far as it is profitable. It must avoid the pitfall, however, of pushing too far beyond, because it may encounter rapidly rising marginal costs at, or near, capacity levels. In such an event, total profits may actually decline in spite of higher output. The maximum profit position will be that level of output, or capacity, where there is the greatest gap between total revenue and total cost, as shown in Figure 6-3.

Another advantage of a break-even chart is that cost can be broken down into *TFC* and *TVC*. In fact, if desirable, the variable cost can be segmented further into a variety of costs, including such items as direct and indirect manufacturing cost, material cost, labor cost, and selling costs.

Putting the values from our hypothetical firm into Figure 6-3 shows the *TFC* of $50 represented by a straight horizontal line. This indicates that the fixed costs remain constant over a given range of output. Total costs, which continually increase, are represented by a line moving upward

Figure 6-3 Break-Even Chart

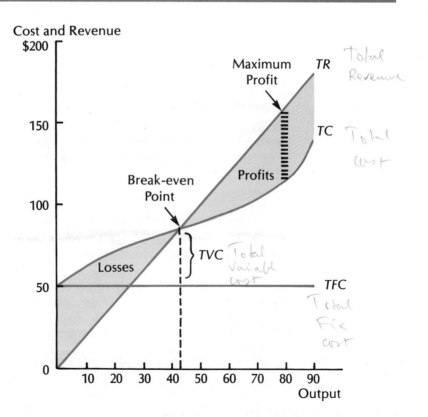

to the right. The difference between *TC* and *TFC* represents the *TVC*. Since the price at which each unit sells is constant, the total revenue is shown by the line moving upward to the right at a constant slope. The break-even point is at 42 units of output. Although profits are made at all levels of production beyond this point, maximum profit is made when production is in the vicinity of 80 units. The same information can be interpolated from Table 6-2, page 99.

Marginal Revenue Versus Marginal Cost

It is only reasonable to assume that anytime a firm can add to its total profit by producing more or fewer units, it will act accordingly. Consequently, the firm's profit picture is often analyzed in terms of what happens to cost and revenue with the addition of one more unit of input or output. Whenever the production and sale of a marginal unit adds more to revenue than it does to cost, profits are sure to increase, or losses diminish, whatever the case may be. If the production of one more unit adds more to cost than it does to revenue, the opposite is true. We have available two such concepts that tell us how much is added to revenue and how much is added to cost with each additional unit of output. To determine the point of maximum profit for the firm, all we have to do is observe their relationship.

Marginal revenue, *MR*, measures the increase in total revenue per additional unit of output, and marginal cost, *MC*, measures the increase in total cost per additional unit of output. Therefore, anytime *MR* is greater than *MC*, profits will rise or losses will diminish. On the other hand, if *MR* is less than *MC*, profits will decrease, or losses will increase. A firm will profit by increasing its output so long as its *MR* > *MC*. It will pay to reduce output whenever *MR* < *MC*.

In most cases marginal revenue is a constant or decreasing value, and the marginal cost is a continuously increasing value. Therefore, as a firm adds units of output, it eventually reaches a point at which *MR* = *MC*. This is its maximum profit position, since at any lower level of output *MR* > *MC* and at any greater level *MR* < *MC*. In our hypothetical firm, for example, it can be observed that the *MR* has a constant value of $2, while the *MC*, after reaching a low of $0.63, continuously increases to more than $5 as production reaches 90 units. Comparing the *MR* in column 14 with the *MC* in column 11 in Table 6-2, it can be seen that, at all levels of production up to and including the seventh unit of input, *MR* > *MC*. Therefore, the firm will continue to produce up to that point. It will not add the eighth unit of input, however, since *MR* < *MC* for the output that will be forthcoming. Consequently, the firm will maximize profits, according to the marginal analysis, at a level of output in the vicinity of 80 units. This, of course, corresponds with the maximum profit position indicated on the break-even chart illustrated in Figure 6-3.

Minimizing Losses in the Short Run

Thus far we have been dealing with the pleasant situation of a firm making a profit, but what happens if the firm is suffering a loss? Suppose, for example, that in our problem the average revenue received by the firm was only $1, as determined by the forces of the market. Assuming that the costs remained the same, it would be evident from reexamining Table 6-2 that our firm would not be able to make a profit at any level of production. It would, however, minimize its losses with 6 units of input, or 78 units of output. What then should the firm do—continue to operate or shut down? The answer will depend on the relationship of cost to revenue and on whether we are talking about the short-run or the long-run period.

In economics the **short run** is a period of time in which some factors of production are fixed. The **long run** is a period of time in which all factors of production, including machinery, buildings, and other capital items, are variable. In the short run, for example, it may be possible for a firm to increase its output within a given range by adding more workers, putting on another shift, buying more raw materials, and manipulating other variable factors without increasing the size of its fixed plant and equipment. If given enough time, however, it could increase its output greatly in the long run by adding to its capacity with the construction or purchase of new plant and equipment. Consequently, in the long run even the fixed factors become variable. The actual length of this period is rather nebulous and varies with different industries.

If a firm is operating at a loss in the short run, and we will assume it is minimizing its losses, the question still remains whether it should continue to operate or shut down. The answer will depend very much on the relationship of its fixed to its variable cost and the relationship of the variable cost to its total revenue.

Assume that a firm has a *TFC* of $60,000 and a *TVC* of $40,000 for a *TC* of $100,000. At the same time suppose its *TR* is $50,000. It is obvious that the firm is suffering a loss of $50,000. Nevertheless, it is better for it to continue to operate in the short run rather than shut down. Notice that by operating, the loss is only $50,000; but if it were to shut down, its loss would be greater. If it were to close down, its total cost would drop by the amount of its variable cost, $40,000; but keep in mind that its revenue would drop to zero. Furthermore, it would still have its fixed cost of $60,000 to pay, and its loss would be $60,000 instead of $50,000.

PURE PROFIT

From an economic point of view, profit is a residual of income over and above all economic costs, both explicit and implicit, that results from the operation of a business. Profits are dynamic in that they are constantly changing in amount. New business firms are established in the hope of making a profit, and other businesses fail because of lack of profit. Starting a business involves a risk, but the opportunity for profit induces thousands of individuals annually to try to become successful entrepreneurs.

Pure profit is a return to the entrepreneur from the operation of the business. It may be either large or small. It excludes any return from the use of the other factors of production utilized in the input mix. If the profit is too small or if the firm suffers a loss, it may go out of business. That amount of profit that is necessary to induce the entrepreneur to stay in business is called **nominal profit.** It is measured by the opportunity cost of the services of the entrepreneur. Usually nominal profit is considered as an economic cost of doing business. When it is, the nominal profit position becomes a no-profit position as far as the business operation is concerned. Any amount over and above the nominal profit can be called **pure profit.** Under conditions of pure competition, profit, in addition to being residual and dynamic, is a temporary phenomenon. The conditions of pure competition are such that anytime a pure profit exists, forces come into play to eliminate such pure profit. This is so because of the nature of pure competition, as we shall soon see.

Conversely, in a monopoly, if a pure profit situation exists, the monopolist may be able by various means to effectively block the entry of new firms into the industry. Thus, profit becomes more than a temporary phenomenon. Furthermore, since the output of the monopoly becomes the total supply on the market, the monopolist can influence the market price by changing output. In this way the price can be set where it will yield the greatest profit. Under a condition of monopolistic or imperfect competition—which frequently occurs—profits may be larger than they would be under pure competition.

SUMMARY

In providing a supply of goods or services for the market, the cost of production is affected by physical factors such as the law of diminishing marginal productivity (or law of diminishing returns) and returns to scale. The most widely recognized of these factors, the law of diminishing returns, means that as additional units of a factor of production are combined with a fixed quantity of other factors, a point will be reached where the output resulting from the use of an additional unit of the variable input factor will not be as large

as was the output resulting from the addition of the preceding unit.

In analyzing a firm's cost the economist considers not only the explicit cost but also the imputed cost of using one's own factors of production, such as labor or land, in the productive process. Imputed costs are generally measured in terms of alternative uses to which the factors of production could be applied. Costs may be classified as fixed or variable. Total cost is a combination of both. Cost may also be broken down into unit cost, such as average fixed cost, average variable cost, average total cost, and marginal cost. The price received per unit of output, as determined by the forces of demand and supply in the market, is known as average revenue to the firm. Marginal revenue is the increase in total revenue that results from the sale of an additional unit of output.

A firm can analyze its profit position by means of a break-even chart on which are plotted total revenue, total cost, total fixed cost, and total variable cost. In addition to ascertaining the break-even point, a firm can also determine its maximum profit level on such a chart. The maximum profit position of a firm can also be determined by marginal analysis. A firm will maximize its profits or minimize its losses by operating at the point where marginal revenue equals marginal cost. Even if a firm is suffering a loss, it will benefit the firm to continue operating in the short run so long as it is recovering its variable cost and is making a contribution to overhead.

Profit is the residual of income over and above all economic costs that result from the operation of a business. That amount of profit that is necessary to induce the entrepreneur to stay in business is called nominal profit. Any amount over and above the nominal profit is referred to as pure profit.

NEW TERMS AND CONCEPTS

Production function
Marginal product
Law of diminishing marginal productivity, or diminishing returns
Average product
Constant returns to scale
Decreasing returns to scale
Increasing returns to scale
Opportunity cost

Explicit costs
Implicit or imputed costs
Fixed costs
Overhead
Average fixed cost
Variable costs
Average variable cost
Total cost
Average total cost

Marginal cost
Average revenue
Total revenue
Marginal revenue
Break-even point
Short run
Long run
Nominal profit
Pure profit

DISCUSSION QUESTIONS

1. Does the size of the marginal product have an effect on the average product? Explain.
2. Explain the law of diminishing marginal productivity.
3. How do you distinguish between explicit and implicit (imputed) costs?
4. Explain why the average variable cost decreases, reaches a minimum, and then rises again, while the average fixed cost continues to decrease as output increases.
5. Is it true that whenever marginal cost is rising, the average variable cost and the average total cost must also rise? Why?
6. How is maximum profit position determined on a break-even chart? What components are needed to construct a break-even chart?
7. Why is the point at which marginal revenue equals marginal cost the maximum profit position?
8. What is pure profit and how is it measured?

SUGGESTED READINGS

Cohen, Kalman J., and Richard M. Cyert. *The Theory of the Firm: Resource Allocation in a Market Economy*, 2d ed. Englewood Cliffs, NJ: Prentice-Hall, Inc., 1975.

Cole, Charles L. *Microeconomics; A Contemporary Approach*. New York: Harcourt Brace Jovanovich, Inc., 1973.

Friedman, David D. *Price Theory*. Cincinnati: South-Western Publishing Co., 1986.

Hadar, Josef. *Elementary Theory of Microeconomic Behavior*. Reading, MA: Addison-Wesley Publishing Co., 1974.

Marshall, Alfred. *Principles of Economics*. New York: Macmillan Publishing Co., 1961.

McCloskey, Donald N. *The Applied Theory of Price*, 2d ed. New York: Macmillan Publishing Co., 1986.

McKenzie, Richard. *Microeconomics*. Boston: Houghton Mifflin Co., 1986.

Watson, Donald S., and Malcolm Getz. *Price Theory and Its Uses*, 5th ed. Boston: Houghton Mifflin Co., 1981.

7
PURE COMPETITION: A MODEL

■

Many types of competition exist in the U.S. economic system. Since there are over 12 million firms, exclusive of farms, doing business in hundreds of industries, it is possible to find various degrees of competition within each industry and numerous shades of competition between different markets. Market situations may range all the way from perfect or pure competition to pure monopoly. Although there are fundamental differences between types of competition, sometimes conditions in a firm or an industry will contain elements of more than one type. Furthermore, a firm may find itself in one type of competitive market in selling its products but a different type of competitive market in buying its raw materials or hiring labor.

The basic types of market structure are pure competition, pure monopoly, monopolistic competition, and oligopoly. Among the distinguishing characteristics of different types of markets are the number of firms in an industry, the presence or absence of product differentiation, and the ability of any or all firms in an industry to influence the market price. Since pure competition affords a theoretical standard by which we measure the economic and social value of other forms of market structure, we shall first analyze the purely competitive industry.

CHARACTERISTICS OF PURE COMPETITION

Pure competition is an ideal set of market conditions that assumes the following characteristics.[1]

1. *There are numerous sellers in the market, all selling an identical product.* There are no quality differences, no brand names, no advertising,

---

1. Although the phrase "pure competition" is sometimes used interchangeably with the phrase "perfect competition," there is a degree of difference in the meanings of the two. **Perfect competition** implies that there is perfect information about markets and prices on the part of all buyers and sellers, perfect mobility of the various factors of production, and perfectly free entry into and exit from an industry. In short, perfect competition is more idealistic and is characterized by a higher degree of competition.

nor anything else that would differentiate the products of various sellers.

2. *All consumers and sellers are informed about markets and prices.* If one seller is putting a product on the market at a lower price than others, all consumers are aware of this. Furthermore, if one producer can offer a good on the market at a lower price than competitors because of certain cost advantages, other producers will soon learn why and how it can be done.

3. *There is free entry into and exit from the market.* Anyone who desires to produce and sell goods in a particular market may do so, without any undue encumbrances. This, of course, would exclude the protection of patent rights, the absence of excessive capital requirements, the availability of the necessary factors of production, freedom from government regulations, and other conditions that may hinder or deter a person or firm from going into the production of a particular type of good or service. Pure competition also assumes that there is perfect mobility on the part of the factors of production.

4. *No individual seller or consumer can influence price. Price is determined by market supply and market demand.* There must be enough sellers in the market so that each one's contribution to the total supply is infinitesimal. Consequently, whether a firm increases or decreases production has no appreciable effect on the total supply. Under such circumstances each seller must accept the market price as determined by aggregate demand and supply. The seller will not be able to obtain a greater price for his or her product because all products of that kind are identical. This does not preclude the possibility, however, that the market price could be changed by the actions of many, or all, firms. If an individual producer increased output by 50 or 100 percent, for example, the change in total supply would be so insignificant that it would not affect the market price. On the other hand, if each of a large number of producers increased output by 10 percent, this could affect supply appreciably and result in a change in market price.

PRICE AND PROFIT IN THE SHORT RUN

Under pure competition each producer faces a perfectly elastic demand curve; that is, the producer's entire supply can be sold at the market-determined price. Profit will depend upon the difference between the average total cost of production and the selling price, multiplied by the number of units sold. Since producers are in business to make a profit, each producer will try to produce that number of units whose sale will yield the greatest profit.

Acting alone, a producer can do little or nothing to change the market price. It will make no appreciable difference on price if a given producer sells much or nothing. This is not true, however, for the industry as a whole. If a great many or all producers increase or decrease production, the total market supply will be affected. This will result in a change in price, assuming that demand does not change.

A case in point is the production of wheat in the United States, where there are more than one-half million producers. Whether Farmer Yoshino increased production from 100 to 1,000 or even to 10,000 bushels will have little, if any, effect on a market price of $4 per bushel when there is a total supply of more than 2.0 billion bushels on the U.S. market each year and over 14 billion bushels on the world market. On the other hand, if each wheat farmer in the United States increased output by a mere 2 percent, it would increase the total U.S. wheat supply by more than 40 million bushels and no doubt would tend to lower the market price.

Under a condition of pure competition in an industry that is producing a standardized commodity, how many units of the commodity will each producer undertake to produce? This question cannot be answered exactly, but we can acquire an understanding of the factors that help to determine the amount that each one will produce. Within the assumed short-run conditions we shall see how each producer will attempt to set output where marginal cost becomes equal to marginal revenue. For the sake of simplicity, we assume that no new factories will be built in the industry and that existing plants will not be enlarged. But it is assumed that each firm is free to vary its volume of production from zero to its maximum existing capacity.

Adjustment of Production to Price in the Short Run

Just how much will the single firm undertake to produce? In most real situations it would probably be impossible to say. It is not likely that the entrepreneur could predict exactly what the cost would be at different levels of production. In addition, the producer is likely to be satisfied with a "good" or "reasonable" amount of profit, which would mean he or she would refrain from attempting to squeeze out the very last possible cent of profit from the business.

Nevertheless, it is realistic to assume that the producer is motivated by the desire to make as much profit as possible. This assumption does not deny the fact that the producer probably has values and interests other than those that relate to money. But for the purpose of economic analysis, it is necessary to give attention here only to those matters that affect the profit possibilities of a productive enterprise operating under conditions of pure competition.

Therefore, to arrive at a logical determination of the firm's output, we proceed on the assumption that the entrepreneur will undertake to produce that amount which will maximize the firm's profit or minimize its loss. What that volume of production will be depends upon the firm's cost and revenue relationships.

Let us assume for a certain producer that total cost, average total cost, marginal cost, average revenue and marginal revenue, and total revenue are as shown in Table 7-1 and Figure 7-1. The difference between *AR* (or price) and *ATC* represents profit per unit. Profit per unit multiplied by the output measures total profit. Remember that a firm will maximize its profits (or minimize its losses) at the point where marginal cost equals marginal revenue *(MC = MR)*. A close inspection of Table 7-1 and Figure 7-1 reveals that at a price of $1.80 per unit, the equilibrium output, 13 units, corresponds with the point of intersection between the marginal cost and marginal revenue curves.

The point where *MC = MR* is called the equilibrium point because once the firm reaches that position, there is no incentive to move to any other level of output. If it is not operating at that point, the firm is motivated by the prospect of greater profit to change its output until the equilibrium position is attained. If *MC < MR*, an expansion of output will increase profit. If *MC > MR*, a contraction of output will increase profit. When *MC = MR*, total profit is at the maximum.

In this case if the price is $1.80 and fewer than 9 units or more than

Table 7-1   Cost and Revenue Schedule

Units of Output	TC	ATC	MC	TR	AR and MR	Total Profit or Loss
1	$10.08	$10.08	—	$ 1.80	$1.80	−$8.28
2	11.22	5.61	$1.14	3.60	1.80	− 7.62
3	12.12	4.04	0.90	5.40	1.80	− 6.72
4	12.84	3.21	0.72	7.20	1.80	− 5.64
5	13.44	2.69	0.60	9.00	1.80	− 4.44
6	13.98	2.33	0.54	10.80	1.80	− 3.18
7	14.52	2.07	0.54	12.60	1.80	− 1.92
8	15.12	1.89	0.60	14.40	1.80	− 0.72
9	15.84	1.76	0.72	16.20	1.80	0.36
10	16.74	1.67	0.90	18.00	1.80	1.26
11	17.88	1.63	1.14	19.80	1.80	1.92
12	19.32	1.61	1.44	21.60	1.80	2.28
13	21.12	1.62	1.80	23.40	1.80	2.28
14	23.34	1.67	2.22	25.20	1.80	1.86
15	26.04	1.74	2.70	27.00	1.80	0.96
16	29.28	1.83	3.24	28.80	1.80	− 0.48
17	33.12	1.95	3.84	30.60	1.80	− 2.52

Figure 7-1 Cost and Revenue Curves

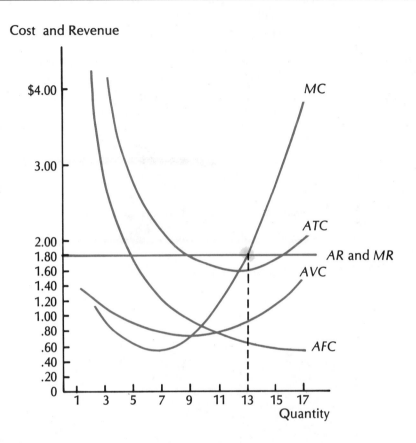

15 are produced, the producer will lose money. It is only when 9 to 15 units are produced that *AR* (price) is above *ATC*. Note that after producing 13 units, *MC* rises above *MR*. Although some profit could be realized by producing and selling 15 units, maximum profit cannot be increased by producing more than 13 units, the output for which *MC* and *MR* are exactly equal. If *MC* and *MR* did not coincide exactly for the production of a whole unit, then it would be most profitable to produce the whole number nearest to where they are equal.

Now suppose that the price, instead of $1.80, falls to $1.61, as shown in Figure 7-2. Note that at this price *ATC*, *MC*, AR_1, and MR_1 are practically equal at the point of intersection of the *MC* and MR_1 curves. What does this signify? It means that the most the producer can hope for is to break even. By producing 12 units, *AR* will be just equal to *ATC*. If any more units are produced, *ATC* and *MC* will rise above MR_1 and AR_1 and a loss will be incurred. If the producer stops short of producing 12 units, *ATC* will be greater than AR_1 and a loss will also be incurred.

For another example, assume that the price (AR_2 and MR_2) has fallen to $1.20 as shown in Figure 7-2. How many units will be produced? We can see that no matter how many units are produced, the producer cannot hope to make a profit because, for any number of units, *ATC* is above AR_2. The point at which the loss can be minimized is the production of 11 units, the number that is nearest the intersection of *MC* and MR_2. The producer will not produce more than 11 units, however, because beyond that point *MC* rises above MR_2.

In this case it will pay the firm to continue to operate in the short

Figure 7-2   Cost and Revenue Curves

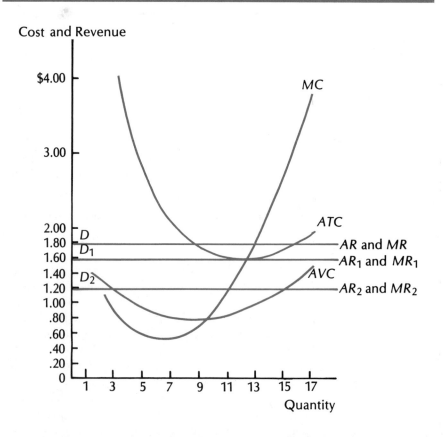

run rather than shut down. It will pay the firm to continue to operate so long as it can recover its variable cost. Whether it can do so may be ascertained by comparing the *AVC* with the *AR* at the equilibrium level. If *AR* = *AVC*, it will recover its variable cost. If *AR* > *AVC*, it will also recover a part of its fixed cost, or as stated earlier, it will make a contribution to overhead. How much of a contribution it will make can be observed from the graph. Although the fixed cost is not drawn on the chart, remember that since *ATC* = *AFC* + *AVC*, the *AFC* will be represented by the difference between the *ATC* and *AVC* curves at the point of equilibrium.

On the other hand, visualize a situation in which the market price may be only $0.60 for the firm in question. Not only would the firm suffer a loss at any level of output, but even at the equilibrium level, or point of minimum loss, the *AR* would be less than the *AVC*. In this situation, the firm would not recover its variable cost and would find it less costly to shut down rather than operate in the short run. In such a case *AR* < *AVC* at the equilibrium point.

Short-Run Equilibrium Price

We may conclude, therefore, that the competitive **short-run equilibrium price** is that price which results from the interaction of demand and supply over a short period of time.

What might be called "short-run equilibrium price" is not a stable price, for at the given market price prevailing during the short-run period, **submarginal producers**—those whose total cost is greater than their revenue—could not break even. These producers would eventually improve their efficiency or disappear. If they disappeared, the market supply would decrease, which would cause the price to rise. If they improved their efficiency, the supply would increase, which would cause the market price to decline. Moreover, the presence of **supramarginal producers**—those who are making profits—would attract newcomers into the industry, and this would result in an increase in the market supply of the good and a decrease in the market price.

PRICE AND PROFIT IN THE LONG RUN

Under conditions of pure competition, economic profits are residual, dynamic, and temporary. Profit is *residual* insofar as it is revenue that remains after deducting both explicit and implicit costs, including a nominal profit as an imputed cost of the entrepreneur's service. Profits are *dynamic* insofar as they are constantly changing in amount and among firms. Under purely competitive conditions profits are *temporary*, in that, if profits are being made, long-run forces that tend to reduce or eliminate economic or pure profit will come into play. On the other hand, if losses are generally being suffered, market forces tend to bring about adjustments that may cause profits to appear.

Profit Differentiation among Firms

It should be remembered that under conditions of pure competition all firms pay an identical price for input factors, and all sell their finished goods, or output, at a uniform market price. It is still possible, however, for profits among firms to differ. One of the main reasons for this difference is that, even though all firms have the same unit cost for inputs, some firms use their inputs more efficiently. In the short run some of them may be using better production techniques, they may be spreading their fixed cost over a larger range of output, and they may be using other measures to lower per unit cost of output. At any given market price, therefore, it is possible to have some firms making a profit, others breaking even, and still others suffering a loss. This is demonstrated in Figure 7-3.

A change in the market price, as it moves up or down, can affect the profit status of each firm. A change in the per unit cost of inputs, likewise, can affect the profit of each firm by altering its average cost curve. In the long run it is assumed that the submarginal firms will reorganize their productive factors to make a profit or else will drop out of business. Remember that pure competition assumes that all sellers are informed about markets, prices, and costs. Therefore, if for some reason one firm is able to produce at a lower cost, others will know how it can be done. In the long run, adoption of similar production techniques will enable the others to adjust their factors to reduce costs.

Figure 7-3   Profit, Break-Even, and Loss Positions

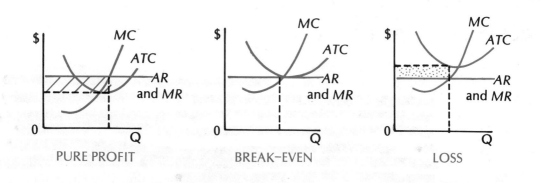

How Profits Disappear

Under pure competition, competitive forces tend to eliminate pure profit. This is due to the freedom of firms to enter into and exit from the industry. If a profit is being made by firms in the industry, outsiders can gather information on how to produce and share in the profits being made. Indeed, they have both the incentive and the freedom to do so.

It is true that no individual supplier can influence price under conditions of pure competition; but if a number of new firms enter the market, the addition of their supplies to the total market supply could very well result in a decrease in market price. If profits still remain even at the lower price, firms will continue to enter the industry, continuously lowering prices until a point is reached at which the price will equal the average total cost and pure profit will be eliminated. On the other hand, if the price were below cost and firms in the industry were suffering losses, firms would drop out of the industry. In the long run the market supply would be reduced, causing price to rise and losses to disappear in the industry. The process took place recently, for example, in the computer industry. It expanded during the 1960s and 1970s as prices and profits rose, but it contracted in the 1980s when prices and profits fell and many firms either merged or dropped out of the industry. This whole process can be demonstrated graphically, as in Figure 7-4.

Assume that the intersection of demand (D) and supply (S) in Figure 7-4 establishes a market price of $5 per unit. This then will be the AR for each of the firms in the industry. Assuming that these cost and revenue

Figure 7-4 Long-Run Equilibrium Price and Profit

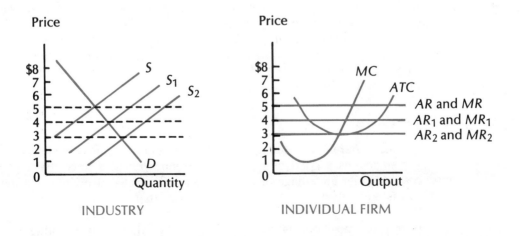

relationships are typical for the industry, individual firms will be making profits. These profits, however, will induce new firms to enter the industry. As they enter, total supply on the market will increase, and market price will be lowered to $4, as shown by the intersection of S_1 and D. This in turn will lower the AR and MR curves for each of the firms in the industry, thereby reducing profits. Since profits still exist even at this price, firms will continue to enter the industry, increasing the market supply to S_2 and reducing the price to $3 per unit.

At an AR and MR of $3, there will be no pure profit for the firms in the industry. At this point there is no further incentive for additional firms to enter the industry. Not only are all the firms in equilibrium because they are operating at the point where $MC = MR$, but also equilibrium exists in the industry because there is no incentive for firms to enter or leave. There is no excess profit to attract new firms. On the other hand, since existing firms will be covering all explicit and imputed costs, including a nominal return to the entrepreneur, they will not be inclined to withdraw from the industry.

You can visualize what would happen if the initial market price were such that losses existed in the industry. As firms dropped out of the industry, the total supply on the market would decrease, raising the market price and the MR and AR of the individual firms. This process would continue until the price was raised sufficiently to eliminate losses. At that point, there would be no further incentive for firms to leave the industry, and equilibrium would again be established.

Before leaving this topic, it should be remembered that we demonstrated the movement from a short-run profit position to a long-run, no-pure profit equilibrium by adjustments in the market price or average revenue. It is also possible, however, that the long-run profit squeeze may be accelerated by an upward pressure on the cost of inputs. As new firms enter the industry, their combined demand for inputs may very well increase the total demand for raw material, labor, capital, and other inputs. This in turn could raise the market price of inputs and the ATC curve for individual firms, causing a reduction in profits. Consequently, the competitive forces in the economy work from two angles—the downward pressure on prices and the upward pressure on cost—to eliminate profits in the long run.

The Long-Run Cost Curve

Under pure competition, or highly competitive conditions, the consumer obtains a good or service in the long run at a price that equals cost. Another advantage of competition is the fact that price in the long run is equal to *minimum* average total cost, that is, the lowest point on the ATC curve. Although the typical firm may be in equilibrium at a no-pure profit position, as shown in Figure 7-4, there may be other firms operating at a larger scale that are making a pure profit with the given market price. Pure competition assumes that all firms are informed about any cost advantages that may arise as a result of larger-scale operations. Consequently, the no-pure profit firms, observing the larger-scale operators making a profit, will be inclined to enlarge their operations. As they move toward the larger scale of operations, of course, the total supply in the market will increase, forcing market price downward. If industry equilibrium comes into existence at the larger scale of operations and the firms reach a no-pure profit position, competition may very well lead some aggressive innovators to try operating on a still larger scale in the hope of reducing cost to make profits.

If the firm is successful and does make a profit at the larger scale of operations, existing producers will follow suit and others will enter the industry at this new, larger scale of operations. As they do so, the supply will increase once more, forcing the price down still further. Eventually a point of diminishing returns will be reached on the scale of operations. This will be known as the **optimum scale of operation**. At any larger scale there will be no further cost advantages arising from size. In fact, *ATC* may increase owing to inefficiencies arising from excessive bigness. By joining all the short-run *ATC* curves, we can develop a long-run *ATC* curve, as shown in Figure 7-5.

At any scale of operations up to the optimum scale, it is said that **economies of scale** exist because long-run *ATC* decreases as the size of the plant increases. Beyond the optimum scale, however, **diseconomies of scale** come into existence, causing the long-run *ATC* to bend upward.

Figure 7-5 Long-Run Average Total Cost Curve

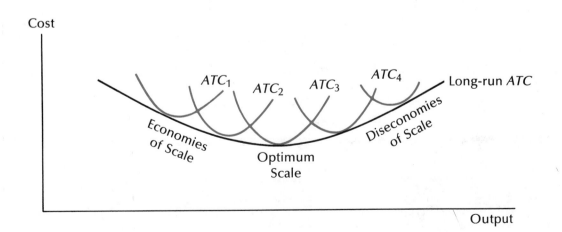

THE SOCIAL IMPACT OF PURE COMPETITION

Theoretically there are two major virtues of industry-wide and economy-wide pure competition: (1) competition stimulates initiative and productive energy, and (2) competition results in minimum prices to consumers. Under an assumed condition of pure competition throughout the economy, efficiency in all divisions of production would be promoted and only the most efficient entrepreneurial undertaking would survive. The existence of high profits in any field of production would induce most of the producers to increase their outputs and encourage additional entrepreneurs to enter the field, with the result that the supplies of goods or services would increase and prices would decline. The demand for the factors of production would be competitive, which would enable the owners of each of the factors to obtain fair and reasonable prices for what they had to sell. Potential entrepreneurs would be encouraged to discover and to produce new types of goods and services that would be desired by consumers.

As a consequence of economy-wide competition, profits either would disappear or would be reduced to the minimum necessary to induce only the most efficient entrepreneurs to undertake the risks of production. At the same time, the prices of goods and services would be at the lowest possible level consistent with the practice of personal freedom by all individuals.

Pure competition would serve the consumer very well. It would result in greater production, the use of more resources and labor, lower prices, and less profits than would exist under noncompetitive conditions. However, competition is not without its disadvantages. It frequently results in an unnecessary duplication of plant and equipment; it often brings forth an endless and sometimes needless variety of models and fashions; and at other times it causes a waste of resources, especially in the extractive industries. Although competition benefits the economy as a whole, it can cause financial hardship for individual producers and displacement of workers as business firms are forced out of business by more efficient producers. It is also possible that in some industries, such as public utilities, many firms, each operating at a small scale, would not be able to provide a good or a service as cheaply as a few firms producing at a much larger scale.

SUMMARY

There are several types of models of economic competition, ranging from pure competition at one extreme to pure monopoly at the other. In between are monopolistic competition and oligopoly.

Pure competition is an ideal set of market conditions in which there are numerous buyers and sellers of an identical type of product. These consumers and sellers are well informed about market conditions and prices.

Although there is free entry into and exit from the market, no individual consumer or seller can influence the market price, which is determined by total supply and total demand. Under conditions of pure competition, each firm will operate at its maximum profit, or equilibrium, position as determined by the intersection of its marginal cost and marginal revenue curves. A firm that is suffering a loss may continue to operate, rather than shut down, in the short run so long as it is recovering its variable cost and making a contribution to overhead.

In the long run, economic forces will come into play to reduce price and to eliminate economic or pure profit under conditions of pure competition. Consumers eventually will receive the product at a price that is equal to the cost of production. A long-run cost curve can be constructed from a series of short-run cost curves for firms at different scales of operations. Competitive forces arising from economies of scale in the long run will result in a lower price to consumers. The price eventually will reach the lowest point on the average total cost curve at the optimum scale of operation.

NEW TERMS AND CONCEPTS

Pure competition
Perfect competition
Short-run equilibrium
   price

Submarginal producers
Supramarginal producers
Optimum scale of operation

Economies of scale
Diseconomies of scale

DISCUSSION QUESTIONS

1. What are the various types of market structures that may exist?
2. What characteristics or conditions must be present for pure competition to exist?
3. Explain why the individual seller in pure competition can have no effect on the market price.
4. By examining a marginal revenue and marginal cost graph, how can you ascertain the following: (a) whether the firm is making a profit or suffering a loss; (b) if the firm is suffering a loss, whether it should shut down or continue to operate in the short run.
5. Explain how a short-run equilibrium price is achieved.
6. What is meant by the optimum scale of operation?
7. Explain how profits disappear in the long run under conditions of pure competition.
8. What are the social benefits of pure competition?

SUGGESTED READINGS

Dooley, Peter C. *Elementary Price Theory*, 2d ed. Englewood Cliffs, NJ: Prentice-Hall, Inc., 1973.

Friedman, David D. *Price Theory*. Cincinnati: South-Western Publishing Co., 1986.

Hailstones, Thomas J., and John C. Rothwell. *Introduction to Managerial Economics*. Englewood Cliffs, NJ: Prentice-Hall, Inc., 1985.

Kamerschen, David R., and Lloyd M. Valentine. *Intermediate Microeconomic Theory*, 2d ed. Cincinnati: South-Western Publishing Co., 1981.

Mansfield, Edwin. *Microeconomics: Theory and Applications*, 4th ed. New York: W. W. Norton & Co., 1985.

Maurice, S. Charles. *Economic Analysis, Theory and Application*, 4th ed. Homewood, IL: Richard D. Irwin, Inc., 1982.

Stigler, George J. *The Theory of Price*. New York: Macmillan Publishing Co., 1987.

8

IMPERFECT COMPETITION: THE WORLD OF REALITY

◼

MONOPOLY

At the other end of the competitive scale from pure competition is **pure monopoly**. This is a market condition in which there is only <u>one producer or seller</u> of a commodity. Furthermore, it assumes that there are <u>no close substitutes</u> for the particular good or service. This latter assumption, of course, makes it difficult for a pure monopoly to exist. It may be, for example, that Ford Motor Company has a monopoly on the production and sale of Ford cars. But as long as car buyers can turn to Plymouths, Chevrolets, Toyotas, and numerous other makes of autos, Ford does not truly have pure monopoly power.

In many cases a landlord will have a monopoly on the location of a certain rental property. After all, the landlord is the only one who has that particular piece of property to rent. But since there may be several other choices of similar property near that location, it cannot be claimed that the landlord is a monopolist. Like pure competition, pure monopoly is more of an abstraction than a reality.

Because of the complexity of our markets today, it is rather difficult to determine who is and who is not a monopolist. A firm may produce a multitude of commodities, many of which are sold in the market in competition with identical or similar products. But among its products there may be one item for which there is no competition. Is this firm then a monopolist or not? Even a pure monopolist can claim to be in competition with other firms, not for the sale of a particular good or service, but for the acquisition of the consumer's dollars. Although there are a number of near monopolies in the U.S. economy today, pure monopoly is nonexistent except for government-regulated public utilities.

The Characteristics of Monopoly

The major characteristic of monopoly is the degree of <u>control over price</u> that can be exercised by the seller. In pure competition the individual supplies of many sellers make up the market supply. But with a monopoly the individual supply of the monopolist is identical with the market supply.

123

On the demand side, since the monopolist is the only supplier, the total demand on the market becomes a demand for that supplier's product or service. Therefore, any time the monopolist increases or decreases supply, it will affect the market price. Instead of having to take the market price as given and adjust output to the most profitable position, as the case may be under pure competition, the monopolist can adjust output, within limits, to attain the most favorable market price. The monopolist does not have absolute control over the market price, of course, because customers cannot be forced to buy at prices they are not willing to pay.

Sources of Monopoly

Monopolies may develop from a number of sources. But the essence of obtaining and maintaining a monopoly is the erection of barriers to the entry of other firms into the industry. If a monopoly can effectively block the entry of new firms into the business or industry, it can continue to enjoy its monopoly profits.

Economies of Scale.

In some industries it is uneconomical for firms to operate competitively. The "heavy industries," such as steel and heavy machinery, which require the centralized control of vast amounts of capital to achieve the economies of large-scale production, tend to be monopolistic. In such industries pure competition is not feasible, for if many firms were to supply the market, none could produce enough to take advantage of the low per unit cost associated with economies of scale. Even though most of the largest firms within these industries are not pure monopolies, they tend to have monopolistic characteristics.

Natural Monopolies: Public Utilities.

Some industries by their very nature tend to foster monopoly and repel competition. For example, confusion, waste, and inconvenience would result if several natural gas utility companies were to compete for the trade of consumers in an urban area.

In addition to waste through duplication of assets, just think of what the condition of our streets would be if three or four gas companies were tearing up streets for the purpose of repairing gas lines. Visualize the unsightliness of three strings of telephone wires and poles of competing companies traversing the streets and lawns in a new residential subdivision. And what about the safety of passengers and pedestrians if buses from four different transit companies were to race each other from corner to corner to pick up passengers?

In such cases, where one or two firms can adequately supply all the service needed, it is desirable to limit the number of firms within a given territory. Under these circumstances, it becomes imperative for the government to exercise its powers to regulate services and prices. This is done by granting a monopoly franchise to one or a few firms subject to control by a public service commission.

Control of Raw Materials. Another effective barrier to entry is the ownership or control of essential raw materials. Although it is difficult to gain complete control of raw materials, and in many cases there may be close substitutes for a particular raw material, this method of blocking competition was effective for years in the production of aluminum. The Aluminum Company of America retained its monopoly position for years through its control of nearly all sources of bauxite, the major ingredient of aluminum production. In Africa and elsewhere most of the diamond mines are owned by the DeBeers Company of South Africa, and a large portion of the world's molybdenum supplies are controlled by one company.

Patents. A patent gives the holder the exclusive right to use, to keep, or to sell an invention for a period of 17 years. In spite of safeguards against an undesirable amount of monopoly arising from the granting of such a temporary exclusive right, the control of patents is an important source of monopolistic power for some large corporations.

Possible procedures in using patents and the patent laws to stifle competition vary. Patents granted for useless devices or processes increase the likelihood that inventors of worthwhile innovations will encounter lawsuits for infringement. By making slight changes in a patented device or process, the owner may file an amendment to a patent and thus prolong its life. Perhaps the most effective method for maintaining control that a patent gives a manufacturer is to scare away new rivals by threats of infringement suits.

Patent controls and improvement have played an important role in the development of many of today's well-known giant corporations. At the present time nearly two-thirds of all new patents are obtained by corporations.

Competitive Tactics. A firm may eliminate its rivals or block the entry of new firms through the use of aggressive production and merchandising techniques. Sometimes unfair tactics are employed to drive out competition. We have seen the use of temporary selling below cost to weed out or bankrupt smaller competitors, the defaming of competitors' products, the pirating of administrative personnel, the application of undue pressure on suppliers or financial sources, and sometimes outright blackmail. Although many of these tactics have since been declared illegal, there is still much aggressive competition taking place in our economy that makes it difficult for new firms to enter some industries.

PURE MONOPOLY PRICE

It is important to keep in mind the definite and clear concept of what is implied by pure monopoly. The concept of pure monopoly implies a situation where there is a single seller of a good for which there is no available close substitute. Whether the power of the monopolist is exercised to obtain the highest possible price for what is sold depends largely upon whether the monopolist is deterred by fear of possible government regulation or potential competition. Another important consideration is the desire to achieve or to maintain the goodwill of the public, since this affects the sales of the firm's product.

Pure monopoly occurs under one of two possible conditions: (1) the supply may consist of a single unique good or a limited number of nonreproducible units of a good for which there is no available close substitute; or (2) the supply may be reproducible. In this discussion we are primarily interested in the second condition because most goods are reproducible.

Determination of Monopoly Price

Within limits a monopolist can produce and maintain supply at virtually any level. The price will be uniform for all consumers and can be set by the seller at that point which will yield the greatest total profit. The location of this point depends upon the demand for the product and the costs of production.

The Monopolist's Demand Curve. Under pure competition, demand for the output of a single firm can be represented by a straight horizontal line. The individual producer is unable to influence the market price by either increasing or decreasing supply. The producer is able to sell any quantity offered at the current market price.

The monopolist's situation, however, is different. The monopolist is the only supplier of the good, and the demand curve for the monopolist's product slopes downward to the right *because it is the market demand curve of all consumers.* The less essential the product, the more elastic the demand. Hence, the first question to be considered by the monopolist is, "How many units of my good can I expect to sell at various prices?" The number of units to be produced will be determined by the answer.[1]

The monopolist's position is reflected in Figure 8-1. Since there is only one producer, the demand curve for the individual firm is also the demand curve for the entire industry. *D* is the demand curve and also the average revenue *(AR)* curve for the firm. The total revenue at 1,100 units is $8,800; at 1,000 units it is $10,000; and at 900 units it is $10,800. Thus, the monopolist can obtain a higher price and larger revenue by limiting supply. If sales were increased from 1,000 to 1,100, total revenue would decrease. Of course, if demand were elastic, it would be more profitable to increase output.

---

1. The student may find it helpful to review the discussion of elasticity of demand in Chapter 5.

Figure 8-1 The Monopolist's Demand Curve

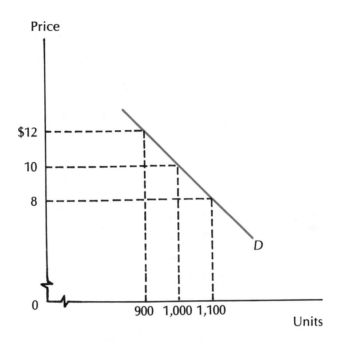

The Monopolist's Cost Curves. As in the case of most other producers, the monopolist's cost per unit usually decreases for a while as the number of units produced increases. If production is pushed to the point where marginal cost *(MC)* increases, however, before long the average total cost *(ATC)* will also increase. The *ATC* increases when the increase in average variable costs becomes great enough to offset the decrease in average fixed costs. How long the monopolist will continue to increase production after *MC* begins to rise will depend upon the number of units that can be produced before the *MC* of the next unit produced is greater than the corresponding marginal revenue *(MR)*.

Relationships between the Monopolist's Cost and Revenue Curves. Assume that the monopolist's cost and revenue situation is as shown in Table 8-1. The level of production at which profit is maximized is reached when 8 units are produced. Since *MC* and *MR* are also equal for 9 units, the same amount of profit, $24.48, will be realized if 9 units are produced. But if more than 9 units are produced, profit will decrease because *MC* rises above *MR*. If 12 units are produced, there will be a loss of $2.64.

Table 8-1   Costs and Revenues for a Monopoly

change in Revenue over the change in product sold.

Units of Output	TC	ATC	MC	TR	AR	MR	Total Profit or Loss
1	$ 20.00	$20.00	—	$ 16.48	$16.48	—	− 3.52
2	34.72	17.36	$14.72	31.48	15.74	$15.00	− 3.24
3	45.12	15.04	10.40	45.00	15.00	13.52	− 0.12
4	52.16	13.04	7.04	57.04	14.26	12.04	4.88
5	56.80	11.36	4.64	67.60	13.52	10.56	10.80
6	60.00	10.00	3.20	76.68	12.78	9.08	16.68
7	62.72	8.96	2.72	84.28	12.04	7.60	21.56
8	65.92	8.24	3.20	90.40	11.30	6.12	24.48
9	70.56	7.84	4.64	95.04	10.56	4.64	24.48
10	77.60	7.76	7.04	98.20	9.82	3.16	20.60
11	88.00	8.00	10.40	99.88	9.08	1.68	11.88
12	102.72	8.56	14.72	100.08	8.34	0.20	− 2.64

Since *ATC* is less at 10 units than at 9 units, and at 10 units *AR* is still greater than *ATC*, it might appear at first glance that it would be more profitable to produce the larger number. However, this conclusion is not justified, because after 9 units, the cost of producing another unit would be greater than the amount of revenue received from its sale (*MC* = $7.04, *MR* = $3.16). Thus, it is the relationship between *MC* and *MR* that is significant in determining the point at which the producer limits supply.

The relationships of the cost and revenue curves may be plotted as shown in Figure 8-2. *AR* is the monopolist's demand curve. It slopes downward to the right, indicating that as the price decreases, a larger number of units will be bought. *MR* shows that as the number of units sold increases, the marginal revenue per unit decreases. *ATC* reflects the behavior of average total cost as an increased number of units are produced. *MC* indicates the decreasing or increasing amount of cost that is incurred as additional units are produced by the monopolist. The shapes of these cost curves are the same as those of a competitive firm and are traceable to the law of diminishing returns.

Because the monopolist is faced with a negatively sloped *AR* curve (demand), the *MR* curve will always be less than the *AR* curve, and the *MR* curve will decline at a faster rate. Remember that in pure competition, where the seller has a horizontal *AR* curve (demand), every time an additional unit is sold at the market price, that same amount is added to the total revenue. Consequently the *AR* and *MR* curves are equal. The monopolist, however, faces a situation where, in order to sell a larger quantity, price must be lowered.

Figure 8-2 Cost and Revenue Curves for a Monopoly

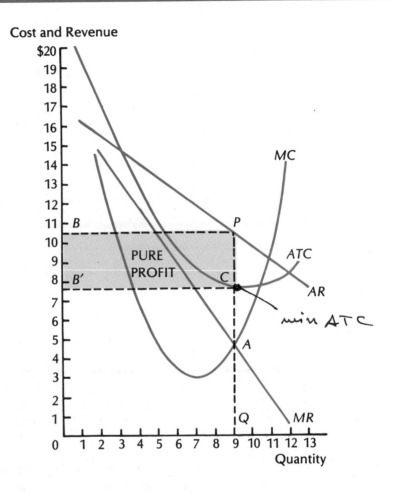

For example, the monopolist may be able to sell one unit for $10 or two units for $9 each. This does not mean that one unit can be sold for $10 and two more for $9 each, because one of the two buyers who would pay $9 is the same one who is willing to pay $10. The monopolist's choice, then, is to sell a single unit for $10 or both of them for $9 each. If the latter is chosen, AR will be $9 but MR will be $8. This can be seen from Table 8-2.

In short, the AR of the monopolist will decline because a lower price is received on the additional goods that are sold. The MR will decline at a faster rate than the AR because in selling a larger number of units, the monopolist also takes a lower price on the units that could have been sold at a higher price had the monopolist elected to sell fewer units. Thus, if three units are sold for $8 each instead of two units for $9 each, total revenue will increase by $8 from the sale of the third unit, as such, minus $1 less on each of the two previous units that could have been sold for $9 if only two units had been sold.

Under the conditions represented in Figure 8-2, at a production level of nine units, MC and MR are exactly equal. Beyond point A it would become less profitable to produce an additional unit. The MC of additional units would be more than the MR. Demand being what it is, the price at which nine units would sell is $10.56. This is shown by the lines PB and PQ, which indicate price and quantity, respectively. The total revenue from the sale of nine units, then, would be $95.04. In the figure the total revenue is represented geometrically by the area 0QPB.

Table 8-2 Marginal Revenue—Competition versus Monopoly

	Pure Competition				Monopoly		
Quantity	Price	TR	MR	Quantity	Price	TR	MR
1	$5	$ 5	—	1	$10	$10	—
2	5	10	$5	2	9	18	$8
3	5	15	5	3	8	24	6
4	5	20	5	4	7	28	4

The cost of producing nine units is $70.56. The total cost is represented by the area 0QCB', which is less than the area 0QPB by the size of the area embraced within BPCB'; this area represents the net profit of $24.48 ($95.04 − $70.56).

It should not be difficult to visualize what would happen if additional firms were to enter this industry. The increase in supply and decrease in market price that would result would soon eliminate profits. But if the monopolist can effectively block entry of new firms, prices and profits can be maintained. Consequently, it is often said that monopoly results in a higher price, the use of fewer resources, and greater profit than would be the case under pure competition.

Restraints on Monopoly Price

People often assume that monopoly implies an exorbitant price. There may be some justification for the belief that goods produced by a firm that is a monopoly, or virtually so, will be sold at a price that will exploit the public. It would be a mistake, however, to think that monopoly always means an exorbitant price. The monopolist cannot charge more for a product than the consumers are willing to pay. In Figure 8-1 it can be seen that all the monopolist desires to sell cannot be sold at a given price. For example, 1,000 units can be sold at $10 per unit, but notice the that 1,200 units cannot be sold at that price. Furthermore, the monopolist cannot raise the price to $12 and still hope to sell as many units as were sold at $10. Even if a firm is a monopoly, it cannot arbitrarily set a price and sell all it wants to sell at that price. It can alter its supply to attain the best possible price for itself, but it still must price within the limits of consumer demand. It may very well be, however, that the price which is most profitable to the monopolist, and within the reach of a few consumers, would deprive a large number of consumers from enjoying the product.

Several other major economic considerations may deter the monopolist from selling its goods at the highest possible price. These include the monopolist's lack of specific knowledge concerning demand, elasticity, and unit production costs; a desire to discourage competition; a desire to maintain good customer relations; and a possible fear of governmental regulation.

MONOPOLISTIC COMPETITION

Pure competition and pure monopoly are the extremes in a wide range of market conditions, which includes oligopoly and monopolistic competition. Oligopoly, which will be discussed later in the chapter, is a market condition with relatively few firms. **Monopolistic competition** is a market condition in which there are a relatively large number of firms supplying a similar but differentiated product, with each firm having a limited degree of control over price. Monopoly indicates some degree of control over market supply or price. On the other hand, pure competition indicates that no individual supplier can influence price. Putting the two terms together indicates that there is some degree of control over price, but that it is limited.

Differentiated Products

The major characteristic of monopolistic competition is product differentiation. Product differentiation permits a limited degree of control over price. In monopolistic competition there must be a sufficiently large number of sellers that the actions of any one have little perceptible effect on the others.

Some idea of the nature of monopolistic competition and its distinction from other forms of competition is apparent in the case of coffee. Assume that there were a large number of firms selling coffee of an identical quality, that there were no brand names, and no advertising claims, and that the coffee was all packaged in the same type of container. Assume further that a price of $2.70 per pound were established by the supply and demand on the market. Under pure competition no seller could get more than the market price for his or her coffee. Why would a consumer purchase any one seller's coffee at a higher price when identical coffee for $2.70 per pound could be obtained from several other sellers? On the other hand, if there were only one seller, the market price could be changed by limiting or expanding the monopolist's supply on the market.

More realistically, we have a relatively large number of coffee producers supplying a similar but differentiated product. It is different because one coffee is "good to the last drop," another is "mountain grown," another is "decaffeinated," and one is "freeze-dried." There are many different blends packaged in a variety of containers. Although they may all be selling for about the same bulk line price as determined in the market by the aggregate demand and supply for coffee in general, it is the product differentiation, whether real or psychological, that permits an individual firm to have some degree of control over the price at which it will sell. However, it is the similarity among the coffees that limits this degree of control.

Consumers buy a particular brand of coffee because they like the taste, admire the package, or are swayed by advertising. Consequently, if the maker of a particular brand, let us say Old Judge Coffee, decided to raise the price a little above the market level, all consumers would not be lost, as would be the case under pure competition. We can assume that most of the Old Judge consumers would be willing to pay a few cents more than the general market price because of the difference in Old Judge. But the seller cannot raise the price too much above the market price. When the price differential becomes too great, consumers may still feel that Old Judge is different, but not that different! When the price reaches a certain level, they will shift to other brands of coffee.

On the other hand, if Old Judge were to lower its price by a few cents from the average market price of $2.70, it would probably gain very few new sales by the substitution effect. Consumers buy certain brands because they feel there is something different about them. If their feeling is strong, they are not going to leave their particular brand favorite and shift to Old Judge for the sake of just a few cents. But if Old Judge reduces its price substantially, many of the consumers may feel that the quality difference is not great enough to deter them from making a switch to the lower-priced Old Judge coffee. In such a case, a point may be reached where the sales of Old Judge coffee would increase substantially, provided other coffee producers did not react by lowering their prices.

Product differentiation gives the individual supplier a certain price range within which prices may be raised or lowered without substantially affecting either the supplier's sales or the sales of competitors. This is the monopolistic aspect of monopolistic competition. But if Old Judge raises its price too high compared with other brands, it will lose consumers; and if it lowers its price sufficiently, it can draw consumers away from other brands. This is the competitive aspect of monopolistic competition.

As a result, we will usually find products at a variety of prices within a general market price range in monopolistic competition. With a large number of sellers, there is less concern about competitors' reactions to a firm's reduction in price. But instead of strong price competition, the firms may stress product differentiation, use heavy advertising, and emphasize packaging to sway consumers. With a large number of firms in the market, however, there is less likelihood of firms engaging in collusive practices to fix price or to limit output.

Short-Run Price and Profit

The demand curve faced by the monopolistic competitor is not a horizontal, perfectly elastic demand curve characteristic of pure competition. Nor is the firm's demand curve identical with the market demand as is the case with monopoly. Even though there are a large number of firms, remember there may not be so many as there are in pure competition, and their products are differentiated. Consequently, the firm will be able to sell more by lowering its price. But since this degree of control is limited by the fact that the firm's supply is a small portion of the total supply on the market, that it has many competitors, and that its product is still similar though differentiated, its demand curve will slope downward to the right. Furthermore, it will tend to be more elastic than the demand curve for the total industry. Of course, the more closely monopolistic competition approaches pure competition, the closer to horizontal will be the demand curve of the individual firm. The more market conditions move in the direction toward oligopoly or monopoly, the less elastic the individual firm's demand curve will be and the more closely it will approach the industry demand curve.

Again, keep in mind that when the demand, or average revenue, curve slopes downward to the right, the marginal revenue curve will move in the same direction but at a steeper slope. Typical short-run cost and revenue curves for a firm engaged in monopolistic competition are shown in Figure 8-3. Figure 8-3a depicts the general range of prices established in the industry around the intersection of total supply and demand. Figure 8-3b shows a monopolistic competitor making a profit. Note that the price, although slightly higher than the average price established by supply and demand in the market, is still within the general price range at which most producers will sell their products. With this price and the accompanying cost the firm will produce 30,000 units and enjoy profits as shown in the rectangle.

Long-Run Equilibrium

If short-run profits are generally available in the industry, however, they will be an invitation for new firms to enter. As these new firms

Figure 8-3   Possible Equilibrium under Monopolistic Competition

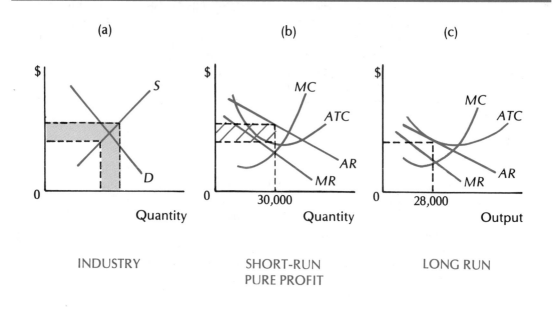

(a)   (b)   (c)

INDUSTRY   SHORT-RUN   LONG RUN
                   PURE PROFIT

enter the market with their similar but differentiated products, the total supply on the market will increase. This, in turn, will decrease the market price and lower the average revenue of each firm in the industry. So long as there are no severe restrictions to entry, the process will continue until supply and price are such that profits for the average firm will be eliminated, as shown in Figure 8-3c. Notice that at the point of equilibrium, 28,000 units of output, the firm will be making no pure profit in the long run. Furthermore, its total sales will have dropped somewhat as a result of competition in spite of the total increase of sales in the market.

Of course, if firms in the industry had been suffering losses in the short run, the opposite reaction on price would have occurred. As firms dropped out of business, the total supply on the market would have decreased, forcing the market price upward. Average revenues for the firms in the industry would have risen until losses were eliminated and equilibrium was established at a no-profit, no-loss position in the long run. Thus, in the long run under conditions of monopolistic competition, consumers will receive a differentiated product at a price that is equal to the average total cost of production for the firm.

Notice, however, that even though the consumer receives the product at a price that equals the cost of production in the long run, this price is not as low as it would be under conditions of pure competition. Because of the slope of the *AR* curve, it cannot touch the *ATC* curve at its lowest point as does the horizontal *AR* curve characteristic of pure competition. Hence, even if costs were identical, the equilibrium price under monopolistic competition must be higher than the price under pure competition.

OLIGOPOLY

Oligopoly is a market condition in which relatively few firms produce identical or similar products. It might involve two or three firms or a dozen or more, depending on the nature of the industry. However, there must be few enough firms that the actions of any one on matters of price and output will have a noticeable effect on the others. The basic characteristics of oligopoly are (1) the ability of individual firms to influence price and (2) interdependence among firms in setting their pricing policies. If only three firms supply a particular good, any one of them could influence the market price by altering the amount it offers for sale. An increase in supply by any one firm would increase total supply and tend to depress the market price. If one firm cut its price, it would gain a larger share of the market at the expense of the other two firms. But the other firms might react by lowering their prices also. This retaliation would again affect all firms' market shares—and might wipe out the initial gain of the price-cutting firm. Whether or not the firms would gain from such price competition would depend on the elasticity of demand for the product.

An oligopolist may be reluctant to engage in price competition because of the possible reaction of competitors. Consequently, many forms of nonprice competition, of which product differentiation is very prevalent, are found among oligopolists. Oligopolistic conditions sometimes lead to collusive practices, such as price leadership, pooling, and other techniques designed to fix prices or to limit quantity.

Price Determination

Pricing under oligopoly is more difficult than it is under other market conditions. The firm may be faced with a price situation where it may or may not be able to determine what amount can be sold at various prices. What will happen to sales when an oligopolist changes price will depend in large part on the reaction of competitors. In fact, an oligopoly is often described as a market situation in which the number of sellers is so few that each must take into consideration the reaction of its rivals. This, of course, is a different situation from that of monopolistic competition, where the number of competitors is so large that an individual seller can ignore the reactions of its competitors. Fear of retaliation by competing firms can be a strong force limiting price competition under oligopolistic conditions.

Three reactions by rivals are possible when an oligopolist changes supply and/or price. (1) Competitors may choose to ignore the price change. In this event the demand and average revenue curve for the individual firm will be known with a reasonable degree of accuracy and may appear as D shown in Figure 8-4. (2) A change in price by an oligopolist may be met by a similar change by rivals. If they do follow suit, the demand or average revenue of an oligopolist may appear as D_1. Notice that the demand curve D_1 will tend to be less elastic, since the gain in sales resulting from lower prices will be lessened if competitors lower their prices also. On the other hand, the firm initiating a rise in a price will not lose as many sales, as it otherwise would, if rivals increase their prices also. In short, the substitution effect resulting from the price change will be lessened if other firms follow suit regarding the price change.

(3) A third situation may arise. Rivals may follow suit for a decrease in price but ignore a rise in price. If one firm were to reduce price, its increase in quantity sold might be less than anticipated as rivals cut prices also. This would tend to eliminate any **substitution effect,** or increase in

Figure 8-4   Possible Demand Curves for an Oligopolist

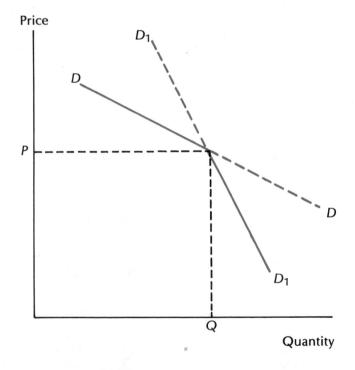

sales at the expense of other firms. The price-cut initiator would experience some increase in sales, however, as total industry sales expand in response to the lower price charged by all firms. But if a firm raised its price and its rivals did not, the decrease in sales might be greater than anticipated as a result of its loss of sales to rivals through the substitution effect.

In this third case the oligopolist's demand curve would be the same as that of D for any price above P, but identical with D_1 for any price below P. The demand curve would appear as DPD_1 as shown in Figure 8-4, and is referred to as a *kinked demand curve*. This situation can lead to price stability, since the demand curve of the individual firm will tend to be inelastic if price moves downward and elastic when its price moves upward. Under these circumstances, price P may become the maximum revenue point for the firm, and Q becomes the equilibrium output. There would be little incentive for the firm to change its price or output.

Price Rigidity

The tendency toward price rigidity in oligopoly contributes to nonprice competition. As a result, great emphasis is placed on product differentiation, and there is tremendous stress on advertising as part of the competition among sellers. Sellers are constantly offering a great variety of styles, promotional deals (rebates), guarantees, and the like. But they seldom engage in price competition. Witness, for example, the pattern of competition in the production and sale of automobiles, soaps, toothpaste, tires, and coffee, where the emphasis is generally on nonprice competition. Sometimes oligopolists practice administered pricing. An **administered price** is a predetermined price set by the seller rather than a price determined solely by demand and supply in the marketplace.

The tendency toward price stability associated with oligopoly, however, often leads to collusive practices. This occurs especially where there is a high degree of inelasticity for the product and there are relatively few firms in the industry. The highly inelastic demand, especially with a kinked demand curve, makes price competition unprofitable not only for the individual firm but also for the industry as a whole. The fewness of firms makes it easier for them to enter into an agreement, either tacit or formal, to limit output or to fix price. Court dockets in recent years have been replete with antitrust suits against such collusive practices in several industries.

PURELY COMPETITIVE VERSUS MONOPOLISTIC PRICING

The weight of economic evidence indicates that a high degree of competition is beneficial for the consumer. As stated before, there is a tendency toward lower prices, the use of more resources, and less pure profits in the long run under competitive conditions. In an industry, the amount of profit for each firm tends to decline to the point where *AR* is equal to *ATC*. This means that the consumer will be able to purchase the good at a price equal to the lowest possible average total cost of production for a given scale of operation.

In most cases of monopolistic competition there is a tendency, in the long run, for monopoly profits to decline and for cost-revenue relationships to become adjusted, as shown in Figure 8-5. Since the demand (the *AR* curve) for the output of a single firm under imperfect competition slopes downward to the right, the marginal revenue curve slopes downward also, but *below* the average revenue curve. Therefore, the two cost curves and the two revenue curves cannot all coincide at the point where the average revenue and the average total cost curves coincide, as would be the case under pure competition. As a result of the less than perfectly elastic demand, the long-run equilibrium price will be higher under any form of imperfect competition than it will be under pure competition for identical cost conditions.

In Figure 8-5, *ATC* and *AR* coincide at *A*, and *MC* and *MR* intersect at *B*. Thus, 0*Q* units would be produced, price being at *P*. If either fewer

Figure 8-5   Possible Long-Run Price under Monopolistic Competition

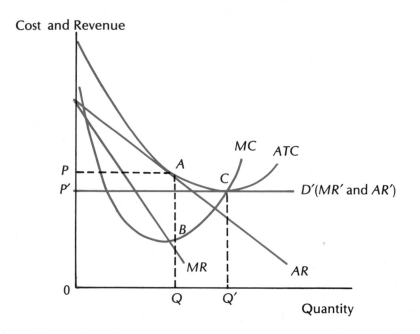

or more units were produced, a loss would result because, for any other quantity, *AR* lies below *ATC*.

Since there is a tendency for production to be adjusted to the point where *MC* and *MR* are equal, the result of monopolistic competition in the long run might appear to be the same as that of pure competition. Such a conclusion would be erroneous because, under monopolistic competition, the price where *MC* = *MR* is not the same as the price where *AR* = *ATC*.

In Figure 8-5 *D'* represents the straight-line curves for marginal revenue *MR'* and the average revenue *AR'*, which coincide under pure competition. The point where *MC* and *MR'* are equal (Point C) is also the point where *ATC* and *AR'* are equal. Thus, under pure competition the price would be at *P'* and 0*Q'* units would be produced. Consequently, under pure competition (assuming that it is feasible and possible), the price is lower and the supply greater than under monopolistic competition.

This analysis assumes, however, that the scale of operation for the small firm in pure competition is the same as that for a larger firm in some form of imperfect competition. Although the scale of operation of firms in monopolistic competition may be similar to those in pure competition and, therefore, their cost curves nearly identical, oligopolies and monopolies generally operate at much larger scales of operation. With the resulting lower average total cost curve of the oligopoly or monopoly, it is possible to have an equilibrium price lower than that possible under purely competitive conditions. Nevertheless, the monopolist's or oligopolist's price is not equal to the lowest point on its average total cost curve. This can be seen in Figure 8-6.

Figure 8-6   Possible Equilibriums under Pure Competition, Monopoly, and Oligopoly

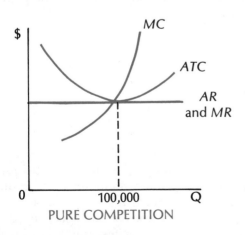
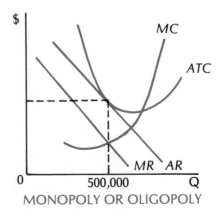

COMPETITION AMONG CONSUMERS

Just as there can be different types of competition among sellers, there can be varying degrees of competition among consumers. Pure competition among consumers exists in cases where there are numerous consumers, who are well informed about price and market conditions, purchasing a commodity under identical conditions, and where no individual consumer is large enough to change the total demand or influence the market price. The numerous shoppers in a given locality certainly form a purely competitive consumers' market for the products of the local grocery store.

We use the term **monopsony** to refer to a condition in which there is only one purchaser for a good or service. Monopsonies can be found in local areas where there may be only one granary to service the local farmers. Sometimes a near monopsony will exist when a large-scale employer moves into a predominately rural area. Such an employer may be the only major consumer of labor in the area.

Oligopsony exists when a few consumers dominate the market. In the tobacco market, for example, there are numerous producers but relatively few buyers. It is quite possible for any of the major producers of cigarettes to influence the market demand and, consequently, the market price for raw tobacco by their decisions to buy more or less tobacco. A similar situation exists in the commercial jet aircraft market, where there are only a few purchasers. The authors of a college textbook face an oligopsonistic market in the publication of their manuscript, as do rookie professional baseball players in selling their athletic abilities.

Monopsonistic competition, a condition in which there are many purchasers who offer differentiated conditions to sellers, is very prevalent in the U.S. economy. In any large community, for example, a great number of firms hire labor, offering a variety of working conditions and fringe benefits. Toy manufacturers deal with a monopsonistically competitive market in the distribution of their products.

MARKET STRUCTURE IN THE UNITED STATES

The variety and complexity of our market certainly confirm the notion of a mixed economy, as referred to in Chapter 3. Not only is the economy in this sense mixed for the total economic system, but it also may be mixed for an individual firm. Quite often a firm dealing in a purely competitive market in buying its raw material, labor, and other units of input will have a monopoly or near monopoly in selling its finished product. At other times a **bilateral monopoly** may exist. This is a situation in which a monopsonist faces a monopolist. The monopsonist is the only consumer on one side of a market, and the monopolist is the only seller on the other. There are many times, too, when a multiproduct firm will sell some of its goods in a competitive market, sell others as an oligopolist, and perhaps have a monopoly in the sale of one product.

Of course, influence on supply and price will depend on the nature of the market in which the seller is dealing. The type of market will also condition the seller's initiating actions as well as reactions to changes by others. Furthermore, as we have already seen, the type and degree of competition influence the price and output policies and the profit picture of individual firms and of industries in total.

Concentration Ratios

It is difficult to measure the degree of competition, monopoly, oligopoly, or monopolistic competition that exists on the seller's side of the market—or how much competition, monopsony, or oligopsony exists on the consumer's side. The **concentration ratio** is the percentage of total shipments in a given industry that is accounted for by the four leading firms in that industry. For example, based on recent data from the Census of Manufacturers, concentration ratios ranged from 14 percent in the soft drink industry to 93 percent in the motor vehicle industry. It is certain that imperfect competition (which includes monopoly, oligopoly, and monopolistic competition) exists in a substantial portion of the U.S. markets for goods and services.

Workable Competition

Economists for the past few decades have been suggesting a concept referred to as **workable competition.** This implies that it is not necessary to have all the conditions of pure competition to serve the best interest of the consumer. It also implies that some forms of imperfect competition may be workable under suitable conditions. To have workable competition at least three basic conditions have been suggested: (1) There must be a reasonably large number of firms; (2) there must be no formal or tacit agreement regarding price and output; and (3) new firms should be able to enter without serious impediment or disadvantage. Others might add to this the fact that no firm should be large or powerful enough to coerce other firms. But even here, it is difficult to ascertain the exact meaning of workable competition. What is meant by a reasonably large number of firms? Is it 5, 10, or 25? Obviously it will depend on the type of industry. What is meant by "no serious impediment to entry"? Would an exceptionally large capital requirement qualify as a serious impediment?

It is easy to see that trying to decide on those industries in which workable competition does or does not exist depends largely upon the interpretation of the person making the judgment. Some economists, for example, would consider the automobile industry, with its relatively few major producers, an example of workable competition; but others would not. More would classify the steel industry as workable competition, but still some economists would disagree. Here again we face that perennial problem of implementing economic theory or knowledge. Nevertheless, many industries fitting the categories of oligopoly or monopolistic competition could readily qualify as cases of workable competition.

HOW MUCH MONOPOLY IS TOLERABLE?

Capitalism suggests that prices should be determined by competition whenever possible. Most students of the subject "competition versus monopoly" feel that, as time has gone on, there has been a noticeable tendency for competition to diminish and be replaced by monopoly, oligopoly, or monopolistic competition.

We should not assume that pure competition has ever existed in the production and sale of most goods and services. For example, an antecedent of modern factories—the blacksmith shop—enjoyed a considerable degree of monopoly within its market area. Although not much capital was required to set up a blacksmith shop, that capital was not always easy to command; nor did everyone possess the requisite skill and brawn to be a blacksmith. Also, while the number of productive establishments relative to the total population may have been greater than that of today, we should recognize that in earlier times the market areas were very much restricted because of the lack of transportation facilities.

Is monopolistic power increasing? Unfortunately we have no adequate measuring devices by which to judge the extent of monopolistic practices and conditions at present as compared with those in the past. For example, it is true that there are numerous giant industrial and business firms. At the same time, better means of communication and transportation have enlarged market areas. Nevertheless, the absolute size of some firms and the rate of increase in the number of business mergers in recent years give the impression that there are relatively fewer sellers now. This is the opinion of many economists. If this opinion is correct and the tendency continues, what does it portend for our economic order and for the economic and political welfare of the people?

Under pure competition, price tends to equal production costs. At the same time, in the production of most articles the existence of a sufficient number of firms to provide the conditions necessary for pure competition is neither possible nor desirable. Moreover, where competition is keen and there are many small establishments, most of which are unable to make much profit, prices may be high because few, if any, of the establishments are of sufficient size to enable them to realize the economies of large-scale production. One large plant may be able to supply a greater variety and quantity of better articles at lower prices than a large number of small concerns that, in spite of real competition, are unable to reduce their costs. Would it be wise, for example, to have 100 or more firms of the more than 200 that entered the industry in the past 70 years still producing automobiles? Certainly if the industry had to support that many firms, producers would not be able to operate on the large scale that makes automobile prices today as competitive as they are. It seems obvious, therefore, that it should not be an aim of public policy to eliminate large-scale production merely for the purpose of maintaining the existence of many firms in an industry.

Nevertheless, the history of monopolies and oligopolies over the centuries seems to prove that when production is controlled by too few producers, the state must stand ready to insure consumer protection against any exploitative practices on the part of the monopolists and oligopolists. As individuals in society have become more interdependent, therefore, and as the economies of large-scale production have grown more apparent and desirable—implying in many cases a decrease in the number of producers—the need for the adoption of a sound public policy for dealing with business and industry has become evident in our growing and complex economy.

ANTITRUST LAWS

During the past century a series of antitrust laws have been enacted in the United States. The primary purpose of these laws has been to maintain competition and prevent restraint of trade. They also restrict unfair competitive practices by businesses, both large and small. A few of the more notable laws are explained here.

Sherman Antitrust Act

The first two sections of the Sherman Antitrust Act of 1890 declare that: (1) "every contract, combination . . . or conspiracy in restraint of trade or commerce among the several states is hereby declared to be illegal"; and (2) "every person who shall monopolize, or . . . combine or conspire to monopolize any part of the trade or commerce among the several states . . . shall be deemed guilty of a misdemeanor. . . ." Section 7 provides for triple damages by making it possible for an injured party to "recover threefold the damages sustained by him and the costs of the suit" from a defendant who has been convicted of violating the law.

Although the statute condemns "every contract" intended to restrain trade by means of monopoly, courts have generally held that the restraint must be "undue" and "unreasonable" before it is illegal. Of course, what is reasonable depends upon the judgment of the court. This "rule of reason" was emphatically enunciated by the United States Supreme Court in 1911 in the famous Standard Oil case.

In the case against the United States Steel Corporation by the government in 1920, the Court held that mere bigness was not a proof of violation. This principle was also invoked in the International Harvester case of

1927. Subsequent cases, however, have held otherwise, beginning particularly with the Alcoa case in 1945, in which Judge Learned Hand indicated that the concentration of economic power is undesirable even in the absence of unfair practices.

Clayton Act

In spite of the Sherman Antitrust Act and of several convictions under the law, the tendency toward corporate combinations continued. In an attempt to "put teeth" into the Sherman Antitrust Act, the Clayton Act was passed in 1914. It prohibits (1) price discriminations that would result in a lessening of competition or tend to create monopoly; (2) tying clauses in contracts whereby buyers of goods are required to agree not to use the product of a competitor of the seller; (3) the acquisition of the stock of one corporation by a competing corporation for the purpose of lessening competition; and (4) interlocking directorates.

The Clayton Act exempted labor organizations from the application of the Sherman Act—at least it seemed to. The Act was often referred to as labor's *Magna Carta,* because it states that "the labor of human beings is not a commodity or article of commerce." Many labor leaders thought that under this law unions could not be considered trusts or monopolies subject to antitrust action. They were disappointed, however, when in 1921 in *Duplex Printing Press Company* v. *Deering* the Supreme Court held that the Sherman Act applied to unions under certain conditions.

The Clayton Act was amended in 1936 by passage of the Robinson-Patman Act, which was primarily designed to prevent "unfair" competition in trade by the giving or the receipt of discounts or services when such act would amount to discrimination and result in a substantial reduction of competition. Unfortunately it is often very difficult to apply the law to particular cases.

Section 7 of the Clayton Act was amended in 1950 by the Anti-Merger Act, otherwise known as the Celler-Kefauver Amendment, so that now it is illegal for one corporation to acquire the assets, as well as the stock, of another company where the acquisition of such assets might (1) "substantially lessen competition between them," (2) "restrain commerce," or (3) "tend to create a monopoly."

Federal Trade Commission Act

The Federal Trade Commission Act of 1914 declares "that unfair methods of competition in commerce are hereby declared unlawful. The commission is hereby empowered and directed to prevent persons, partnerships, corporations, except banks, and common carriers subject to the acts which regulate commerce, from using unfair methods in commerce."

Originally the functions of the Commission were to investigate reports of violations of the Sherman Antitrust Act and other antitrust laws and to recommend needed legislation for the control of monopolies. The Wheeler-Lea Act of 1938 gave the Commission the power of initiative to restrain business practices that it considers detrimental to the public interest, including false advertising and the adulteration of manufactured products.

The Public Utility Holding Company Act

The purposes of the Public Utility Holding Company Act of 1935, the provisions of which are administered by the Securities and Exchange Commission (SEC), are (1) to eliminate the issuance of securities on the basis of fictitious asset values, (2) to eliminate and prevent an unnecessary "pyramiding" of holding companies in the public utility industry, (3) to limit powers of holding companies over their subsidiaries, and (4) to prevent the development or extension of holding companies. The law contains what has been called a "death sentence clause," which requires the dissolution or simplification of holding companies that are considered unjustifiably complex.

Several other acts have been passed to regulate businesses, and court interpretations of these various acts have been numerous. It should be kept in mind that these actions have been taken in an effort to protect, preserve, and promote competition in the U.S. economy.

There was considerable relaxation in the application of antitrust laws in the 1980s as a rash of mergers and takeovers took place throughout major industries in the U.S. economy. In fact, a legislative bill was discussed in Congress in 1986 that was intended to remove many antitrust restrictions in order to permit U.S. firms to compete better against the flood of imports coming into the country.

SUMMARY

Pure monopoly is a market condition in which there is one seller. The fact that the monopolist is the only producer and the fact that there are no close substitutes for the product give the monopolist the ability to set the price by altering the total supply. Monopolies may arise from a number of possible sources, such as economies of scale, the nature of the industry, the control of raw materials, the granting of patents, or the use of various types of competitive tactics.

A monopolist's ability to retain monopoly profits depends in large part on existing barriers to the entry of new firms into the industry. But monopolists do not always charge the maximum possible price because they may not know their true cost and revenue, they may desire to discourage competition, they may desire to promote better customer relations, or they may fear government regulation.

Monopolistic competition is a market condition in which a large number of firms produce similar, but differentiated, products. Product differentiation tends to give each firm a limited degree of control over the price of its product. Just as with pure competition and monopoly, the firm in monopolistic competition will maximize its profits, or minimize its losses, at the point where marginal cost equals marginal revenue. Pricing under monopolistic competition, however, is likely to be higher than it would be under conditions of pure competition.

Oligopoly is a market condition where there are relatively few firms producing identical or similar products. Because of the limited number of firms, each firm must consider the reaction of rivals in matters relating to output and price. A peculiar characteristic of oligopoly is the kinked demand curve, which exists when rivals follow if a firm drops prices but do not follow if a firm raises prices. This and other conditions of oligopoly tend to result in price stability in an oligopolistic industry.

Competition among consumers also varies. In the consumers' market there exist pure competition, monopsony, monopsonistic competition, and oligopsony. The economy is made up of a complex mixture of many types and degrees of competition among both consumers and sellers. It is generally agreed that a large amount of competition is beneficial to the total economy.

There are, however, some merits, as well as disadvantages, to other forms of competition in certain industries. Workable competition is described as a condition in which there is a reasonably large number of firms in an industry, there is no agreement among the firms regarding output or price, and new firms are free to enter the industry without serious impediment or disadvantage. Over the years a series of antitrust laws have been designed to promote competition and restrict unfair competitive practices. In recent years there has been some relaxation of antitrust laws.

NEW TERMS AND CONCEPTS

Pure monopoly	Administered price	Bilateral monopoly
Monopolistic competition	Monopsony	Concentration ratio
Oligopoly	Oligopsony	Workable competition
Substitution effect	Monopsonistic competition	

DISCUSSION QUESTIONS

1. What is the economic justification for granting a monopoly franchise to a public utility?
2. How can a monopoly exercise control over price? Is this control absolute? Explain why or why not.
3. What is the relationship between the average revenue curve for a monopolist and the demand for the product of the monopolist's particular industry?
4. Why do the average revenue curve and the marginal revenue curve of a monopolist diverge, whereas these curves are identical for a firm in pure competition?
5. How does product differentiation give a business firm engaged in monopolistic

competition a certain degree of control over price?

6. Is it possible for a monopoly or an oligopoly to make a profit and still have a lower price than a firm engaged in pure competition that is selling its product at a price equal to its cost of production? Explain.

7. Why does an oligopolist have to be concerned about the actions or reactions of rivals?

8. Explain the "kinked demand curve" characteristic of oligopoly. How does it tend to lead toward price stability?

9. Do you think antitrust laws should be relaxed to permit U.S. firms to compete better against imports?

SUGGESTED READINGS

Adams, Walter. *The Structure of American Industry*, 7th ed. New York: Macmillan Publishing Co., 1985.

Chacholiades, Miltiades. *Microeconomics*. New York: Macmillan Publishing Co., 1986.

Demsetz, Harold. *The Market Concentration Doctrine: An Examination of Evidence and a Discussion of Policy*. Washington, DC: American Enterprise Institute for Public Policy Research, 1973.

Fisher, Franklin M. *Antitrust and Regulation*. Cambridge, MA: MIT Press, 1985.

Miller, Roger L. *Intermediate Microeconomics: Theories, Issues, and Applications*. New York: McGraw-Hill Book Co., 1977.

Telser, Lester G. *Competition, Collusion, and Game Theory*. Chicago: Aldine Publishing Co., 1971.

Watson, Donald S., and Malcolm Getz. *Price Theory and Its Uses*, 5th ed. Boston: Houghton Mifflin Co., 1981.

Weiss, Leonard W. *Case Studies in American Industry*. New York: John Wiley & Sons, 1980.

PART 3

MONEY, CREDIT, AND BANKING

9
MONEY AND ECONOMIC ACTIVITY

■

Money may be regarded as the lubricant of the economic system. Not only does it facilitate trade and exchange, but the amount and flow of money also affect the circular flow of economic activity and the price level.

For many years economists held that money was passive and that it had no substantial effect on the economy. They maintained that one must remove the veil of money to understand how the economy really operated. For this reason they frequently gave explanations of the economic system in terms of a barter economy. The classical economists endeavored to show the passive nature of money by the following types of explanation. Assuming full employment, they asked what would happen to the economy if everyone woke up some morning to find double the amount of money in their pockets, cash registers, and vaults. Since people could not buy any more goods and services because of the full-employment conditions, they held that the value of goods in terms of money would double but that the total real purchasing power of each individual would remain the same. Although this is a simplified version of their concept, classical economists truly underemphasized the role of money in the economy.

On the other hand, some economists today reverse the situation, for they visualize money as a panacea for most of the ills of the economic system. Thus, they advocate manipulation of the money supply to remedy many undesirable economic situations.

THE SUPPLY OF MONEY AND ECONOMIC ACTIVITY

What is the effect of money on the economy? From observation and analysis it is evident that changes in the volume of money can have a definite effect on the level of economic activity and on the price level, depending on the conditions existing in the economy. It is also quite true, however, that money cannot cure all or even most of the weaknesses of a particular economy. Changes in the money supply, however, can cause an acceleration or deceleration in the circular flow of economic activity.

The Monetary Equation

One way that we can explain the effects of money on the economic system is in terms of its quantity. The **quantity theory of money** attempts to explain the relationship between the quantity of money and the price level. It assumes that any money received generally will be spent directly or indirectly to buy goods and services. This is known as the **transactions approach**.[1] The theory is expressed by a simple formula:

$$MV = PT$$

The various elements in the formula represent the following:

M is the total money supply. For our purpose this includes all types of money and credit.

V is the velocity of money, or the number of times that the money supply turns over in a given period of time, such as a month or a year. Velocity can be determined by dividing the money supply into the total spending in the economy.

P is the price level, or the average price per transaction. We should keep in mind that *P* has no practical value and that this formula is merely a tool of analysis to determine the relationship between the four elements *M*, *V*, *P*, and *T*, rather than a formula to determine actual price level.

T is the total transactions in the economy. For our purpose we will consider it as the total physical units of goods and services produced and sold in the economy over a given period of time.[2]

The formula merely states that money times velocity, which equals the total spending in the economy, is equal to the average price times the total units produced and sold. The formula, $MV = PT$, then, is a simple truism.

---

1. Another approach is known as the **cash balance approach**. It puts more emphasis on what individuals and firms do with their money—that is, spend it or save it—and the length of time they may hold on to their money. According to the cash balance approach, $M = KTP$, or $P = M/KT$, where M = the money supply, T = total transactions, P = the price level, and K = that fraction of a year's transactions over which the community desires to hold cash. In this formula K is the reciprocal of V in the transaction formula.

2. In the formula $MV = PT$, it is possible to let T represent either (1) the sale of goods and services currently produced over a given period of time or (2) the sale of goods and services whether currently or previously produced. Since the latter concept includes the resale of all commodities previously produced, such as used cars, existing homes, and second-hand furniture, it is a much broader concept. The first concept is used here because the level of production and employment, and therefore the circular flow, is affected primarily by the sale of goods and services currently being produced rather than by the resale of old commodities.

Stable Money Supply. We can do more with the formula if we isolate the element of price. This can be done by simple conversion. It follows mathematically that if $MV = PT$, then the following formula is also true:

$$P = \frac{MV}{T}$$

With this formula in mind, let us assume for a very simple example that the total money supply in the economy is $5, that this amount of money is spent four times, and that four transactions take place. If $M = $5, V = 4$, and $T = 4$, then $P = 5, the average price per transaction. When these values are used in the formula, they appear as follows:

$$P = \frac{MV}{T} = \frac{$5 \times 4}{4} = \frac{$20}{4} = $5$$

Other things remaining unchanged, if the money supply remains stable, there will be no change in either the level of economic activity or the price level. In short, the circular flow will remain stable.

Increase in Money Supply. Now let us see what effect a change in the money supply can have on the level of economic activity and the price level. Since the effect of a change in the money supply will depend to some degree on the status of employment, let us assume a full-employment economy. This implies full employment of resources and productive capacity as well as labor. Under such conditions if we increase the money supply, for example from $5 to $10, higher prices will result. When we are at full employment, it is almost impossible to increase the total output of goods and services quickly, that is, in the short run. Therefore, the additional money available will be used by individuals and firms to bid against each other for existing goods and services. This situation will cause prices to rise, which means that inflation will result. In terms of our formula:

$$P = \frac{MV}{T} = \frac{$10 \times 4}{4} = \frac{$40}{4} = $10$$

Since total spending will now increase to $40, provided that the velocity remains the same, and since our transactions cannot increase, the price level will rise to $10 per unit.

An exception may result if individuals for some reason decide to save the additional money they receive rather than to spend it. In such a case the velocity would decrease. For example, if the money supply were increased to $10 but $5 of it were saved, only $20 would be spent. In calculating the formula under such conditions, the velocity would be equal to 2 ($20 ÷ $10 = 2$) instead of 4. However, this is a rare occurrence. Usually an increase in the money supply in a full-employment period leads to higher prices, and rising prices usually induce people to spend their incomes faster to beat further price increases, which in turn increases V. Therefore, sizable increases in the money supply in a full-employment economy may lead to serious inflation.

If we make the same change under different circumstances, we will obtain different results. If we increase the money supply in an economy that is operating at less than full employment, it will likely lead to an increase in the level of economic activity instead of a rise in prices. For example, if the money supply were increased to $10, the additional money could be used to purchase additional goods and services that could be produced by the unemployed work-force personnel, unused resources, and idle capacity existing in the economy. If production were increased in proportion to the increase in the money supply, the price level would remain stable. Thus, the formula would have new values (M and T would be doubled), but the same price level would result:

$$P = \frac{MV}{T} = \frac{\$10 \times 4}{8} = \frac{\$40}{8} = \$5$$

If we continued to increase the money supply, it might lead eventually to full employment, and any further increases in the money supply would again bring on higher prices. For example, if we push the money supply to $15 while V and T remain at 4 and 8, respectively, the price level will move up to $7.50 per unit, as shown below:

$$P = \frac{MV}{T} = \frac{\$15 \times 4}{8} = \frac{\$60}{8} = \$7.50$$

An increase in the velocity of money can have an effect similar to an increase in the money supply. In fact the two frequently go hand in hand to compound the effect on the price level. Individuals and firms could negate the influence of the increased money supply to increase prices and/or raise the level of economic activity if they were to increase their savings when the money supply was increased.

Decrease in Money Supply.   A decrease in the money supply can bring about a reduction in the level of economic activity and/or a decline in the price level. For example, if total spending were reduced as a result of a reduction in the money supply, fewer goods might be produced, causing a reduction in employment and transactions. On the other hand, if we were to reduce the money supply to $3 while V remained at 4 and T at 4, the price level would fall to $3, as can be seen from the formula:

$$P = \frac{MV}{T} = \frac{\$3 \times 4}{4} = \frac{\$12}{4} = \$3$$

This situation assumes, of course, that the goods would be sold at lower prices rather than permitted to pile up in inventories.

The decrease in the price level caused by a decrease in the money supply could be offset easily by an increase in velocity. This will often occur in a full-employment economy when individuals are in a frame of mind to buy goods and services. They will increase velocity to compensate for a relative scarcity of money. Many times, however, a decrease in the money supply and a decrease in the velocity work hand in hand to aggravate a price decline, especially during a recessionary period.

Changes in Money Supply and Velocity. In general, we can say that an increase in the money supply will lead to an increase in the level of economic activity if we are in a state of less than full employment. This will mean more production, employment, and income to those in the economy. If we are at full employment, however, an increase in the money supply will merely lead to inflation. On the other hand, a decrease in the money supply will lead to a decrease in the level of economic activity and/or a decline in prices.

Similar effects can be brought about by variations in the velocity of money. If individuals spend their incomes faster or save a smaller portion of them, the turnover of the total money supply will be greater and total spending will be increased. This could lead to an increase in the level of economic activity and/or a price increase, depending upon the circumstances existing in the economy. A decrease in velocity, which results from spending at a slower rate or saving a larger portion of income, will lead to a decrease in production and/or a decline in prices. Thus, it would appear that the amount and flow of the money supply can affect business activity in the economy. This was demonstrated in the circular flow in Chapter 4.

As was stated previously, whenever planned investment is greater than planned saving, an increase in economic activity or a rise in prices

Table 9-1   Relationships of Investment, Saving, the Government Budget, and the Money Supply

Conditions Tending toward a Stable Level of Economic Activity and a Stable Price Level	Conditions Tending toward a Decrease in the Level of Economic Activity and/or a Decline in the Price Level	Conditions Tending toward an Increase in the Level of Economic Activity and/or an Increase in the Price Level
Planned I = Planned S	Planned I < Planned S	Planned I > Planned S
Balanced government budget Stable money supply	Surplus government budget Decrease in money supply	Deficit government budget Increase in money supply

follows. In the absence of a change in velocity, however, an increase in the money supply is required to give businesses the means to increase their investment. The increased investment may come about from an increase in the amount of currency or through an increase in bank credit.

Likewise, it is frequently by means of an increase in the money supply generated by bank credit that government deficit spending is financed. On the other hand, a decrease in investment or a government surplus could result in a diminution of bank credit, which would reduce the money supply.

From all indications, there is some relationship between investment-savings decisions and the status of the government budget on the one hand and changes in the money supply on the other. Furthermore, a change in any of these may affect the GNP and the price level. These relationships are shown in summary form in Table 9-1.

Effect of Changes in Money Supply in the United States

Whatever the source of money, a definite correlation can be shown between the level of production, the price level, and the money supply. Table 9-2 shows the relationships that have existed for the past few decades.

In the early 1960s increases in the money supply (column 2) showed a closer relationship with the level of business activity than they did with the price level (column 4) because the economy operated at less than full

Table 9-2 Money Supply, Production, and the Price Level, 1960–1986

Year	Money Supply (billions)	Total Production (current dollars)	Consumer Price Index (1967 = 100)	Total Production (1982 dollars)
1960	$142	$ 515	88.7	$1,665
1965	170	705	94.5	2,088
1970	217	1,016	116.3	2,416
1975	291	1,598	161.2	2,695
1980	414	2,732	246.8	3,187
1985	627	3,993	322.2	3,574
1986	730	4,209	328.4	3,677

Source: *Economic Report of the President* (Washington, DC: U.S. Government Printing Office, 1987).

employment during most of the first half of the decade. During the 5-year period 1960–1965, as shown in Table 9-2, the money supply increased 19 percent; the real GNP 26 percent; and the price level 6.5 percent, or 1.3 percent annually.

In the latter half of the decade, when we reached full employment, however, the additional increases in the money supply helped to contribute to the substantial rate of inflation that occurred in the economy. Between 1965 and 1970 the money supply grew 28 percent; real production 16 percent; and the price level 23 percent, or 4.6 percent annually.

Prices continued to rise in spite of the slowdown that occurred in the economy with the recession of 1970. Subsequently, President Nixon in August, 1971, imposed a wage-price freeze followed by mandatory controls. With the removal of compulsory controls early in 1973, price increases accelerated. By the end of that year inflation was at a double-digit annual rate, and prices continued at undesirable levels in spite of our negative economic growth rates during the 1974–1975 recession.

Although inflation did slow to a rate of 4.8 percent in 1976, it resumed its upward climb in 1977 and reached double-digit levels in 1978 and 1979. Continued economic expansion, sizable increases in the money supply, and huge federal deficits added to the inflationary impact. In the period 1975–1980 the money supply increased by 43 percent; real production rose 18 percent; and the price level increased by 53 percent, or at an average annual rate of more than 10 percent.

Much of the increase in prices during the 1970s, of course, was a combination of cost-push, structural, and social inflation rather than demand-pull inflation. In addition, the energy crisis and crop shortages caused additional price pressures that aggravated the inflationary spiral.

By the end of the 1970s, it was calculated that *embedded inflation* was 7 to 9 percent annually. Embedded inflation is defined as increases in the price level resulting from built-in factors in the pricing mechanism, including oil price increases, contractual wage increases, and various forms of income and benefits indexed to the CPI.

Fortunately in the 1980s, especially beginning in 1982, the rate of inflation slowed down considerably. After experiencing double-digit inflation through 1981 and most of 1982, the annual rate of inflation in 1982 through 1986 was 4 percent or less. Much of this disinflation was due to the rapid fall in oil import prices and the continued importation of other low-priced goods. For the period 1980-1985 the money supply increased 51 percent, real output increased 12 percent, and the price level rose 31 percent.

CHANGES IN THE PRICE LEVEL

Prices are constantly moving up or down depending on business conditions. Prices in general may be moving in the same direction. On the other hand, some may be rising, some may be declining, while others are remaining stable. Even if one could remember all the individual price changes, it would be of no great consequence. Such details may cause one to lose sight of what is happening to prices generally in the economy. It is convenient, therefore, to have a device by which to measure the general or average movement of all prices in the economy. For this reason, we construct price indexes.

Whether we observe the Producer Price Index, the Consumer Price Index, the Spot Market Price Index, or one of the numerous other price indexes calculated by various government agencies, it is worthwhile to know something about the makeup of such an index. A **price index** compares the average of a group of prices in one period of time with the average of the prices of the same group of commodities or services in another period. Prices are determined for a base period, and the prices in all subsequent years are measured in relation to the base-period prices.

A Hypothetical Price Index

When calculating price indexes, it is essential to hold the items whose prices are to be measured constant both in quantity and in quality. Only in this way can an accurate price index be obtained. Table 9-3 includes a hypothetical set of figures that show the general principle by which an index is calculated.

Assume that it costs $500 per month to buy the five basic commodities (*a, b, c, d*, and *e*) in 1967. The price index in column 4 represents the comparison of the cost of the five commodities in any year with their cost in the base year 1967. The index for 1967 must be 100 since the cost of the commodities in 1967 was 100 percent of their cost in the base year (1967). By 1977, however, these same commodities cost $910. Therefore the index for 1977 was 182; that is, the prices were 182 percent of what they were in 1967 ($910/$500 = 182 percent). This means that the price

Table 9-3   Hypothetical Price Index

(1) Year	(2) Commodities	(3) Price or Cost	(4) Price Index, Base Year 1967	(5) Price Index, Base Year 1980
1960	*abcde*	$ 445	89	36
1967	*abcde*	500	100	40
1970	*abcde*	580	116	47
1977	*abcde*	910	182	74
1980	*abcde*	1,235	247	100
1987	*abcde*	1,610	322	130

of these commodities increased 82 percent. By 1987 the commodities cost $1,610 and prices were 322 percent of what they were in 1967, or 222 percent greater than they were in 1967.

As you can see, the index gives us a means of comparing prices at any time with the level that existed in the base year. The index for any given year can be obtained simply by dividing the cost in the given year by the cost in the base year. Any one year can be compared with another simply by noting the change in the index.

It is necessary to change the base year occasionally because our spending habits change over the years, new products enter the market, and the comparison of current prices with prices in some much earlier period may become meaningless. A change in the base year does not change the actual prices but merely changes the year with which current prices are compared. For example, if the base year for the index in Table 9-3 were changed to 1980, the cost of buying the commodities in 1987 would still be the same, but the index would read 130 ($1,610 ÷ $1,235 = 130 percent) instead of 322 as it did when the index was based on 1967 prices.

Changing the base year is a fairly simple matter; the difficulties occur when the products that are being analyzed change. For a periodic revision of current index numbers, the construction of a new index is not that simple. With changes in the basic commodities and changes in the weights of the various commodities, the absolute cost of buying the new "market basket" of goods and services may be more or less than the absolute cost of buying the former package of goods and services.

The Consumer Price Index

The **Consumer Price Index (CPI)** compares the price of a group of 400 basic commodities and services out of the more than 1,400 required by an average family of four in a moderate-sized industrial community. These items are weighted according to the percentage of total spending applied to each of several categories, such as food, rent, apparel, transportation, and medical care. A separate index is calculated for each of the categories as well as a composite for all commodities. Indexes are calculated for each of 28 metropolitan areas, for several nonmetropolitan urban areas, and also for the United States as a whole.

The Bureau of Labor Statistics (BLS), which calculates the CPI, uses the Laspeyres' formula for the actual mathematical calculation of the index.[3] The BLS has used a number of different base periods for the CPI,

---

3. In its simplest form, the formula reads:

$$R_i = \frac{\Sigma \, q_0 p_i}{\Sigma \, q_0 p_0}$$

where the q_0's are the average quantities of each item used by families in the wage-earner group in the base period, the p_0's are the prices for these items in the base period, and the p_i's are the prices in the current period.

but it now uses a 1967 base year. The CPI was scheduled to be changed to a 1977 base year in 1982. The change was postponed indefinitely, however, owing to federal budget restraints.

wage?

Components of CPI. As mentioned earlier, the CPI market basket is made up of various components. The current categories and their weights are: all items (100 percent), food and beverages (19.8 percent), housing (37.7 percent), apparel (5.1 percent), transportation (21.6 percent), medical care (6.3 percent), entertainment (4.2 percent), and other goods and services (5.3 percent). Since prices of some goods and services rise faster than others, it is essential to use appropriate geographic areas and item categories when utilizing the index for specific purposes. Figure 9-1 gives some indication of how the prices of medical care have been rising faster than the prices of apparel and entertainment. Weights for the various categories are to be updated in 1987.

The New Index. Before 1978, the market basket of items in the CPI was based on the needs and spending pattern of families of "urban wage earners and clerical workers." Since the proportion of such workers in the labor force had been declining over the years, the BLS decided to expand the scope of coverage to "all urban families." Some groups, particularly labor unions, objected to the change, since the CPI historically had been computed on a wage earner family basis. As a result, the BLS now publishes two CPIs—the original index for wage earners and clerical workers (CPI-W) and a new index for all urban families (CPI-U). After several years of experimentation and analysis, the BLS will decide whether to continue both indexes or to retain only one of them.

Limitations of CPI. The CPI merely measures the relative change in the cost of living. It does not measure the actual cost of living. A higher index in one city may not necessarily indicate that prices are actually higher in that city than they are elsewhere. It may simply mean that the cost of living has increased more rapidly in one city than it has in other cities since the base period.

Assume that the actual monthly dollar cost of living and Consumer Price Index for the two cities are as shown below:

	1982		1987	
City	Cost of Market Basket	Base-Year CPI	Cost of Market Basket	Current-Year CPI
A	$1,500	100	$2,100	140
B	$1,800	100	$2,400	133

Figure 9-1 Consumer Price Index, 1970–1986 (1967 = 100)

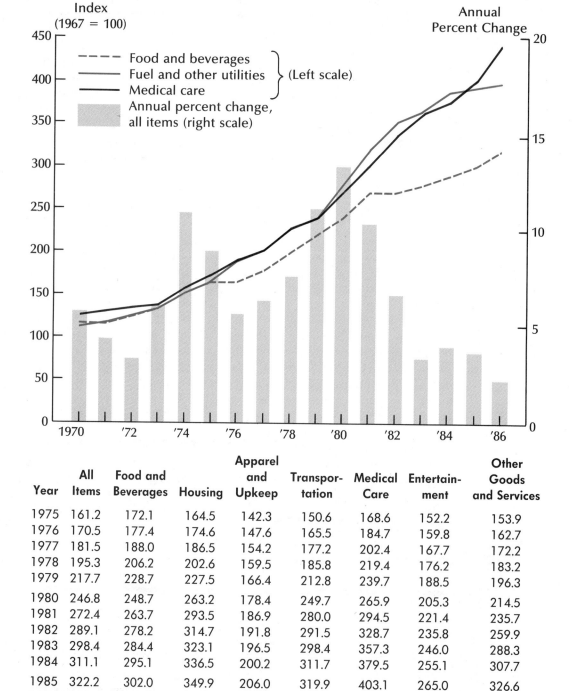

Year	All Items	Food and Beverages	Housing	Apparel and Upkeep	Transportation	Medical Care	Entertainment	Other Goods and Services
1975	161.2	172.1	164.5	142.3	150.6	168.6	152.2	153.9
1976	170.5	177.4	174.6	147.6	165.5	184.7	159.8	162.7
1977	181.5	188.0	186.5	154.2	177.2	202.4	167.7	172.2
1978	195.3	206.2	202.6	159.5	185.8	219.4	176.2	183.2
1979	217.7	228.7	227.5	166.4	212.8	239.7	188.5	196.3
1980	246.8	248.7	263.2	178.4	249.7	265.9	205.3	214.5
1981	272.4	263.7	293.5	186.9	280.0	294.5	221.4	235.7
1982	289.1	278.2	314.7	191.8	291.5	328.7	235.8	259.9
1983	298.4	284.4	323.1	196.5	298.4	357.3	246.0	288.3
1984	311.1	295.1	336.5	200.2	311.7	379.5	255.1	307.7
1985	322.2	302.0	349.9	206.0	319.9	403.1	265.0	326.6
1986	328.4	311.8	360.2	207.8	307.5	433.5	274.1	346.4

Source: *Economic Report of the President*, 1987.

If 1982 is selected as a base year, both of these costs would represent 100 for the respective cities in 1982. Notice that the monthly cost of living in both cities increased by $600 between 1982 and 1987. But the CPI rose more in city A with the lower dollar cost of living. Thus, it is possible for a city with an actual lower cost of living to have a higher consumer price index number than a city with a higher cost of living. The median cost of living for a family in Atlanta in the fall of 1985 was $27,695; in New York City it was $35,443. The CPI in October, 1985, for Atlanta, however, was 336 while that for New York was 322.

Another limitation of the CPI is that it is not a completely pure price index. The BLS admits that there may be certain elements of quality improvement reflected in the index. Ascertaining to what extent a rise in the price of a commodity or service is due to a general rise in quality is difficult. Various studies indicate that the size of the upward bias involved with the collection and processing of data for the index approximates one to two percentage points annually.

Finally, it should be remembered that the CPI endeavors to measure changes in the prices of consumer goods and services only. Since these account for only about two-thirds of the total spending, the CPI does not give a full account of what is happening to prices. It does not take into consideration changes in the prices of machinery, equipment, buildings, or raw materials. A broader price measure is the "GNP implicit price deflators," which include changes in the prices of all goods and services produced by our nation's economy. Still another index, the PPI, measures changes in producer prices only.

CPI, COLA, and Indexation.   In recent years much additional interest has been generated in the composition, structure and measurement of the CPI. Today nearly 10 million industrial workers have their wages tied to the CPI through cost-of-living adjustment (COLA) clauses. In addition, military pensions and Social Security payments are adjusted for the cost-of-living changes. The federal food stamp and school lunch programs are related to the CPI. It is estimated that more than 50 to 60 million U.S. citizens have some type of income or benefits indexed to the CPI. Moreover, federal income tax payments have been indexed to the CPI since 1985.

Value of Money

In addition to measuring changes in the price level, price indexes are also useful for determining the value of money. The value of money is based upon the goods and services that a given amount of money will buy. If prices rise, a given amount of money will buy less and the value of money decreases. If prices fall, the value of money increases since a given amount of money will buy more. Although the inherent value of the money has changed little, its value relative to goods and services has changed substantially over recent years.

The value of the dollar can be determined at any time by dividing the dollar by the price index and multiplying by 100. Thus, the value of the dollar in 1967, using 1967 = 100, was $1.00 ($1.00 ÷ 100 × 100 = $1.00). In 1980 the dollar was valued at $0.40 ($1.00 ÷ 247 × 100 = $0.40) compared with 1967. In 1986 it was valued at $0.31 ($1.00 ÷ 328 × 100 = $0.31).

We should keep in mind that the value of the dollar is only a relative comparison. There is nothing inviolable about this value. You can easily show that the dollar in 1986 was worth about 88 cents instead of 31 cents simply by using 1982 as the base year instead of 1967: $1.00 ÷ 113 × 100 = $0.88. In fact, you can always make the dollar equal to a dollar by using the current year as the base year.

Real Income

Although the purchasing power of the dollar has declined in recent decades, we have many more dollars in income today than we had previously. As a result, the total purchasing power of the average individual has changed noticeably in the past several decades. It is true that total purchasing power increased in the 1950s and 1960s, but it declined in the latter part of the 1970s and early 1980s. Unfortunately, prices in the 1970s rose faster than incomes.

Table 9-4 Money Wages versus Real Wages, 1977–1986
Average Weekly Earnings in Nonagricultural Industries

Year	Weekly Money Wage	% Increase in Money Wage over 1977 Wage	CPI (1977 = 100)	Real Wage (1977 $)	% Change in Real Wage over 1977 Real Wage
1977	189.00	—	100.0	189.00	—
1978	203.70	7%	107.6	189.31	0
1979	219.91	16	119.9	183.41	−3%
1980	235.10	24	136.1	172.74	−9
1981	255.20	35	150.0	170.13	−10
1982	267.26	41	159.3	168.09	−11
1983	280.70	49	164.4	171.26	−9
1984	292.86	56	171.4	173.48	−8
1985	299.09	59	177.5	171.60	−9
1986	304.85	61	180.9	171.07	−9

Source: *Economic Report of the President, 1987.*

We can obtain some idea of the total change in purchasing power for the average individual from Table 9-4. In this table, the money wage (column 2) represents the average gross weekly earnings in all private nonagricultural industries. Column 5 is the real wage, or the purchasing power of the money wage in constant dollars. The real wage in column 5 is determined by dividing the money wage in column 2 by the Consumer Price Index (1977 = 100) in column 4. Column 6 is the percentage change in real wages in each year compared with 1977.

Some interesting observations can be made from Table 9-4. Notice that the money wage increased substantially in the period from 1977 to 1986; but because of price increases, the real wage actually declined by about 9 percent. In effect, price increases obliterated most of the advantages of higher wages during that period. Although the average worker had $115.85 more weekly pay in 1986 than in 1977, his or her purchasing power was about 9 percent less in 1986.

Effects of Price Changes

Inflation benefits those whose incomes rise with increases in business activity and prices. For example, business profits, wages of industrial workers, and salespersons' commissions are very susceptible to change. They change with increases or decreases in business activity and prices. It is to their advantage when prices are increasing. But since their incomes usually decrease faster than do prices, they are at a disadvantage when prices are decreasing. Others, such as civil service employees, some executives, schoolteachers, and pensioners whose incomes tend to remain fixed or relatively stable in spite of changes in business conditions and prices, are at a disadvantage in periods of rising prices. These individuals suffer from inflation, but they gain during a period of deflation, provided they maintain their income and their jobs. It seems, then, that whenever prices move substantially in either direction, inequities will develop.

Changes in the price level also affect creditors and debtors, each in a different manner. Inflation is beneficial to debtors but detrimental to creditors. While deflation works a hardship on debtors, it enhances the value of creditors' dollars. To illustrate, suppose you had borrowed $50,000 to build a home in 1977 with the stipulation that you repay the entire amount plus interest in one lump sum in 1987. In 1977, the creditor gave up $50,000, or the equivalent of a good three-bedroom home. When you repaid in 1987, however, the $50,000 that the creditor received would purchase only about one-half of the same type of house, since the cost of such homes had risen to about $100,000. The money the creditor was repaid had less purchasing power than the money given up in 1977. On the other hand, you would be making repayment with dollars that had one-half the purchasing power of those that you borrowed. Increased income that accompanied rising prices would have made it easier for you to repay the loan. If prices had fallen, the situation would have been reversed. You would have been repaying with dollars of greater value than those that you initially borrowed.

SUMMARY

Money affects the level of economic activity and the price level. These effects can be explained by the use of the monetary equation which states that $MV = PT$, or $P = MV/T$. In short, an increase in the money supply in periods of less than full employment will tend to bring about an increase in the level of economic activity. During full-employment periods, however, increases in the money supply will lead to inflation. A decrease in the money supply will bring about a decrease in the level of economic activity and/or a decrease in prices.

Although the monetary formula, $MV = PT$, is merely a tool of analysis, the actual price level can be measured through a price index. The most common index is the Consumer Price Index (CPI) calculated by the Department of Labor. It is currently maintained on a 1967 base year. The price index is useful for determining the value of the dollar and for determining the real income of the workers in the economy. It shows that while the average weekly money wage in nonagricultural industries increased between 1977 and 1986, the real wage, or purchasing power of the money wage, actually decreased. Indexing various forms of income and benefits to the CPI is a common practice.

Changing price levels bring about a redistribution of income. Those whose incomes increase faster than does the price level will experience an increase in real income. Individuals with stable incomes, however, will experience a decrease in purchasing power as the price level rises faster than do their money incomes. Changing price levels also affect creditors and debtors.

NEW TERMS AND CONCEPTS

Quantity theory of money   Cash balance approach   Consumer Price Index (CPI)
Transactions approach   Price index

DISCUSSION QUESTIONS

1. Under what conditions will an increase in the money supply have more influence on the price level than it will on the level of economic activity?
2. Do you think the money supply should be increased a specific amount each year for the purpose of financing normal increases in business activity and stabilizing the level of economic activity?
3. The monetary formula serves as a tool of analysis rather than as a device for con-

structing a consumer price index. Explain.
4. It is said that the CPI is not a completely pure price index. Explain.
5. Assume the following: $M = \$2,000$, $V = 10$, and $T = 1,000$. Using the monetary formula, what will be the value of P? If the amount of money doubles, what will be the new price level?
6. In evaluating the cost of living for a particular city, can an individual rely on the Consumer Price Index as a specific indica-

tion of how much it will cost to live in that particular city? Why or why not?

7. Distinguish between money wages and real wages. Are real wages today higher or lower than they were in 1986? Explain.

8. What is the level of the CPI today? What category of prices within the CPI has increased the most since 1986?

SUGGESTED READINGS

Fergus, James T. "Cost-of-Living Comparisons: Oasis or Mirage?" *Economic Review*. Federal Reserve Bank of Atlanta (July/August, 1977).

Horvitz, Paul M., and Richard A. Ward. *Monetary Policy and the Financial System*, 5th ed. Englewood Cliffs, NJ: Prentice-Hall, Inc., 1983.

Kamerschen, David R. *Money and Banking*, 9th ed. Cincinnati: South-Western Publishing Co., 1988.

Marcoot, J. L. "Revision of the CPI Is Now Underway." *Monthly Labor Review* (April, 1985).

McCulloch, J. Huston. *Money and Inflation: A Monetarist Approach*, 2d ed. New York: Academic Press, 1982.

Money in the Economy. Federal Reserve Bank of San Francisco, 1981.

Motley, Brian, and John L. Scadding. "Monetary Policy and Velocity." *Weekly Letter*. Federal Reserve Bank of San Francisco (June 7, 1985).

U.S. Department of Labor, Bureau of Labor Statistics. "The Consumer Price Index." *Handbook of Methods, Vol. 2*. Washington, DC: U.S. Government Printing Office, 1984.

———. *Revising the CPI: A Brief Review of Methods*. Washington, DC: U.S. Government Printing Office, 1980.

10

MONEY: ITS NATURE, FUNCTION, AND CREATION

■

Most of us use money every day. We see it, touch it, and spend it. But how many of us can define it adequately? Money is generally defined too narrowly. Some define it as the currency of a nation; others think in terms of legal tender. It is often referred to as the medium of exchange. Such definitions, however, automatically exclude the largest portion of our money supply—credit. In order to include all segments of our money supply, a broad definition is essential. Thus, we can say that **money** is anything that is commonly accepted in exchange for goods and services.

THE NATURE OF MONEY

Commodity money is that type in which some commodity actually serves as money. Many commodities, such as stones, shells, various crops, metal, and paper, have served as money in various countries of the world. United States history reveals that tobacco, corn, wampum, warehouse receipts, and bank notes, in addition to metal coin and paper currency, have served as money. In fact, many of these monies were given legal-tender status, which means that they were acceptable in payment of debts, both public and private.

There are two basic types of modern money, each of considerable importance: metallic money and paper money. **Metallic money** is a special type of commodity money in which some metal, such as gold, silver, or copper, is used. **Paper money** is in the form of bills and notes. Paper money may or may not be backed up by gold or silver. Although we have had various types of commodity money in the United States, all our currency today is in the form of paper money and coins.

Classification of Money

Money may also be classified according to its inherent value as full-bodied money or credit money.

Full-Bodied Money. **Full-bodied money** is money in which the intrinsic value of the material content is equal to the monetary value (face value).

For example, the inherent value of a $10 gold piece was equal to its monetary value of $10. Not only could you use the $10 gold Eagle to buy $10 worth of groceries, but also if it were melted, you could sell its gold content for $10 in cash in the gold market.

Credit Money. **Credit money** is money in which the intrinsic value of the material content is less than the monetary value. It may be made of either metal or paper, or it may be in the form of checking deposits. Credit money is frequently referred to as **token money**. Most coin money in the United States is token money. Sometimes money that is not backed 100 percent by reserves of coin or bullion is also referred to as credit money.

Representative Money. **Representative money** is money, usually paper, that serves in place of metallic money. It may represent either full-bodied or token money. Gold certificates that circulated in the United States before 1933 were a good example of the former. The only type of representative token money we have today is the silver certificate. For decades, instead of coining the silver, the government held it in the form of bullion and issued silver certificates that circulated in the economy. But even these are now being retired. One of the advantages of representative money is that it is more portable than metallic money.

Fiat Money. The government also issues credit money in the form of bills or circulating promissory notes. Sometimes it is referred to as **fiat money**, which is money backed up by the promise of the government to redeem it or to exchange it for other types of money.

In fact, most of our currency is in the form of Federal Reserve notes, which are issued by the Federal Reserve Banks with the approval of the United States Treasury. At one time the gold reserve required for these notes was 25 percent. The other 75 percent of the backing was in the form of additional gold certificates, government securities, or note assets of the bank. Today there is no gold reserve behind these notes.

Demand Deposits. Banks issue credit money in the form of notes and demand deposits. The largest portion of our money supply is in the form of **demand deposits** (bank checking deposits), which are mostly credit money. For the time being it will suffice to say that checks written against these deposits serve as money. Since the monetary value of a check is greater than the intrinsic value of the paper on which it is written, it is, of course, credit money. We shall see later how demand deposits may arise.

Measures of the Money Supply

Today virtually all the money in the United States is credit money. The total amount in the economy in mid-1986 was approximately $730 billion. Of this about 25 percent, $184 billion, was in the form of currency. About $308 billion, or 42 percent, was in the form of demand deposits. The remainder was in the form of traveler's checks and other checkable deposits.

Over 90 percent of the total currency is in the form of Federal Reserve notes. These notes are issued by the twelve Federal Reserve Banks. They are obligations of the U.S. government as well as the Federal Reserve Banks and must be fully collateralized. Although gold backing is no longer required for these notes, many are still secured by some gold, with most of the remainder secured by government securities or certain other types of bank assets. Federal Reserve notes, like other kinds of paper currency, are produced by the Department of the Treasury.

There is also a small quantity of other types of bills in circulation. This includes National Bank notes, which were issued by the various national banks and secured by government bonds deposited with the Comptroller of the Currency. Also in this category are Federal Reserve Bank notes, which are like the National Bank notes except that they were issued by the Federal Reserve district banks. In addition, silver certificates are still outstanding. All three are now obligations of the United States Treasury and are secured 100 percent by other types of money. They are now held mainly by collectors.

The remainder of the currency is composed of coins, which include dollars, half dollars, quarters, dimes, nickels, and pennies. This, then, is the currency that we use in everyday transactions of the economy.

The most commonly used measure of the money supply is M1, which is composed of currency in circulation, traveler's checks, demand deposits in commercial banks, and other checkable deposits (such as NOW and ATS accounts). Since these deposits are subject to immediate withdrawal, or use via check writing, they serve as readily as cash for purchases. A broader measure of money, M2, is composed of M1 plus savings and

Table 10-1   Total Money Stock of the United States, 1986
                 (in Billions of Dollars)

	M1	M2	M3	L
Currency	$183.5			
Demand deposits	307.8			
Other checkable deposits	232.7			
Other	6.4			
Total	$730.4	$2,804.7	$3,488.1	$4,111.8

Source: *Economic Report of the President*, 1987.

small time deposits, overnight repurchase agreements (RPs), Eurodollars, and certain money market mutual fund (MMMF) balances. M3 consists of M2 plus large time deposits, longer-term RPs, and institutional MMMF balances. The largest money supply designation is L, which is composed of M3 plus other liquid assets. These money supply measures are shown in Table 10-1.

FUNCTIONS OF MONEY

Money performs four essential functions in our complex economy: (1) a standard of value, (2) a medium of exchange, (3) a store of value, and (4) a standard of deferred payment.

Standard of Value

Money serves as a standard of value or as a unit of account. This means that we can measure the value of all other commodities in terms of money. Without money it would be extremely difficult to compare the values of different commodities. How much would one horse be worth? We might say that it would be worth six pigs, twenty bushels of wheat, eight pairs of shoes, or one-half of a cow. Without money we would have to compare the value of the horse in terms of each article or commodity for which we might trade it. With money as a standard of value, however, we can express the value of the horse in terms of money. Since the values of all other commodities are also expressed in terms of money, it is an easy matter to compare the value of the horse with other commodities by looking at their respective dollar values. If the horse is valued at $350, we know that it is equivalent in value to any other commodity or combination of commodities whose value is also equal to $350.

Medium of Exchange

In a barter economy, the exchange of goods and services is extremely cumbersome. If a farmer would like to trade a lamb for a pair of shoes, the farmer must find someone who has a pair of shoes and wants to trade them for a lamb. Thus, a problem of **double coincidence of wants** arises. The farmer may be forced to exchange the lamb for two bushels of wheat, the wheat for a set of books, and the books for the shoes.

In a monetary economy, the individual can simply sell the lamb for cash and then spend the cash for the shoes. Thus, money serves as a medium of exchange. It is an economic catalyst. Money eliminates the need for a double coincidence of wants, and it also facilitates the exchange of goods and services.

Store of Value

Money serves as a store of value insofar as we can convert excess goods into money and retain the money. It may be difficult to accumulate and to hold wealth in the form of commodities, because some commodities are too bulky to store, others are perishable, and for some the cost of storage may be prohibitive. If money is to be a good store of wealth, it must possess stability. People would be reluctant to store their wealth in the form of money if they knew the purchasing power of the money would decline substantially during the period in which the money was to be held. When a nation has an unstable currency, its citizens may store their wealth in the form of some foreign currency or in gold or silver. If the value of money declines, perhaps they will be prompted to spend their wealth if it is in the form of money.

Standard of Deferred Payment

In our economy, a great many purchases are made for which we do not pay cash. Instead the consumer agrees to pay the purchase price over a period of time. Thus, money becomes a standard of deferred payment. If a family buys a home, it may take 20 years or more to pay for it. The creditor is trusting that the money to be received from the family over the years will be usable and that its purchasing power will not decline to any serious extent. Just as in the case of the store of value, it is important that money be stable if it is to serve as a standard of deferred payment.

Sound money must be able to perform all four functions. The United States dollar has done reasonably well in this respect. Some monies do only a partial job. In some Latin American nations and in some other nations, where price levels have risen drastically in recent years, currency is experiencing difficulty in fulfilling its functions because of the serious inflation. Even in the United States, when higher than usual inflationary rates exist, some citizens and foreigners alike seek to hold their wealth in some commodity other than United States dollars, such as real property, gold, and certain foreign currencies.

CREATION OF CREDIT MONEY

In spite of the fact that demand deposits compose the largest part of our money supply, they are the most mystifying part of it. Demand deposits are credit money. There are two types of demand deposits. A **primary deposit** is one that arises when you put money into your checking account. Such deposits are considered part of the money supply. This kind of deposit is offset, however, by a decrease in currency outside banks that is counted as a part of the total money supply.

A **derivative deposit** arises, on the other hand, when you borrow money from the bank. It is so named because the deposit derives from the loan. Instead of giving cash, the bank may open a checking account in your name. The checks written against your account serve as purchasing power. The bank honors the checks though you put no cash into the bank. Thus, there has been an increase in the money supply to the extent of the demand deposits created. Because of the complexity of the monetary aspect of demand deposits, it will be explained gradually.

Personal IOUs

Assume that Farmer Jim Lee needs $6,000 to buy food, seed, and fertilizer, and to pay the help that he must hire to work his farm. Suppose that Jim requests his grocer to accept his IOU with the promise that he will pay when the crops are harvested. If the merchant does not know Jim or if she doubts his ability to repay the IOU, she will refuse the offer. Jim may encounter the same difficulty when he tries to buy seed and fertilizer from the supplier. When he attempts to hire workers, he may endeavor to pay them in IOUs, with the promise to redeem them when the crops are harvested. The workers, however, may protest that they will be unable to buy food, shelter, and family necessities with Jim's IOUs. What Jim is really trying to do is obtain credit, but because he is unknown, there may be uncertainties about his ability to repay. Since his personal IOUs are not negotiable, he will find it extremely difficult to operate on credit. But if Jim could get his IOUs accepted in exchange for groceries, feed, fertilizer, and labor, his IOUs would be serving as a form of money.

Demand Deposits

Since in our example Jim Lee is unable to use his own credit, let us assume that he goes to the only bank in the community to borrow funds. In discussing his problems with the bank official, he will be told that if he wants a loan, he will have to put up collateral. Assume that Jim has equipment valued at $10,000, which he pledges as collateral for a $6,000 loan. For safety purposes, collateral in excess of the amount borrowed is generally required. If the loan is for 1 year, Jim will be asked to sign a note payable to the bank stating that he will repay the $6,000 plus 10 percent interest ($600) at the end of the year.

If the bank gave Jim $6,000 in legal-tender currency, he could easily buy the commodities needed. People would certainly accept the currency without question. If the bank were to lend cash, however, its ability to make loans and thus to make profit in the form of interest income would be limited. Suppose that the bank had $100,000 in cash reserves. If it lent all the money at 10 percent, it would make only $10,000 a year in interest. It was this limitation that led banks to search for a more profitable method of lending money.

If Jim Lee were to come to the bank today to borrow $6,000, the bank, instead of giving him the loan in the form of cash, would grant the loan by creating a derivative deposit for him. In this case Jim would put no money into the bank, but he would write checks against the created demand deposit. These checks, which are drafts against the bank to pay the bearer a stipulated amount, serve as money, and people usually accept them in good faith in exchange for goods and services. Thus, there is an increase in the money supply to the extent of the demand deposits created. Checks, of course, can be written against these deposits. This process is illustrated in Figure 10-1. Since the bank does not lend currency, it might seem that there is no limit to the amount of loans which it can make in the form of demand deposits. It will, however, need to keep sufficient cash on hand to provide for those who want to redeem the checks.

If everyone who received a check cashed it, and if the money were kept out of the bank permanently, the bank would need a reserve equal to the amount of checks written, or to the amount loaned in this case. If the bank had $100,000 in reserves to start with, it could lend only $100,000, because when checks equal to this amount were written and cashed, the reserve would become depleted. If the bank gave additional loans in the form of demand deposits, it could not honor the checks written against such loans.

In actual practice, however, this will not happen for three reasons: (1) Not all people cash checks immediately. Some of the checks may be endorsed and continue to circulate in the community before being cashed. (2) Some people, instead of cashing checks, will deposit them in the bank

Figure 10-1   Loan Made by Creating Credit Money

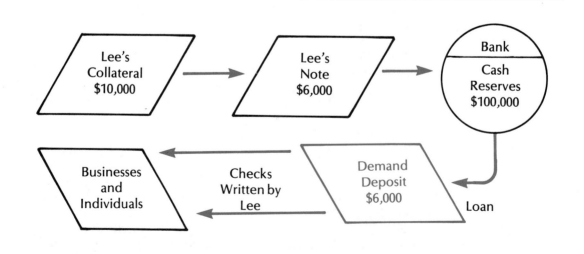

where they will be credited to the depositors' accounts. In this case no money leaves the bank. A bookkeeping entry merely transfers the cash from the account of the person who wrote the check to the account of the depositor of the check. There is no decrease in the cash reserve of the bank. (3) Even if someone cashes a check and takes the money out of the bank, the chances are very good that when the money is spent it will eventually come into the hands of another person who will deposit the cash in the bank. In such a case the decrease in cash reserves resulting from redemption of the check will be offset by the return of cash by the person making the deposit.

As a result of these three factors, the bank can keep less money on hand than the value of its checks outstanding. The possibility of all check holders coming to the bank to redeem their checks at the same time is very remote. Thus, the amount of checks that can be written and the extent of loans that can be made in the form of demand deposits are limited only by the bank's ability to take care of those who want to cash their checks immediately. Since banks are interested in making a profit, they are encouraged to make as many loans as is reasonably safe. However, because some banks in the past overextended loans in relation to reserves, they were caught short. To prevent such abuses of the credit system, the states and the bank regulators placed restrictions on the amount of loans that could be made by a bank. For example, depending on their size, banks are now generally required to keep 3 to 12 percent cash reserves behind demand deposits. The amount of this reserve requirement will limit a bank's ability to make loans.

If the bank is required to keep a 10 percent cash reserve behind its demand deposits (loans) and $100,000 is deposited in the bank, two alternatives are available to the bank for lending money:

1. The bank can hold $10,000 in cash as reserve against the $100,000 deposit and lend the remaining $90,000 to those who request loans. If it does this, its income will be limited to $9,000 ($90,000 × 0.10) if it charges 10 percent interest on the loans.

2. The bank can hold the entire $100,000 as cash reserves. In this case the $100,000 cash reserves can be used to back $1,000,000 in the form of demand deposits ($100,000 is 10 percent of $1,000,000).

Since the bank already has $100,000 on deposit as a result of the original primary deposit, it can extend its credit another $900,000 in the form of derivative demand deposits. If the bank followed this second alternative, its interest income on loans would be $90,000 ($900,000 × 0.10). The biggest difficulty involved in following the second alternative would be in maintaining proper reserves, $100,000, with $1,000,000 in demand deposits outstanding. If the bank in any one day had more checks drawn against it than it had new deposits, it would have a net withdrawal of funds from the bank. Technically, this is known as an **adverse clearing balance**.

Such an event would decrease the bank's total reserves. Thus, unless the bank had excess reserves, that is, unless the bank had reserves over and above that which it was required to maintain, it might easily get into difficulty. In such a case any adverse clearing balance would leave the bank short of its required reserve.

Banks, therefore, will follow the first alternative rather than the second. They will tend to hold $10,000 in reserve against the original primary deposit of $100,000 and to make loans to the extent of $90,000.

Multiple Expansion of Bank Credit

Even if the bank holds $10,000 in cash reserves against the original deposit of $100,000 and lends $90,000 in cash, there will be an expansion of credit. This will come about because what an individual bank may fear to do—that is, hold the entire $100,000 in reserve and lend $900,000 in the form of demand deposits, because of the possibility of an adverse clearing balance—the banking system as a whole can do through a multiple expansion of bank credit.

The individual bank holds a 10 percent reserve against the original deposit and lends the remainder in the form of cash or demand deposits, as shown in Figure 10-2. There will be an increase in the money supply since there will exist $100,000 in demand deposits in addition to the continued circulation of $90,000 in demand deposits or cash as a result of the loan.

Although the individual bank in the preceding situation increases the money supply to a limited degree, the cumulative action of all banks will increase the money supply nine times. This is brought about because the $90,000 in cash that is loaned will find its way into other banks. These

Figure 10-2 Loans Actually Made by an Individual Bank

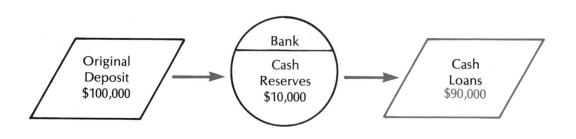

Bank holds part of the primary deposit as a reserve against that deposit and lends the remainder in cash.

banks in turn will hold a portion of this money in reserve and will lend the remainder, which will eventually flow into other banks. For example, when the borrower of the $90,000 spends the money, it will come into the hands of others, and eventually the $90,000 will be deposited in other banks, which will hold $9,000 cash reserve against the $90,000 deposits. These banks in turn will have $81,000 to lend. This process can continue until the total loans outstanding will be equal to $900,000 and the original $100,000 will be held as reserves in various banks. At that time banks can lend no more money. This process, known as the **multiple expansion of bank credit**, is demonstrated in Figure 10-3.

Figure 10-3   Multiple Expansion of Bank Credit

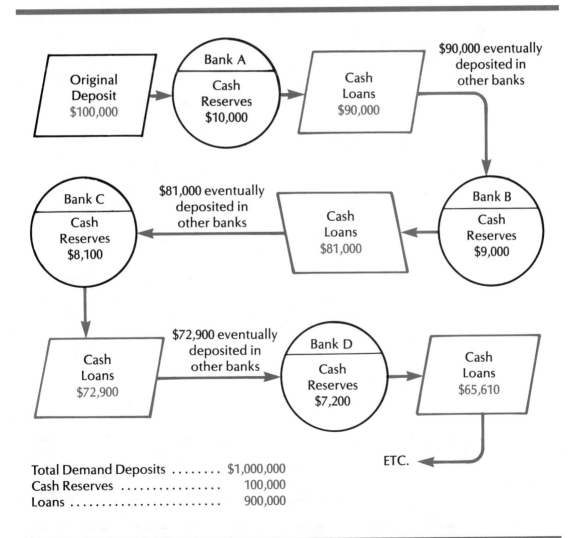

Total Demand Deposits $1,000,000
Cash Reserves   100,000
Loans   900,000

Another way of looking at this process is in tabular form as shown in Table 10-2. This table shows how $1,000 deposited in a bank (Bank A) can be expanded into $10,000 in demand deposits and loans of $9,000.

If there is a 10 percent reserve requirement, it is assumed that Bank A will hold $100 against the original deposit of $1,000. Thus, it will have $900 in cash that it can lend. People who borrow this money spend it and circulate it in the community until it finally ends up in other banks, as people make deposits there. If all these deposits were made in Bank B, that bank would hold a $90 reserve against its deposits of $900 and lend the remaining $810. This process continues until all the money is tied up in reserves in various banks. At such time the total deposits will equal $10,000, the reserves $1,000, and the total loans outstanding $9,000.

It should be kept in mind that the expansion of credit which increases the money supply results when the banks make direct loans in the form of demand deposits or in the form of cash, which subsequently leads to demand deposits. Actually, depositors can write checks equivalent to $10,000, and these checks serve as money. Thus, in place of a mere $1,000 in cash, we now have $10,000 in checks buying goods and services.

Keep in mind also that just as we can observe the multiple expansion of bank credit whenever there is a net increase in deposits at the bank, we can also see a multiple contraction of bank credit whenever there is a net withdrawal of deposits.

Effect of Changes in the Reserve Requirement

If the banks were required to keep a larger amount of reserves, their ability to expand credit would be reduced. If we assume the reserve re-

Table 10-2 Expansion of Bank Credit, 10 Percent Reserve Requirement

Bank	Deposit	Reserve	Loan
A	$ 1,000	$ 100	$ 900
B	900	90	810
C	810	81	729
D	729	73	656
E	656	66	590
F	590	59	531
G	531	53	478
H	478	48	430
I	430	43	387
J	387	39	348
Etc.	Etc.	Etc.	Etc.
	$10,000	$1,000	$9,000

quirement to be 20 percent, instead of the 10 percent used in our previous examples, the bank would need to hold twice as much in reserves. This would reduce the bank's ability to extend credit by approximately one-half, as shown in Table 10-3. A reserve requirement of only 5 percent would increase the bank's ability to extend credit from $9,000 to $19,000.

Remembering the relationship of the money supply to the level of economic activity, we can relate this explanation of credit to the circular flow. If the reserve requirement on demand deposits can alter the bank's ability to extend credit, and if changes in the money supply can alter the circular flow, then it appears that we can influence the circular flow and encourage its acceleration or deceleration by changing the reserve requirement. This is exactly what happens in our economy. We use the reserve requirement along with several other monetary measures as tools to stabilize economic activity and the price level.

Table 10-3 Expansion of Bank Credit, 20 Percent Reserve Requirement

Bank	Deposit	Reserve	Loan
A	$1,000	$ 200	$ 800
B	800	160	640
C	640	128	512
D	512	102	410
E	410	82	328
Etc.	Etc.	Etc.	Etc.
	$5,000	$1,000	$4,000

MONETARISTS VERSUS FISCALISTS

Through the 1940s and 1950s most economists, following Keynesian economic analysis, believed that investment was the primary determinant of economic activity. Moreover, they recommended that fluctuations in the economy could be remedied with the use of fiscal measures dealing with government revenues and expenditures. Accelerating government spending, or even using deficit spending, would improve a sluggish or recessionary economy. On the other hand, reduced government spending, or a surplus budget, could be used to combat inflation. Followers of this theory are today known as the *Fiscalists*.

In the 1960s and 1970s, however, a good many economists began accepting the theory of Milton Friedman, then at the University of Chicago, that the primary determinant of economic activity was the size of the money supply. His studies indicated a close relationship between the size of the money supply and the level of economic activity and/or the price level. A growth in the money supply, according to Friedman, led to an increase in economic activity and/or the price level. A decrease or tightening of the money supply led to a decrease in economic activity and perhaps a recession and unemployment. Moreover, there existed a time lag between changes in the money supply and the level of economic activity. This made the use of discretionary monetary measures to stabilize the economy more haphazard. Therefore, Friedman suggested the adoption of a constant rate of increase in the money supply, such as 3–5 percent, annually. This has become known as the monetary rule. Followers of this theory are known as *Monetarists*.

Few economists today believe that either investment or the money supply is the sole determinant of the level of economic activity. Most suggest that both have an effect, and that a combination of fiscal and monetary measures is needed to help bring about stable economic growth and stable prices. They also recommend the combined and coordinated use of fiscal and monetary policies for this purpose.

In the 1970s other economic theories regarding the level of economic activity came into existence. These are the rational expectations hypotheses and supply-side economics, which will be explained in Chapter 21.

SUMMARY

Money is broadly defined as anything that is commonly accepted in exchange for other commodities. There are various types of money, such as commodity money, metallic money, and paper money. Furthermore, money may be full-bodied, or it may be credit money.

In mid-1986 the U.S. money supply, M1, amounted to approximately $730 billion. Of this total, about $308 billion was demand deposits and $184 billion was currency. The remainder was traveler's checks and other checkable deposits. Money has four basic functions. It serves as a standard of value, a medium of exchange, a store of value, and a standard of deferred payment.

Money in the form of credit is created by banks and other financial institutions. It may come in the form of demand deposits or in the form of cash that subsequently generates demand deposits. In either case, banks can lend more money than they actually have in cash.

To prevent the banks from overextending credit in the form of demand deposits, the banks are required to keep a certain amount of reserve behind their loans (demand deposits). This reserve requirement becomes a limiting factor to the amount of credit that may be issued by a bank. In general, the total amount of credit created through the establishment of demand deposits will be some multiple of the actual cash reserves of the bank.

Although an individual bank may not extend credit to the full extent permissible because of the fear of adverse clearing balances, the banking system as a whole is capable of extending credit to the full extent.

Changes in the reserve requirement can affect the supply of money that is made available by banks. Changes in the money supply can affect the level of economic activity and the price level. Therefore, changes in the re- serve requirement can affect business activity and prices.

NEW TERMS AND CONCEPTS

Money
Commodity money
Metallic money
Paper money
Full-bodied money
Credit money

Token money
Representative money
Fiat money
Demand deposits
Double coincidence of wants

Primary deposit
Derivative deposit
Adverse clearing balance
Multiple expansion of bank
   credit

DISCUSSION QUESTIONS

1. Would it be possible for some commodity to serve as money in a modern economy? If so, how and under what circumstances?
2. What is the distinction between M1, M2, and M3? Which do you think is the best measure of the money supply? Why?
3. What effect will a rapidly rising price level have on money in regard to its function as a store of value?
4. Explain how a derivative demand deposit increases the money supply whereas a primary deposit does not.

5. What would happen to the money supply if, as some have advocated, a 100 percent reserve requirement for demand deposits were established?
6. How do reserve requirements on bank deposits affect the bank's ability to create credit?
7. In your opinion, should banks be permitted to create credit? Why or why not?
8. Do you see any relationship between the multiple expansion of bank credit and the velocity of money?

SUGGESTED READINGS

Duprey, James N. "How the Fed Defines and Measures Money." *Quarterly Review*. Federal Reserve Bank of New York (Spring/Summer, 1982).

Kaufman, George G. *Money, the Financial System and the Economy*, 3d ed. Boston: Houghton Mifflin Co., 1983.

Klein, John J. *Money and the Economy*, 5th ed. New York: Harcourt Brace Jovanovich, Inc., 1982.

The Story of Checks. Federal Reserve Bank of New York, 1981.

The Story of Money. Federal Reserve Bank of New York, 1981.

Your Money and the Federal Reserve System. Federal Reserve Bank of Minneapolis, 1982.

11

THE FEDERAL RESERVE AND THE MONEY SUPPLY

∎

A few banks did exist during colonial and early post-colonial days, but the first attempt at centralized banking came when the federal government chartered the First Bank of the United States in 1791 for a 20-year period. The primary functions of the First Bank were to perform as a commercial bank for individuals and business, to act as a banker's bank, to serve as a fiscal agent for the federal government, and to endeavor to keep some order in the banking business by exercising certain restraints on state banks. Opposition to the bank led to the defeat of the recharter movement in 1811. For the following 5 years only state banks existed.

In 1816, however, the Second Bank of the United States was chartered for a 20-year period. Although it was designed to perform functions similar to those of the First Bank, it had a greater amount of capital stock and operated on a more widespread scale. Despite its efficient operation, there was considerable opposition to the Second Bank. Some opponents disliked the idea of central authority, others objected to its strict regulations, some objected to foreigners owning a certain amount of the stock of the bank, and still others thought the bank to be unconstitutional. Political difficulties between the bank officials and the presidential administration were instrumental in defeating the Congressional bill to recharter the bank in 1836.

Between 1836 and 1863 there was no central authority in the banking system. As a result, abusive banking practices became prevalent. Because of the existence of widespread malpractices, this period became known as the "wildcat banking period."

The National Banking Act of 1864 brought some order to the banking business by creating the National Banking System. Its stringent requirements and provisions for note security ended many unsound operations of the banks. The system, however, had several noticeable weaknesses, such as the perverse elasticity of the money supply, the gravitation of reserves toward the money center, and the lack of assistance to the farm sector of the economy because real estate could not be used as collateral for loans. After several years of research and study, the National Banking System was supplanted in 1913 by the Federal Reserve System with the passage of the Federal Reserve Act.

STRUCTURE OF THE FEDERAL RESERVE SYSTEM

The Federal Reserve System (hereafter called the Fed) is a complex and intricate system composed of a Board of Governors, a Federal Advisory Council, a Federal Open Market Committee, 12 Federal Reserve Banks, branch banks, member banks, and several minor organizations. It is an instrument of the government, and yet it is not owned by the government. It is owned by the member banks, but its most important officials are appointed by the government. Each body within the Fed has its individual function, but the functions of each are interrelated.

The Board of Governors of the Federal Reserve System

At the apex of the Fed is the Board of Governors (the Federal Reserve Board, or the FRB) in Washington. Its primary function involves the formulation of monetary policy for the U.S. economy. The FRB is an agency of the federal government, but it has considerable autonomy. It consists of seven members who are appointed by the President of the United States with the consent of the Senate. Each member must be selected from a different Federal Reserve district. Each member is appointed for 14 years and is ineligible for reappointment after having served a full term. Appointments are staggered so that a new appointee is assigned every 2 years. The President of the United States selects the Chairman and the Vice-Chairman of the Board.

The FRB has numerous powers, including the supervision of the Federal Reserve Banks. It must approve the Reserve Bank officers and has the right to suspend or to remove officers if necessary. It must authorize loans between Federal Reserve Banks, it reviews and determines discount rates established by the Reserve Banks, it establishes reserve requirements within legal limits, and it regulates loans on securities, in addition to many other functions.

Federal Advisory Council

The Federal Advisory Council (FAC) is a committee of twelve members, one from each Federal Reserve district, selected annually by the board of directors of each Federal Reserve Bank. The members are individuals of prestige and banking acumen who are required to meet at least four times a year with the FRB. The FAC serves primarily in an advisory capacity to the FRB. It confers with the FRB on business conditions and other matters pertinent to the Fed.

In addition to the Federal Advisory Council, a number of other committees and conferences assist the FRB with various functions. One of the most important of these is the Conference of Presidents of the Federal

Reserve Banks, which convenes periodically and meets with the FRB once or twice a year.

Federal Open Market Committee

The Federal Open Market Committee (FOMC) is also composed of twelve members, including the seven members of the FRB and the President of the Federal Reserve Bank of New York. The other four members of the Committee are Federal Reserve Bank representatives who serve 1-year terms on a rotating basis. The FOMC engages in the buying and selling of government securities in the open market for the express purpose of influencing the flow of credit and money. Its actions help in stabilizing the price level and the growth of economic activity. The Committee meets every 4 or 5 weeks.

Federal Reserve Banks

The Fed divides the United States into 12 geographic districts. Each district has a Federal Reserve Bank named after the city in which it is located. The districts are organized on the basis of the concentration of financial activity. As a result, the St. Louis district geographically is about one-half the size of the Kansas City district, but it does as much financial business as the latter. Several of the districts have branch banks. The Federal Reserve Bank of Cleveland, for example, has branches in Pittsburgh and Cincinnati. Puerto Rico and the Virgin Islands are included in the New York district for check clearing and collection. See Table 11-1 and Figure 11-1 for a list of the district banks and branches.

Each Federal Reserve Bank is controlled by a board of directors consisting of nine members divided equally into three classes. Class A directors are elected by the district member banks to represent them on the board. Class B directors are elected in the same manner, but are nonbankers, for they are to be employed by and represent industry, commerce, and agriculture. Class C directors are appointed by the Fed's Board of Governors and may not be affiliated in any way with any bank. One of the Class C directors is appointed chairman of the district Reserve Bank's board of directors by the FRB. The chairman serves also as a Federal Reserve agent and is responsible for the issuance of Federal Reserve notes.

The public nature of the Fed is attested to by the fact that nonbankers constitute a majority on the board of directors of each Reserve Bank. The board of directors of each Reserve Bank appoints a president and vice-president for the Bank. These officers must be approved by the FRB and are responsible for the day-to-day operation of the Reserve Bank.

Federal Reserve Banks supervise member banks in their districts and conduct periodic examinations of banks' operations. In the event that any member bank chronically engages in unsound banking practices, the Re-

Table 11-1   Federal Reserve Districts and Banks

District	Federal Reserve Bank	Branches
1	Boston	None
2	New York	Buffalo
3	Philadelphia	None
4	Cleveland	Cincinnati, Pittsburgh
5	Richmond	Baltimore, Charlotte
6	Atlanta	Birmingham, Jacksonville, Miami, Nashville, New Orleans
7	Chicago	Detroit
8	St. Louis	Little Rock, Louisville, Memphis
9	Minneapolis	Helena
10	Kansas City	Denver, Oklahoma City, Omaha
11	Dallas	El Paso, Houston, San Antonio
12	San Francisco	Los Angeles, Salt Lake City, Portland, Seattle

serve Bank has the authority to remove its officers and directors. Although this authority is seldom exercised, its presence helps to keep member banks in line.

In addition to serving as central banks, or banker's banks, the Federal Reserve Banks also serve as fiscal agents for the federal government. They handle the detailed work of issuing and redeeming government bonds, they hold deposits and disburse funds for the Treasury, and they perform many other fiscal duties. They supply money for the business community in the form of Federal Reserve notes and regulate the member banks' ability to create money in the form of demand deposits.

Federal Reserve Member Banks

There are approximately 14,481 commercial banks in the United States. Roughly 41 percent (5,960) belong to the Federal Reserve System, and they are known as **member banks**. About 4,425 of these are national banks. When the Federal Reserve System was established, each national bank was required to join or to forfeit its charter. Membership is also open to state banks that can qualify. Many of them cannot qualify because of the

Figure 11-1   The Federal Reserve System

* ∗ Board of Governors of the Federal Reserve System
* ● Federal Reserve Bank Cities
* · Federal Reserve Branch Cities

Source: Adapted from *The Federal Reserve Bulletin*. (Washington, DC: Board of Governors of the Federal Reserve System, monthly.)

high minimum capital requirement, and some do not like the System's restrictions and regulations. Others are reluctant to join because as non-members they are permitted to use certain major facilities of the System anyway. Although less than one-half of all commercial banks belong to the System, these banks do 70 to 75 percent of the total commercial banking business in the United States.

Each member bank is required to buy stock of the Federal Reserve Bank of its district. The original stock subscription called for an amount equal to 6 percent of the member bank's own paid-up capital and surplus. To date, the member banks have purchased all the stock in the Federal Reserve Banks. As a result, we have a unique system in which the member banks completely own the Federal Reserve Banks, but most of the regulation or control of these Banks resides with the Board of Governors.

Although the member banks are operated for profit, the Federal Reserve Banks are operated strictly in the public interest. The Fed pays a 6 percent dividend on its stock. Any profits over this amount are turned over to the United States Treasury. In 1986, for example, the Treasury received over $15 billion from the Fed.

Obligations and Benefits of Membership

In addition to the purchase of Federal Reserve Bank stock, each member bank is obligated to maintain sufficient monetary reserves to meet the requirements set by the FRB under the law. Member banks also must remit at par checks drawn against them when presented for payment by the Federal Reserve Bank. Member banks are required to maintain most of their legal reserves with the Federal Reserve Banks. In addition, member banks are subject to examinations and regulations by the Federal Reserve Banks. All member banks must insure their deposits with the Federal Deposit Insurance Corporation. Moreover, member banks must comply with various federal laws, regulations, and conditions regarding adequacy of capital, mergers, and the establishment of branches and loan and investment limitations.

Benefits of membership include the ability to borrow from Federal Reserve Banks when the need arises; the privilege of using Federal Reserve facilities for collecting checks, settling clearing balances and transferring funds by wire to other cities; and the ability to obtain currency as needed. Other advantages of membership include sharing in the information facilities provided by the System and participating in the election of the Board of Directors of the Federal Reserve Bank. Since 1980, however, many of these regulations and benefits have been applied to all depository institutions.

Monetary Control Act of 1980

Congress enacted the Depository Institutions Deregulation and Monetary Control Act of 1980 to lessen regulation and promote competition among depository institutions. Depository institutions include commercial banks, savings banks, savings and loan associations (S&Ls), and credit unions.

The major purposes of the Act are to achieve competitive equity among financial institutions and improve the effectiveness of monetary policy by making the fulcrum on which that policy operates more stable. Many of the differences between commercial banks and other financial institutions were diminished by the Monetary Control Act.

The Act permits all financial institutions to have demand deposits and NOW accounts. S&Ls are allowed to extend their loan business beyond mortgages into other types of consumer credit, such as auto loans. The Act permits the payment of interest on checking accounts. It also provided for the phase-out of all limitations on interest rates paid by depository institutions by 1986. FDIC and FSLIC insurance coverage was increased to $100,000 per account.

The Act requires that all depository institutions be subject to the same reserve requirements as Federal Reserve member banks. Reserve requirements for nonmember depository institutions were to be phased in over an 8-year period. S&Ls, according to the Act, are permitted to borrow from the Federal Reserve Bank if necessary. The Federal Reserve Banks now act as clearinghouses for all depository institutions. The Act also requires Federal Reserve Banks to charge fees to both member banks and nonmember institutions for certain Fed services.

FEDERAL RESERVE CONTROL OF THE MONEY SUPPLY

Through its control over bank credit and other checkable accounts, the Federal Reserve System can affect the money supply. Thus, its actions have an effect on the level of economic activity and/or the price level. The Fed has many instruments or measures through which it can control bank credit. Some of these are referred to as **general controls** because they affect the overall supply of money. Others are referred to as **selective controls** because they affect the use of money for specific purposes in our economy. Let us see exactly how these controls are utilized in an attempt to stabilize the flow of economic activity or the price level.

GENERAL CONTROLS

In using its general controls, the Fed can influence the total amount and flow of credit and money; but these controls do little to encourage or to restrict the use of money for specific purposes. There are occasions, however, when the Fed, by tightening credit as a hedge against inflation, for example, may cause a shortage of money for many specific uses in the economy. In fact, it may cause a shortage of money for some specific activity that the Fed has no desire to restrict. If offsetting measures are not available in such situations, the advantages of a generally tight money supply must be weighed against the adverse effects of a money shortage for specific uses.

Reserve Requirements

We learned in Chapter 10 that a bank's ability to extend credit is affected by the amount of reserves it must hold for its demand deposits. We found that an increase in the reserve requirement would decrease the bank's ability to increase the money supply, and vice versa. Earlier in this chapter we learned that the member banks are required to keep most of their reserves in the Federal Reserve Banks. Now we can add the fact that the Board of Governors (FRB) has the authority to determine, within limits, the amount of reserves that the member banks must hold against demand deposits. Such reserve requirements as designated by the FRB are referred to as the **required reserve**. Any reserve over and above this amount that a bank may have is an **excess reserve**. Both are important to the potential size of the money supply.

Reserve Requirements. Before 1980, the Fed could regulate only member bank deposits and reserves, but the Monetary Control Act of 1980 made *all* depository institutions subject to the Fed's reserve requirements. For purposes of setting reserve requirements, deposits are divided into two broad categories. *Transaction accounts* are those used to make payments to others. They include regular checking accounts; negotiable orders of withdrawal (NOW) accounts; automatic transfer service accounts (ATS); share drafts of credit unions; and accounts that permit payment by automatic teller, telephone, or preauthorized transfer. *Nonpersonal time accounts* include time deposits or certificates of deposit (CD) that are transferable or held by depositors other than natural persons (large CDs that require at least 14 days' notice before withdrawal is made).

Reserves against transaction accounts are 3 percent on the first $29.8 million and 12 percent on deposits in excess of that amount. The $29.8 million breaking point is adjusted annually by formula. Additionally, the Act authorizes the FRB to impose a "supplemental" reserve requirement of up to 4 percent under certain conditions. The Fed will pay interest on such supplemental reserves. Reserve requirements against nonpersonal time deposits are to be set, again by the FRB, at between 0 and 9 percent. Table 11-2 shows the current reserve requirements.

Effect of Lower Reserve Requirements. The FRB uses its power judiciously. During periods of low production, income, and employment, the FRB may decrease the reserve requirements in the hope of increasing the money supply and bringing about an expansion of business activity. To show

Table 11-2 Reserve Requirements Established by the Monetary Control Act of 1980

Type of Accounts	Minimum	Maximum	Current as of December, 1986
Net transactions accounts			
$0 to $29.8 million	3%	3%	3%
Over $29.8 million	8%	14%	12%
Nonpersonal time accounts	0%	9%	3%

Figure 11-2   Reserve Requirement at 10 Percent

how this is accomplished, let us use a hypothetical example in which the banking system as a whole has no excess reserves on which to expand credit. Assuming a 10 percent reserve requirement, the situation at the beginning might appear as shown in Figure 11-2.

The banks are holding $100,000 cash reserves (10 percent) against total deposits of $1,000,000 ($100,000 in primary deposits and $900,000 in derivative deposits or loans). The banks in this situation cannot create any more credit. If the reserve requirement were decreased to 5 percent, however, the banks would have to hold only $50,000 in required reserves against the $1,000,000 in demand deposits. This would free $50,000 of the existing reserve. If it were left on deposit with the Fed, it would become excess reserve. The banks could then extend another $1,000,000 in demand deposits. This is shown in Figure 11-3.

Thus, a decrease in the reserve requirement can increase the bank's ability to extend credit, and this in effect provides for an increase in the money supply. *Notice that reduction of the reserve requirement does not necessar-*

Figure 11-3   FRB Lowers Reserve Requirement to 5 Percent

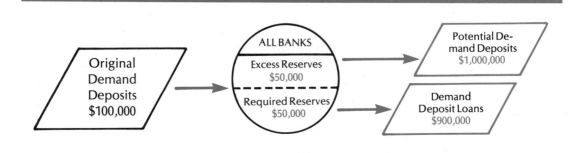

ily increase credit or the money supply, but merely the banks' ability to increase credit. There will not be an increase in credit or in the money supply until businesses or others actually borrow the money in the form of demand deposits. Frequently in a period of slackness or recession, the FRB will lower the reserve requirement, but businesspeople will be reluctant to borrow and spend money because of the poor return on capital investment. There are situations, therefore, in which the lowering of the reserve requirement may not result in an increase in the money supply.

Effect of Higher Reserve Requirements.   The FRB can decrease the banks' ability to expand the money supply by raising the reserve requirement. Assume once again a situation such as we had in Figure 11-2, in which the banks were "loaned up to the hilt." If the FRB increased the reserve requirements from 10 percent to 20 percent, the banks would actually be short of required reserves. In such a case they would have to increase their reserve or recall some of the loans outstanding. (See Figure 11-4.) The action of the banks in recalling loans would reduce the demand deposits a total of $500,000. Thus, it would in effect decrease the money supply by $500,000.

Actually the FRB would not do this, for it would greatly disturb and disrupt business activity. It is more inclined to use its power to prevent undesirable conditions from developing. For example, it tries to ease the money supply by lowering reserve requirements when the economy enters a period of declining business activity in the hope that it will help arrest the downward action. On the other hand, the FRB endeavors to tighten up on the money supply by raising reserve requirements and by using other methods when the economy begins to reach the full-employment, or the inflationary, stage of business activity. It knows that further increases in the money supply through the extension of demand deposits probably will lead to higher prices. Let us demonstrate this point by setting

Figure 11-4   FRB Raises Requirement to 20 Percent

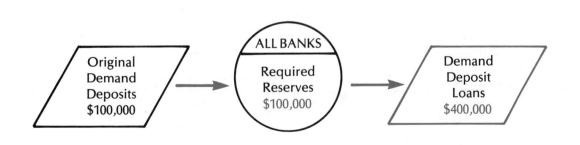

up a new hypothetical case. Assume that there is a 10 percent reserve requirement and that the banks have excess reserves. The situation might appear as shown in Figure 11-5.

With $33,333 in excess reserves and a 10 percent reserve requirement, the banks can increase demand deposits by $333,333. If business activity is good, businesses will borrow and there will be an increase in the money supply. If the economy is at full employment, however, the increased money supply will merely lead to higher prices. Under these circumstances, the FRB could absorb the excess reserves by increasing the reserve requirement. This would decrease the banks' ability to extend credit and thus would act as a deterrent to inflation.

In our case in Figure 11-5, if the FRB increased the reserve requirement to 15 percent, the banks would need $100,000 in legal reserves against the $666,667 total deposits outstanding. The excess reserves of $33,333 would then become a part of the required reserve. The banks would have no excess reserves and would lose their ability to extend additional credit. After such a change the status of the banks' reserves in relation to demand deposits would be as shown in Figure 11-6. Notice that a change in the reserve requirement does not affect the total amount of reserve funds held by member banks. Instead, it changes the volume of demand deposits and the volume of loans that member banks can support with existing reserves.

In fact, it is possible to have an increase in the reserve requirement causing a decrease in the banks' ability to extend credit and still have an increase in the money supply. Return to the situation in Figure 11-5 where the banks had excess reserves and assume the reserve requirement was raised to 12 percent instead of 15 percent. In such event the banks would need $80,000 in reserve behind the $666,667 in total demand deposits ($666,667×0.12 = $80,000). This would then leave $20,000 in excess reserves which could serve as a basis to increase demand deposits another

Figure 11-5   Banks Have Excess Reserves, 10 Percent
Reserve Requirement

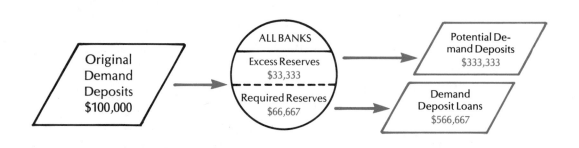

Figure 11-6 FRB Raises Reserve Requirement to 15 Percent

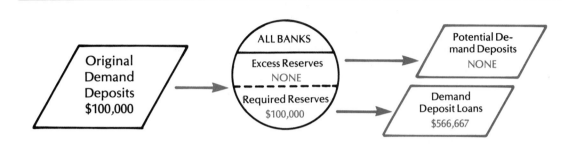

$166,667 ($20,000 ÷ 0.12). Consequently, demand deposits could be increased from $666,667 to a total of $833,333 ($100,000 ÷ 0.12) in spite of the higher reserve requirement.

Since the status of reserves in the individual banks will vary, some banks will be more affected than others by changes in the reserve requirements. For this reason, the FRB is somewhat cautious in the use of reserve requirements to control credit. Because of the rather quick and widespread effect on the potential money supply, the reserve requirement is usually changed by only one-quarter or one-half of a percentage point at a time.

Principle to Remember.   Regarding the Fed's control over the money supply through the use of reserve requirements, we may summarize by saying that an increase in the reserve requirements will decrease the banks' ability to extend credit. Conversely, a decrease in the reserve requirements will increase the banks' ability to extend credit.

Discount Rate

The **discount rate** is the interest rate at which the member banks may borrow funds from the Federal Reserve Banks. As you know, if you wish to borrow $100 at 12 percent from a bank for 1 year, you would have to sign a note payable to the bank (which becomes a note receivable for the bank). The bank would then discount your note for you. Instead of giving you the face value of the note, the bank would deduct the interest and pay you $88. However, you would repay the bank $100. The difference, $12, represents the interest, or discount.

There are two methods by which a bank may borrow from the Fed. The first is by rediscounting its customers' notes or other eligible commercial paper. It involves a sale of eligible paper to the Federal Reserve Bank. The second method is by borrowing on the bank's own promissory notes secured by its customers' notes, government securities, or other satisfactory collateral. The latter is the more popular and convenient method. Borrowings by the first method are called **discounts** and by the second method, **advances**; however, today both methods are generally referred to as discounting. In both methods the discount rate governs the cost of borrowing. Discount facilities are a privilege of the bank rather than a right. Furthermore, credit through this process is extended primarily on a short-term basis to enable a bank to adjust its reserve position when necessary because of such developments as a sudden withdrawal of deposits or an unusually large seasonal demand for credit.

Discounting Process.   Assume a bank has among its assets a considerable number of notes receivable that it discounted at 12 percent in exchange for loans in the form of cash and demand deposits. If a bank is low on reserves, it may discount these notes, called commercial paper, at its Federal Reserve Bank. If the notes are used, this means that the bank can obtain money on the notes immediately instead of waiting until payments on the notes are due.

However, if the Reserve Bank were to charge the bank 12 percent interest for borrowing funds, the bank would have to pay interest to the Reserve Bank in an amount equal to that which it would secure on its notes receivable. In effect, it would make nothing on its own loans to individuals and businesses. Thus, when the discount rate is high compared with the commercial loan rate, the banks will be reluctant to use this discounting process to build up or replace their reserves. If the discount rate is low, however, they will be more inclined to replace or to build up their reserves by discounting. Since reserves increase the banks' ability to extend credit, a decrease in the discount rate may bring about an increase in the money supply.

This process can be demonstrated graphically, but we must look at an individual bank instead of all banks. Assume that an individual bank has no excess reserve, as indicated in Figure 11-7. Keep in mind that the individual bank does not necessarily lend demand deposits to some multiple of its reserve. It holds the proper fractional reserve against its primary deposits. The remainder becomes excess reserves that it can hold or lend. Thus, in our example the individual bank will hold $10,000 in required reserves against the original $100,000 deposit and lend the remaining $90,000 in cash or demand deposits. As the $90,000 filters through the multiple expansion of bank credit, however, total demand deposits will be increased by some multiple of the original deposit.

According to the situation in Figure 11-7, the Acme National Bank will be unable to make further loans without excess reserves. It can build up its reserves through the discounting process. If the Acme Bank has made loans up to $90,000, it no doubt has among its assets $90,000 in notes receivable. Suppose that the bank is receiving 12 percent interest on these notes and that it can rediscount them at 10 percent or use them

Figure 11-7 Individual Bank, 10 Percent Reserve Requirement

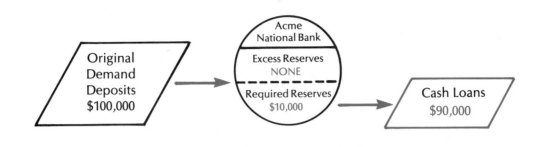

as collateral to secure an advance from the Federal Reserve Bank. If the bank discounted $50,000 worth of the notes, it could still net 2 percent on them. This would mean an annual income of $1,000. However, when it receives the $50,000 cash (or, as usually happens, a $50,000 credit is made to its reserve account in the Reserve Bank), it can lend this cash or $50,000 in demand deposits and make 12 percent on these new loans. Thus, by discounting it will actually be making 14 percent on the $50,000, 2 percent net on the discounted notes plus 12 percent on the new loans. It will have interest income of $7,000 (2 percent on $50,000 in old loans plus 12 percent on the $50,000 in new loans) compared with $6,000 (12 percent of $50,000) if it had not discounted. In such circumstances it is profitable for the bank to discount its commercial paper, to build up its excess reserves, and to make additional loans. (See Figure 11-8.)

If the Federal Reserve Bank were to lower the discount rate, it would be even more profitable for the member bank to discount. On the other hand, if the Federal Reserve Bank raised the discount rate to 11 percent, it would be less profitable for the Acme Bank to discount. If the discount rate were raised to 12 percent, it would not profit the bank to engage in the discounting process. Thus, banks can be encouraged to expand or contract credit by changes in the discount rate. However, changes in the discount rate do not automatically lead to changes in the money supply. Businesses and individuals must increase their loans to make changes in the money supply effective.

Changing the discount rate also has a secondary effect. The commercial loan rate is influenced greatly by the bank discount rate. For example, the **prime loan rate**, that is, that rate at which the individuals and firms with the best collateral can borrow, is usually a few percentage points above the discount rate. Thus, if the discount rate in Cleveland is 7 percent, the prime loan rate may be 9–10 percent. Usually when the discount rate is lowered, the commercial loan rates are lowered. This may encourage businesses to borrow. On the other hand, if the discount rate is raised,

Figure 11-8   Individual Bank Discount Notes, 10 Percent
Reserve Requirement

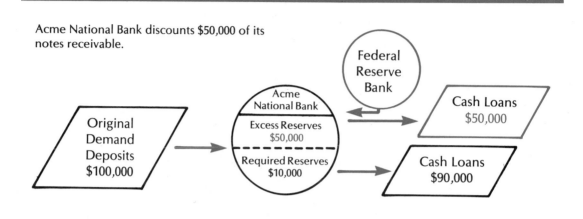

Acme National Bank discounts $50,000 of its notes receivable.

the commercial loan rates may be increased. This, in turn, may discourage businesses from borrowing. It should be remembered, however, that the funds may still be available but at a higher cost.

When business activity is falling, the Federal Reserve Banks lower the discount rate to encourage banks to discount and increase their ability to expand credit, and the banks encourage businesses to borrow by lowering the commercial loan rate. During full-employment inflationary periods, the Federal Reserve Banks raise the discount rate to discourage discounting, which in turn has a restrictive effect on the expansion of credit and discourages borrowing by pushing up commercial loan rates.

Of course, the Fed uses its best judgment in the use of the tools of control. The discount rate is usually changed by very moderate amounts, one-quarter or one-half of a percentage point at a time, so that the change will not cause a serious disruption in business activity. This action is primarily preventive rather than remedial. Sometimes, in fact, changes in the discount rate lag behind changes in the commercial loan rates. In such cases the Fed may raise or lower the discount rate to reduce the spread between the two rates.

The discount rate for each district is determined by its Federal Reserve Bank with the approval of the FRB. Although the Reserve Banks initiate changes in the discount rate, the Board still has authority "to review and determine" discount rates. The discount rate often varies slightly for short periods between districts because of differences in the money markets. Usually when a district changes its rate, most of the others follow suit, since factors of national scope generally cause the change.

Principle to Remember. It is important to remember that a decrease in the discount rate will generally encourage banks to extend credit and businesses to borrow, thus tending to increase the money supply. An increase in the discount rate will discourage banks from expanding credit and businesses from borrowing, thus tending to limit increases in the money supply.

Federal Funds Market

In addition to borrowing from the Reserve Bank, a bank can adjust its reserve position by borrowing from other banks that have surplus reserves. This interbank borrowing takes place in a fairly well-organized market, known as the **Federal Funds Market**. The federal funds rate, over which the Fed has some influence, is the rate at which banks are willing to borrow or to lend immediately available reserves on an overnight basis. It is a very sensitive indicator of the tightness of bank reserves. The federal funds rate may be higher or lower than that prevailing at the discount window, depending on the status of excess reserves.

Open-Market Operations

One of the most important and continuously used instruments of monetary management is the Federal Reserve **open-market operations**. The Federal Open Market Committee has control over a portfolio consisting of government securities including bonds, bills, certificates, and notes. If the FOMC wants to encourage the expansion of credit, it can direct the Fed's Open Market Account Manager at the "trading desk" located in the Federal Reserve Bank of New York to buy securities from member banks and individuals. This increases member bank reserves and enables the banks to make more loans. All member banks hold government obligations, and the Fed can induce member banks to sell or buy government bonds and other securities by offering to buy them at a premium price or sell them at a discount.

Bill short
Note med.
Bond long
terms

Purchase of Securities. When the Fed buys securities, it increases the excess reserves of the banks and permits them to expand credit. This is demonstrated graphically in Figure 11-9. Suppose that banks have no excess reserves and, therefore, cannot extend any additional credit. Under such conditions, if the Fed buys $50,000 of government securities from banks, it puts the money directly into the banks or credits their reserve accounts. This increases excess reserves and expands the banks' ability to make loans by $500,000 through the multiple expansion of bank credit. See Figure 11-10.

Figure 11-9   10 Percent Reserve Requirement

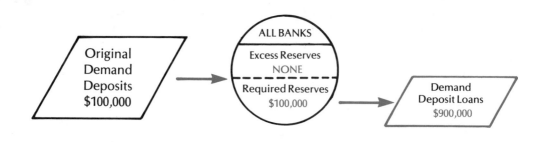

Practically the same result can be accomplished by purchasing securities from individuals or businesses, since these sellers will usually deposit the money received from the sale of securities in banks. These deposits in turn increase bank reserves and may result in a potential increase in the money supply. See Figure 11-11.

In this case the potential expansion of credit is somewhat less than it is when the Fed buys government obligations directly from the member banks because the banks must hold $5,000 in required reserves against the new deposits of $50,000 made by the individuals and businesses that sold the bonds.

Sale of Securities.   During times of inflation the Fed may wish to absorb some of the excess reserves in existence. It can do so by selling government securities to the banks. To buy bonds, banks in all probability will have to give up some excess reserves, which in turn will decrease their ability

Figure 11-10   FOMC Buys Securities from Banks, 10 Percent Reserve Requirement

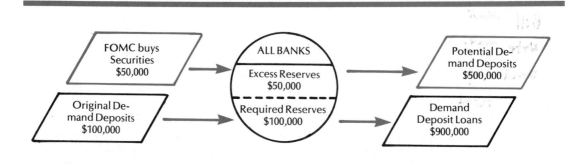

Figure 11-11   FOMC Buys Securities from Individuals and Businesses, 10 Percent Reserve Requirement

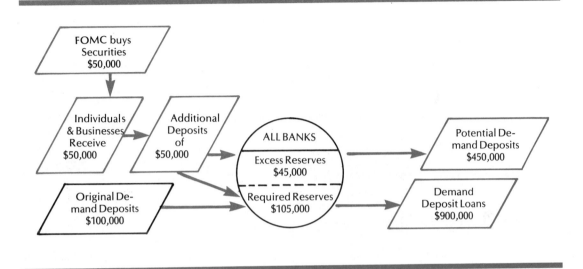

to extend credit. If the Fed sells bonds to individuals or businesses, it is assumed that they will withdraw funds from banks to pay for the bonds. This will reduce excess reserves and decrease the banks' ability to extend credit.

Most of the Fed open-market operations are, in fact, transacted with about two dozen specialized security dealers located in New York City, where the Federal Reserve Bank of New York serves as the Fed's agent for the purchase and sale of securities. Billions of dollars, mostly in short-term government securities, exchange hands daily in this market.

Principle to Remember.   We must remember that the Fed's ability to affect the money supply through its open-market operations is restricted. Although the purchase of bonds from the banks will increase bank reserves, it does not mean that businesses will borrow. On the other hand, selling bonds will not prevent an expansion of credit unless a sufficient amount is sold to absorb all the excess reserves. The effectiveness of the Fed's endeavor to limit expansion of the money supply will depend on the status of excess reserves.

Nevertheless, the purchase of securities in the open market by the Fed will increase the member banks' ability to expand credit, whereas the sale of securities will decrease the member banks' ability to create credit. In this way, the supply and the cost of credit can be affected by the actions of the FOMC.

Moral Suasion

Moral suasion is the term applied to a host of different measures that the Fed uses to influence the activities of banks. In addition to altering reserve requirements and discount rates and engaging in open-market operations, the Fed employs various measures to encourage banks to act one way or another. It does this by sending to banks letters in which it encourages or discourages the expansion of credit. At other times the Fed issues public statements giving the status of the economic situation and endeavors to persuade businesses and banks to expand or to restrain credit. During personal interviews, the Fed officers may warn against speculative loans or suggest that banks become more liberal with their loans. The Fed may ration credit and suspend the borrowing privileges of banks if necessary. In general, moral suasion will affect the money supply only to the extent that banks and businesses are willing to cooperate.

SELECTIVE CONTROLS

All the controls that have been mentioned thus far are general controls because they affect the money supply in general, regardless of the use to which the money may be put. If commercial loan rates are forced up through an increase in the discount rate, for example, individuals or businesses desiring to borrow are affected. The Fed, however, does have certain discretionary controls that affect the specific uses of money and credit in the economy.

For example, the Fed currently has the authority to set stock market margin requirements. This affects the amount of stock that may be purchased on credit. The higher the margin requirement, the greater the down payment required to purchase shares of stock. This reduces the opportunity for speculation in the stock market, holds down the demand for stocks, and moderates the prices of stocks. At various times in the past, the Fed has also had control of the conditions or terms of installment sales. Such controls, which established the down payment and the length of time in which an installment loan had to be repaid, had the effect of limiting total demand.

FEDERAL RESERVE POLICY

The Fed is an independent organization and, as such, exercises a considerable amount of autonomy. The FRB is responsible only to Congress. Hence, it may or may not agree with the economic policies of a given administration. However, since both have the same objectives (high-level production, employment, and income, along with stable prices), their actions usually complement each other.

The 1970s

By mid-1970, when unemployment reached 5.5 percent, the money supply was eased, and by the end of 1971 the discount rate was down to 4.5 percent. Expansion of business activity and the resurgence of inflation after the recession of 1970 led to a tighter monetary effort by the Fed through open-market operations. In a series of moves the discount rate within a year's time was moved to a new high of 8 percent and prime rates at commercial banks reached 12 percent. Furthermore, the reserve requirement at larger banks was raised 0.5 percent.

With the recession of 1974, however, the Fed liberalized the money supply through open-market operations, the prime rate receded from its peak of 12 percent to around 10 percent, reserve requirements were lowered, and a decline in the discount rate was anticipated. The stock market margin was also lowered, this time to 50 percent. These trends continued into 1975, and by April the discount rate had fallen to 6 percent and the prime rate was about 8 percent.

When the inflation rate began moving toward the double-digit level in the late 1970s, the Fed tightened the potential money supply with open-market operations, and some reserve requirements on long-term CDs were increased. The Federal Funds rate was pushed up, and the discount rate was raised by small increments from 5.25 percent in August, 1977, to 8 percent in September, 1978. The discount rate was then increased dramatically by more than one full percentage point to 9.5 percent about a month later. By the end of the year the prime rate at commercial banks reached 11.75 percent.

When inflation reached the double-digit level in 1979, the Fed announced in the fall of that year that it was shifting its anti-inflationary emphasis from that of control of interest rates to more control of the money supply.

The 1980s

In early 1980, the Fed kept the money supply tight in an effort to combat the double-digit inflation. The Fed was given the authority to impose controls on the use of credit cards, add to existing reserve requirements, and impose reserve requirements on the growing number of money market mutual funds. By mid-1980 the discount rate was 13 percent and the prime rate reached 21.5 percent. Although some of the credit controls and reserve requirements imposed earlier in the year were lifted as a result of the 1980 recession, the Fed continued a tight money policy through 1981 to control inflation. The discount rate reached a record level of 14 percent.

The occurrence of another recession in 1982 caused the Fed to back off a bit on its tight money measures. By mid-1982 the inflation rate dropped to 6 percent, unemployment reached 9.5 percent, and the prime rate was down to 16.5 percent. In the last half of 1982, as unemployment exceeded the double-digit level, the Fed, in a series of moves, lowered the discount rate from 14 to 8.5 percent. A strong economic recovery began in 1983 and continued throughout 1984; the inflation rate dropped to 4 percent or less, and the discount rate was held at an 8.5 to 9.0 percent level. But as the economic recovery slowed and unemployment remained at 7 percent or above, the discount rate was lowered to 7.5 percent in mid-1985 and eventually to 5.5 percent in August of 1986. At that time, the prime rate was down to 7.5 percent at most banks, where it remained until the spring of 1987.

RECOMMENDED CHANGES IN FEDERAL RESERVE STRUCTURE AND POLICY

Studies conducted over the past 15 years have recommended certain changes in the structure and policies of the Federal Reserve System. These recommendations include the following: that the discount rate be determined by the FRB instead of by the Federal Reserve Banks; that the open-market operations be vested in the FRB; that the FRB consist of five members only, eligible for reappointment after a 10-year term; that, although the autonomy of the Fed should be maintained, the term of office of the Chairman of the FRB should be made coterminous with that of the President of the United States; that all insured commercial banks be required to join the System; that the reserve requirement for all classes of banks be identical; and that reserve-requirement limitations be set at 8 to 18 percent. The Monetary Control Act of 1980, discussed earlier in this chapter, addressed some of these concerns.

Others suggest that the term of office of Board members be reduced from 14 to 4 years, that 12 members instead of 7 be appointed by the President, that the System be forced to obtain its operating funds from Congress, and that the Secretary of the Treasury be made Chairman of the Board of Governors as a means of curbing its independence.

Arthur Burns, a past Chairman of the Board of Governors, was concerned that the influence of the Fed on money matters and its ability to regulate the money supply was diminishing. He cited the fact that a number of banks had left the Federal Reserve System. He indicated, moreover, that the majority of the newly chartered commercial banks were electing not to join the System. This is emphasized by the fact that in 1960, 46 percent of the commercial banks belonged to the System, but currently only 41 percent of the commercial banks are members. Furthermore, the amount of commercial banking business done by member banks dropped from 83 percent of the total in 1960 to 72 percent currently. Burns suggested that all commercial banks be required to join the Federal Reserve System.

Burns also pointed out that gaps and duplications exist in banking requirements and regulations. This occurs because the Fed, the Office of the Comptroller of the Currency, the FDIC, and the individual states all have regulatory authority over the banks. As a means of establishing more uniform and effective policies and measures, Burns suggested that more of the authority to regulate and establish monetary requirements be centralized in one source. Others have suggested that Congress should set the targets for monetary growth and interest rates, and that the Fed just carry out the necessary measures to reach those targets.

On the matter of policy, an outspoken critic of the Fed has been Professor Milton Friedman, formerly of the University of Chicago. For years he has contended that the lag between implementation of certain monetary measures and their impact on the money supply and the level of economic activity is somewhat indeterminable and considerably longer than the Fed anticipates. In fact, he suggests that the Fed aggravates fluctuations in economic activity and the price level because of this. For example, the Fed may implement measures to tighten the money supply to combat inflation, but the major impact of the tight money may not be felt until several months later when the economy may be sluggish or in a downturn and may actually be in need of monetary expansion.

To avoid this situation, Professor Friedman and other monetarists recommend that the money supply be increased at a rate of 3 to 5 percent annually regardless of the condition of the economy. This, they believe, would do more to stabilize economic activity and the price level than the current policy of tampering with the money supply in an attempt to modify business and price fluctuations.

In response to some of these criticisms of the Fed's independence, Congress passed the Full Employment and Balanced Growth Act of 1978. This legislation amended the Employment Act of 1946 by requiring the Fed to indicate each year what measures it intends to use to work toward the achievement of our national economic goals. However, the continuation of tight money policies, which resulted in high and volatile interest rates during the recessions of 1980 and 1982, aggravated some of the more vocal critics of Fed policy. This brought into focus again the matter of the Fed's independence. Nevertheless, the Fed today keeps Congress and the administration informed about the target rates it sets for changes in the money supply and interest rates.

INCREASED COMPETITION IN BANKING

Not only did the Monetary Control Act of 1980 increase competition among banks in local areas, but by mid-1985 competition was further increased because more and more states began to permit branch banking. This allows banks, especially larger city banks, to have branches throughout a state. Branch banking was followed by interstate banking, which permits a bank in one state to have branches, or own other banks, in some other states. The interstate banking movement was accelerated by the depressed economy in the early 1980s which resulted in many bank failures. Several state legislatures allowed larger and stronger out-of-state banks to take over failing banks and S&Ls within their states. Many of the S&Ls were subsequently converted into commercial banks. This, of course, increased competition even for the larger banks within the state. In addition, a number of foreign banks which, from their home bases abroad, had done business with U.S. firms began to operate banks within the United States. Some examples include Barclays Bank of London, the Bank of Tokyo, and the Sumitomo Bank of Japan.

Banks have also been subject to increased competition from other financial institutions. Many of these institutions, such as brokerage houses and large firms like Sears and General Electric, began accepting deposits and making loans. These so-called nonbank banks have been doing business similar to commercial banks while escaping much of the banking regulation. This is possible because, in most cases, they do not both accept deposits and make loans through the creation of credit. Although the U.S. Comptroller of the Currency favors allowing nonbank banks to do banking business, the Federal Reserve objects to their banking operations. However, it must be stated that commercial banks, in turn, are performing many services that were formerly the prerogative of other financial institutions, such as brokerage houses. The net result of all these changes has been that the sharp distinction between banks and other financial institutions has faded in recent years.

SUMMARY

The Federal Reserve System is a complex system composed of several bodies, organizations, and committees. The Board of Governors sets the overall policy for the System. The 12 Federal Reserve Banks act as central banks, regulate member banks, and serve as fiscal agents for the federal government. The Federal Reserve Banks exercise a considerable amount of autonomy. Of the 14,481 commercial banks in the United States, approximately 41 percent belong to the Federal Reserve System. However, these banks carry on 70 to 75 percent of the total banking business in the nation. Consequently, the Fed has a substantial influence on our banking system.

The Federal Reserve System has a certain amount of control over the nation's money supply, primarily through its ability to affect the volume and cost of bank credit. Some of its controls are general in that they affect the total potential money supply. Others are selective, since they affect the use of credit for particular purposes. The current figures for most monetary controls can be found at any time in the *Federal Reserve Bulletin*.

The Fed can affect the ability of the banks to extend credit through its regulation of the reserve requirements. An increase in bank reserve requirements decreases the banks' ability to extend credit, while a decrease in the reserve requirement has the opposite effect. A change in the discount rate also affects the amount of credit by influencing the borrowing of both banks and businesses. In general, an increase in the discount rate will discourage banks from borrowing to increase their reserves. It also will discourage borrowing by businesses, since an increase in the discount rate generally will force up the commercial loan rate.

The Federal Open Market Committee of the Federal Reserve, through the purchase of securities, can increase banks' reserves and, therefore, affect their ability to extend credit. When the FOMC sells securities to banks, it absorbs their excess reserves and therefore reduces their ability to extend credit. At other times, the Fed uses moral suasion to influence the credit policies of banks. The banks' ability to extend credit also will be affected by the ease with which they can borrow from Federal Reserve Banks. The Federal Reserve has the authority to set stock market margin requirements, which affect the amount of stock that may be purchased on credit.

The general policy of the Federal Reserve has been to use its controls to help stabilize the level of economic activity and the price level. When the economy is moving at a pace that is too fast and inflation is likely to result, the Fed usually tightens the money supply to reduce the inflationary tendencies in the economy. On the other hand, the Fed lowers reserve requirements, reduces discount rates, engages in the purchase of securities from member banks and individuals, and uses moral suasion in an endeavor to offset declines in the economy.

The Depository Institutions Deregulation and Monetary Control Act of 1980 brought about numerous changes in the banking and finance industry. In recent years competition in the banking industry has increased as a result of deregulation and the growth of branch banking, interstate banking, foreign banking, and nonbank banks.

NEW TERMS AND CONCEPTS

Member banks	Excess reserve	Prime loan rate
General controls	Discount rate	Federal Funds Market
Selective controls	Discounts	Open-market operations
Required reserve	Advances	Moral suasion

DISCUSSION QUESTIONS

1. Do you agree with the policy of electing nonbankers to the board of directors of each Federal Reserve Bank? Why or why not?
2. Should all commercial banks be required to become members of the Federal Reserve System? Why or why not?
3. It has been suggested that labor unions be given representation on the board of directors of each Federal Reserve Bank. Do you agree with this suggestion? Why or why not?
4. Since the federal government owns no stock in the Federal Reserve Banks, why should the government appoint the Federal Reserve Board of Governors?
5. Does the lowering of reserve requirements automatically increase the money supply? Why?
6. In what way can a change in the discount rate affect commercial loan rates?
7. What will be the effect of the purchase of bonds from individuals by the Federal Open Market Committee compared with the purchase of bonds from the banks insofar as the expansion of the money supply is concerned?
8. Do you think that the independence of the Fed ought to be modified in any way?

SUGGESTED READINGS

Bartels, Andrew H. "Volcker's Revolution at the Fed." *Challenge*. (September/October, 1985).

Bowden, Elbert V., and Judith L. Holbert. *Revolution in Banking*, 2d ed. Englewood Cliffs, NJ: Prentice-Hall, 1984.

Federal Reserve Bulletin. Washington, DC: Board of Governors of the Federal Reserve System, monthly.

Federal Reserve System: Purposes and Functions. Washington, DC: Board of Governors of the Federal Reserve System, 1984.

Friedman, Milton. "The Case for Overhauling the Federal Reserve." *Challenge* (July/August 1985).

The Hats the Federal Reserve Wears. Federal Reserve Bank of Cleveland, 1982.

McCulloch, J. Huston. *Money and Inflation: A Monetarist Approach*. New York: Academic Press, Inc., 1982.

Meek, Paul. *Open Market Operations*. Federal Reserve Bank of New York, 1978.

Wallich, Henry C. "Banking Reform." *Challenge* (September/October, 1985).

West, Robert C. "The Depository Institutions Deregulation Act of 1980: A Historical Perspective." *Economic Review*. Federal Reserve Bank of Kansas (February, 1982).

PART 4

PRODUCTION, INCOME, AND EMPLOYMENT

12

GNP, NATIONAL INCOME, AND INPUT–OUTPUT ANALYSIS

■

Instead of using hypothetical figures when discussing the circular flow of economic activity as we did in previous chapters, we can use actual dollar measurements. The United States Department of Commerce keeps a running tab on the dollar value of the goods and services produced in our economy. This is broken down into various components, which makes it easier to analyze.

THE GROSS NATIONAL PRODUCT

The dollar value of total production in the United States can be determined by adding the value of all the end products and services produced in a given period. In many cases, however, it is difficult to distinguish intermediate products (those used in the production of other products) from end products (those consumed directly). Should we count a tire as an end product, or should we count it as part of the value of an automobile? Is corn an end product, or is some of it included in the value of bacon when hogs are slaughtered? When we count the value of all the end products, we may count some items twice. For accuracy in calculating the total production, however, it is essential that we count goods and services only once.

The value of our total production can also be obtained by counting the value added to commodities and the value of services. This can be done in each instance by comparing the cost of materials with the market price of the finished product. The difference is the value added by the producer. It represents the amount that must be paid for wages, rent, and interest, as well as the profit the producer will receive on the product. Thus, the summation of the total value added to all the products by the various producers plus the value of the services rendered by others will equal the total production of the economy.

If we consider the production of an automobile, we can demonstrate the idea of value added. If the iron ore and the other basic raw materials originally cost $600, they might be worth $1,200 after being processed into pig iron and other materials, $2,400 after being refined into steel ingots, and so on down the line until they finally take the shape of the automobile at a value of $12,000. If we were to sum the value of the product at the end of each of these productive stages, the total value might be $36,000, as shown in Table 12-1. Obviously there has been much double counting in the process. However, if we were to start out with the value of the basic commodities and add to it only the value added by each productive process, the total value added would be equal to the total price of the end product, as shown in the third column of Table 12-1. Of course, the total value added will represent the total production that has taken place. Likewise, it will be equal to the total payments to the owners of the factors of production.

Our total production is not actually measured by the value-added method. It is measured from two principal points of view: as the summation of end products produced by the economy and as the summation of costs incurred in producing those products.

Now that we have some idea of how total production is measured, we can consider the basic concept of production and its modifications. The basic concept is the **gross national product (GNP)**, which by definition is the current market value of the total goods and services produced by our nation's economy over a given period of time. The GNP is stated on a yearly basis. The 1986 GNP was $4,208.5 billion.

Table 12-1 Value-Added Example

Stage of Production	Value at End of Each Stage of Production	Value Added by Each Stage of Production	
Iron ore and other raw materials	$ 600	$ 600	Value of basic commodities
Pig iron and other processed materials	1,200	600 ⎫	
Steel ingots, etc.	2,400	1,200	Represents
Sheet steel, etc.	4,200	1,800	payments for:
Auto parts	6,000	1,800 ⎬	Wages
Assembly	9,600	3,600	Rent
			Interest
			Profits
Automobile delivered at showroom	12,000	2,400 ⎭	
	$36,000	$12,000	True measure of production

Our total production each year uses up a certain amount of capital goods. Machinery, equipment, buildings, and tools depreciate with use. Some become obsolete and lose their value. Thus, the GNP must be reduced by the amount of depreciation and obsolescence, generally called **capital consumption allowance**. Since capital consumption allowances totaled $455.1 billion in 1986, the **net national product (NNP)** amounted to $3,753.4 billion. Capital consumption allowances generally are about 10 percent of our total production.

National Income

The NNP can be reduced to another meaningful concept called the **national income (NI)**. The NI has a twofold definition. First, it is the total factor costs of the goods and services produced by the nation's economy. In this sense, it is equivalent to the amount that was paid for the use of land, labor, capital, and entrepreneurship to obtain a given GNP. Second, the NI represents the aggregate earnings (in the form of wages, rent, interest, and profit) arising from the production of the GNP. In this sense, it is equivalent to the earnings or income of the owners of the factors of production which were used in producing the GNP. Thus, the "total factor cost" and "aggregate earnings" are merely two sides of the same coin. The value of the NI can be obtained by adding all the earnings of labor and property in a given period. It can also be obtained by subtracting capital consumption allowances and indirect business taxes, such as sales taxes, from the GNP and making a few other minor allowances. After making such adjustments, in 1986 the value of the NI was $3,387.4 billion.

Personal Income

As far as individuals are concerned, the national income figure can be reduced to a more appropriate concept, personal income. By definition **personal income (PI)** is the current income received by persons from all sources. It includes transfer payments from government and business, but it excludes transfer payments among persons. A **transfer payment** occurs when a payment of money is made for which no current goods or services are produced. For example, a veteran attending college may receive $400 per month. This is truly a part of the veteran's personal income, although there are no current goods or services in exchange for the money. It is true that the veteran may have earned it, but it is payment for service in a previous period. Retired persons on business or government pensions are also receiving transfer payments.

Not only individuals but also nonprofit institutions are classified as "persons" for this purpose. Personal income is measured on a before-tax basis. It includes such things as wages, salaries, proprietor's income, rental income, interest, dividends, and transfer payments. Personal income is found by subtracting from NI corporate income taxes and undistributed profits, because neither of these segments of corporate profit is passed on to individuals. This will leave only corporate dividends to be counted as part of the personal income. Table 12-2 shows this by subtracting all corporate profits, along with an inventory valuation adjustment, and then adding corporate dividends and personal interest income to the total. We also subtract Social Security payments and net interest.

We must then add government and business transfer payments and make a few other minor adjustments. After doing this for 1986, we find that the PI was $3,487.0 billion. It is easy to see that the biggest factor

Table 12-2 National Income Accounts for 1986 (Billions of Dollars)

Gross national product (GNP)			$4,208.5
Less:	Capital consumption allowance — *depreciation*	$455.1	
Equals:	Net national product (NNP)		$3,753.4
Less:	Indirect business tax and nontax liability	348.7	
	Business transfer payments	23.2	
	Statistical discrepancy	5.4	
Plus:	Subsidies less current surplus of government enterprises	11.3	
Equals:	National income (NI)		3,387.4
Less:	Corporate profits and inventory adjustment	299.7	
	Contributions for social insurance	376.1	
	Net interest	294.9	
	Wage accruals less disbursements	.0	
Plus:	Government transfer payments	490.5	
	Personal interest income	475.4	
	Personal dividend income	81.2	
	Business transfer payments	23.2	*Gross Inc.*
Equals:	Personal income (PI)		3,487.0
Less:	Personal tax and nontax payments	513.3	
Equals:	Disposable personal income (DPI)		2,973.7 *Net Inc.*
Less:	Personal consumption expenditures	2,762.4	
	Consumer interest payments to business	93.6	
	Personal transfer payments to foreigners	1.4	
Equals:	Personal saving (S)		116.3

Source: *Economic Report of the President* (Washington, DC: U.S. Government Printing Office, 1987).

accounting for the difference between PI and NI is corporation income taxes when we consider that corporations paid over $100 billion in taxes in 1986.

Disposable Personal Income

We are well aware that we do not have the opportunity to spend every dollar we earn. There is quite a gap between our earnings and our take-home pay. The main cause for this difference is the fact that we pay federal and in some cases state and local income taxes. What remains of personal income after these deductions have been made is **disposable personal income (DPI)**. Since we can make the decision on whether or not to spend it and the direction in which it will be spent, this income is sometimes called **discretionary income**. More frequently, however, the term "discretionary income" is applied to that portion of disposable income remaining after paying for such items as food, rent, utilities, basic transportation, and other necessities. In 1986, income remaining to persons after deductions of personal tax and nontax payments to government, disposable personal income, was $2,973.7 billion. Of this total amount we as individuals spent $2,762.4 billion on personal outlays and saved $116.3 billion.

Allocation of the Gross National Product

The GNP is allocated to four major sectors of our economy: consumer, business, net exports, and government. Approximately 66 percent of the total production of our nation was in the form of consumer goods and services. That part of total production in the form of machinery, equipment, buildings, and inventories is known as private investment. About 16 percent of 1986 output was in the form of private investment. Net exports, about −2.5 percent of output, represent the difference between exports from and imports to the United States. Government, the fourth sector, must buy goods and services to perform its necessary functions. About 21 percent of our 1986 output went to the government. It is interesting to observe that state and local governments made 58 percent of total government purchases and that 76 percent of the federal purchases were for national defense purposes. The allocation of the GNP to the four sectors is shown in Table 12-3.

Sources of the Gross National Product

When the four sectors of the economy—consumer, business, exports, and government—purchase goods and services, they must pay for them. These payments to the sellers of the goods and services are in turn used to compensate the factors involved in the production of GNP. As was

Table 12-3 Gross National Product or Expenditure for 1986

		Billions of Dollars	% of GNP
Personal consumption expenditures		$2,762.4	65.6%
Durable goods	388.3		
Nondurable goods	932.7		
Services	1,441.4		
Gross private domestic investment		686.5	16.3
Nonresidential structures	143.6		
Producers' durable equipment	314.9		
Residential structures	216.6		
Change in business inventories	11.4		
Net exports of goods and services		−105.7	−2.5
Exports	373.0		
Imports	478.7		
Government purchases		865.3	20.6
Federal	367.2		
State and local	498.1		
Gross national product		$4,208.5	

Source: *Economic Report of the President*, 1987.

pointed out in our circular flow charts in Chapter 4, these factors are paid in the form of wages, rent, interest, and profit. These productive factors are considered the source of GNP. Table 12-4 shows a breakdown of the payments to the various factors of production. The allocation of GNP and the distribution of NI can also be seen in Figure 12-1.

Final Sales and GNP

GNP data usually include a figure for *final sales*. The difference between final sales and GNP represents net inventory change. When final sales are larger than the GNP, it means that a net inventory reduction took place to meet some of the demand for goods and services. When final sales are less than the GNP, it means that excess production was added to inventories. In 1982, for example, final sales were $3,191 billion and the GNP was $3,116 billion, which indicated that in that recession year inventories were reduced by $75 billion. In 1986 inventories were increased (decreased) by $11.4 billion, and final sales were $4,197.1 billion.

Table 12-4   National Income by Distributive Shares for 1986

		Billions of Dollars	% of NI
Compensation of employees		$2,498.3	73.8%
Wages and salaries	$2,073.8		
Supplements of wages and salaries	424.5		
Rental income of persons		15.6	0.5
Net interest		294.9	8.7
Proprietors' income		278.9	8.2
Business and professional	252.5		
Farm	26.4		
Corporate profits		299.7	8.8
Profits before tax	236.6		
Inventory valuation adjustment	6.3		
Capital consumption adjustment	56.8		
National income		$3,387.4	

Source: *Economic Report of the President*, 1987.

Quarterly Reports on the GNP

To keep citizens informed and to have figures available as a guide for the implementation of national economic policies, the Department of Commerce publishes quarterly reports on the GNP and related figures. These quarterly reports are expressed in annual rates. This is accomplished in effect by adjusting the actual production in any given quarter for seasonal fluctuation and then multiplying the seasonally adjusted figure by 4 to convert it into an annual rate. For example, actual production for a given quarter may be $1,200 billion. The seasonally adjusted output may be $1,175 billion, which, when multiplied by 4, equals a seasonally adjusted quarterly total at an annual rate of $4,700 billion.

The quarterly system makes it easier to analyze movements in the GNP. Any quarter can be compared against another or can be measured against the annual total. With this method it is easy to spot the high and low quarters of business fluctuations, especially when looking at the constant dollar, or real GNP, figures. Downswings and upswings in the economy can be recognized at an earlier date than they would be if the GNP were published on a yearly basis only. Observe the rate of change, for example, in Table 12-5.

Figure 12-1 Allocation of GNP and Distribution of National Income, 1986

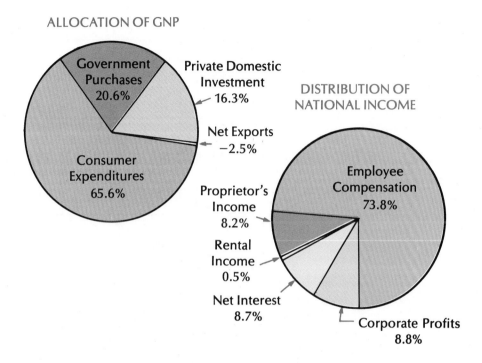

ALLOCATION OF GNP

Government Purchases 20.6%

Private Domestic Investment 16.3%

DISTRIBUTION OF NATIONAL INCOME

Net Exports −2.5%

Consumer Expenditures 65.6%

Proprietor's Income 8.2%

Employee Compensation 73.8%

Rental Income 0.5%

Net Interest 8.7%

Corporate Profits 8.8%

Source: *Economic Report of the President*, 1987.

Table 12-5 Gross National Product, Seasonally Adjusted Quarterly Totals at Annual Rates, 1985–1986 (Billions of Dollars)

Year	Quarter	Current Dollars	1982 Constant Dollars
1985	I	$3,909.3	$3,547.0
	II	3,965.0	3,567.6
	III	4,030.5	3.508.8
	IV	4,087.7	3.622.3
1986	I	4,149.2	3,665.9
	II	4,175.6	3,661.4
	III	4,240.7	3,686.4
	IV	4,268.4	3,702.4

Source: *Federal Reserve Bulletin* (February, 1987)

Figure 12-2   National Circular Flow, 1986

PRODUCT FLOWS (BILLIONS)		
Consumers	$2,762.4	
Domestic investment	686.5	
Net exports	−105.7	
Government purchases	863.3	
GNP	$4,208.5	

Comp. to employees		$2,498.3
Rental income		15.6
Net interest		294.9
Proprietors' income		278.9
Corporate profits		299.7
NI		$3,387.4
Indirect taxes, CCA, and other		821.1
GNP		$3,208.5

INCOME FLOWS (BILLIONS)

Source: *Economic Report of the President*, 1987

Not only is the GNP given in quarterly figures, but also it is frequently revised. A preliminary estimate for a given year usually appears during February of the following year. A more accurate figure is released later in the spring, and final revision is made available during the summer.

Frequently the various accounts of the GNP will not balance when checked against each other. This may be due to the fact that information for various tables is collected from different sources. These differences are usually adjusted by writing the differences off to a statistical discrepancy. In dealing with the GNP and related figures it should be remembered that the data are approximations rather than precise figures.

GNP and the Circular Flow

The GNP is produced by numerous businesses and individuals, who in turn make payments to the various factors of production for their contributions to the GNP. Incomes received are used, in turn, to purchase goods and services. This sets up a circular flow of goods and services and money incomes such as that explained in Chapter 4 and demonstrated in Figure 12-2.

GNP AS A MEASURE OF ECONOMIC PROGRESS

Since GNP is a measure of the total production of goods and services, it is frequently used as a measure of economic progress. Also, when GNP changes, our incomes change; and a change in income affects our standard of living. Consequently, many people like to measure the standard of living by the size of the GNP. However, whenever we use GNP as a measure of economic progress or the level of the standard of living, we must keep certain modifications in mind.

Changes in the Price Level

We know that GNP is the current market value of the total goods and services currently produced by our nation's economy. So GNP can be increased merely by increasing the price of goods and services produced. Therefore, comparing one year with another can be very misleading unless we make corrections for changes in the price level between the two years. In effect, we have to remove the element of price increases from the current GNP. This is true for all the hundreds of thousands of different commodities that constitute the GNP. Instead of adjusting each item individually, however, we adjust them all simultaneously by using the **GNP implicit price deflators**. This is an index that takes into account not only the price changes but also some change in the quality of various products. Thus, by dividing the total GNP for any year by the value of the implicit price deflator for that particular year, we can adjust current GNP to a GNP in constant dollars, or as it is often called, **real GNP**, as Table 12-6 shows.

If we were to use the current dollar GNP as a measure of economic progress, we would be misled into believing that the GNP increased 163 percent between 1975 and 1986. If we look at the GNP in constant dollars, we can readily observe that the physical output of goods and services increased by 36 percent during this period. The real GNP tells us what we want to know much better than the GNP in current dollars.

Looking at the GNP of 1982 as compared with that of 1981 in current dollars, we would be led to believe that production increased by $113 billion, or 3.7 percent. However, since 1982 was a period of high prices and the implicit price index increased more than 6 percent, we can get a true picture of the change in production only by looking at the real GNP. There was a 2.5 percent decrease in output and not a 3.7 percent increase between 1981 and 1982 as one might initially think. The real GNP more clearly shows the recession in the economy in 1982, as well as those of 1980 and 1974–1975.

Table 12-6 Current Dollar GNP Converted to 1982 Constant
Dollar GNP

Year	Current GNP (billions)	Implicit Price Deflators (1982 = 100)	1982 Constant Dollar GNP (billions)
1975	$1,598	59.3	$2,695
1976	1,783	63.1	2,827
1977	1,991	67.3	2,957
1978	2,250	72.2	3,115
1979	2,508	78.6	3,192
1980	2,732	85.7	3,187
1981	3,053	94.0	3,249
1982	3,166	100.0	3,166
1983	3,406	103.9	3,279
1984	3,765	107.9	3,490
1985	3,998	111.5	3,585
1986	4,209	114.5	3,676

Source: *Economic Report of the President*, 1987.

Changes in the Population Size

Another modification that we should make before using the GNP as a measure of economic progress is the adjustment for population. It is true that the physical amount of goods and services produced in 1986 was about 1.4 times as much as we produced in 1975. We must keep in mind, however, that more people were sharing the goods and services we produced. It is necessary, then, to correct our real GNP in order to take into account the increase in population. This can be done simply by dividing the real GNP in any year by the total population in that year.

We can obtain a better measure of the average amount of goods and services received per person by first reducing our GNP to disposable personal income, which is the spendable income or income after taxes. If we divide total DPI by the total population, we will get per capita DPI. This amount can be adjusted for changes in the price level to give per capita DPI in constant dollars, or the **real per capita disposable income**. Other things remaining the same, a comparison of the real per capita DPI for any two years will give us a fair indication of what is happening to our standard of living. We must remember, however, that many people make less than, and others make more than, the value of the per capita DPI.

Table 12-7   Current and 1982 Constant Dollar per Capita Disposable Personal Income

Year	Current Dollar Total DPI (billions)	Population (millions)	Current Dollar Per Capita DPI	1982 Constant Dollar Per Capita DPI
1975	$1,143	216.0	$ 5,291	$ 8,944
1980	1,918	227.7	8,421	9,722
1985	2,828	239.2	11,817	10,563
1986	2,974	241.5	13,312	10,780

Source: *Economic Report of the President*, 1987.

Table 12-7 shows that current dollar total DPI increased more than 160 percent between 1975 and 1986. When we divide this total by the population, however, it shows that the current dollar per capita DPI rose less than 152 percent during the period. Finally, after adjusting the current dollar per capita incomes for price changes, we see that the real per capita DPI rose only 21 percent during the 11-year period. This is the best measure that we have of the standard of living or the measure of economic progress in our country. Although this is not perfect, it is closer to the truth to say that our standard of living increased about 21 percent than it would be to say that it more than doubled. Even so, there are other reservations we should make in utilizing GNP figures as a yardstick for our standard of living and economic progress.

Value of Nonmonetary Transactions

The GNP for the most part takes into account only goods and services for which there have been monetary transactions. If you buy a new desk, it is entered in the GNP, but if you make it yourself out of old lumber, it does not become a part of the GNP. If you hire a commercial gardener to mow your lawn, the value of the service is entered in the GNP. If you mow your own lawn, however, it does not go into the GNP. There are many goods and services that, because they do not involve monetary transactions, never enter the GNP. Nevertheless, they are just as important to our standard of living as most of the items that are counted in the GNP. This is a substantial defect when we want to use the GNP as an indicator of our standard of living. For example, if we assume the current minimum-wage value of $134 per week and apply a standard 40-hour week to ordinary household chores done by members of the family, it would add over $240 billion annually to our gross national product.

It is also estimated by the Internal Revenue Service and others that billions of dollars' worth of services are exchanged in the so-called **underground**, or **subterranean, economy**. A dentist may do some oral surgery for an accountant in exchange for some financial advice without any monetary payments involved. A lawyer may perform legal work for a schoolteacher, who in exchange tutors the lawyer's child. In recent years there have been some formal barter organizations started. These organizations are composed of individuals with various skills such as plumbers, lawyers, mechanics, carpenters, dentists, and the like, who perform services for each other in exchange for organization credits instead of cash payments. The earned credits can then be used to obtain services from other members of the organization. It is estimated that activities equivalent to 10 to 15 percent of the reported GNP are currently taking place in the underground economy.

Types of Goods and Services Produced

We usually think that the more goods and services we produce, the higher our standard of living; but there are exceptions. Sometimes the nature of the goods and services is such that we cannot raise our standard of living through their consumption. For example, as a nation we produced $4,209 billion in goods in 1986. Out of that total output, however, $279 billion, or 6.6 percent, was in the form of military production. While it is true that tanks, ships, missiles, and weapons may protect our society, they do not add directly to our enjoyment or standard of living as do food, new homes, autos, clothing, medical care, and numerous other consumer commodities and services.

Thus, in comparing the GNP of various years to get an indication of our change in living standards, we may be misled if we neglect to consider the type of goods and services produced in each of those years. Likewise, it is difficult to compare the standard of living in two different countries by comparing the respective value of their GNPs, for if one country is highly militarized while the other is not, it can make a substantial difference.

Handling of Durable Goods

Durable goods are added to GNP in the year they are produced. When we produce an automobile, a refrigerator, a set of golf clubs, a suit, or a bicycle, there is value added into the GNP for that commodity. Although we receive services from the commodity in subsequent years, national income accounting handles it as though it were entirely consumed in the year in which it was produced. Normally, as our incomes increase during prosperity periods, we tend to produce more of these durable items; but we do not fully use them in one year. This tends to exaggerate the value of our GNP. On the other hand, in recessions we tend to decrease our production of durable goods, but we still get service out of the items produced previously. This service is a form of real income. Since there is no accounting in the GNP for the length of service of durable goods bought in previous years, GNP frequently underestimates our standard of living, especially during periods of declining business activity.

External or Social Costs

Another reservation that must be kept in mind when utilizing GNP data is the absence of social cost. When a firm produces goods and services, such internal factors as machine depreciation are considered as costs of production. Consequently, these costs are subtracted from GNP to obtain net national product and national income. In addition to internal costs, however, external, or social, costs are involved in the production of goods and services. Effluents from a chemical plant into a stream or river, for example, may pollute the water, making it unsuitable for drinking, swimming, or fishing. This is a social cost to the community. Smoke from a factory may pollute the surrounding air, creating offensive odors or contributing to lung diseases. Noise from an airport may create a sound hazard and decrease property values in the area.

Since these external costs are not borne by the individual firm, they are not included in its total cost or the value added that enters the GNP. They are, however, real economic costs that must be borne by society in the form of deterioration of the environment. As GNP increases, these external, or social, costs become larger and larger. Consequently, the net national product and the national income are overstated by several billions of dollars annually because these costs are not subtracted from GNP.

Value of Leisure

Lastly, the GNP makes no allowance for leisure time. The problem is, even if we wanted to take it into account, how would we value it? It means more to some people than it does to others. Nevertheless, it should be considered when using the GNP as a measure of economic progress. We can now produce as much as or more than we formerly did in a calendar year, even though we have more holidays and vacation time.

Certainly this must be considered a substantial improvement in our standard of living. This does not, however, show up anywhere in our GNP figures. At present there is some movement toward a shorter workweek. If this comes, it will raise our economic standard of living, provided we maintain at least the same output of goods and services.

In summary, GNP figures are a fairly good indication of the total production of goods and services by our nation's economy. They can be used as a measure of economic progress or of the standard of living if we use them in the right way. Do not be like the politicians who boast that our total production of goods and services increased some fabulous amount during their party's administration, or like their opponents who charge that price increases obliterated all the advantages of higher incomes and wages. Get the facts straight and use them properly. This is important because we will see as we go along that the level of the GNP, along with the price level and the level of unemployment, will serve as a guide to the use of government action in an effort to stabilize the circular flow of economic activity.

FLOW OF FUNDS

The GNP records transactions only of those goods and services that are currently produced. It does not measure the financial transactions of goods sold during the current period that were produced at a previous time. For example, suppose Ms. Rodriguez purchased a new auto for $10,000 in March, 1986. When she bought it, there would be an entry in the GNP for $10,000. However, if she sold it through a used-car dealer for $7,000 in October, 1986, this later transaction would not be entered in the GNP. Only the profit or commission of the used-car dealer would enter the GNP as a payment for services rendered. Nevertheless, total monetary transactions as a result of the two sales totaled $17,000.

Furthermore, since the GNP measures only the value added by the producers, it eliminates double accounting. The financial transactions required to get a good produced, however, are much greater than the total value added. This frequently happens in the sale of intermediate products. For instance, in our example in Table 12-1, page 207, we eliminated the double accounting by entering only the value added into the GNP. To get the $12,000 car produced, however, intermediate transactions of $36,000 were necessary.

When you consider the resale of homes, automobiles, commercial property, and millions of other commodities that take place each year, it is easy to see why the GNP, although it does a good job of measuring current production, does not begin to measure the total financial transactions taking place within the economy in a given period. In 1986 we had a GNP of $4,208.5 billion, but the total flow of funds for that year was probably four times as great.

The initial **flow-of-funds system of national accounts**, published by the Federal Reserve, encompasses all transactions in the economy that occurred as a result of cash payments or extensions of credit. This system is broader than the GNP account, since the flow of funds arises from the transfer of existing assets as well as the sale and purchase of currently produced goods and services. It records the sale of old as well as new homes, and the purchase of used as well as new autos. It also includes purely financial transactions, such as a transfer of securities from one person to another.

NATIONAL WEALTH

Another important concept in the study of economics is that of wealth. Wealth is composed of such things as machinery, equipment, buildings, land, and other economic goods. It is obvious that by applying labor and knowledge to this wealth we can produce additional goods and services, or income. Of course, the greater the base of wealth with which a nation has to work, the more goods and services it can produce and the higher its standard of living will be. Consequently, it is advantageous for any nation to add continually to its stock of wealth. As indicated in Chapter 1, there are various estimates of wealth. The one shown in Table 12-8, calculated by the U.S. Bureau of Economic Analysis, indicates that total wealth exceeded $9.6 trillion in 1984. Our national wealth and our productive capacity have been increasing continuously. Table 12-9 shows the delineation of the national wealth in 1984.

Table 12-8 National Wealth (Billions of Dollars)

	Current Dollars	1972 Constant Dollars
1950	$ 723	$ 723
1960	1,287	1,816
1970	2,539	2,715
1980	7,753	3,705
1984	9,626	4,071

Source: U.S. Bureau of the Census, *Statistical Abstract of the United States: 1986* (Washington, DC: U.S. Government Printing Office, 1985).

Table 12-9   Net Stock of Fixed Reproducible Tangible Wealth in the
United States, 1984 (Billions of Dollars)

Business		$6,258
Equipment	$1,529	
Nonresidential structures	1,708	
Residential structures	3,021	
Government		2,133
Military equipment	346	
Other equipment	132	
Nonresidential structures	1,583	
Residential	72	
Households, consumer durables		1,235
Net Stock of Wealth		$9,626

Source: *Statistical Abstract of the United States*, 1986.

INPUT-OUTPUT ANALYSIS

For years economists and forecasters have relied on gross national product and related data to interpret changes and developments in our economy. Through the GNP it is easy to trace the allocation of total production to the major sectors of the economy—consumer, domestic investment, net exports, and government. Through the related national income and personal income, one can see how much income was distributed in the form of wages, rent, interest, and profit.

In 1964 the Department of Commerce published the **input-output tables**, which provided a more detailed breakdown and permitted a closer analysis of production in our complex economy. The input-output analysis was not new, having been originated by Professor Wassily Leontief a few decades before. Previously the necessary data for this type of analysis had been rather scarce. The Department of Commerce study, however, provided a major breakthrough in the utilization of this powerful tool of economic analysis. In 1979 the input-output tables were expanded and updated through 1972.[1] Unfortunately they have not been updated since then.

The input-output studies divide the total economy into 85 basic industries and about 300 subgroups. Through the construction of a matrix, the tables show the various inputs used by each industry in producing its final product. One table shows how the output of each industry is dis-

1. *Survey of Current Business* (February, 1979).

tributed to other industries or to final users. Consequently, one can trace the flow of output from one industry as it becomes input to another and finally ends up as consumer or producer goods.

Table 12-10 shows, for example, that for every dollar of output in 1972, the automobile industry used 7.4 cents' worth of steel and 2.8 cents of rubber and plastic products. It spent about 1 cent for glass, 7.5 cents for screw machine products, and so forth. Included in the $1 value of its auto product was a value-added item of 32.9 cents, which included compensation of employees, corporate profits, and indirect business taxes. These values are circled in the table.

This means that for every $1 billion in auto sales, the industry used $74 million in steel products. Further analysis shows us that to produce the $74 million worth of steel, the steel industry in turn spent $1.5 million for coal (0.0208 × $1.00 × 74 million = $1.5 million); $3.5 million for iron ore; $2.5 million for electricity, gas, and water; and about $1.4 million for chemicals. It paid $30 million for value added. Thus, it is possible to determine the likely impact on 85 different industries that would result from a $1 or $2 billion increase in the demand for automobiles. Conversely, the adverse effect on other industries from an automobile strike or shutdown could be estimated in advance. This permits sectoral analysis that is sometimes called **mesoeconomics**.[2]

Table 12-11 shows how much of an industry's product goes to each of the other basic industries. For example, 13.7 percent of the steel industry's output was sold to the auto industry for its input. Nearly 7 percent of total steel output became input for new construction, and 10.2 percent was used for heating, plumbing, and structural products. About 2.0 percent of steel production was used in the manufacture of farm equipment, and 4.7 percent was used by the metal container industry, as shown by the circled items in the table. From a table like this, a firm in the steel industry may be able to determine whether or not it is keeping up with its industry in the sale of products to various other industries.

Input-output data can become very complex when one is trying to analyze the flow of inputs and outputs among 85 industries in the economy. Anytime the input-output relationship of one industry to another changes, the matrix, or set of tables, has to be modified. Although the Department of Commerce studies have updated the input-output tables to 1972 only, it plans further revision. This tool of analysis will permit better interpretation of the total effect of output changes at the industry and national levels. Furthermore, input-output data are compatible with the national income accounts, so that the two can be used interchangeably in analysis.

Moreover, some developing nations have constructed input-output ta-

---

2. Dr. Lee E. Preston of the University of Maryland feels that it is important that economists and other researchers study our economy as a set of dynamically interrelated sectors and industries. Input-output analysis would be the basis of this research.

Table 12-10 Interindustry Structure of the United States Input-Output Direct Requirements Per Dollar of Gross Output, 1972

For the composition of inputs to an industry, read the column for that industry.

Commodity Number / Industry Number	29 Drugs, Cleaning and Toilet Preparations	30 Paints and Allied Products	31 Petroleum Refining and Related Industries	32 Rubber and Miscellaneous Plastics Products	33 Leather Tanning and Finishing	34 Footwear and Other Leather Products	35 Glass and Glass Products	36 Stone and Clay Products	37 Primary Iron and Steel Manufacturing	38 Primary Nonferrous Metals Manufacturing	39 Metal Containers	58 Misc. Electrical Machinery and Supplies	59 Motor Vehicles and Equipment	61 Other Transportation Equipment	76 Amusements	77 Medical, Educ. Services and Nonprofit Org.	78 Federal Government Enterprises
5 Iron and ferroalloy ores mining		.00044						.00111	.04720	.00038		.00058					
6 Nonferrous metal ores mining		.00197		.00002				.00187	.00074	.07815		.00051					
7 Coal mining	.00019	.00003	.00113	.00048	0.00066	.00004	.00027	.00607	.02080	.00044	.00002	.00023	.00043	.00010		.00024	.01448
26 Printing and publishing	.00419	.00861	.00010	.00061	.00019	.00060	.00170	.00042	.00092	.00038	.04595	.00158	.00033	.00054	.00413	.01040	.00477
27 Chemicals and selected chemical products	.06492	.20697	.02633	.04476	.06580	.00841	.02513	.02548	.01858	.01412	.00244	.02046	.00177	.00078	.00158	.00417	.00064
28 Plastics and synthetic materials	.00084	.09532	.00003	.13939		.00051		.00430		.00745	.00129	.00955	.00088	.00305			
29 Drugs, cleaning and toilet preparations	.05438	.00216	.00033	.00021	.03558	.00174		.00052	.00004		.00107		.00002	.00019	.00027	.01599	.00319
30 Paints and allied products	.00120	.01019	.00009	.00115		.00071	.00226	.00194	.00046	.00136	.01879	.00033	.00297	.00715	.00217	.00013	.00003
31 Petroleum refining and related industries	.00582	.01454	.07416	.00299	.00461	.00216	.00365	.00962	.00473	.00465	.00168	.00196	.00163	.00335	.00217	.00505	.00433
32 Rubber and miscellaneous plastics products	.04488	.00247	.00171	.04310	.00009	.06789	.04161	.00568	.00109	.00726	.00107	.03201	.02826	.01476	.00076	.00610	.00212
33 Leather tanning and finishing				.00005	.08491	.17330		.00005									.00001
34 Footwear and other leather products	.00007	.00006	.00003	.00005		.02404		.00003	.00005	.00001		.00030	.00002	.00002	.00271	.00010	.00020
35 Glass and glass products	.01618	.00094	.00008	.00429	.00009	.00026	.08262	.00068	.00011	.00042	.00002	.00375	.01104	.00506	.00006	.00112	.00019
36 Stone and clay products	.00068	.00526	.00287	.00214	.00339		.01469	.11026	.00688	.00258	.00113	.02831	.00376	.00592	.00002	.00016	.00007
37 Primary iron and steel manufacturing	.00003	.00158	.00041	.00728	.00019	.00073	.00240	.00610	.19298	.00770	.34150	.12113	.07423	.08488		.00010	.00007
38 Primary nonferrous metals manufacturing	.00039	.01086	.00148	.00092		.00386	.00163	.00225	.02150	.40345	.08772	.02141	.01149	.03123		.00063	.00019
42 Other fabricated metal products	.00566	.00357	.00161	.01002	.00951	.01197	.00054	.01144	.01158	.00733	.01123	.00913	.02865	.01949	.00011	.02036	.02045
68 Electric, gas, water, and sanitary services	.00643	.00654	.02030	.01536	.05168	.00484	.04001	.03278	.03334	.02578	.00957	.02721	.00481	.00514	.01157	.01376	.00333
69 Wholesale and retail trade	.02899	.03393	.00947	.02673	.00480	.03749	.03285	.02524	.03793	.03969	.03201	.01170	.05167	.04984	.01459	.01226	.01214
70 Finance and insurance	.00655	.00551	.00644	.00639	.00141	.00665	.00716	.00884	.00587	.00641	.00659	.00277	.00353	.00597	.01542	.01214	
81 Scrap, used, and secondhand goods	.00089	.00047	.00001	.00098		.00018	.00559	.00104	.02078	.04756	.00014		.00178	.00080			
VA Value added	.40076	.34894	.24003	.47808	.26518	.42661	.53401	.47861	.40682	.24817	.30815	.47734	.32870	.36756	.52366	.67756	.74953
EC Compensation of employees	.20275	.25010	.10258	.30219	.23778	.36754	.36965	.31811	.31473	.18395	.21890	.35437	.19126	.32688	.38905	.51489	.78453
IBT Indirect business taxes	.00615	.00709	.13025	.04171	.00207	.00121	.00976	.01174	.01647	.00679	.02039	.00228	.01140	.00142	.08477	.00430	
PTI Property-type income	.19186	.09174	.00720	.13418	.02533	.05785	.15460	.14876	.07562	.05743	.06887	.12069	.12703	.03926	.08984	.15837	-.03500
T Total	1.00000	1.00000	1.00000	1.00000	1.00000	1.00000	1.00000	1.00000	1.00000	1.00000	1.00000	1.00000	1.00000	1.00000	1.00000	1.00000	1.00000

Source: *Survey of Current Business* (February, 1979).

Table 12-11 The Use of Commodities by Industries, 1972 (Percent Distribution, Based on Producers' Prices)

For the distribution of output of a commodity, read the row for that commodity.

Commodity Number	Industry Number / Name	11 New Construction	36 Stone and Clay Products	37 Primary Iron and Steel Manufacturing	38 Primary Nonferrous Metals Manufacturing	39 Metal Containers	40 Heating, Plumbing, and Structural Metal Products	41 Screw Machine Products and Stampings	42 Other Fabricated Metal Products	43 Engines and Turbines	44 Farm and Garden Machinery	45 Construction and Mining Machinery	58 Misc. Electrical Machinery and Supplies	59 Motor Vehicles and Equipment	60 Aircraft and Parts	61 Other Transportation Equipment	62 Scientific and Controlling Instruments	Total Commodity Output
5	Iron and ferroalloy ores mining		1.3	133.7	.7								0.2					100.0
6	Nonferrous metal ores mining		1.3	1.2	84.9		.8	.1	(*)	(*)	(*)	(*)	.1	.5	(*)		(*)	100.0
7	Coal mining		1.7	14.0	.2	(*)	.2	.1	.1	(*)			(*)				(*)	100.0
9	Stone and clay mining and quarrying	35.4	32.2	3.5	.1		(*)											100.0
10	Chemical and fertilizer mineral mining		5.4	6.4	(*)													100.0
26	Printing and publishing	.1	(*)	.2	.1		(*)	(*)	(*)	(*)	(*)	(*)	(*)	.1	.2	.1	.1	100.0
27	Chemicals and selected chemical products	1.3	1.5	2.6	1.3	1.3	.1	.2	.8	(*)	(*)	(*)	.3	.4	(*)		(*)	100.0
30	Paints and allied products	15.8	.8		.9	2.6	3.9	.6	3.1	.1	.4	.4	(*)	5.4	.7	2.6	.2	100.0
31	Petroleum refining and related industries	6.5	.5	.6	.4	(*)	.2	.1	.2	.1	(*)	.1	.7	.3	.2	.1	.1	100.0
32	Rubber and miscellaneous plastics products	5.5	.4	.2	.8	(*)	.4	.4	1.7	(*)	.9	.7	.7	8.8	.2	.9	.7	100.0
35	Glass and glass products	2.9	.2	.1	.2	(*)	2.2	.2	.3	.3	(*)	(*)	.1	12.8	(*)	1.1	.7	100.0
36	Stone and clay products	60.6	10.9	1.6	.4	(*)	.3	.2	.5		.1	.4	.3	1.6	.1	.5	.1	100.0
37	Primary iron and steel manufacturing	7.0	.3	20.0	.5	4.7	10.2	8.2	5.4	2.0	2.0	3.2	.3	13.7	1.2	3.1	.4	100.0
38	Primary nonferrous metals manufacturing	10.8	.1	3.4	41.4	1.8	4.9	2.2	3.9	1.1	.2	.2	2.2	4.0	2.5	1.7	1.2	100.0
39	Metal containers		(*)	.3				.4	.1								.2	100.0
40	Heating, plumbing, and structural metal products	70.0	(*)				1.4			.7		.3	.3	.1		3.1	.1	100.0
41	Screw machine products and stampings	.5	(*)	2.1	.4	(*)	3.0	3.0	2.2	1.0	1.2	.8	.3	43.3	1.2	.8	1.4	100.0
42	Other fabricated metal products	19.7	1.1	2.7	1.1	.3	3.4	1.0	3.4	.4	.4	.5	.6	11.7	1.3	1.6	.9	100.0
43	Engines and turbines		.1	.1		.1	(*)	.1	.4	10.8	6.0	4.4		9.2	.2	5.8		100.0
44	Farm and garden machinery							.1	(*)	.1	4.4			.1		.1		100.0
VA	Value added	4.6	.6	1.3	.5	.1	.5	.4	.6	.2	.2	.3	.2	1.8	.7	.4	.3	100.0

Source: *Survey of Current Business* (February, 1979). (*) Less than 0.00005

bles to learn more about their economies. Likewise, several U.S. firms have developed input-output analysis for their own companies.

SUMMARY

The actual production and income of our economy are measured in dollars. The basic concept in this measurement is the gross national product, the current market value of the total goods and services produced in the nation's economy over a given period of time. The net national product is GNP minus capital consumption allowances. The national income is the aggregate income arising from the current production of goods and services. Personal income is the total income received by persons from all sources. The total personal income remaining after the payment of personal taxes is known as disposable personal income. (See Figure 12.3)

The GNP is distributed to four major sectors in our economy: consumers, private investors, net exports, and the government. These sectors must make payments for the goods and the services received. Such payments to the producers become the source of wages, rent, interest, and profits to the factors of production. In this way, the GNP affects incomes.

The GNP is frequently used as a measure of economic progress. When it is used for such a purpose, however, certain reservations must be kept in mind. For example, the GNP should be valued in constant dollars to obtain a true picture of the changes in the real output of goods and services. Population changes should be taken into account by using the per capita disposable personal income for comparison. Other minor qualifications, such as the exclusion of nonmonetary transactions, the type of goods produced, the exaggerating effect of durable goods, the social cost of production, and the lack of a value for leisure, should also be considered.

National wealth is another important economic concept because it is a basis of our productive capacity. Current estimates place our wealth at more than $9.6 trillion. Input-output tables permit analyses of the flow of production from one industry to another and eventually to the final user.

NEW TERMS AND CONCEPTS

Gross national product
  (GNP)
Capital consumption
  allowance
Net national product (NNP)
National income (NI)
Personal income (PI)
Transfer payment

Disposable personal income
  (DPI)
Discretionary income
GNP implicit price deflators
Real GNP
Real per capita disposable
  income

Underground, or
  subterranean, economy
Flow-of-funds system of
  national accounts
Input-output tables
Mesoeconomics

Figure 12-3 Relation of Gross National Product, National Income, and Personal Income: 1986

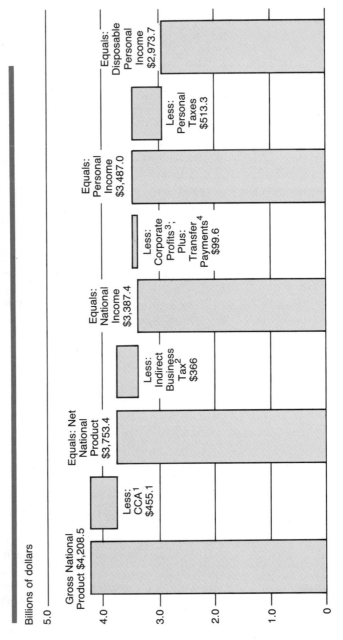

Billions of dollars

[1]Capital consumption allowances. [2]Less: Current surplus of government enterprises plus subsidies. [3]Also-Less net interest and contributions for social insurance. [4]Also-Plus personal interest and personal dividend income.

Source: Chart prepared by U.S. Bureau of the Census.

DISCUSSION QUESTIONS

1. Explain how the gross national product gives rise to our total personal income.
2. Does the share of the national income that is in the form of corporate profit seem excessive? Why or why not?
3. Has the government's share of the GNP been increasing or decreasing in the past 10 to 15 years?
4. Why is it important to reduce the GNP and national income to constant dollar values when using them as measures of economic progress?
5. Should the performance of household chores and other nonmonetary services be included in the gross national product? Why?
6. Do you think we should include in the GNP an adjustment for the social (external) costs of production? Why or why not?
7. How can the input-output tables be used to measure the impact on the economy of a strike in a major industry, such as the steel or auto industry?
8. Is it true that as we produce more and more goods and services we deplete our wealth? Why or why not?

SUGGESTED READINGS

Carlson, Keith M. "Recent Revisions of GNP Data." *Review*. Federal Reserve Bank of St. Louis (January, 1986).

Economic Report of the President. Washington, DC: U.S. Government Printing Office, 1987.

"Input-Output Structure of the U.S. Economy: 1967." *Survey of Current Business* (February, 1974).

Leontief, Wassily. "Why Economics Needs Input-Output Analysis." *Challenge* (March–April, 1985).

Mattera, Philip. *Off the Books: The Rise of the Underground Economy*. New York: St. Martin's Press, 1985.

Meadows, Edward. "Tracking the Ever-Elusive Gross National Product." *Fortune* (May, 1978).

Mohn, N. Carroll, William A. Schaffer, and Lester C. Sartorius. "Input-Output Modeling: New Sales Forecasting Tool." *Business Review* (July, 1976).

"New Application of Input-Output." *Business Economics* (January, 1971).

Okun, Arthur M. "Should GNP Measure Social Welfare?" *Brookings Bulletin* (Summer, 1972).

13
PERSONAL INCOME DISTRIBUTION

■

The fact that we have the highest total income and one of the highest per capita incomes in the world does not mean that the United States is the land of milk and honey for all its citizens. Some individuals have sufficient income to provide for a high standard of living, while others live on limited incomes. In fact, a surprising number have no more than a subsistence level of living.

When we state that the per capita disposable personal income for the United States for 1986 was approximately $13,312, we should remember that this figure is obtained by taking the total disposable personal income for the nation and dividing it by the total population. This does not mean that every person in the economy received an income of $13,312 per year. Many received less, and others received more than the average figure.

INDIVIDUAL, FAMILY, AND HOUSEHOLD INCOME

The U.S. Department of Commerce collects and records distribution of income figures based upon two categories. A **family** refers to a group of two or more persons living in the same dwelling who are related by birth, marriage, or adoption. A **household** includes all persons, related or unrelated, who occupy a housing unit. A person living alone is counted as a household. The U.S. median household income (that amount below which one-half of the households are receiving) in 1984 was $22,415 per year.

Table 13-1 reveals some interesting facts. For example, 7.9 percent of the households received less than $5,000 per year, and 21.1 percent received less than $10,000 per year. These amounts cannot be considered even a subsistence income today. However, over 50 percent of households were earning more than $20,000 and 28.1 percent over $35,000 per year. Many of those in the higher income brackets were there as a result of having two or more members of the household at work. In 1984, for example, in 45 percent of families both the husband and wife were working. In these families, the wife's earnings provided 30 percent of the family

Table 13-1   Income Distribution of Households, 1984

Money Income before Taxes	% of Total Households	Money Income before Taxes	Cumulative % of Total Households
Under $5,000	7.9%	Over $ 0	100.0%
$ 5,000–9,999	13.2	Over 4,999	92.8
10,000–14,999	12.2	Over 9,999	79.0
15,000–19,999	11.4	Over 14,999	66.8
20,000–24,999	10.4	Over 19,999	55.4
25,000–34,999	16.9	Over 24,999	65.0
35,000–49,000	15.3	Over 34,999	28.1
50,000 and over	12.8	Over 49,999	12.8

Source: *Statistical Abstract of the United States*, 1986.

income. A household in the $35,000-and-over bracket can consider itself among the well off today.

Families in the lowest income brackets receive a relatively small percentage of total income, as Table 13-2 shows. In 1984 those in the highest-fifth income group received 42.9 percent of total income, while those in the lowest-fifth income category received less than 5 percent of the total income.

This distribution is not necessarily unjust, however. So long as there exist differences in skills, abilities, and ambitions among income earners, incomes will differ. Naturally when the lowest income recipients are grouped into one category and the highest income recipients are placed in another category, the lowest category of income recipients will receive a total income less than their proportion of the population and the highest

Table 13-2   Money Income of Families: Percent of Aggregate Income Received by Each Fifth

	1960	1984
Highest Fifth	41.3%	42.9%
2d-Highest Fifth	24.0	24.4
Middle Fifth	17.8	17.0
Next-to-Lowest Fifth	12.1	11.0
Lowest Fifth	4.8	4.7
	100.0%	100.0%

Source: *Statistical Abstract of the United States*, 1986.

income group will receive a share of income larger than their proportion of the population.

Although the actual percentage distribution of total income among income groups according to fifths has not changed much since 1960, income distribution by size of income and our level of living has improved noticeably because our total income and per capita income have increased. Rather than a pyramid shape with a few families at the apex and the majority of families at the bottom, relatively few families are at the upper and lower extremes and the bulk are in the middle income groups.

There are income differences among races and between sexes. In 1984, for example, the median income for white households was $23,647, while that for black households was $13,471. The percentage of black households in middle and higher income groups is less than the percentage of white households, but in recent years more black households have been moving into middle and upper income levels. The median income of households of Spanish origin was $16,992. The median income of full-time male workers in 1983, $22,508, was more than that of females, $14,479. But here too women have been making progress in securing better-paying jobs.

Differences of income are also based on educational attainment. The median income of a household headed by a college graduate in 1983 was $40,943, compared with $25,387 for a household headed by a high school graduate. As expected, there are also income differences according to the age of income recipients.

Unfortunately, not only are many families receiving very limited incomes, but a large number of them have very few, if any, financial assets. Liquid assets are an important supplement to current income, especially during periods of family emergency when additional spending power is needed. **Liquid assets** include United States savings bonds, savings accounts, and checking accounts, but exclude currency. For example, recent data show that about one-third of the families have liquid assets of less than $2,000. In fact, one out of every six families has no liquid assets.

Income by Geographic Area

Income diversity also exists among geographic areas in the United States. Some areas are known as conventionally high income areas, while others are known for their low incomes. These differences arise because of the locations of industries, differences in the cost of living, the accidental location of materials, the need for skilled labor in some areas, the presence or absence of labor unions, and numerous other factors. The highest personal income areas in the nation are New England, the Mideast, and the Far West. The highest income states are Alaska, Connecticut, New Jersey, and Massachusetts. The lowest personal income areas are in Arkansas and Mississippi. The average per capita personal income for all the states is shown in Table 13-3. Notice that in about two-thirds of the states the personal incomes are below the national per capita income of $13,451.

Table 13-3 Per Capita Personal Income by States and Regions, 1985

United States	**$13,451**	Southeast	$11,705
New England	15,387	Alabama	10,510
		Arkansas	10,180
Connecticut	17,627	Florida	13,397
Maine	11,423	Georgia	12,158
Massachusetts	15,790	Kentucky	10,585
New Hampshire	14,308	Louisiana	11,015
Rhode Island	13,592	Mississippi	9,035
Vermont	11,599	North Carolina	11,314
		South Carolina	10,514
Mideast	14,844	Tennessee	10,934
		Virginia	14,164
Delaware	14,337	West Virginia	10,112
District of Columbia	17,909		
Maryland	15,356	Southwest	12,782
New Jersey	16,368		
New York	15,237	Arizona	12,454
Pennsylvania	12,959	New Mexico	10,741
		Oklahoma	12,103
Great Lakes	13,337	Texas	13,165
Illinois	14,397	Rocky Mountain	12,377
Indiana	12,276		
Michigan	13,298	Colorado	14,413
Ohio	12,979	Idaho	10,605
Wisconsin	12,883	Montana	10,728
		Utah	10,166
Plains	13,296	Wyoming	12,955
Iowa	12,779	Far West	14,722
Kansas	14,046		
Minnesota	14,071	California	15,255
Missouri	12,784	Nevada	13,981
Nebraska	13,699	Oregon	12,165
North Dakota	13,034	Washington	13,267
South Dakota	11,207	Alaska	17,756
		Hawaii	13,542

Source: *Survey of Current Business* (April, 1986).

Changing Income Distribution

Is income diversity or inequality bad for the economy? The answer is yes and no, depending on the degree of inequality. If most families are without sufficient income to provide for the basic necessities of life, it is detrimental to the welfare of society as well as disruptive to the operation of an economic system. On the other hand, a certain amount of income inequality is beneficial for the economic system. First, income serves a functional purpose since it is the means by which we pay individuals for their productive efforts. One of the ways to recognize the differences in productivity is by the payment of a higher income to those who produce the most. If everyone received the same income regardless of productivity, much of the incentive in the economy would be destroyed. Would young people sacrifice to attend college or to learn a trade if they could not better their income? What would happen to risky business ventures which eventually enrich our standard of living if we were to remove the incentive of large profits as a reward for success?

Second, savings are essential to the development of capital formation, which is responsible for most of the increased productivity in our economy. The higher the income, the greater the ability to save. Thus, high incomes that permit savings are beneficial. If we had perfect equality in the distribution of income, it would result in a minimum of personal savings and would hamper to some extent the economic growth.

Equitable Distribution of Income.   An equal distribution of income does not imply a just or equitable distribution. It is true that we should have an equitable distribution of income; that is, income should be distributed according to some standard. Equity, however, means different things to different people, depending on their particular value judgment. For example, to some individuals the only equitable distribution would be an equal distribution of income. Others, however, would consider an equal distribution inequitable because the individuals who contribute the least to the economy would be rewarded as much as those who contribute the most.

The old saying that individuals should "contribute according to their ability and share according to needs" is advocated by some, especially those with little ability. This practice, too, would discourage incentive. Even though a policy of this type has been tried in some socialistic economies, it was soon recognized that differences in income were necessary to induce individuals into the more difficult and complex occupations in the economy.

In our capitalistic system we think of an equitable distribution as one in which income distribution is made according to the economic contribution of the individual. As a result, we are sure to have some diversity in the distribution of income. Our main task is not to eliminate income inequality. Rather, we should endeavor to keep the inequality from becoming too great. The best way to accomplish this is by raising the incomes of the lower income groups through higher productivity, rather than by taking income away from the higher income groups.

Changes in Income Distribution.   While it is true that we have inequality in the distribution of income, two important changes took place within the economy in the few decades before 1970. The median real income of households increased, and income inequality lessened to some extent. The median income, in constant dollar figures, nearly doubled between 1950 and 1970. The lessening of income inequality during that period did not come at the expense of higher income groups. Rather than decreasing the income of those in the higher income groups, the number of households in the lower income groups declined.

In more recent years, the median real income of households has stabilized. Between 1970 and 1984, money income of households, in current dollars, rose from $8,734 to $22,415, a 157 percent increase. But in terms of constant dollars, real income of households actually declined 4 percent. This decline was the result of prices rising faster than income during much of that time period.

Although gains in real income have been limited in recent years, there is still some shifting of households into higher constant dollar income brackets. For example, the percentage of households in the income brackets above $35,000 increased from 21.6 percent in 1970 to 28.1 percent in 1984. This movement is evident in Figure 13-1 and Table 13-4. The shift toward higher income levels includes black and other minority households.

Figure 13-1   Shifts of Households into Higher Income Groups since 1970 (Constant 1984 Dollars)

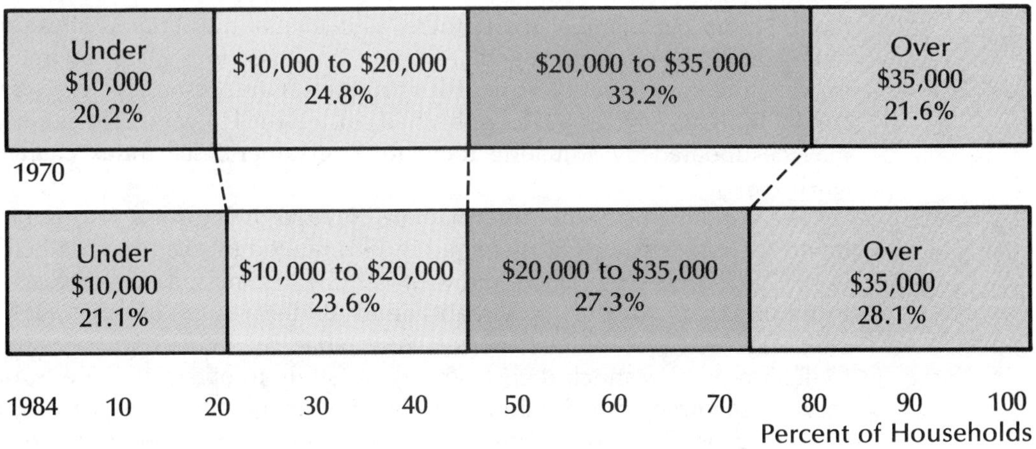

Source: Data from *Statistical Abstract of the United States*, 1986.

Table 13-4   Changes in Percentage Distribution of Household Income
(Constant 1984 Dollars)

Money Income before Taxes	Percent of Households	
	1970	1984
Under $5,000	8.8%	7.9%
$ 5,000–9,999	11.4	13.2
10,000–14,999	10.9	12.2
15,000–19,999	13.9	11.4
20,000–24,999	8.8	10.4
25,000–34,999	24.4	16.9
35,000–49,999	11.9	15.3
50,000 and over	9.7	12.8
Median Income	$23,363	$22,415

Source: *Statistical Abstract of the United States*, 1986.

URBAN FAMILY BUDGETS

Income is only one side of the economic picture for individuals and families. The other side is the cost of living. A high income means little if it is insufficient to provide the necessary goods and services to take care of a family. This brings up an interesting question: Just how much does it cost to provide the average family with the commodities required for a decent standard of living? Since costs vary in different parts of the country, since some families are larger than others, and since some families require more per member than others, estimates of the actual cost of providing family needs vary. A good estimate, however, is available by updating the Bureau of Labor Statistics (BLS) budgets. (Unfortunately, the Urban Family Budgets have not been published since 1981. However, the budgets may be updated by adjusting them for Consumer Price Index changes since 1981.)

The annual cost of an "intermediate" level of living for a four-person family residing in the U.S. mainland in 1986 ranged from a high of $35,838 in the New York City area to a low of $27,054 in Dallas, Texas, according to the BLS estimates of the Urban Family Budget. Honolulu was higher still, with a $37,403 budget figure. The *intermediate* budget was designed to determine how much it costs an urban family to obtain the goods and services required to maintain a "modest but adequate" level of living in various areas. The urban family is composed of a 38-year-old employed husband, a wife not employed outside the home, an 8-year-old girl, and a 13-year-old boy.

The average intermediate budget for the urban United States in 1985 was $30,328. A *lower* budget, at a less adequate level of living, as calculated by the BLS was $18,280, and a *higher* budget was $45,404. The budgets, however, do not show how an "average family" actually spends, or is supposed to spend, its income. The budgets merely give the total cost of a representative list of goods and services considered essential to provide food, clothing, housing, medical care, transportation, and some participation in social activities.

The budgets calculated by the BLS and updated to 1986 are shown in Table 13-5. Of the $30,328 average intermediate budget figure, about 72 percent is allocated to family consumption items. About 23 percent is spent for food, and 21.8 percent goes for housing. The total figure also includes clothing, personal taxes. Social Security, insurance, and occupational expenses.

When we compare the household income by income level and the urban family budget for recent years, it indicates that about 60 percent of the households have insufficient incomes to maintain even the "modest but adequate" BLS budget. Even if we subtract from this group single people, who are included as households in the income studies, a substantial portion of the total households in the United States have incomes inadequate to provide a moderate level of living. However, many of these households have less than four members as described in the BLS budget.

The recent census data show that over 27.5 million persons, or about 11.7 percent of the total population of the United States, are 65 years of age or older. Much interest has arisen in recent years regarding the cost of living for the retired couple. For this reason, the BLS computed a "retired couples budget" for the same cities for which it calculated the urban family budget. Generally the retired couples budget was about 40 to 50 percent of the urban family budget.

THE NATURE AND EXTENT OF POVERTY

Because of his concern about the number of families in our economy that were living on substandard incomes, President Kennedy directed his Council of Economic Advisers to undertake a study of poverty in the United States. Although he did not live to see its fruition, the study served as a basis for designing the war-on-poverty program instituted by the passage of the Economic Opportunity Act in August, 1964. The findings of the Council of Economic Advisers are contained in large part in the 1964 *Economic Report of the President*.

The Poverty Level

Realizing that the measurement of poverty is not simple, the *Report* defined "poor" as "those who are not now maintaining a decent standard

Table 13-5 Intermediate Urban Family Budget, 1986

	Total Budget [1]
Urban United States	**$30,328**
Nonmetropolitan areas [2]	27,723
Metropolitan areas	30,890
Atlanta, GA	28,000
Baltimore, MD	29,961
Boston, MA	34,850
Buffalo, NY	31,850
Chicago, IL–Northwestern IN	30,508
Cincinnati, OH–KY–IN	31,163
Cleveland, OH	31,574
Dallas, TX	27,054
Denver, CO	30,613
Detroit, MI	29,054
Honolulu, HI	37,403
Houston, TX	27,440
Kansas City, MO–KS	29,509
Los Angeles–Long Beach, CA	29,855
Milwaukee, WI	32,062
Minneapolis–St. Paul, MN	31,300
New York, NY–Northeastern NJ	35,838
Philadelphia, PA–NJ	31,696
Pittsburgh, PA	29,737
St. Louis, MO–IL	29,226
San Diego, CA	30,559
San Francisco–Oakland, CA	32,309
Seattle-Everett, WA	30,090
Washington, DC–MD–VA	33,183

1. Includes clothing and personal care, other family consumption, gifts and contributions, personal income taxes, basic life insurance, occupational expenses, and Social Security.
2. Places with population of 2,500–50,000 in 1960.

Source: U.S. Bureau of Labor Statistics. *Autumn Urban Family Budget and Comparative Indexes for Selected Urban Areas*, 1982. Updated to 1985.

of living," or those whose basic needs exceed their means to satisfy their needs. Since the needs of various families differ, and since there is no precise way of determining the number of families that have insufficient resources to meet their particular needs, the *Report* utilized what was thought to be a minimum acceptable standard of living for an American family. It considered a number of studies and established $3,000 (before taxes and expressed in 1962 prices) as the line of demarcation between poverty and nonpoverty.

This poverty-level income has been adjusted upward to account for price increases and changes in consumption patterns. Thus, the comparable poverty level income for 1984 was $10,609 annually for a four-person family. As a result of continuing price increases, the poverty level income rose to $11,500 by 1986.

Incidence of Poverty

The President's *Report* indicated that nearly one-fifth of our total 186.6 million population in 1962 was poverty-stricken. The *Report* also indicated a heavy concentration of poverty among nonwhites, the poorly educated, the elderly, rural dwellers, Southerners, and families headed by women. This is still the case today. Because of the seriousness of the poverty situation, Congress passed the Economic Opportunity Act in August, 1964. This Act provided funds to launch the war on poverty. Before the Office of Economic Opportunity (OEO), which was established under the auspices of the Economic Opportunity Act, was dismantled in the early 1970s, several billion dollars were spent on various programs designed to reduce or eliminate poverty.

Progress against Poverty

Since 1962, considerable progress has been shown in our fight against poverty. The progress has resulted not only from specific measures designed to reduce poverty, but, in large part, from the overall expansion of the economy in the past 25 years. Data for 1984 indicated that 11.6 percent of all families were considered below the poverty level, as compared with 22 percent in 1962. Furthermore, the number of persons considered to be living in poverty was reduced from more than 39 million to 34 million during that period, despite the fact that the U.S. population increased by 50 million in the interim. When income is adjusted for receipts of cash transfers (such as Social Security payments, unemployment compensation, and welfare) and in-kind transfers (such as food stamps, rent subsidies, and Medicare), the incidence of poverty is reduced by nearly 30 percent.

In 1984 the incidence of poverty among nonwhite families was 31 percent, compared with 9 percent among white families. The incidence of poverty among families headed by females was more than three times greater than that among families headed by males. Moreover, the occurrence of poverty was higher in the south than in other regions of the country.

The incidence of poverty in the short run is affected by business cycles, especially recessions. Between 1979 and 1983, which included the recessions of 1980 and 1982, the number of persons in poverty increased by 8.3 million and the percent of families in poverty rose from 9.2 to 12.2 percent. The incidence of poverty diminished, however, with the economic expansion of 1983–1986.

PERSONAL INCOME IN OTHER NATIONS

Data on personal income and poverty reveal that the process of economizing (mentioned in Chapter 2) is a real problem with many families. Economizing occurs not so much because our incomes are low in absolute terms, but because they are low relative to our desired standard of living. What we bemoan as a low level of income in the United States is actually high compared with many other parts of the world. Comparative income figures for the United States and other countries can be estimated from the data shown in Table 13-6, since income is closely related to production.

For decades, U.S. per capita production and income exceeded that of all other nations in the world. In recent years, however, some nations including Switzerland, Sweden, and Norway have on occasion surpassed the United States. Among the other leading industrial nations, the U.S.

Table 13-6 Per Capita Gross National Product for Selected Countries, 1983 (1983 U.S. Dollars)

Switzerland	$15,633	United Kingdom	$7,999
United States	14,093	Soviet Union	6,815
Norway	12,930	New Zealand	6,813
Canada	12,662	Italy	6,149
Sweden	10,744	Spain	4,057
Denmark	10,684	Mexico	2,097
West Germany	10,672	Brazil	2,086
Australia	9,727	Argentina	1,915
Japan	9,697	People's Republic	
France	9,473	of China	395
Belgium	8,245		

Source: *Statistical Abstract of the United States,* 1986.

per capita output is still 11 percent above that of West Germany, 60 percent greater than that of Japan, 95 percent above that of Great Britain, and more than double that of the Soviet Union.

SUMMARY

Although the per capita income for the United States is among the highest in the world, we have an unequal distribution of income, and many households are receiving relatively low incomes. While the median household income in 1984 was $22,415, about one-quarter of households received incomes of less than $10,000 in that year. Forty-five percent of the households received less than $20,000. Families in the highest fifth in income rank received 43 percent of total national income, while those in the lowest fifth shared less than 5 percent of total income.

There are a number of reasons for this unequal distribution of income. There are income differences among races and between sexes. There are differences in income based on educational attainment and according to the age of the income recipients. In addition, those in the lower income brackets own very few financial assets. Income also varies according to the geographic areas within the nation. Personal income is highest in New England and lowest in the Southeast.

The intermediate-level urban family budget, which required about $30,328 a year in 1986, calls for more spending than the actual income of many families. As a result, most families must continuously economize. According to our government standards, 11.6 percent of our families are still classified as poor. Presently many programs costing several billion dollars are being conducted through numerous federal and state agencies in an effort to reduce or eliminate poverty in the United States.

The relative inequality in the distribution of our income has been decreasing over the past several decades. Fortunately, our problem is not so much one of choosing between basic necessities, but rather one of determining which of the numerous additional goods and services desired should be purchased. The average incomes in the United States are rather high compared with the rest of the world. In some recent years Switzerland, Sweden, and Norway have surpassed our level of per capita production and income. However, U.S. income and output per capita remain above most leading industrial nations including West Germany, Japan, Great Britain, and the Soviet Union.

NEW TERMS AND CONCEPTS

Family   Household   Liquid assets

DISCUSSION QUESTIONS

1. How might *equality* in the distribution of income not be *equitable*?
2. Does our current progressive income tax, which requires those in higher income brackets to pay a higher tax rate, tend to exaggerate or modify the unequal distribution of income in the economy? Explain your opinion.

3. It is possible to raise the income level of all families and individuals in the economy without substantially changing the distribution of total income. Explain.

4. Do you think that the incidence of poverty in the United States will ever drop below 5 percent? Why or why not?

5. Do you see any relationship between geographic distribution of income and migration of people within the United States?

6. In your opinion, is the urban family budget too meager?

7. It has frequently been proposed by various government agencies and other groups that the federal government, through some type of payment, should guarantee each U.S. family an annual income of at least $10,000. Do you agree or disagree? Why?

8. What causes the great disparity of income among various nations throughout the world?

SUGGESTED READINGS

"Annual Cost of City Workers Family Budget." *Monthly Labor Review* (April, 1983).

Brimmer, A. F. "Income Equity: The Growing Gap between the Rich and the Poor." *Black Enterprise* (August, 1982).

Buchele, R., and M. Aldrich. "How Much Difference Would Comparable Worth Make?" *Industrial Relations* (Spring, 1985).

Corcoran, Mary, and Greg Duncan. "New Evidence on Earnings Differences between the Races and Sexes." *Economic Outlook U.S.A.* (Spring, 1978).

Danziger, S., and P. Gottschalk. "The Poverty of Losing Ground." *Challenge* (May/June, 1985).

Garnick, Daniel H., and Harold L. Friedenberg. "Accounting for Regional Differences in Per Capita Personal Income Growth, 1929–1979." *Survey of Current Businesss* (September, 1982).

Hailstones, Thomas J., and Frank V. Mastrianna. *Contemporary Economic Problems and Issues,* 8th ed. Cincinnati: South-Western Publishing Co., 1988. Chapter 4.

Hauver, J. A., et al. "Federal Poverty Thresholds: Appearance and Reality." *Journal of Consumer Research* (June, 1981).

Sorrentino, Constance. "Youth Unemployment: An International Perspective." *Monthly Labor Review* (July, 1981).

14

DETERMINANTS OF GNP AND ECONOMIC GROWTH

∎

In Chapter 12 we saw that the GNP is allocated to four major sectors of the economy—consumer sector, private investment, net exports, and the government. These sectors, in turn, must pay accordingly for the goods and services they receive. These payments are distributed eventually to the owners of the factors of production who contributed the goods and services to produce the GNP. Thus, in exchange for the physical goods and services received by the four sectors, there arise monetary payments to the factors of production. As we learned in Chapter 1, each factor—land, labor, capital, and entrepreneurship—contributes toward the total product; and their owners are paid in the form of rent, wages, interest, and profits, respectively. In national income accounting, the total product is represented by the GNP, and the payments to the factors of production are in the form of wages and salaries, rental income, net interest, proprietor's income, and corporate profits. It is reasonable to assume that the total demand by the four sectors determines the size of the GNP, and that the size of the GNP determines our earned income.

Table 14-1 shows the GNP and the payments to the factors of production for 1986. According to the table, the total demand by consumers, investors, exporters, and the government led to a GNP of $4,208.0 billion. When these sectors demand goods and services, they must make payment for them. This sets up a circular flow of economic activity—with the flow of goods and services to the four sectors according to their economic contribution. The greater the demand by consumers, private investors, exporters, and the government, the greater the income distribution to the factors of production. The less the demand, the smaller the income payments. It is primarily the demand by these four sectors that determines the total production, employment, and income in our economy.

MULTIPLIER AND ACCELERATOR

If each of the sectors demanded the same quantity of goods and services in a current year as they did in the previous year, the same GNP and the same income would result for the current year. If any of the four

Table 14-1 National Product and Income Account, 1986
(Billions of Dollars)

Product Flow		Income Flow	
GNP	$4,208.5	GNP	$4,208.5
Consumer purchases	$2,762.4	Capital consumption	
Private investment	686.5	allowances, indirect	
Net exports	−105.7	business taxes, etc.	$ 821.1
Government		National income	$3,387.4
purchases	865.3		
		Compensation to	
		employees	2,498.3
		Proprietor's income	278.9
		Rental income	15.6
		Net interest	294.9
		Corporate profit	299.7

Source: *Economic Report of the President*, 1987.

sectors changed its demand, however, there might be a change in the level of economic activity and a change in the level of income. For example, if an increase of $20 billion occurred in private investment while a decrease of $20 billion in consumption took place, there would be no substantial change in total income. If investment increased by $20 billion, however, and consumption, net exports, and government remained the same, the net increase in spending would accelerate the level of economic activity. To be effective, a net change would have to take place.

The Multiplier Effect

What would be the result of a net increase of $20 billion in private investment? Would it increase income by $20 billion? Actually it would increase the GNP and our total income not just by $20 billion, but by some larger amount. This comes about because of the **multiplier effect**. "Multiplier" is a sophisticated name for a very basic idea. We all know that when one person spends money, it becomes income to the recipient. The recipient in turn may spend the money, and it becomes income to a third party, and so on. The total income resulting from the continual respending of a given amount of money will be larger than the actual amount of the money initially spent.

For example, suppose that $20 billion is spent by private investors; this may result in an increase of $20 billion, $40 billion, $60 billion, and so on, as it is respent. The only limiting factor to the creation of income resulting from the respending of the original $20 billion will be a failure of someone along the line to respend the money that is received. This would be the case if a person were to save a portion of the money, to spend it abroad, or to put it into a bank or an insurance policy where it was not all reinvested by the financial institution. In other words, any time that we withdraw money from the circular flow, it will not be available to respend and create more income.

Relationship to Consumption and Savings.   Savings of money constitutes the biggest leakage factor from the income stream. Thus, the multiplier will depend on the relationship of savings to income, or of consumption to income. For example, let's assume that people spend four-fifths of their income and save one-fifth. The multiplier will be 5, which means that a net increase in investment of $20 billion would increase gross income by $100 billion. This effect is demonstrated in Table 14-2.

According to this table, an increase in investment of $20 billion, when originally spent, will become income of $20 billion to A. If A saves one-fifth, or $4 billion, and spends the rest, the $16 billion respent by A becomes income to B. When B in turn spends four-fifths of the $16 billion income, it will create $12.8 billion income for C. This process of receiving income and respending, which creates incomes for others, will continue until the original amount of money is all held in savings by the various individuals. At that time, no more income will be generated.

Through this process the original investment of $20 billion brings about an increase of $100 billion in gross income.[1] Thus, the multiplier has a value of 5. The **multiplier** is simply the relationship between a change in effective demand (investment or consumption or government spending)

Table 14-2 Multiplier Effect (Billions of Dollars)

Net Increase in Investment		Increased Income	Increased Spending (Spend 0.80)	Increased Savings (Save 0.20)
$20	A	$ 20.0	$16.0	$ 4.0
	B	16.0	12.8	3.2
	C	12.8	10.2	2.6
Multiplier	D	10.2	8.2	2.0
effect	E	8.2	6.6	1.6
	F	6.6	5.2	1.4
	G	5.2	4.2	1.0
		Etc.	Etc.	Etc.
		$100.0	$80.0	$20.0

---

1. The increase in net income, of course, will be something less than this amount.

and the resulting change in income. The change in income is the result of respending, so the level of consumption has a direct influence on the size of the multiplier.

Higher Consumption.   The more people respend, or the less they save, the greater will be the multiplier effect. For example, if individuals and businesses were inclined to save only one-tenth of everything they received in income, the multiplier would be equal to 10. An increase of $20 billion in investment would bring about a $200 billion increase in income because the money would turn over more frequently before it was all saved.

Compare Table 14-3 with Table 14-2. In this case A, the recipient of the original investment spending, saves one-tenth, or $2.0 billion, of the income of $20 billion, and respends $18 billion. Thus, the amount of income created by the respending is greater than it was in the previous example, in which only $16 billion was respent. The total effect of this stronger inclination to respend, or **propensity to consume**, will be a greater increase in income. The total income of the economy, in this case, increased by $200 billion, out of which income recipients spent $180 billion and saved $20 billion.

Table 14-3   Multiplier Effect (Billions of Dollars)

Net Increase in Investment		Increased Income	Increased Spending (Spend 0.90)	Increased Savings (Save 0.10)
$20	A	$ 20.0	$ 18.0	$ 2.0
	B	18.0	16.2	1.8
	C	16.2	14.6	1.6
Multiplier	D	14.6	13.2	1.4
effect	E	13.2	11.8	1.4
	F	11.8	10.6	1.2
	G	10.6	9.6	1.0
		Etc.	Etc.	Etc.
		$200.0	$180.0	$20.0

Lower Consumption.   The lower the propensity to consume, the less the multiplier. If the income recipients were to save one-half of everything they received, this would result in a multiplier of only 2. In Table 14-4, observe that a $20 billion increase in investment will increase incomes by only $40 billion, of which people will spend one-half and save the other half.

Table 14-4 Multiplier Effect (Billions of Dollars)

Net Increase in Investment		Increased Income	Increased Spending (Spend 0.50)	Increased Savings (Save 0.50)
$20	A	$20.0	$10.0	$10.0
	B	10.0	5.0	5.0
	C	5.0	2.5	2.5
Multiplier	D	2.5	1.3	1.2
effect	E	1.3	0.7	0.6
	F	0.7	0.4	0.3
		Etc.	Etc.	Etc.
		$40.0	$20.0	$20.0

Calculation of Multiplier.   As we study the tables, it becomes evident that the multiplier depends on the spending and saving habits of the individuals and businesses in the economy. In fact, the size of the multiplier depends directly upon the propensity to consume, that is, the relationship between income and consumption. To calculate the multiplier, the average propensity to consume or the marginal propensity to consume may be used. The **average propensity to consume (APC)** is the percentage of total income spent on consumption out of any given level of income.[2] Although the multiplier can be based on the average propensity to consume, it is more accurate to base it on the marginal propensity to consume. The **marginal propensity to consume (MPC)** is simply the part of the last increment of income received by individuals and businesses that will be spent on consumption. Since the spending and saving habits of individuals and businesses change as incomes change, we can better tell what income recipients will do with their next increment of income by observing what they did with their previous increment.

The *MPC* will decrease as income increases. When people have low incomes, they must spend practically everything. Thus, ability to save is limited. While it is true that people spend more money on necessities, conveniences, and luxuries as their incomes increase, total spending is usually a smaller percentage of the new higher total income. As their incomes increase, the amount and the percentage of saving by individuals will increase since their ability to save increases. For example, let's study the case of a recent college graduate. Let us assume that she has a salary of $2,000 per month, of which she spends $1,800 and saves $200 (10 percent

---

2. Using the average propensity to consume, we can find the multiplier with the formula: $k = 1/(1 - APC)$.

of income). When her salary increases to $2,200, she may spend $1870 and save $330 (15 percent of income). The graduate is spending more money and is also saving more; but the percentage of total income that is now being spent on consumption has declined while the percentage of saving has increased.

Some individuals may continue to consume at a pace equivalent to their increase in income. In fact, there are always some who spend more than they earn no matter what their income. The general tendency in any economy, however, is for the marginal propensity to consume to decrease as real income increases, provided other things remain unchanged. We can now state our formula for the multiplier in terms of the marginal propensity to consume as follows:

$$k = \frac{1}{1 - \dfrac{\Delta C}{\Delta Y}} = \frac{1}{1 - MPC} = \frac{1}{MPS}$$

In this formula:

k is the multiplier

ΔC is the change in consumption

ΔY is the change in income

1 represents the total increase in income

When the marginal propensity to consume, $\dfrac{\Delta C}{\Delta Y}$, is subtracted from 1, the total increase in income, we get the marginal propensity to save (MPS). Dividing the MPS, $1 - (\Delta C/\Delta Y)$, into 1 gives us the multiplier. Thus, a rule of thumb for figuring the multiplier is simply to say that the multiplier is equal to the reciprocal of the MPS.

In order to calculate the MPC (or MPS), we must observe two time periods and compare the change in income with the change in consumption between the two periods. Since we either spend (consume) or save our income, we can say at any time that income equals consumption plus saving. Thus, let us use the following data to work out the multiplier.

$$Y \quad = \quad C \quad + \quad S$$

Period I $\$6,000 = \$4,800 + \$1,200$

Period II $7,200 = \ \ 5,700 + \ \ 1,500$

In Period I, we spent $4,800 of the $6,000 and saved $1,200. In Period II, with incomes increased to $7,200, we spent $5,700 and saved $1,500. The MPC will equal three-fourths, since income was $1,200 higher in Period II, out of which we spent $900 and saved $300. This is calculated as follows:

$$\frac{\Delta C}{\Delta Y} = \frac{\$900}{\$1,200} = 0.75$$

Now if we put these figures into our formula, we find:

$$k = \frac{1}{1 - MPC} = \frac{1}{1 - 0.75} = \frac{1}{0.25} = 4$$

The size of the multiplier based on the *MPC* is 4, or we can say that it is the reciprocal of the *MPS*. Using the *MPC* gives us a good indication of what individuals and businesses will do with the next increment of income they receive. Table 14-5 gives the value of the multiplier at various sizes of the marginal propensity to consume and save. It can be seen that the multiplier is related directly to the *MPC* and inversely to the *MPS*.

Various estimates of the actual multiplier for the United States place it somewhere between 2 and 3, depending on the level of employment and business activity. In determining the value of the multiplier, it is best to use the disposable personal income of an individual or a nation. It gives the best reflection of what is done with increased incomes. The difficult part in calculating the multiplier is to hold all other factors constant. For example, we might show that the $20 billion of increased investment was accompanied by an increase in disposable personal income of $60 billion for the nation. But part of the increase in disposable personal income could be due to a tax reduction or to a reduction of savings. Increased spending and consequently increased disposable personal income might result from such things as better products, more advertising, or scare buying. Thus, the change in income should be adjusted for such factors to determine a true multiplier.

Table 14-5 Relationship of *MPC* and *MPS* to the Multiplier

MPC	MPS	Multiplier (k)
9/10	1/10	10
5/6	1/6	6
4/5	1/5	5
3/4	1/4	4
2/3	1/3	3
1/2	1/2	2
1/3	2/3	1 1/2

Accelerator

Granting that we have a multiplier and can estimate its size, we can see that an increase in spending by investors, consumers, or government will bring about an increase in income by some multiple of the original spending. However, that is not all. As the increased income resulting from the multiplier effect is being respent, the demand for consumer goods and services will increase. This increased demand may lead businesses to increase demand for machinery, equipment, and buildings to produce the additional goods and services. They will, in turn, increase their investment to obtain the capital equipment needed to increase production. The relationship between this secondary, or induced, investment brought about by the spending of the increased income resulting from the multiplier on the original investment is known as the **accelerator effect**.

Following our example, we can assume that our original, or autonomous, investment of $20 billion will increase income by $100 billion, out of which people spend $80 billion and save $20 billion. When merchants see the additional $80 billion flowing over their counters, they will increase their orders of goods and services. This means that the producers will increase output. To do this, manufacturers and others may have to purchase new and modern equipment, buildings, and other items, which will result in an increased investment in capital goods. They might finance this investment by using savings or by borrowing from the banks. At any rate, secondary or induced investment will take place. For our purposes, let us say that this secondary investment amounts to $8 billion. This is shown in Table 14-6.

Some economists feel that because of the difficulty in distinguishing between original and secondary investment, it is impossible to measure the accelerator. They have a point. After all, on what basis are we going to make a distinction between the two? We could say that any investment which occurs in the first six months of the year is original and that which takes place in the last six months is induced. But what about the businesspeople who are induced to expand in April because of increased business activity in the first quarter of the year? Should their investment be called induced or original? Or what about the executive who, in the fall of one year, plans to expand in the fall of the next year? Is this induced invest-

Table 14-6 Relationship of Original and Secondary Investment
(Billions of Dollars)

	Investment	Increased Income	Increased Spending .80	Increased Saving .20
Original, or autonomous, investment	$20 — Multiplier →	$100	$80	$20
Secondary, or induced, investment	$ 8 ← Accelerator			

ment? An arbitrary division between original and induced investment would not give us a true measure of each. Nor could we ask each business whether a particular investment was original or induced. Despite the difficulties of measuring it, we do know that the accelerator effect exists.

Interaction of Multiplier and Accelerator

Just as we have a multiplier effect on the original investment, we can have a similar multiplier effect on the secondary investment. Through the multiplier effect the original investment brings about increased income, which when spent brings about secondary or induced investment. The multiplier effect on the secondary investment further increases income. This in turn leads to tertiary investment, which generates more income, and so forth. Thus, the multiplier and accelerator serve to augment each other and to boost income and investment. This is shown in Table 14-7.

If we measure the original increase in investment, $20 billion, against the initial increase in income, $100 billion, we get a multiplier of 5. Or if we measure the total investment over the period, $32 billion, against the total increase in income, $160 billion, we could still get a multiplier of 5. The 5 is known as the **simple multiplier**. However, if we measure the original increase in investment, $20 billion, against the total increase in income resulting from the interaction of the multiplier and accelerator, $160 billion, we find the multiplier is 8. We call the 8 the **supermultiplier**.

Because of the problems in distinguishing between the original and secondary investment, the accelerator and supermultiplier are extremely difficult to measure. Therefore, we usually talk in terms of the simple multiplier. We can get some idea of the simple multiplier by observing the changes over two consecutive national income periods. We can compare the total change in investment that occurred with the total change in income. In our example, the effect that we obtain from investing a

Table 14-7 Interaction of Multiplier and Accelerator (Billions of Dollars)

	Investment		Increased Income	Increased Spending .80	Increased Saving .20
Original, investment	$20——Multiplier	→$100	$ 80	$20
	←Accelerator				
Secondary investment	8←Multiplier	→40	32	8
	←Accelerator				
	4←Multiplier	→20	16	4
Totals	$32		$160	$128	$32

Figure 14-1   Multiplier and Accelerator Action

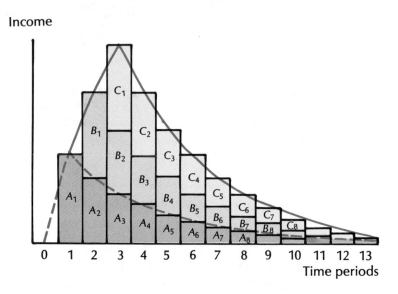

total of $32 billion is a total increase in income of $160 billion. This result clearly shows the simple multiplier is 5.

The cumulative effects of the multiplier and accelerator are demonstrated in Figure 14-1. The increase in income shown by A_1 results from the original investment. In the second period, a portion of this money is spent creating additional income. The process continues through the third and fourth periods, and so on. The effect of the original investment eventually will end, as shown by the dashed line. If secondary investment, shown by B, starts to take place in period 2, however, this will further augment income in that and subsequent periods. By period 3, tertiary investment, shown by C, takes place to augment income further in the third and subsequent periods.

The dashed line shows the effect of the simple multiplier and the increase in economic activity resulting from the original investment. After the spending of the original investment takes place, economic activity increases but at a decreasing rate. The solid line shows what happens when respending brings about induced investment. Economic activity surges to a higher level before the rate of increase begins to decline. The net result is that income will reach a higher level with induced investment than it would with the original investment only.

In effect, the cumulative action of the multiplier and accelerator intensifies fluctuations in business activity. Although there is no certitude regarding the length of time that elapses between the original investment and the respending of it after it becomes income to others, most estimates place the time somewhere between 3 and 3.5 months.

Effects of Multiplier: An Example

The effect of the multiplier on the economy is shown in the hypothetical situation in Table 14-8. From this table it can be seen that consumers spend $2,850 billion of their income on consumer goods. The $210 billion in consumer savings plus $390 billion in capital consumption allowances plus $150 billion in undistributed profits forms the basis for the $750 billion private investment plus net exports. The government purchases its $900 billion in goods and services by collecting $360 billion in indirect taxes, $226 billion in corporation and Social Security taxes, and $314 billion in personal income taxes. If each sector of the economy reacts in a similar fashion in a subsequent period, we will have the same output and income.

What would happen if businesspeople increased their investment in plant and equipment by $50 billion in the subsequent period? Assuming a marginal propensity to consume of two-thirds, and provided taxes, capi-

Table 14-8 GNP: Product and Income Flow, Period I
(Billions of Dollars)

Product Flow			Income Flow		
Gross national product		$4,500	Gross national product		$4,500
			Minus:		
Consumer purchases		$2,850	Capital consumption		
Goods	$1,650		allowance	$ 390	
Services	$1,200		Indirect business tax	360	
Domestic investment		720	National income		$3,750
Construction	360		Minus:		
Plant and equipment	300		Corporate taxes, Social		
Inventories	60		Security payments, etc.	226	
Net exports		30	Undistributed profits	150	
Government purchases		900	Personal income		3,374
Federal	376		Minus:		
State and local	524		Personal taxes	314	
			Disposable personal		
			income		3,060
			Consumer expenditures	2,850	
			Savings	210	

tal consumption allowances, and undistributed profits remained the same, the following changes would take place:

1. Spending on plant and equipment would increase from $300 billion to $350 billion.

2. Private investment would increase from $720 billion to $770 billion.

3. With a multiplier of 3, the GNP would increase to $4,650 billion.

4. The increase in GNP would increase the national income to $3,900 billion, personal income to $3,524 billion, and disposable personal income to $3,210 billion, assuming that taxes and other things remained constant.

5. Since the marginal propensity to consume is two-thirds, people would spend $100 billion of their additional $150 billion increase in income and save the remainder, $50 billion.

6. The additional spending of $100 billion on consumer goods and services would increase consumer purchases on the product flow side to $2,950 billion, and the $50 billion in additional savings would offset the original increase in investment.

After these changes take place, the hypothetical GNP would appear as shown in Table 14-9.

Table 14-9   GNP: Product and Income Flow, Period II
(Billions of Dollars)

Product Flow			Income Flow		
Gross national product		$4,650	Gross national product		$4,650
			Minus:		
Consumer purchases		2,950	Capital consumption		
Goods	$1,710		allowance	$ 390	
Services	1,240		Indirect business tax	360	
Domestic investment		770	National income		3,900
Construction	360		Minus:		
Plant and equipment	350		Corporate taxes, Social		
Inventories	60		Security payments, etc.	226	
Net exports		30	Undistributed profits	150	
Government purchases		900	Personal income		3,524
Federal	376		Minus:		
State and local	524		Personal taxes	314	
			Disposable personal		
			income		3,210
			Consumer expenditures	2,950	
			Savings	260	

If we know the multiplier, we can estimate the amount of investment that is needed to reach a particular level of GNP. For example, with an average multiplier of 3, we know that a $1,500 billion investment is necessary to bring about a GNP of $4,500 billion. Thus, if private investment were $700 billion, and government purchases were $800 billion, which in effect means we have a total private plus government investment of $1,500 billion, the GNP would be $4,500 billion. If we had a multiplier of 3, it would mean that the average propensity to consume would be two-thirds. Therefore, people would spend $3,000 billion and save or pay in taxes $1,500 billion of their income. In 1986, for example, it took a total investment (private investment, plus government spending minus net imports) of $1,446 billion to give us a GNP of $4,209 billion. This indicates an average multiplier of something less than 3, based on the average propensity to consume.

Production, Employment, and the Multiplier

The multiplier is also useful in deciding what additional investment may be necessary to reach a stage of full employment in a forthcoming period. We can determine what amount of GNP is necessary to maintain full employment in the following manner. If we multiply the number of people available for work by the average number of hours worked per person per year, and then by the average productivity per work hour, we obtain the total current potential production, or GNP, of the economy. Thus, our formula becomes:

Labor Force × Hours per Worker × Output per Work-Hour =
Potential GNP

For example, let us assume the normally employed labor force in a given year is 110.6 million, the average number of working hours per person per year is 1,820 (35 hours per week), and the productivity per work-hour is $20.14. Putting these numbers into our formula, we obtain a potential or full-employment GNP of:

$$110.6 \text{ Million} \times 1,820 \times \$20.14 = \$4,054 \text{ Billion}$$

If we produce anything less than $4,054 billion, we will not be fully employed. Some workers will be without jobs, and others will be on short hours. This happened during the recession of 1982 when the size of the labor force was approximately 112 million and the GNP was $3,166 billion. We operated at less than full capacity, and unemployment was 10.7 million workers, or 9.5 percent of the labor force. This was 4.5 percentage points above what is usually considered a normal level of unemployment.

It might be possible to avoid such excess unemployment, at least to a degree, if it could be anticipated. To this end, forecasting the GNP has become a very useful technique of economic analysis. Estimates of intended investment by businesses can be obtained through the Securities and Exchange Commission and the Department of Commerce. Another excellent source is the McGraw-Hill *Survey of Business Investment*. It is possible to ascertain consumer spending plans from surveys published by the University of Michigan and the Conference Board. Estimates for government expenditures can be obtained by studying various proposed governmental budgets.

Suppose that by using various sources and methods it was estimated that the GNP for a forthcoming period would be $4,500 billion:

Consumer purchases	$2,900
Domestic investment	800
Net exports	30
Government	770
Estimated GNP	$4,500

If a GNP of $4,650 billion is needed for full employment, it is obvious that we will have some degree of unemployment. If consumers, businesses, and the government follow through as indicated, total production will be 3.2 percent below that amount needed for full employment. This could mean excess unemployment of 3.7 million people, or total unemployment of 7 to 8 percent of the labor force.

When faced with such a situation, the logical thing to do would be to encourage increased spending by any or all four sectors. But how much additional spending would be necessary? The answer depends in large part on the size of the multiplier. The gap between the estimated and the full-employment GNP is $150 billion. It is not necessary, however, to increase spending by this amount. If the multiplier were 3, an original increase of $50 billion in investment, for instance, would increase the GNP by $150 billion to $4,650 billion. Out of the $150 billion of higher income, people would spend $100 billion on consumer goods (assuming a marginal propensity to consume of two-thirds). This would in effect give us sufficient output to maintain full employment since the GNP would then be:

	Estimated GNP	Increased Investment (in billions)	Final GNP
Consumer purchases	$2,900		$3,000
Domestic investment	800	+$50	850
Net exports	30		30
Government	770		770
GNP	$4,500		$4,650

Actually when it is observed that the estimated GNP may be less than that needed for a high level of employment, the administration and agencies of the federal government may take steps to encourage consumption and private investment. They can use indirect governmental measures to bolster the level of economic activity. If consumers and businesses are conservative and do not respond to the stimulus, the government, as a last resort, can use more direct measures, including deficit spending, in an effort to raise the level of economic activity.

ESTIMATING FUTURE GROWTH OF THE ECONOMY

It is important for macroeconomic analysis to know what may happen to the economy in the future. Will we have sufficient savings and credit to finance expansion? Will we have the resources to expand at the same rate in the future as we have in the past? These and many other questions are of interest from economic, social, political, and military points of view. Likewise, the future of our economy is important from a microeconomic point of view. A firm should have some idea of what its total income will be in 5, 10, or 15 years so that it may plan properly. There are several methods of obtaining a reasonable estimate of our GNP for the future. These are all estimates and do not purport to measure precisely the rate of growth or the level of economic activity for any particular year in the future.

A number of growth projections, based on an annual real growth rate of 3 percent, indicate that the GNP will be nearly $4 trillion by 1995 in terms of 1985 constant dollars. If a 3 percent annual inflation is injected into the forecasts, it means that the current dollar GNP in 1995 will be close to $7.2 trillion. That, of course, is a tremendous quantity of goods and services to produce, distribute, and finance.

By 1995 the U.S. population is projected to be in the vicinity of 260 million, compared with 239 million in 1985. Some geographic areas will grow at faster rates than others, and there will be some change in the age structure of the population. The labor force will grow to more than 130 million, and the length of the workweek will decline. Per capita production in current dollars will be in the neighborhood of $30,000 annually, and average family income will be well in excess of $45,000 annually. It is anticipated that the distribution of income will show an increase in the percentage of families in the middle- and upper-income groups. The long-run decline in the incidence of poverty will continue. Of course, for a number of reasons not all industries will grow at the same rate.

One factor common to most of these forecasts is that they are based for the most part on population increases anticipated in the future. The rate of population increase, however, could continue its shift downward, as it has been doing in recent years, or it could reverse itself. Thus, the projection of the GNP would have to be scaled downward or upward accordingly.

SUMMARY

The level of economic activity is determined by the aggregate demand of the four basic sectors in our economy: consumer, investment, net exports, and government. If a net change in the aggregate demand occurs, it will cause a change in the level of economic activity.

If an initial increase in demand by any of the sectors takes place, it will increase the size of the GNP not only by the initial increase but also by some multiple thereof. This multiplier effect is measured by the relationship between the original increase in investment (consumption or government) and the increase in income that results from it. The size of the multiplier varies directly with the marginal propensity to consume and inversely with the marginal propensity to save.

In calculating the multiplier, based on the marginal propensity to consume, the formula is $k = 1/(1 - MPC)$. The multiplier is usually considered to be somewhere between 2 and 3 for our economy.

The increased income resulting from the multiplier effect causes a greater demand for goods and services. This respending in turn may induce secondary investment in the economy. This phenomenon is referred to as the accelerator effect. Just as there is a multiplier effect on the original, or autonomous, investment (consumption or government spending), so too can there be a multiplier effect on the secondary investment. This in turn will increase incomes still more and perhaps bring about tertiary investment. The relationship between the original investment and the total increase of income resulting from the interaction of the multiplier and accelerator is known as the supermultiplier. Period analysis is used in an endeavor to plot the combined effects of the multiplier and the accelerator.

The multiplier is useful for calculating the additional amount of investment or government spending that may be required to bring the economy from a state of low economic activity and employment up to a point of higher employment. It can also be used to determine the total amount of investment and government spending that is needed in the economy to maintain a given level of economic activity.

Methods exist to estimate the level of economic activity for future dates, essentially in terms of the GNP. The usual procedure is to determine the size of the labor force for a future date, to determine the total work-hours for the given year, and then to multiply the total number of work-hours by the projected productivity per work-hour. Such calculations, however, give only rough estimates since the assumptions that must be made are subject to change.

NEW TERMS AND CONCEPTS

Multiplier effect
Multiplier
Propensity to consume
Average propensity to
 consume (APC)

Marginal propensity to
 consume (MPC)
Accelerator effect

Simple multiplier
Supermultiplier

DISCUSSION QUESTIONS

1. The marginal propensity to consume determines the size of the multiplier. Explain and illustrate.
2. What are the similarities and differences between the multiplier and the velocity of money? (Refer to Chapter 9 for a review of the velocity of money).
3. If a tax reduction is proposed to stimulate the economy, what effect will the multiplier have on the size of the tax reduction?
4. Why is it so difficult to measure the accelerator effect?
5. It is said that the supermultiplier actually contains some measure of the accelerator. Explain.
6. On the basis of the relationship of private investment plus government spending to GNP last year, what is the approximate size of the multiplier for the U.S. economy?
7. What reservations must be kept in mind when using GNP estimates of the future?
8. Of what practical use is a prediction of the gross national product for a future period to a business firm today?

SUGGESTED READINGS

The American Economy: Prospects for Growth through 1991. New York: McGraw-Hill Book Co., 1978.

"America's Restructured Economy." *Business Week* (June 1, 1981).

Baily, Martin Neil. "Productivity in a Changing World." *The Brookings Bulletin* (Summer, 1981).

Council of Economic Advisers. *U.S. Long-Term Economic Growth Prospects: Entering a New Era.* Washington, DC: U.S. Government Printing Office, 1978.

Fair, Ray C. "A Forecast from an Econometric Model and Its Estimated Uncertainty." *Economic Outlook U.S.A.* (Spring, 1978).

The Global 2000 Report to the President. Washington, DC: U.S. Government Printing Office, 1980.

Hailstones, Thomas J., and Frank V. Mastrianna. *Contemporary Economic Problems and Issues,* 8th ed. Cincinnati: South-Western Publishing Co., 1988.

The New American Boom: Exciting Changes in Life and Business between Now and the Year 2000. Washington, DC: Kiplinger, Inc., 1986.

15

INCOME-EXPENDITURE ANALYSIS

■

John Maynard Keynes, a British economist, was primarily responsible for the early development of the income-expenditure analysis of the economy. Subsequently many others improved and expanded the original Keynesian presentation, and it has developed into an excellent tool of economic analysis. Modern monetary, fiscal, and psychological policies are difficult to understand without a knowledge of the principles of the income-expenditure analysis. Although the principles have been widely accepted, controversy still arises concerning economic policies based upon them. However, it is possible to accept Keynesian tools of analysis without agreeing with the economic policies of Keynes, other economists, or political figures. It is possible, for example, to accept the income-expenditure analysis of unemployment without agreeing with the President's Council of Economic Advisers regarding what we should do about unemployment.

INCOME-EXPENDITURE ANALYSIS AND CLASSICAL TRADITION

The development of the income-expenditure analysis involved a breaking away from classical tradition. We will begin with a brief description of some major classical doctrines. The principles and doctrines of classical economics are not listed in any one place. They were developed over many years by various economists, and certain basic assumptions and principles were accepted as the foundation of economic analysis. Thus, a complete understanding of the classical tradition requires a good background in the history of economic thought. Nevertheless, the basic principles and assumptions that were in dispute can be summarized here.

Full Employment

Of greatest importance is the classical assumption that the economy can be in equilibrium only at full employment. If the economy is not at full employment, the situation is merely a temporary deviation from full employment. According to the classical theory, the economy operates on a basis of free trade and laissez-faire. Competition, the regulator of the economy, is an important factor in maintaining or moving the economy toward full employment. Competition will force prices downward to insure that all goods are moved off the market. Competition likewise will insure that all savings are invested, since it will force the interest rate down until it becomes profitable for businesses to borrow and to invest all available funds. Also, because of competition, unemployment for extended periods of time is improbable if not impossible. If workers are unemployed for any reason, it is assumed that they will compete for jobs against each other, and against those still employed, by offering to work for a lower wage. As a result of this competition, wages will be forced down. As wage rates decline, it becomes profitable for the entrepreneurs to hire more workers.

Thus, the normal tendency of the economy, according to the classical tradition, is to move toward full employment. If the economy is at less than full employment, the deviation is only temporary. Such a temporary deviation may be caused by several factors but primarily by monopolistic restrictions, labor union interference, and government intervention in the economy.

Income Equals Expenditures

Since the classicalists maintain that the primary purpose of money is its use as a medium of exchange, they maintain that all income will be spent. People will use money to buy the current goods and services they need. What they do not spend on current consumption, they will spend to build up their inventories of consumer goods or invest in capital goods. If anything is saved, it will be borrowed by others and spent in various ways, especially for capital goods investment. Thus, any decrease in consumption will be offset by an increase in investment. Fluctuations in the interest rate will insure that all the savings will be borrowed.

Supply Creates Demand

The classical theory holds that production which creates supply also creates an equivalent amount of monetary purchasing power (demand). It is also assumed that all the income will be spent. Thus, supply and demand will always be equal. This is often referred to as Say's law.[1] If supply creates its own demand and the goods can be moved off the market, then, according to the classical presentation, there should be no reason why the economy should not move right up to, and maintain equilibrium at, full employment.

---

1. Jean Baptiste Say was a French economist who, along with others, espoused the theory that supply creates demand. He explained the theory in his book, *A Treatise on Political Economy*, published in 1830.

The income-expenditure analysis contends that purchasing power does not automatically become demand for goods and services. People may have the purchasing power, or potential demand, and not use it. After producing goods and exchanging them for money, individuals may decide to hold on to the money as savings instead of spending it. In such a case, the total demand for goods and services may be less than the supply, and goods produced may not be moved off the market. Thus, there will be no incentive to increase production or to move to a higher level of employment.

According to the income-expenditure analysis, a problem arises in an economy when individuals substitute a desire for savings in place of a demand for goods and services, and this savings is not offset by borrowing and investing. As goods are produced, supply is created, which also creates purchasing power; but some of the purchasing power may be held in idle balances. As a result, the total supply will be greater than the effective demand for goods and services. It is only when savings is offset by investment that the economy will maintain equilibrium.

Before leaving this exposition on classical economics, it should be emphasized that there is much more to the classical doctrine than the few principles and assumptions mentioned. In fact, the bulk of our present microeconomic theory developed from the classical theory. The advocates of the Keynesian income-expenditure analysis do not wish to overthrow the entire classical tradition. Economic theory would be in a sad state without it. Both the classical doctrine and Keynesian economics have a place in current economic analysis. In fact, the more recent development of supply-side economics is based in large part on classical tradition.

INCOME-EXPENDITURE ANALYSIS

The income-expenditure analysis can be described as a theory of output, employment, and income. In explaining what determines the actual level of employment at any given time, the theory is centered on effective demand. **Effective demand** is defined as the actual demand for goods and services by both consumers and businesses. This effective demand is measured by the spending of current income. Total output, and therefore total employment and income, is determined by effective demand. The income derived from the output of goods and services in turn determines the total effective demand. If spending for consumer and capital goods is high, effective demand will again be high. Thus, a continued high rate of spending will assure a strong effective demand, which in turn will assure a high level of production, employment, and income. This action gives us the circular flow of economic activity previously described in Chapter 4.

The heart of the income-expenditure theory centers on the concept of effective demand. Difficulties arise when the effective demand is less than total output or income. This means that some of the goods produced will not be moved off the market. Since the cause of unemployment is inadequate effective demand, the theory concentrates its efforts in large part on the analysis of effective demand and its three important basic components of consumption, investment, and government spending.

As employment increases, income will increase. The increased income will cause consumption to increase. However, consumption will increase by less than the increase in income. In short, the marginal propensity to consume declines as the real income of the individuals and the economy as a whole increases. This point is integral and exceptionally important to current economic analysis.

Although the absolute amount of consumption increases with higher income, consumption decreases relative to income. Therefore, as the economy expands, there is an increasing difference between the amount of production, which is equivalent to income, and the amount of consumption. Investment, which is expected to absorb this difference, is not always forthcoming. Therefore, there may be less total effective demand than is necessary to clear from the market all the goods the economy is capable of producing. In such a case, production, employment, and income will be cut back.

Of great significance is the fact that consumption is generally less than total output, and as a result, investment is necessary to absorb the difference between what is produced and what is consumed. Furthermore, as output increases, the marginal propensity to consume declines. This means that the higher the output, the greater the gap between output and consumption. Thus, the higher the output and employment, the greater the amount of investment required to maintain a given level of employment. Lastly, the theory contends that because of the relative stability of the consumption function, effective demand will fluctuate primarily according to changes in investment.

The relationship between income and output on the one hand and the consumption function on the other is an important key to the income-expenditure analysis. It is this relationship that determines the amount of investment needed for any given level of employment. Furthermore, because of the nature of the consumption function, as output increases a larger amount of investment is required to move to a higher level of output, income, and employment. In the income-expenditure analysis, the third element of effective demand, government spending, is considered a means of raising the total effective demand when the first two basic elements, consumption and investment, are inadequate to maintain a satisfactory level of production and employment for the economy.

Equilibrium-Level Investment

The economy reaches equilibrium at a point where total investment is equal to the difference between total output (or income) and total consumption. Since output equals income, the value of both is shown on the income-output line moving upward to the right at a 45° angle in Figure

Figure 15-1 Income-Output and the Consumption Function
(Billions of Dollars)

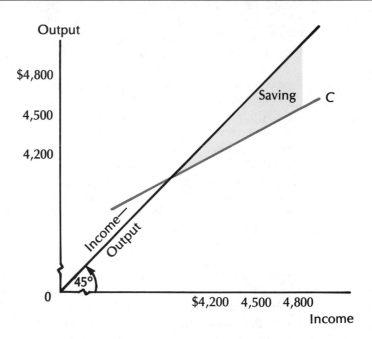

15-1. Line *C* is the consumption function representing the propensity to consume at various levels of income and employment. As income increases, consumption will increase but not so much as income. Therefore, consumption can be represented by a line moving in the same direction as income, upward to the right, but at less of an angle.

At very low levels of income, consumption may actually exceed income. This can result if people borrow money in addition to their regular incomes in order to buy goods and services. It may also occur as a result of inventory depletion, since it is possible to sell more than is currently being produced by supplying goods out of inventory. In most instances, however, consumption will be less than income. This difference between income and consumption represents saving, as shown in Figure 15-1. Therefore, it is necessary to have sufficient investment to fill the gap between output and consumption if all the goods and services are going to be moved off the market. Since there will be a larger gap between output and consumption at the higher levels, at any given time it will require increasing amounts of investment to move the economy to higher levels of output.

The level of economic activity, then, will be determined by the amount

Figure 15-2 Effective Demand Greater than, Equal to,
and Less than Total Output (Billions of Dollars)

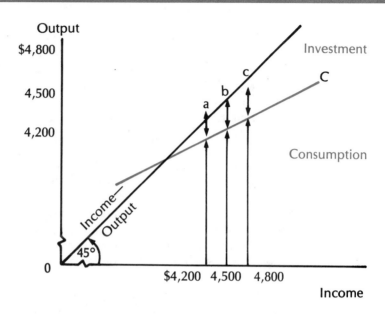

of investment. Output will adjust itself to the point where investment just fills the gap between output and consumption. At this point, total effective demand will equal total output, and all the goods and services will be moved off the market. At any lower output level with this given investment, total effective demand will be greater than output, and planned investment (represented by the double-pointed arrow) will be greater than planned savings, as illustrated by point *a* in Figure 15-2. Thus, if the economy were at a lower level, such as point *a*, economic activity would rise until the equilibrium position, such as point *b*, was reached. At point *b* in Figure 15-2 it can be observed that total effective demand, composed of consumption and investment, equals total output and that investment equals savings. At any higher level of output, such as point *c* in Figure 15-2, with the given investment (as designated by the double-pointed arrow), total effective demand will be less than output. Thus, if the economy were operating at a higher level, not all the goods produced would be moved off the market. This would bring about a decrease in economic activity until it reaches the equilibrium point, where investment is just sufficient to fill the gap between output and consumption, investment is equal to savings and total effective demand is equal to total output.

Relationship of Investment to Savings

In analyzing Figure 15-2, it should be kept in mind that the difference between the income line and the consumption line represents savings. In this way we can relate investment to savings and see their relationship to the level of economic activity as pointed out in Chapter 4. At point *a* in Figure 15-2, for example, it can be seen that the planned amount of investment, as shown by the double-pointed arrow, is more than that necessary to fill the gap between output and consumption, planned savings. Therefore, planned investment is greater than planned savings. This means that the total effective demand, made up of both consumption and investment, will be greater than output. As a result, there will be an increase in economic activity as businesses increase production to satisfy the demand. As the economy moves upward, income increases, the marginal propensity to save increases, and the gap between output and consumption widens. The economy comes into equilibrium at point *b* where investment will fill the gap between output and consumption. At this point, investment is equal to savings. Therefore, total effective demand is equal to total production. All goods produced will be cleared from the market, and the economy will be in equilibrium.

With this given amount of investment and consumption, there is no incentive to move to a higher level of output because it would not be profitable to do so. For example, if the economy did move up to point *c* without a change in investment, it would soon fall back to point *b*. Note in Figure 15-2 that at point *c* investment is insufficient to fill the gap between total output and consumption. Therefore, planned investment is less than planned savings. This means that total effective demand is less than total output and not all production will be moved off the market. As a result, businesses will curtail their activities. This will bring about a decline in output, employment, and income. As income decreases, the marginal propensity to save decreases and the gap between output and consumption becomes less and less, until point *b* is reached, at which investment is just sufficient to fill the gap between output and consumption. Here once again investment will equal savings, total spending will equal total income, total effective demand will equal total output, and the economy will be in equilibrium.

Principle to Remember.   Thus, with any given amount of investment there is only one point of equilibrium. If the economy is at any other level of economic activity, forces come into play to accelerate or decelerate the level of economic activity until it comes to its equilibrium point. The direction in which the economy moves will depend on the relationship of investment to savings. Whenever planned investment is greater than planned savings, there will be an increase in the level of economic activity if we are at less than full employment. If planned investment is less than planned savings, there will be a decrease in the level of economic activity.

When investment is equal to savings, there will be a stable flow of economic activity and the economy will be in equilibrium.

The Problem of Unemployment

In Figure 15-2, page 265, point *b* is the equilibrium level for the economy. Here total output is $4,500 billion, which gives a total income of $4,500 billion. Total consumption is $4,050 billion, and savings equals $450 billion. However, the amount of spending on investment, $450 billion, offsets the savings. Therefore, total spending equals total income, and total effective demand equals total output. The economy is at an equilibrium point from which there is no incentive to move. This is fine if the economy is at a position of high-level employment. But an important problem arises if the economy is in balance at an undesirably high level of unemployment. For example, suppose that a GNP of $4,650 billion were necessary for full employment. The economy would be stuck at a level of $4,500 billion output, and there would be no incentive, according to the income-expenditure theory, to move it up to a level of $4,650 billion.

Increased Investment. The income-expenditure approach does not deny the possibility of increasing the level of employment through increased consumption. Since consumption spending is dependent primarily on income, however, it is thought improbable that the propensity to consume out of any given level of income would change sufficiently to raise the level of economic activity. This is an essential assumption of the income-expenditure analysis.

Since consumption is not likely to increase, increased investment will be necessary to move the economy to a higher level of employment and income. As shown in Figure 15-3, a greater amount of investment is necessary to maintain the economy at point *c* than is required at point *b*. Although at the higher income people will spend more, consumption increases by less than the increase in income. The marginal propensity to consume declines as income increases. This results in a larger gap between income and consumption at the higher level that must be filled with investment. According to the income-expenditure theory, increased consumption from increased income will be helpful in moving the economy toward a higher level; but a move to higher income can only result if an increase in investment or government spending initiates the increase in output.

Greater Consumption. An increase in the propensity to consume out of given levels of income, however, will be helpful in moving the economy toward a higher level of employment because it will decrease the gap between output and consumption. This means that less investment will be required to maintain any given level of economic activity and that it will make it easier to reach and maintain a full-employment economy. In

Figure 15-3   Higher Investment Results in a Higher Level
of Output and Income (Billions of Dollars)

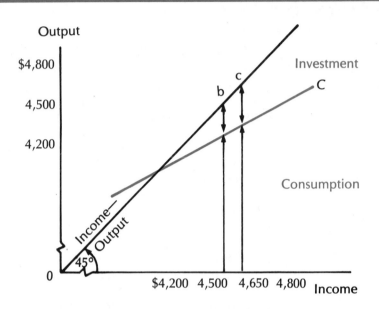

fact, if the propensity to consume were raised to 100 percent, there never
would be any problem with maintaining full employment because the
effective demand for consumer goods would always be equal to the total
output. There would be nothing to stop the economy from moving right
up to and staying at full employment. No investment would be necessary.

Although it is improbable, in the short run at least, that propensity
to consume would increase sufficiently to move the economy substantially
toward full employment, it might increase sufficiently to help reduce the
amount of investment necessary to obtain a higher level of employment.
This is shown in Figure 15-4. The same investment that gives equilibrium
at point b could result in equilibrium at point c if the propensity to consume
were to increase sufficiently.

The amount of investment shown at point b fills the gap between
output and consumption, as measured on line C. Whereas this amount
of investment is insufficient to fill the gap between output and consumption at point c, as measured by line C, it will fill the gap between output
and consumption at point c, as measured on the new consumption line
C_1. In this case, the higher level of consumption makes it possible to
obtain a higher level of output, income, and employment without increasing investment.

Figure 15-4   Higher Consumption Results in a Higher Level
of Output and Income (Billions of Dollars)

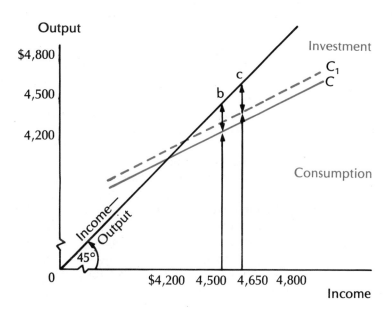

The increased effective demand necessary to move to a higher level of employment need not come from one source; that is, either investment or consumption alone. It could very well, and often does, come from a combination of the two forces. If investment increases, income will increase, and in turn consumption should increase. If consumption increases, effective demand will increase, which in turn will cause firms generally to increase rather than curtail investment. Likewise, they generally will move downward together. On the other hand, it is possible, though improbable, to have the advantages of an increase in one factor offset by a decrease in the other.

If the economy were in equilibrium at less than full employment and it were desirable to move to a higher level of employment, every attempt should be made to increase the level of economic activity. According to the classical approach, employers and employees merely had to wait for the competitive factors to make the adjustments necessary to move the economy to a full-employment position. In the absence of monopolistic restraints, labor union interference, and government intervention, it was only a matter of time before the economy would be back in equilibrium at full employment, according to the classicalists.

According to the income-expenditure approach, however, the private enterprise system is not so competitive as the classicalists anticipated, and laissez-faire not so prevalent as they assumed. Therefore, there may be no automatic adjustment to the full-employment level. Rather than let the economy stagnate in a lull of unemployment and uncertainty, the income-expenditure analysis suggests that the economy can be stimulated to move to a higher position by the use of various measures designed to increase the level of investment and consumption.

Government Spending.   When consumption and investment do not provide the effective demand necessary for high employment, Keynes and other advocates of income-expenditure analysis suggest that government spending be used to bolster the economy. To reach any given level of output and employment, government spending can be used to absorb the difference between output and total effective demand. This means that the total effective demand of private enterprise can be supplemented by the effective demand of government. Therefore, in the economy we have three forces making up the total effective demand, with the third force—government spending—acting as a stabilizer of the economy.

The use of government spending in this way is revealed in Figure 15-5. It shows an initial equilibrium position at point b, where output is equal to $4,500 billion. If the economy were to move up to the full employment level, point c, without increasing either investment or consumption, it could not stay at that level. The total effective demand, composed of consumption and investment, would be less than total output. Investment would be less than savings, spending less than income, and effective demand less than output; therefore, the economy would slide back to equilibrium with unemployment, point b. However, if government spending were injected to fill the gap between total output and total effective demand at point c, investment, plus government spending, would equal savings. As a result, total spending would equal total income, and total effective demand, including government, would equal total output. In such a case, all goods and services produced would be moved off the market and there would be equilibrium at the higher level of output, income, and employment.

Originally it was thought that government spending would increase business activity and encourage consumption and private investment to such an extent that the stimulus of government spending could be removed. This process is known as **pump priming**. It implies that all it takes is a bit of government spending to increase and maintain the flow of goods and services at a higher level.

Although the economy may respond to the stimulus of government spending, there is no assurance that income and consumption will continue at their higher levels when the government spending is removed. As a result, government spending may be required for a considerable period of time before the economy makes the proper adjustment to continue at

Figure 15-5   Government Spending Results in a Higher
Level of Output and Income (Billions of
Dollars)

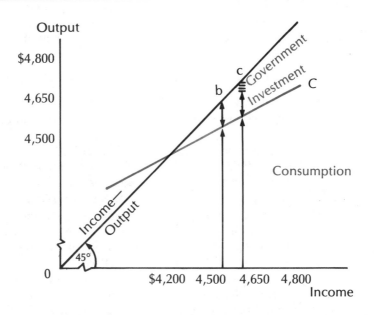

a higher level of consumption and investment. This sustained process of
government spending is part of what is called **compensatory spending**.
It implies that government spending must be sufficient to make up, or
compensate, for the lack of adequate consumption and investment during
periods of unemployment.

When using government spending to bolster the economy, caution
must be exercised in the matter of securing the funds that the government
spends. The government must raise the funds in such a manner that it
does not result in a reduction of consumption or private investment. Government spending should in no way compete with or discourage consumption and private investment. Furthermore, all other efforts to raise effective
demand should be exhausted before resorting to government spending.

In general, then, the income-expenditure analysis disagrees with the
classical viewpoint that the normal equilibrium position for the economy
is that of full employment. The income-expenditure holds that it is just
as easy to have equilibrium in the economy at less than full employment.
Proponents of the income-expenditure analysis usually advocate adopting
means to bolster the economy when it is at less than full employment,

whereas the classicalists would rely on the automatic adjusters supposedly inherent in the free enterprise, laissez-faire economy to make any corrections needed in the level of business activity. According to the income-expenditure approach, government spending can be used as a strong tool for stabilizing the economy, increasing spending as needed, and also decreasing it when feasible. It suggests the use of government spending to offset undesirable fluctuations in the level of investment.

Income-Expenditure Analysis and Business Fluctuations

It can be observed that as output, income, and employment fluctuate with changes in investment, the level of economic activity will fluctuate between two extremes. It will not fall below the point where the consumption function is equal to output (at least not for long) because below that point the effective demand for consumption alone exceeds the total output. Since effective demand is greater than output, entrepreneurs will be induced to increase production and employment to satisfy the excessive demand at this point. Sometimes it is difficult to realize that we can consume more than we produce. This can occur, however, when we supply goods out of inventory to such an extent that we have a net decrease in inventory at the same time that we are consuming all our current production. This occurred in the 1982 and previous recessions when businesses were trying to deplete their inventories. Another way we can consume more than we produce is through failure to replace our worn-out machinery and equipment. The result is a net disinvestment in the economy.

At the other extreme, in the short run the real level of economic activity cannot move upward beyond the full-employment stage. Increased consumption, investment, or government spending at this stage can lead only to higher prices. There may be an increase in the monetary value of the total output brought about by the inflation in the economy, but there will be very little, if any, increase in the absolute or real output of goods and services. Therefore, the economy fluctuates between point *x*, the point where consumption is equal to output, and point *c*, full employment, as shown in Figure 15-6. It does not necessarily fluctuate from one extreme to another. It may move back and forth between various intermediary points. Fluctuations are caused primarily by variations in investment, but they may also result from changes in consumption. Government spending may be used to offset undesirable fluctuations in investment that result in unemployment.

The Problem of Inflation

If investment, consumption, or government spending continues to increase once the economy has reached the full-employment level, inflation will set in. If inflation occurs, measures should be used to discourage further consumption and investment, because increased spending will

Figure 15-6   Level of Economic Activity Fluctuates between
Points *x* and *c* According to the Amount of
Investment (Billions of Dollars)

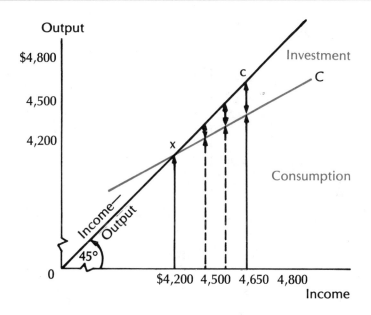

lead to still higher prices as investors and consumers bid for the use of
scarce labor, raw materials, and productive capacity. To combat inflationary tendencies, government spending can be decreased, taxes increased,
interest rates pushed upward, and credit restrained.

Strong inflationary tendencies seldom occur in the absence of large
government outlays. Therefore, the first order of anti-inflationary policy
would seem to be reducing government spending. The large government
outlay, however, often occurs during wartime or emergency periods. It
would be unwise to win the battle against inflation by reducing government spending but to lose the fight against the enemy because of the
lack of war materials. Thus, during wartime and emergency periods when
larger government outlays are necessary, inflation has to be combated
by reducing consumption and private investment. Devices to accomplish
this include controlled material plans, wage and price controls, rationing,
taxation, and credit restraints.

Figure 15-7 illustrates the situation where, because of government
spending, the total effective demand at point *c* is greater than total output.
Normally there would be an increase in output in response to this demand,
but because of the full-employment status of the economy, it is extremely

Figure 15-7 Reduction of Investment and Consumption
Necessary to Allow for Increased Government
Spending in a Full-Employment Economy
(Billions of Dollars)

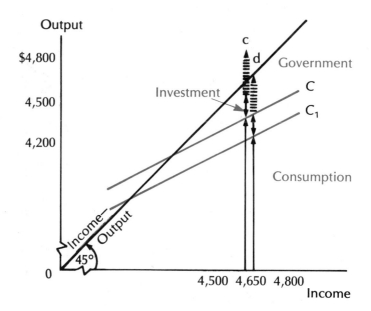

difficult to increase output. As a result of competitive bidding, prices move
upward. The problem, then, is to reduce either consumption or private
investment, or both, to allow a sufficient gap between total effective demand for consumption plus private investment and output to permit the
necessary amount of government spending. At the same time, total effective demand, including government, must not exceed total production.
This could be accomplished if consumption were reduced to line C_1 and
investment reduced as designated at point d in Figure 15-7.

In Figure 15-7, for the sake of clarity the line on which point d is
located is set a little apart from the line on which point c is located. Actually,
the two lines should be superimposed.

INCOME-EXPENDITURE ANALYSIS RESTATED

According to the income-expenditure analysis, as output increases,
income increases. As income increases, consumption increases, but at a
lesser rate. Since the marginal propensity to save increases as income

increases, a larger and larger amount of investment is needed to fill the gap between income and spending for consumption if all the goods produced are to be moved off the market. The economy, of course, comes into equilibrium at a point where investment is equal to saving. At equilibrium, spending on investment will make up for the difference between consumption and output. This means that total spending will equal total income, effective demand will equal output, and all the goods will be moved off the market.

Employment will also fluctuate with investment. It may fluctuate between a low level and the full-employment level, depending on the amount of investment. Thus, investment becomes the important determinant of output and employment. Since the consumption function is relatively stable in the short run, the level of employment cannot be increased without an increase in investment. The higher the level of consumption, however, the less the investment required to obtain any given level of employment.

If the economy becomes stabilized at any undesirable level of employment because of inadequate investment, the adoption of monetary, fiscal, and other measures designed to encourage consumption and investment is recommended. These measures should raise the level of income and output. If the attempt to raise the level of effective demand through consumption and investment is unsuccessful, government spending can be utilized in order to bring the economy to a higher level of employment.

Purpose of Theory

The ultimate purpose of the income-expenditure theory is to explain what determines the level of employment and to show the cause of unemployment. Income-expenditure analysis seeks a practical explanation to the operation of the economic system, in the hope of discovering those variables that cause changes in the level of economic activity. Once the variables are found, pressure can then be applied on them to move the economy to a more favorable position. To solve the problem of unemployment, the theory seeks those variables that could be managed or controlled within the sphere of the private enterprise system. Although many of the advocates of the income-expenditure analysis are not averse to using government action whenever effective demand fails to support a high level of employment, they emphasize that other measures should be utilized before resorting to government intervention to bolster the economy.

Marginal Efficiency of Capital and Rate of Interest

According to the income-expenditure analysis, output, employment, and income depend on effective demand, which is determined by the amount of consumption and investment. Consumption is determined by the size of income and the propensity to consume out of the given level of income. If the propensity to consume remains stable, total effective demand and, therefore, total output and employment will be determined by the amount of investment. An increase in investment will increase employment. In fact, employment will probably not increase except through increased investment.

Investment is dependent upon the marginal efficiency of capital (*MEC*) and the rate of interest (*RI*). The **marginal efficiency of capital** is the expected rate of return on investment, or in other words, the expected profit from a given investment. If the *MEC* is high compared with the *RI*, businesses will borrow and invest. If it is low compared with the *RI*, however, they will not be inclined to invest and may even disinvest. The *MEC*, according to the income-expenditure analysis, is the active factor in determining whether businesses are going to borrow and invest. The rate of interest is a passive factor. Businesses do not borrow just because the interest rate is low; they borrow and invest because of profit expectations. A sizable and favorable gap between the *MEC* and the *RI* will bring about an increase in the level of economic activity. Since the *MEC* is based on profit expectation, it is to some degree psychological and dependent on the attitude and outlook of the business community. The *MEC* will be determined by the expectation of profits compared with the replacement cost of capital assets. In short, it is a measure of the net rate of return on investment (over all cost except the rate of interest). The *MEC* can be enhanced by an increase in productivity, sales, or prices, or by a decrease in the costs of production. By its very nature, the *MEC* is dynamic and subject to sharp fluctuation owing to changes in prices and sales. Thus, it can easily account for variations of investment.

Furthermore, it is the relationship between *MEC* and *RI* that causes expansion, equilibrium, or contraction in the economy. Whenever the *MEC* is greater than the *RI*, it will bring about expansion in business activity. As expansion proceeds, however, the *MEC* eventually declines when sales begin to slacken and the price level stabilizes or begins to decline. In the process of expansion, the increased demand for money and the pressure on bank reserves tend to force the *RI* upward. The decline in the *MEC* and the rise in the *RI* finally bring the two into balance. At this point, there is no further incentive for business to borrow and invest. This point may or may not correspond to the point of full employment. If it does not correspond to full employment, or at least to a high level of employment, monetary measures can be used in an attempt to keep the *RI* below the *MEC* until a high level of employment is reached.

On the other hand, if the *MEC* should become less than the *RI*, the level of economic activity would begin to fall. There would be no point in businesses borrowing to invest in replacement or new productive facilities only to lose money. As a result, there will be a decrease of investment in the economy and consequently a decrease in effective demand. In turn, production, employment, and income will further decline. In fact, according to the income-expenditure theory, depression is a period in which the *RI* exceeds the *MEC*. As the contraction proceeds, the *RI* will begin to decline, and eventually the *MEC* will pick up after the economy has experienced a depression. When they come into balance again, the economy will be in equilibrium.

Thus, whenever *MEC* > *RI*, forces come into play to bring about an increase in the level of economic activity. As the expansion takes place, forces will bring *MEC* and *RI* into balance. Whenever *MEC* = *RI*, there will be a stable flow of economic activity. But whenever *MEC* < *RI*, forces will contract the level of economic activity. As the contraction takes place, forces will bring *MEC* and *RI* into balance again. In this process, the *MEC* is the more important and active factor. It is easier to make artificial adjustments in the *RI*, however, than it is in the *MEC* when a bolstering of the economy through governmental policies is desired.

Determinants of the Rate of Interest

Because of the possibility of manipulating the interest rate to raise employment or combat inflation, it is important to know its determinants. According to the income-expenditure analysis, the *RI* is dependent upon the strength of liquidity preference compared with the quantity of money in the economy. **Liquidity preference** is the desire to hold assets in the form of cash. Firms and individuals often desire to hold money for the sake of holding money. Liquidity may be desired for any one of three reasons: (1) the transactions motive, (2) the precautionary motive, and (3) the speculative motive.

Transactions Motive. Money is saved to carry out future monetary transactions. Many people, for example, save to accumulate sufficient funds for a down payment on a home or an automobile; firms save to buy machinery and equipment. Even those who are paid once a month, like college professors, save for transactions later in the month.

Precautionary Motive. Individuals and firms save for the proverbial rainy day. Individuals like to save so that they will have funds for emergencies, for periods of unemployment, and for retirement. Firms likewise desire to have reserves for various contingencies that may arise. This motive is very substantial when one considers the effects of not only individual savings but also Social Security funds, OASDHI and unemployment compensation funds, industrial pension funds, supplemental unemployment benefits, private insurance policies, and the like.

Speculative Motive. Individuals and firms hold money to take advantage of movements in the price level. They will postpone purchases if they think that the price level, or the prices of the particular goods or services they intend to buy, is going to decline in the near future. Investors will not purchase stocks or bonds if they expect prices to go down or the interest rate to rise. This type of liquidity preference is important in relation to the rate of interest. When it is anticipated that business activity is going to be good, the demand for money for speculative purposes will be great and the interest rate will rise. When the demand for speculative funds decreases, the interest rate will fall. The speculative motive is more dynamic and subject to sharper changes than either the transactions or precautionary motives and has a substantial effect on the rate of interest.

The liquidity preference will vary among individuals and firms. In general, however, it will fall with a rise in prices and increase when prices are declining. The stronger the liquidity preference, the more one has to pay to induce those with the funds to part with their liquidity. Therefore, the rate of interest will vary directly with liquidity preference.

The other factor affecting the rate of interest is the amount of money existing in the economy. The greater the amount of money compared with liquidity preference, the lower the interest rate. To look at it another way, if individuals and firms desire to hold a certain amount of liquid funds and the money supply is increased, it will automatically reduce the relative liquidity preference and lower the rate of interest. If the quantity of money is decreased, the relative liquidity will increase and the rate of interest will rise.

EVALUATIONS OF THE INCOME-EXPENDITURE ANALYSIS

There are many criticisms of the income-expenditure analysis. Some of them are major, but most of them are minor insofar as they affect its use as a tool of economic analysis. Although we will evaluate only a few of the important criticisms here, a close inspection of the income-expenditure analysis and its related criticisms and shortcomings would prove fruitful.

Socialistic

It is often claimed that policies based upon the income-expenditure approach tend to be socialistic because they will lead to government domination of the economy. These opponents claim that as income increases, the gap between output and consumption becomes larger. Since investment may be insufficient to fill the gap between consumption and output, government spending will be used to make up for the inability of private investment to fill this gap. As the economy expands, according to the critics, it will be more difficult for private investment to fill the expanding gap. They conclude, therefore, that increasing amounts of government spending will be required, and that a point will eventually be reached at which government spending will become an unduly large part of the total spending in the economy. They envision something similar to that shown in Figure 15-8.

Figure 15-8 Government Spending Becoming an Ever Larger Part of Total Spending (Billions of Dollars)

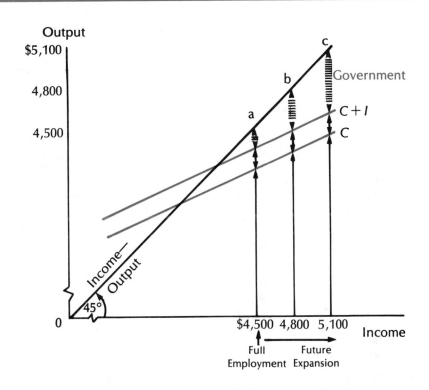

This figure shows a full-employment economy at the $4,500 billion level (point *a*). At this point only a moderate amount of government spending is used to maintain full employment. As the ability of the economy to produce increases to point *b* or *c*, the figure shows a larger amount of government spending required to maintain full employment. There are three major faults with this criticism: (1) It does not allow for a higher amount of investment to maintain the higher level of economic activity. In fact, as shown, the absolute amount of investment has remained stable, which means the ratio of investment to output has decreased. (2) It does not allow for any long-run change in the propensity to consume. (3) It does not allow for an increase in population. If the expansion in the economy results from an increase in population, there probably will not be a decline in the propensity to consume as shown in Figure 15-8. In the long run it is quite feasible that the consumption function for the economy will increase. Furthermore, the absolute amount of investment no doubt

Figure 15-9 Changing Levels of Consumption and Investment Lead to Lesser Increases in Government Spending (Billions of Dollars)

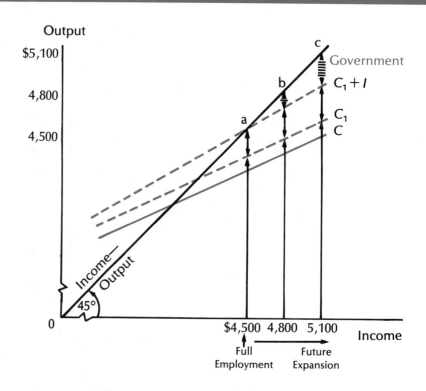

will have to increase to support a higher level of economic activity. Therefore, consumption and investment may change, as indicated in Figure 15-9.

Here it can be seen that a long-run increase in consumption from C to C_1 and the increase in total investment will make it possible to maintain a higher level of employment without a substantial increase in government spending. For example, in Figure 15-9 no government spending would be required to stabilize the economy at point a. In addition, less government spending would be required in Figure 15-9 than in Figure 15-8 at points b and c.

Some people consider the income-expenditure analysis socialistic in character. It might be noted, however, that Keynes, its leading proponent, was endeavoring to find a substitute for socialism or communism. He thought it would be better to improve the free enterprise, capitalistic system than it would be to substitute some collective form of economy. One of the vulnerable aspects of capitalism is its recurring periods of unemployment. If these became frequent, serious, and prolonged, people would be encouraged to look for a change in the economic system as a possible remedy. Keynes implied that it would be better to use the means available, including government intervention, to raise the level of employment rather than change the form of the economy.

Although it is rather evident that the income-expenditure analysis is not socialistic in nature, it cannot be denied that income-expenditure economics is a move away from the concept of laissez-faire and a move toward government intervention. Government action is often suggested when necessary to alleviate unemployment. Whereas the rugged individualist may feel that such government intervention is an infringement upon economic freedom, collectivists suggest government intervention to a much greater degree and even to the extent of government ownership of the means of production. We should avoid either of these extremes. Measures that can operate within the structure of the free enterprise system to promote a high level of employment are needed.

Certain income-expenditure analysts are criticized for their lack of faith in the ability of the private economy to maintain a high level of employment. But a decade of the most serious depression known to the world in the 1930s made pessimists out of some of the sturdiest of capitalistic supporters. More recently the occurrence of four recessions between 1970 and 1982 has dampened the enthusiasm of some regarding the attainment of our goals of full employment and price stability. On the other hand, the fact that free enterprise capitalism has proved in the past that it can establish records of prosperity and employment without large-scale deficit spending should not render the income-expenditure analysis invalid. The fact that an economist is incorrect in an opinion about the future does not invalidate the basic principles of economics, any more than the fact that a meteorologist is wrong in a weather forecast invalidates the laws of physics. Even when the economy is enjoying high levels of prosperity and employment, the income-expenditure analysis can still be used to show that a high level of consumption and investment makes deficit spending by the government unnecessary during such periods. Furthermore, the income-expenditure analysis can be applied to the study of inflation.

Premature Use of Government Intervention

Many proponents of the income-expenditure analysis might be validly criticized for their haste in suggesting the use of deficit spending. It seems that more attention might be given to consumption and investment before resorting to deficit spending. More emphasis on business research, the development of new products, cost-reduction measures, advertising, improved methods of distribution, new forms of energy, and probably many unexplored measures could encourage consumption and investment.

Furthermore, greater stress could be placed on the use of indirect measures to raise employment. The impact of tax reductions, public works spending, worker retraining programs, the extension and increase of unemployment compensation, poverty programs, regional economic development, and other expansionary measures as a means of reducing unemployment and stimulating economic growth is still subject to analysis and evaluation.

What about Today's Problems?

According to the income-expenditure analysis, the primary determinant of economic activity is effective demand. Fluctuations in effective demand, for whatever reason, cause production and employment to increase or decrease and prices to rise or fall. Since it was developed in an era of abundance of labor and resources, the income-expenditure analysis assumed that supply would always be forthcoming in response to an increase in effective demand.

Today, however, production, employment, and prices are being affected increasingly by shortages of materials, international financial manipulation, and a general depletion of the world's natural resources. Consequently, it can no longer be assumed that effective demand is the sole, or even in some cases the primary, determinant of economic activity.

On still another score, the income-expenditure analysis provides the tools to analyze the economy in terms of recession, depression, and full employment. It explains demand-pull inflation, but it does not explain cost-push, structural, or social inflation. Moreover, it does not give us an effective remedy for stagflation, the combination of stagnation and inflation, associated with the 1970s and early 1980s. For analyses or answers to these current problems, we have to look elsewhere.

SUMMARY

The relationship of the various elements of the income-expenditure theory can be summarized as follows:

1. Output, income, and employment depend on effective demand.
2. Effective demand is made up of consumption, investment, and goverment spending.
3. Consumption depends on the size of income and the propensity to consume.

4. The propensity to consume is relatively stable; therefore, assuming nominal government spending to have a neutral effect, changes in employment will result primarily from changes in investment.
5. Investment is determined by the marginal efficiency of capital (*MEC*) compared with the rate of interest (*RI*).
6. The *MEC* is dependent upon profit expectation compared with the cost of capital assets.

7. The *RI* depends upon liquidity preference compared with the quantity of money.
8. Liquidity preference depends on the strength of the transactions, precautionary, and speculative motives for saving.
9. In the absence of sufficient consumption and investment, changes in government spending can be used to influence the level of output, income, and employment.

The relationships are outlined schematically in Figure 15-10. From this outline, one can easily determine what general effect a change in any of the various factors of the economy will have on the level of economic activity. For example, other things remaining the same, an increase in the size of income will result in higher consumption, increase the effective demand, and thereby increase the level of economic activity. A decrease in the propensity to consume, on the other hand, will result in decreased employment if not offset by other changes. An increase in the quantity of money will reduce the rate of interest; this, in turn, will increase investment. An increase in effective demand will result and, therefore, a boost in output, employment, and income will also occur. A reduction in prices will lower profit expectations. This reduces the marginal efficiency of capital, which in turn reduces investment and brings about a decrease in production and employment.

Not only is the outline an aid in analyzing the effects of changes in the various forces in the economy, but it is also useful for the purpose of determining the appropriate measures necessary to improve the level of economic activity, to combat inflation, or even to handle the problems of stagflation. For example, if the economy is in equilibrium at less than full employment, it can easily be visualized that a higher investment will result from lowering the interest rate, and that a lower interest rate can be obtained by increasing the quantity of money. Thus, a liberalization of the money supply can be helpful in raising the level of employment. On the other hand, a decrease in the money supply can be effective in combating inflation. Employment may also be increased through higher consumption. Therefore measures designed to increase the propensity to consume, such as tax reductions, liberal consumer credit, and improved products, will tend to increase the level of production and employment.

This outline can be used as a means of analyzing the effect of governmental monetary, fiscal, and psychological policies on the level of economic activity. Furthermore, it points up the importance of the three strategic variables: the propensity to consume, the marginal efficiency of capital, and the rate of interest. As a result of the many advantages, it would seem worthwhile to keep this outline in mind as a handy reference for analyzing the effect of various factors on the general level of economic activity.

The income-expenditure analysis has been criticized because many of the policies developed from it require government action. Although some economists suggest heavy government intervention, many of our policymakers have been against any undue government interference in the economy.

The income-expenditure analysis has also been criticized because in the long run it will require larger and larger amounts of government spending. This argument, however, neglects the need for increased investment in an expanding economy, it does not allow for a long-range increase in the propensity to consume, and it does not take into consideration an increase in the population.

Moreover, the income-expenditure analysis, having been developed in the 1930s, does not provide the framework to analyze and answer many of the current issues and problems of today's economy.

Figure 15-10   Outline of the Income-Expenditure Analysis

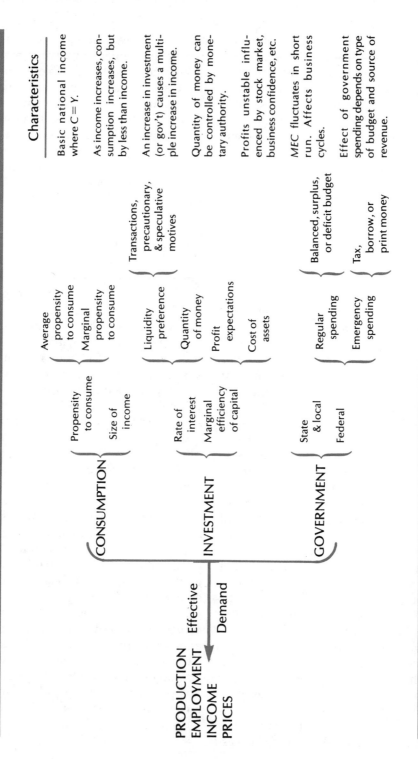

Source: Adapted from *The Economics of John Maynard Keynes: The Theory of a Monetary Economy*, by Dudley Dillard, © 1948, p. 49, by permission of Prentice-Hall, Inc., Englewood Cliffs, New Jersey.

NEW TERMS AND CONCEPTS

Effective demand
Pump priming

Compensatory spending
Marginal efficiency of
  capital (*MEC*)

Liquidity preference

DISCUSSION QUESTIONS

1. Discuss the classicalists' assumption that full employment is the normal equilibrium level for the economy.
2. Explain what is meant by the statement "Supply creates its own demand."
3. What does the income-expenditure analysis cite as the cause of business cycles?
4. Recent empirical data indicate that with rising income the marginal propensity to consume may not decline as much as Keynes and others assumed. If this is true, what happens to the validity of the income-expenditure approach as a tool of analysis?
5. How is it possible to have the consumption function relatively stable but still have different amounts of consumption and different propensities to consume along the consumption function line?
6. Why does a high level of consumption make it easier to maintain a high level of employment?
7. Why is the consumption function not necessarily stable in the long run? What factors may cause it to change?
8. Whenever planned investment is greater than planned savings and the economy expands, exactly what is it that causes investment and savings to come into balance?

SUGGESTED READINGS

Dillard, Dudley. *The Economics of John Maynard Keynes*. New York: Prentice-Hall, Inc., 1983.
Eichner, Alfred S. "Post-Keynesian Theory: A Look Ahead." *Challenge* (May/June, 1979).
Hansen, Alvin. *A Guide to Keynes*. New York: McGraw-Hill Book Co., 1953.
Hicks, John. *The Crisis in Keynesian Economics*. New York: Basic Books, Inc., Publishers, 1975.
Kenyon, Peter. "A Guide to Post-Keynesian Economics." *Challenge* (July/August, 1978).
Keynes, John Maynard. *The General Theory of Employment, Interest, and Money*. London: Collier MacMillan Publishers, 1965.
Lawson, Tony, and Hashem Pesaran, eds. *Keynes' Economics: Methodological Issues*. Armonk, NY: M. E. Sharpe, Inc., 1985.
Leijonhufvud, Axel. *On Keynesian Economics and the Economics of Keynes*. New York: Oxford University Press, 1968.
Lekachman, Robert. *The Age of Keynes*. New York: Random House, Inc., 1966.

16
THE MEANING OF FULL EMPLOYMENT

■

A definite relationship exists between the level of employment and the size of the GNP. When real GNP decreases, unemployment usually increases. In fact, as we shall see, unemployment may develop even when GNP remains constant or increases moderately over any extended period of time. Unemployment is detrimental to the economy because it decreases incomes. This in turn reduces consumer spending, which further decreases demand and eventually GNP.

Previously in referring to full employment we were considering full employment of labor, resources, and productive capacity. In this chapter, however, we are concerned primarily with employed and unemployed labor forces. In this sense, unemployment causes individual hardship to workers and their families. From Table 16-1, it can be seen that we have had periods of full employment and periods of widespread unemployment. As the years pass, the size of the population will increase and the labor force will grow. This will make the problem of maintaining full employment more complex.

THE LABOR FORCE

Customarily, between 40 and 45 percent of our total population are members of the labor force. This seems to be the norm for industrial nations throughout the world. However, the labor force is limited by definition. Many individuals who work just as much as do those in the labor force are excluded because of the nature of their work or because they receive no remuneration for it.

Size and Composition of the Labor Force

To understand the problem of maintaining full employment, let us look more closely at our labor force and our population. In 1986 we had a total population of 241.5 million. Of this total, 180.6 million were in

Table 16-1 Population, Total Labor Force, and Unemployment (Millions)

Year	Total Population	Total Labor Force[1]	Participation Rate	Civilian Unemployment Rate
1929	121.8	49.2	40.4%	3.2%
1933	125.6	55.2	43.9	26.9
1940	132.6	56.2	42.4	14.6
1945	140.5	65.3	46.5	1.9
1950	152.3	63.4	41.6	5.2
1960	180.7	72.4	40.1	5.5
1970	204.9	84.9	41.4	4.9
1980	227.7	108.5	47.7	7.1
1986	241.5	119.5	49.5	7.0

1. Includes armed forces.
Source: *Statistical Abstract of the United States*, various years, and *Employment and Earnings* (January, 1987).

the category of noninstitutional population, that is, all persons 16 years of age or older, including members of the armed forces but excluding persons in institutions.

Total Labor Force.   In 1986, of the noninstitutional population, 119.5 million were in the total labor force. The **total labor force** is made up of all those in the noninstitutional population who are working or are seeking work. Thus, it includes the unemployed as well as the employed. Furthermore, it includes proprietors, the self-employed, and members of the resident armed forces. However, the labor force excludes members of the armed forces stationed overseas, all persons engaged in incidental unpaid family work (less than 15 hours), and all persons engaged exclusively in housework in their homes or attending school. Thus, students as such are not members of the labor force. If they work or look for work during the summer vacation period, however, they become members of the labor force. Likewise, when they graduate, they generally become members of the labor force.

Civilian Labor Force.   By definition the **civilian labor force** consists of "all persons in the total labor force except members of the resident armed forces." Since 1.7 million persons were in the resident armed forces in 1986, the civilian labor force was 117.8 million, and of this total, 8.2 million, or 7.0 percent, were unemployed. The **unemployed labor force** includes all persons in the labor force seeking work, including those who are cur-

Table 16-2   Population and Labor Force, 1986 (Millions)

Total population		241.5
Noninstitutional population		182.3
Total labor force		119.5
Resident armed forces		1.7
Total civilian labor force		117.8
Unemployed labor force		8.2
Employed civilian labor force		109.6
Agricultural employment	3.2	
Nonagricultural employment	106.4	
Persons not in the labor force		62.8
Keeping house	29.1	
In school	9.2	
Unable to work	2.7	
Others	21.8	

Source: *Employment and Earnings* (January, 1987).

rently engaged in emergency relief work. A breakdown of the population and the labor force is shown in Table 16-2.

The **employed civilian labor force** is the difference between the civilian labor force and the unemployed. Technically, it includes all employed workers, including persons who did not work at all during the census week because of illness, bad weather, vacation, or labor disputes. It includes part-time as well as full-time workers. In 1986 the number of employed was 109.6 million, and of this total 3.2 million were engaged in agricultural work and 106.4 million were in nonagricultural employment.

There were 62.8 million persons in the noninstitutional population who were not in the total labor force. It is interesting to keep in mind that 29.1 million of this group were homemakers. Although the homemaker often puts in a harder day than the breadwinner of the house, the homemaker is not included in the labor force. Another 9.2 million of those not in the labor force were in school: high school, college, or elsewhere. Nearly 3 million people were unable to work. The remainder, 21.8 million, was composed of those who are retired, individuals who do not want to work, and those who do not have to work.

The bulk of the labor force is engaged in nonagricultural employment. The largest category, which is trade (wholesale and retail), has 23.8 million. The second largest category is services, with 23.0 million workers. The third largest portion, 19.2 million, is engaged in manufacturing, and government has 16.7 million workers.

Trends in the Labor Force

Our labor force has definite characteristics, but these same characteristics change as time progresses. Some of the most pronounced trends that have been developing in the labor force in recent decades include:

Teenage Employment. The percentage of teenage full-time employment has decreased. Some of the decline is the result of federal and state legislation that restricts the use of child labor. The larger influences, however, are probably compulsory school regulations and the increased educational facilities in the United States today. At present nearly 50 percent of the persons in the 18–19 age group are in school compared with 38.4 percent in 1960. Since more teenagers are in school, there is less chance that they will also be full-time members of the labor force. Some of them, however, are part-time workers in the labor force. It is projected that the labor force participation rate of individuals aged 18–19 will remain stable in the next decade.

Today 31.0 percent of those in the 20–21 age bracket are enrolled in a school of some type, compared with 19.4 in 1960. As more people in their early twenties attend colleges and technical schools, it is expected that the labor force participation rate for this age group will decline from its present rate of about 85 percent. In fact, by 1990 there will actually be fewer persons in the 20–24 age group in the labor force.

Older Workers. The percentage of older workers in the labor force has decreased. This has been the result of the growth and expansion of Social Security and of private pensions. Today only 16.3 percent of males 65 years of age or over are in the labor force compared with 26.8 percent in 1970. It is anticipated that by 1995 this percentage will be reduced to 13.3 percent. However, recent legislation restricting compulsory retirement may impact this trend in the future.

Female Workers. The number and percentage of women in the labor force have increased. The increased amount of clerical and retail sales work and the development of light manufacturing (those occupations in which women historically have been employed) have increased the demand for female labor throughout the United States. In addition, as a result of equal employment opportunity laws, the demand for women at the managerial and professional levels has increased and will continue to increase. Currently, 44.4 percent of the employed civilian labor force is composed of women. Almost 55 percent of the noninstitutional female population are members of the labor force. In 1986, both the husband and wife were employed in almost half of all married-couple families. Table 16-3 shows the number and the percentage of women in the labor force in the past few decades.

Table 16-3 Employment of Women in the Civilian Labor
Force (Millions)

Year	Total Civilian Employment	Female Employment	Female Employment As % of Total
1950	58.9	17.3	29.2
1960	65.8	21.9	33.0
1970	78.6	29.7	37.8
1980	99.3	42.1	42.4
1986	109.6	48.7	44.4

Source: *Statistical Abstract of the United States*, various years, and *Employment and Earnings* (January, 1987).

Skilled and Unskilled Workers. The percentage of unskilled laborers in the labor force has decreased. With increased use of complex machinery and equipment, it has become necessary for more workers to learn how to operate such machinery and equipment. As a result, we have had an increase in the percentage of semiskilled workers, while the percentage of skilled workers in the labor force has remained relatively constant. We have also had substantial increases in the percentage of professional and technical workers, which includes primarily skilled and semiskilled workers, as well as an increase in the percentage of clerical workers.

Service-Oriented Jobs. Another pronounced trend in the labor force is the growing number and percentage of service-oriented jobs. Today nearly 50 percent of our total output is in the form of services. The demand for workers in goods-producing industries, such as manufacturing, construction, and mining, is declining, while the demand for workers in service-producing industries is growing in both absolute and relative terms. Today only 25 percent of nonagricultural workers are engaged in the production of goods, as compared with 38 percent in 1960. On the other hand, the percentage of workers in service industries has risen from 62 percent to 75 percent during the same period. This trend can be observed in Table 16-4. Notice the rising trend of workers in services. The latter category includes workers in the hotel and tourist trade, laundries, advertising agencies, motion pictures, the medical and legal professions, and certain educational services.

Agricultural Employment. There has been a definite move away from agricultural occupations. As a result of increased productivity, we produce more and more agricultural commodities with fewer and fewer farmers.

Table 16-4 Percentages of Nonagricultural Employees in
Goods-Producing and Service-Producing Industries

Industry	1960	1970	1980	1986
Goods-producing				
Manufacturing	31%	28%	22%	19%
Construction and mining	7	6	6	6
Total	38	34	28	25
Service-producing				
Transportation and public utilities	7	6	6	5
Wholesale and retail trade	21	21	22	24
Finance, insurance, and real				
estate	5	5	6	6
Services	14	16	20	23
Government	15	18	18	17
Total	62	66	72	75

Source: *Statistical Abstract*, various years, and *Economic Report of the President*, 1987.

In 1930, for example, 10.3 million farmers provided food for 122 million Americans. Today it takes only 3.3 million farmers to provide more than enough food for 240 million Americans. In short, less than one-third the number of farmers are feeding about twice as many people, and the U.S. is still the world's biggest agricultural exporter.

Organized Workers. There was a substantial increase in the number and the percentage of organized workers in the labor force between 1935 and 1955. For a few decades labor union membership remained fairly stable at about one-fourth of the total labor force. However, since 1970 union membership has decreased as a percent of the civilian labor force. This stabilization and then decline has resulted in large part because the labor force has not been growing as fast in those occupations in which workers traditionally have been organized, such as the unskilled, semiskilled, and craft occupations. A considerable amount and proportion of the increase in the labor force have been in professional, technical, sales, clerical, and other white-collar occupations not traditionally organized by labor unions.

A dramatic drop in union membership occurred between 1980 and 1984. During that time, the organized labor movement lost 2.7 million members. This was the result of the severe drop in employment in the durable-goods-producing and transportation industries, which are highly organized. Competition from imports caused job losses in the auto, steel, appliance, and other heavy industries. Government deregulation of transportation brought competition from increased numbers of nonunionized firms. Widespread layoffs and job terminations in these industries also occurred during the 1980 and 1982 recessions. By 1986, union membership had declined to 18.8 percent of the employed labor force.

Size of the Labor Force.   The size of the labor force has been increasing continuously, primarily as a result of the increase in population. We added 2.4 million persons per year to our labor force during the 1970s. In the early 1980s, the average annual increase was approximately 1.7 million. A sizable part of the growth since 1970 has been due to the influx of women into the labor force. Table 16-5 shows the growth of the labor force.

A slower growth in the labor force, however, is predicted for the next several years. Projections indicate that in the 1980s the labor force will grow by 17 percent, compared with 29 percent for the 1970s. By 1990, the total labor force is expected to reach 125 million. There will be a noticeable increase in the number of women workers, and the ratio of females in the total labor force will rise. There will be greater increases in the number of white-collar and service workers in the next decade. The number of farm workers will decline compared with blue-collar workers.

During the late 1980s and early 1990s, the number and percentage of workers in the 16–24 age group will decline. This should help reduce unemployment among the youth of the nation, which, at an average 21.4 percent in the 1980s, was 3 times more than the adult unemployment rate. But there will continue to be an increase in the ratio of young blacks entering the labor force during the decade. Unemployment rates among black teenagers are usually double what they are among white teenagers.

Table 16-5   Labor Force Participation Rate (Millions)

Year	Total Population	Total Labor Force	Total Labor Force Participation Rate
1950	152.3	63.4	41.6
1960	180.7	72.4	40.1
1970	204.9	84.9	41.4
1980	227.7	108.5	47.7
1986	241.5	119.5	49.5

Source: *Statistical Abstract of the United States*, 1986, and *Employment and Earnings* (January, 1987).

Labor Force Participation Rate. Although the labor force grew in size, the labor force participation rate remained relatively stable until the early 1970s. The **labor force participation rate** is the percentage of the total population in the labor force. Between 1950 and 1970, the total labor force participation rate remained at about 41 percent. Table 16-5 also reveals that the total labor force participation rate has been noticeably higher since 1970. This is due primarily to the increase in the number of women entering the labor force.

EMPLOYMENT ACT OF 1946

It was thought that trouble would arise after World War II when veterans returned looking for jobs. It was thought that many of the wartime entrants into the labor force would hesitate to leave and this would cause a surplus labor force as the veterans returned, especially with the decline of war production. Many women, however, left the factories and offices to manage their homes. Young people reluctantly returned to school, and elderly citizens also left the labor force. Nevertheless, the civilian labor force did rise by 6.5 million within 2 years after World War II.

Some economists and government officials anticipated that we might have between 6 and 8 million unemployed in 1946, mainly because of the termination of wartime industries. However, the economy made a quick transition from wartime to peacetime production. In spite of the fact that government defense spending decreased more than $50 billion from 1945 to 1946, the slack was taken up by large consumer spending, expanded business investments, and strong foreign demand for our products. As a result, the GNP fell only moderately in 1946. Unemployment averaged 2.3 million for the year and never exceeded 4 million in any one month.

Nevertheless, the fear that widespread depression and chronic unemployment might recur with the cessation of war production led, in part at least, to the passage of the Employment Act of 1946. With the long and deep depression of the 1930s still in mind, many individuals, organizations, and public officials supported the Act, which was introduced shortly after the end of World War II.

Purpose of the Act

The original suggestions, known as the Full Employment Bill, would have made the government directly responsible for maintaining full employment and called for a planned federal budget designed to take up any employment slack in the economy. However, that proposal was not enacted. The Employment Act of 1946 that was passed merely declared that it was the government's policy to use measures at its disposal to promote maximum employment, production, and purchasing power. Section Two of the Act reads:

> The Congress hereby declares that it is the continuing policy and responsibility of the Federal Government to use all practicable means consistent with its needs and obligations and other essential considerations of national policy, with assistance and cooperation of industry, agriculture, labor and State and local governments, to coordinate and utilize all its plans, functions, and resources for the purpose of creating and maintaining, in a manner calculated to foster and promote free competitive enterprise and the general welfare, conditions under which there will be afforded useful employment opportunities, including self-employment, for those able, willing, and seeking work, and to promote maximum employment, production, and purchasing power.

Council of Economic Advisers

The Employment Act of 1946 set up a Council of Economic Advisers (CEA) appointed by the President with the advice and consent of the Senate. Each appointee must be a person who is exceptionally qualified to analyze and interpret economic developments and to appraise programs and activities of the government in the light of the provisions and objectives of the Act. The Council reports to the President on current and foreseeable trends. The President in turn makes recommendations for a program to promote a high level of employment.

Specifically, it is the function of the Council "to develop and recommend to the President national economic policies to foster and promote free competitive enterprise, to avoid economic fluctuations or to diminish the effects thereof, and to maintain employment, production, and purchasing power." The Council also analyzes existing programs and activities of the federal government to determine whether they are consistent with the express purpose of the Act, which is to maintain maximum employment.

The Act also requires the President to transmit to Congress an annual *Economic Report*. The *Report* gives a review of economic developments of the past year, the economic outlook for the forthcoming year, and an outline of the measures recommended for adoption to obtain or to maintain the objectives of maximum production, employment, and income. The President customarily delivers this report in late January of each year.

Joint Economic Committee

The *Economic Report* and all supplementary reports, when transmitted to Congress, are referred to the Joint Economic Committee. This Committee is composed of 10 members of the Senate and 10 members of the House of Representatives. The functions of the Joint Committee are (1) to make a continuing study on matters relating to the *Economic Report*, (2) to study means of coordinating programs to further the policy of the Employment

Act, and (3) to file a report with the Senate and the House containing its findings and recommendations with respect to each of the main recommendations made by the President in the *Economic Report*.

Meaning of Full Employment

The Act says nothing about a guarantee of jobs, but it does oblige the government to take steps to maintain a high level of employment. Nowhere in the Act, however, does it define or state what is meant by maximum or full employment. The 1953 *Economic Report of the President*, however, did state specifically that "Under the Employment Act, full employment means more than jobs. It means full utilization of our natural resources, our technology and science, our farms and factories, our business brains, and our trade skills."

It is expected that we will have some unemployment at all times because of job terminations by employees, discharges, and relocations. Also included in this group are people who are chronically unemployed because of certain mental, physical, or psychological handicaps. By the late 1950s a number of organizations, committees, and government agencies studying the problem of unemployment came to the conclusion that the amount of this so-called **frictional unemployment** should be about 4 percent of the total civilian labor force.

In the early 1970s various authorities suggested that perhaps our full employment standard of 96 percent employment and 4 percent unemployment was outmoded. It was proposed that the structure of the labor force was changing and that a new unemployment figure might be more appropriate as a measure of full employment. The labor force now includes larger numbers of young people, women, and minority workers than there were in the late 1950s. These groups usually have higher rates of unemployment than the labor force as a whole. Consequently, it was argued that if more weight were given to these categories in establishing a normal unemployment figure, the current rate would be perhaps 4.5 to 5 percent. A 4.6 percent figure, for example, was suggested in the 1974 *Economic Report of the President*, and a 5.1 percent rate was used as a benchmark in the 1979 *Economic Report*. Today it is generally agreed by government economists and others that 5 to 6 percent is an acceptable **full-employment unemployment rate**.

Any unemployment rate has to be observed with certain reservations. Even when unemployment is higher than our national goal, some categories of workers will still be experiencing lower unemployment rates than the national average. Notice in Table 16-6 that in June, 1982, when total unemployment was 9.7 percent, unemployment among white workers was 8.6 percent and among married men it was 6.5 percent. Even when we reach the full-employment level, we should not become complacent. At that level there are still sore spots of unemployment in the economy. In October, 1978, unemployment was the lowest it had been since the

Table 16-6 Unemployment Rates for Various Categories of Workers

	Unemployment Rates		
Category	October, 1978	June, 1982	June, 1986
Married males, spouse present	2.7%	6.5%	4.4%
Married females, spouse present		7.4	5.3
Adult males	4.1	8.8	6.2
Adult females	5.7	8.3	6.4
White workers		8.6	6.2
Black workers	11.3	18.9	14.9
Hispanic workers		13.8	10.7
All teenagers	16.1	23.2	19.2
Black teenagers	34.7	48.9	41.9
Black female teenagers	39.3	47.1	43.9
Total labor force	5.8	9.7	7.2

Source: *Employment and Earnings* (February, 1983, and August, 1986).

1974–1975 recession. With total unemployment averaging 5.8 percent, unemployment among black workers was 11.3 percent, among teenagers it was 16.1 percent, and the black teenage rate was 34.7 percent. Unemployment was 39.3 percent among black female teenagers.

Not only is it important to hold unemployment to a minimum, but it also is desirable to reduce underemployment. What is the difference between unemployment and underemployment? **Unemployment** refers to the number of workers not employed, whereas underemployment refers to the utilization of the workers. **Underemployment** occurs when a worker is employed but is not working to full capacity. It is possible for the economy to be in a state of full employment and yet be underemployed. Such would be the case if large numbers of workers were on jobs that did not require their full skill or productivity. For example, situations are found in which engineers are driving taxis, artists are painting signs, mechanics are sweeping floors, or skilled secretaries are doing filing work. Annually many individuals are trained for skilled jobs but fail to find job openings. Often college graduates with tremendous potential never reach their full productive capacity. Although much has been done to prevent unemployment, very little has been done on a nationwide scale to reduce underemployment. Underemployment can occur also when workers for some reason or another, such as the occurrence of a recession, do not work a full workweek.

Administering the Act

Since the original implementation of the Employment Act of 1946, the government has had several challenges in maintaining full employment as a result of the eight recessions that have occurred since the Act was passed. A new challenge arose in the recession of 1970 when the economy was characterized by unemployment between 5 and 6 percent along with inflation of more than 5 percent annually. Caution had to be exercised so that measures designed to expand employment would add only minimal inflationary pressures to the economy. A similar situation developed with the recession of 1974–1975 when unemployment reached 9.0 percent, and the economy was simultaneously experiencing double-digit annual inflation.

The problems of stagflation were further aggravated by the recessions of 1980 and especially 1982 when unemployment reached 10.7 percent in the fall of the year, the highest unemployment rate since the Great Depression.

Although in recent years there has been growing agreement on the meaning of full employment, considerable disagreement still arises over the degree of government action that should be taken to prevent either moderate or widespread unemployment from developing. Should government action, including deficit spending, be used to maintain employment for all those in the labor force, including the part-time farmers who are also working in industrial jobs, students who are working after school, the parent who has employed adult children living at home and vice versa, or both members of married-couple families?

These are difficult questions. The Employment Act of 1946 does not give us answers. Some supporters of the Act would like the role of the government to be spelled out more definitively. They would like to see concrete procedures set up by the Act for automatic action whenever unemployment reaches a certain level as specified by the Council of Economic Advisers. It has also been recommended that the Act be amended to include stabilization of the price level as a specific part of its policy.

In its 40 years of operation, the Council of Economic Advisers has proved to be a worthwhile and successful organization. It has performed its task well and has greatly enlightened members of Congress, administrators, and citizens on matters involved in the operation of the economy. Both parties, Democrat and Republican, continuously support the main objectives of the Act.

FULL EMPLOYMENT AND BALANCED GROWTH ACT OF 1978 (HUMPHREY-HAWKINS ACT)

After nearly a year of debate, revision, and finally House-Senate compromise, Congress enacted the controversial Humphrey-Hawkins Bill under the official title of the "Full Employment and Balanced Growth Act of 1978." The Act amends and embellishes the Employment Act of 1946. In particular it includes specific numerical targets and timetables regarding full-employment and inflation rates.

The Humphrey-Hawkins Act is broader in coverage than the Employment Act of 1946. Instead of calling for maximum production, employment, and purchasing power, the Act establishes goals of full employment and production plus increased real income, balanced growth, a balanced federal budget, and reasonable price stability. The Humphrey-Hawkins Act also requires the President to spell out in the *Economic Report* measures designed to accomplish the objectives of the Act. This must be done by January 20 of each year.

The Act, for example, set a goal of 3 percent or less unemployment among adult workers (20 years of age or older) and 4 percent unemployment for the total labor force by the end of 1983. It required, too, that the rate of inflation be reduced to at least 3 percent by that time. In achieving these goals, the Act does give some preference to full employment insofar as it states "the policies and programs designed to reduce the rate of inflation shall not impede the achievement of the goals for the reduction of unemployment." The long-term goal for reasonable price stability was to reduce the rate of inflation to zero by 1988. Subsequently, the target date for full employment was postponed until an unspecified time in the 1980s.

According to the Act, a balanced budget and balanced economic growth are to be sought after the goals concerning unemployment are reached. Moreover, the Act calls for a narrowing of the differences in unemployment rates between various categories of the unemployed.

Two major items were included in the original Humphrey-Hawkins Bill which did not survive to the final Full Employment and Balanced Growth Act of 1978. First was the concept of using the federal government as an "employer of last resort" for the unemployed if unemployment were not reduced to target levels within the 5-year period. This item would have required the federal government to provide or find jobs for those who could not find employment. The second item was the establishment of a broad and specific planning system for the U.S. economy.

UNEMPLOYMENT RATES IN THE UNITED STATES AND ELSEWHERE

Before concluding our chapter on employment, it may be enlightening to compare unemployment rates in the United States with those elsewhere in the world. In some years, the faster economic growth rates of several other nations, such as West Germany, Japan, and France, often have been compared with the slower rate of economic growth in the United States. Likewise, critics have called attention to the fact that unemployment in many countries is lower than it is in the United States. Studies in the

Table 16-7 International Comparisons of Unemployment Rates for Selected Years (Adjusted to United States Definition)

	1960	1970	1980	1984
United States	5.5%	4.9%	7.1%	7.5%
Canada	7.0	5.7	7.5	11.3
France	1.8	3.0	6.5	10.1
West Germany	0.8	0.5	2.9	7.8
Great Britain	2.2	3.0	7.0	13.0
Italy	4.3	3.5	3.9	5.6
Japan	1.7	1.2	2.0	2.8
Sweden	—	1.5	2.0	3.1
Australia	—	1.4	6.1	9.0

Source: *Statistical Abstract of the United States*, 1970 and 1986.

early 1980s revealed that after making adjustments for differences in counting procedures among the various nations, unemployment rates in the United States were still higher than in some industrial nations but not so high as in others. Recent figures for 1984 indicate that this is still true, as shown in Table 16-7.

SUMMARY

In 1986, the total population of the United States amounted to 241.5 million persons. Of this total, 180.6 million were in the noninstitutional population. Since many of these people were managing homes, attending school, or not seeking work, there were only 119.5 million in the total labor force. The total labor force is composed of all those who are working or seeking work, including the resident armed forces. After subtracting the number of persons in the resident armed forces, a civilian labor force of 117.8 million was left in the economy in 1986. Employment averaged 109.6 million and unemployment 8.2 million.

The labor force has certain characteristics, but some of these have been changing in the past few decades. The following trends in the labor force are observable: (1) a decrease in teenage employment; (2) a decrease in the number of older workers; (3) an increase in the number of women in the labor force; (4) a decrease in the percentage of unskilled workers; (5) an increase in the number and percentage of service-oriented jobs in the economy; (6) a move away from agricultural employment; (7) a rising, stable, then declining percentage of the labor force engaged in organized labor activities over the past few decades; (8) an overall increase in the size of the labor force; and (9) growth in the labor force participation rate since the early 1970s.

Although we continuously strive for full employment, the exact concept of full employment is sometimes nebulous. Most economists today seem to agree that if 5 to 6 percent or less of the labor force is unemployed, the economy for all practical purposes is in a state of full employment.

The Employment Act of 1946 declared it to be a policy of the federal government to use the means at its disposal to create conditions favorable to a high level of production, employment, and income. To implement the objectives of the Act, the Council of Economic Advisers (CEA) was created. The function of the Council is to study the economy in light of the objectives of the Employment Act and to make reports and recommendations to the President, who is required to transmit to Congress an annual *Economic Report*. The annual report and all supplementary reports are referred to the Joint Economic Committee, composed of 20 members of Congress. The function of the Joint Committee is to continue study on matters relating to the *Economic Report of the President* and to file its own report to Congress concerning the merits of the *Economic Report*.

The Full Employment and Balanced Growth Act of 1978 established specific unemployment and inflation rate goals for the U.S. economy. The Act required measures to be taken to reduce adult unemployment to 3 percent and total unemployment to 4 percent by 1983 and also to reduce the inflation rate to 3 percent by that time. These target dates were postponed, however.

It is hoped, by the time you have finished this book, that you will be able to analyze the economy well enough to anticipate the recommendations that will be made in the *Economic Report of the President* each January.

NEW TERMS AND CONCEPTS

Total labor force
Civilian labor force
Unemployed labor
 force

Employed civilian labor
 force
Labor force participation rate
Frictional unemployment

Full-employment
 unemployment rate
Unemployment
Underemployment

DISCUSSION QUESTIONS

1. Why are homemakers not included as members of the labor force? Do you think they should be?
2. Should everyone who is seeking work be classified as an unemployed member of the labor force? Explain.
3. Do you think there should be a nationwide compulsory retirement age to make more opportunities available for young people coming into the labor force?
4. Do you think that unemployed persons whose spouses are still working should be counted as unemployed as far as our national employment figures are concerned?
5. Technological development and automation displace more than 2 million workers annually. Does this mean that they all become unemployed? Explain.
6. Could the Council of Economic Advisers function better if it were responsible to Congress, or to an independent agency, rather than being part of the President's administration? Why or why not?

7. Do you think that the federal government should act as an "employer of last resort" as stated in the original Humphrey-Hawkins Bill?

8. It has been suggested that we consider the economy to be at full employment as long as job vacancies are equal to or greater than unemployment. Do you agree?

SUGGESTED READINGS

Bregger, John E. "A New Employment Statistics Review Commission." *Monthly Labor Review* (March, 1977).

Economic Report of the President. Washington, DC: U.S. Government Printing Office, annually.

Employment and Training Report of the President. Washington, DC: U.S. Government Printing Office, annually.

Hailstones, Thomas J., and Frank V. Mastrianna. *Contemporary Economic Problems and Issues*, 8th ed. Cincinnati: South-Western Publishing Co., 1988. Chapter 1.

Shishkin, Julius. "The Labor Market: Matching Up the Statistics and the Realities." *Challenge* (January/February, 1978).

Sorrentino, Constance. "Youth Unemployment: An International Perspective." *Monthly Labor Review* (July, 1981).

Stein, Herbert. "Internal and External Functions of the CEA (Council of Economic Advisers)." *Monthly Labor Review* (March, 1974).

U.S. Department of Labor. "Explanatory Note (for the Unemployment Survey)." *News* (February, 1986).

Weiner, Stuart. "The Natural Rate of Unemployment: Concepts and Issues." *Economic Review*. Federal Reserve Bank of Kansas City (January, 1986).

17
BUSINESS CYCLES

■

One of the striking features of our national income is its dynamism. It does not grow at a steady rate. Sometimes it expands rapidly; at other times it shows only a modest increase or even a decrease. In spite of its overall growth in recent years, it has in the past declined at a rate that was disastrous to the welfare of the country. Fluctuations have been characteristic of the national economy since the early days of our nation.

Why does the economy not continuously produce income at full capacity, with jobs for all who want to work? What is implied by balance, or equilibrium, in the national income, especially with full employment? What are the characteristic features of the so-called business cycle? Can these fluctuations be eliminated by the concerted action of business and government?

Most of us would agree that it would be great to have a national income as large as possible, one that continued to grow as the population increased, without serious fluctuations or adverse side effects, and with jobs for all. As stated by the late President Johnson in one of his last *Economic Reports:*

We seek a free and growing economy which offers productive employment to all who are willing and able to work, generates steady and rapid growth in productivity—the ultimate source of higher living standards—while providing the new skills and jobs needed for displaced workers, and permits every American to produce and to earn to the full measure of his basic capacities.

Much of this sentiment was incorporated into the Full Employment and Balanced Growth Act of 1978, which emphasized not only the national goal of full employment and production, but also the goals of *increased* real income and balanced growth.

ACTUAL VERSUS POTENTIAL OUTPUT

The importance of maximizing income and output is best realized when the losses from operating at less than full capacity are considered. Production losses were staggering during the Great Depression of the 1930s.

Figure 17-1 Actual and Potential Real GNP (Billions of 1982 dollars)

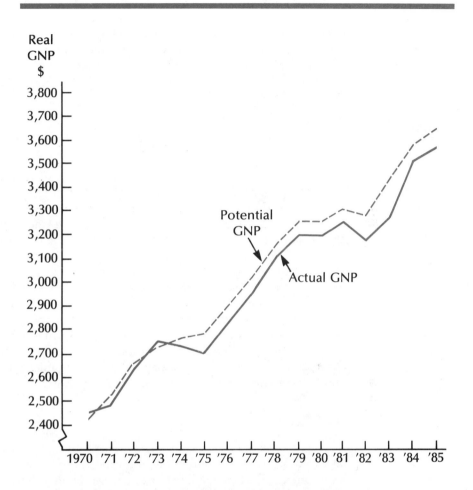

Source: Based on data from *Economic Report of the President*, 1987.

Even in the relative prosperity of the past few decades much has been lost in the way of production and employment as a result of minor depressions or recessions and the failure of the economy to operate at full capacity. Figure 17-1 shows not only the sizable drops in production during the recessions of 1974–1975 and 1982, but also substantial underproduction during the 1970s and 1980s. During this period the average annual increase in productivity per work-hour of U.S. labor slowed markedly from 3 percent to about 2 percent.

A rough estimate places the loss of output during the 1970–1985 period, as a result of the failure to maintain full employment, in excess of $1 trillion in constant 1982 dollars. It is estimated that the loss resulting from the 1982 recession was about $300 billion. Using the potential real growth GNP growth rate (3 percent annually) for the 1970–1985 period would show a much larger production and income loss than that shown in Figure 17-1. In 1985, for example, the potential real GNP gap would be $150 billion, in 1982 constant dollars, instead of the approximately $75 billion shown in the figure.

THE BUSINESS CYCLE

National income is subject to various types of disturbance, but the most pronounced is the business cycle. What is called a **business cycle** may be considered a process of cumulative change over a time span longer than a year. During the cycle all parts of the economy display marked changes in activity as they move through periods usually called prosperity, recession, depression, and recovery. Production, prices, incomes, and employment activities all show characteristic changes during the cycle; in fact, there is no part of the economy that is not affected in some way. Extensive studies have shown that these cyclical fluctuations are found in economies throughout the world. Because of the pervasive character of business cycles and their persistence during many years, it has been assumed that they inevitably accompany all complex modern economies, although they appear most clearly in those economies where free markets and private enterprise prevail.

Types and Length of Cycles

A study of past economic data reveals that there have been many and varied business fluctuations in our economy. Some cycles have been long, others short. Some have been severe, while others have been mild. An analysis of the historical data reveals that business fluctuations may be classified as (1) minor cycles or (2) major cycles.

Minor cycles are those of relatively mild intensity in which the fluctuations are noticeable but not severe. They are shorter but more numerous than major cycles. Evidence seems to indicate that minor cycles occur every 3 to 4 years. In fact, some specific measurements show the average length of the minor cycle in the United States to be 47.6 months, with 26.2 months spent in the expansion stage of the cycle and 21.4 months in the contraction phase of the cycle. Since the end of World War II, we have experienced eight downswings in the economy, in 1949, 1953–1954, 1958, 1960–1961, 1970, 1974–1975, 1980, and 1982. The 1982 recession was the deepest and most prolonged downswing since the Great Depression of the 1930s.

Major cycles are those that show a wide fluctuation in business activity. They are usually characterized by serious depressions. This means widespread unemployment, lower income, and low profits or losses in many cases. Business cycle data indicate that major cycles occur about every 10 years. Since World War II, however, we have experienced no major cycle. This may be due to our use of modern monetary, fiscal, and other measures and our built-in economic stimulus in the form of large-scale defense outlays.

Other types of cycles or fluctuations, such as long-wave (of 50–60 years duration) building cycles, commodity price fluctuations, and stock market price fluctuations, have been revealed by research and economic analysis. In fact, cycles have a certain degree of ubiquity in the study of all aspects of economic activity.

Phases and Measurement of the Cycle

Today business cycles are considered to have four distinct phases: prosperity, recession, depression, and recovery. **Prosperity** exists whenever there is an overall high level of economic activity. A **recession** occurs whenever there is a noticeable drop in the level of business activity. **Depression** is the period in which the level of business activity has dropped as far as it is going to drop in a particular cycle. **Recovery** occurs when the level of business activity begins to rise.

The duration or intensity of any of the four phases has little to do with their definition; that is, a business cycle consists of a series of changes that includes all four phases whether the trough is as deep as we experienced in the 1930s or as slight as we experienced in 1980. The four phases of the business cycle are shown in Figure 17-2.

It has become customary, however, for much of the public and even business analysts to refer to a mild depression as a business recession. In answer to whether a recession took place in the economy in the early part of 1967, the National Bureau of Economic Research (NBER) defined a recession as a period in which the real GNP declines in two consecutive quarters. This in effect changed the conventional meaning of recession. However, it left us without a specific definition of a depression. Consequently, there was much discussion in 1974 and 1975 about whether the economy, which declined in each quarter of 1974 and in the first quarter of 1975, was experiencing a recession or suffering a depression. Since production and employment were down considerably, some individuals began referring to the period as one of depression.

Some analysts consider the combined downswings of 1980 and 1982, often referred to as a double-dip recession, as a depression. This was especially so when unemployment exceeded 10 percent, the use of industrial capacity fell below 70 percent, and we had a record number of bankruptcies.

Although we have more or less definite measurements of the length

Figure 17-2 Phases of the Business Cycle

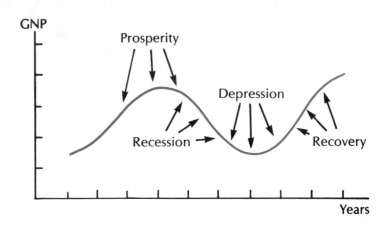

of the total cycle and even the length of the expansion and contraction periods of the average cycle, it is difficult to obtain a conclusive measurement of the average length of each of the four phases of the cycle. The main difficulty of such a measurement stems from the fact that there is no agreement on exactly when we leave one phase of the cycle and go into another.

It is a bit easier to measure the amplitude of a business fluctuation. In measuring the business cycle, however, it is necessary to make allowances for any forces affecting business fluctuations other than those that are inherent in the business cycle. The level of business activity at any time is affected by four forces or types of economic change: (1) the trend, (2) seasonal variations, (3) irregular fluctuations, and (4) cyclical fluctuations.

The **trend** is the directional movement of the economy over an extended period of time such as 20–30 years. It represents the long-run average change (growth or decline) in the economy. **Seasonal variations** are recurring fluctuations in business activity during a given period, usually 1 year. The cause of this fluctuation may be natural or artificial. We produce more farm commodities, for example, in the summer than we do in the winter because of a natural cause, the weather. On the other hand, department store sales increase substantially during November and December due to our custom of giving Christmas presents.

Irregular or **random fluctuations** in business activity result from some unexpected or unusual event. Such factors as a serious flood, plague, pestilence, or drought can affect the economy as a whole or affect certain areas in the economy. **Cyclical fluctuations** are changes in the level of business activity that come about regardless of the trend, seasonal, or

Figure 17-3   Measurements of Business Activity

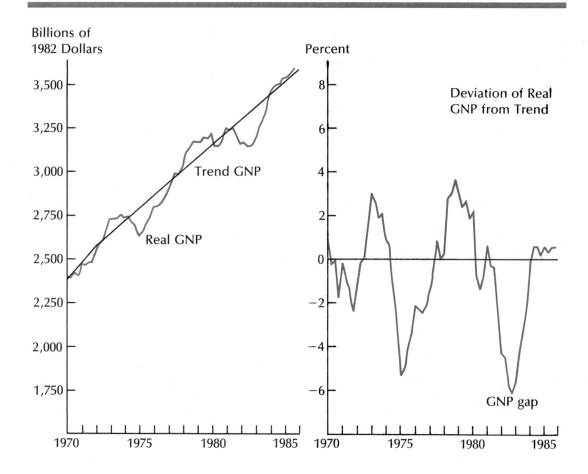

Source: U.S. Department of Commerce, Bureau of Economic Analysis.

irregular forces. Business cycles may occur because of inherent forces in the economy. They may be influenced, however, to a considerable degree by external forces, such as wars, changes in the monetary system, and changes in population.

The intensity of the cycle may be determined by measuring the movement of the seasonally adjusted business activity above and below the trend line. If the actual business data are corrected for seasonal fluctuations and for any possible irregular forces, the actual data can then be compared with the trend line simply by measuring the difference between the actual data and trend line values. In Figure 17-3, for example, the seasonally adjusted business activity is shown by the fluctuating line. The magnitude of the cycle at any point is measured by the difference between the value of the actual data and the trend line value. The value can be calculated also in percentage terms, as shown in the right half of the figure.

Pattern of the Cycle

Although some business cycles are short and others long, some fluctuations intense and others mild, a definite pattern of the cycle appears to exist. Once a downturn has started, there is a cumulative action among several elements in the economy that tends to augment the downswing. During the downswing, however, forces eventually come into play to arrest the contraction and to start an upward movement. Once this upward motion begins, reactions of individuals and businesses are such that the upswing is augmented. During prosperity, however, forces build up that eventually effect a downturn.

The elements or forces operating to bring about business cycles are of two kinds—internal and external. The internal forces, or **endogenous forces**, are those elements within the very sphere of business activity itself. They include such items as production, income, demand, credit, interest rates, and inventories. The external forces, or **exogenous forces**, are those elements usually considered as being outside the normal scope of business activity. They include such elements as population growth, wars, basic changes in the nation's currency, national economic policies, floods, droughts, and other catastrophes that have a pronounced effect on business activity. We will first analyze the endogenous forces. To see how the relationships among the various elements change and how these changes bring about oscillation of business activity, let us look at each phase of the cycle.

DEPRESSION

In addition to an adverse economic effect, depression may have serious social and political consequences. There is naturally more public concern about a serious depression than there is about a mild depression, but unemployed individuals and bankrupt firms are involved regardless of whether the depression is serious or mild.

Cost-Price Relationship

During a depression, production, employment, and income are at a low ebb compared with their respective status during prosperity. If income is low, the demand for consumer goods is low; and a low demand in a period of ample supply generally forces prices down or restrains price increases. Cost, too, is relatively low because unemployed labor, resources, and capacity are bidding against each other for jobs, sales, and rent, respectively. Because sales are off and prices generally are down, profits are low during a depression. This means low investments, because business-people do not invest in new ventures or add to existing capacity unless they anticipate profits.

Inventory Adjustment and Borrowing

Although in the early phases of a depression inventories may be rather high because of previous inventory build-up, they dwindle to a low position as retailers supply goods out of inventory and cut orders from producers. Since production is at a low level, businesses have little need for borrowing for capital expansion. With the decline in commercial loans, bank reserves should be relatively high. Thus, we have a situation in which the banks have the ability to expand credit, but businesses are reluctant to borrow because profit expectations are dim. In addition, many firms that would like to borrow for refinancing are poor risks; and the banks are not too eager to accommodate them. Banks tend to become more selective during depressions. In total, business loans fall off substantially. This tends to make excess reserves relatively high; and with the excess reserve high and demand for loans low, the normal reaction is to force interest rates down.

Liquidity Preference and Saving

During the contraction phase of the cycle when prices are declining, the value of money rises. Individuals and businesses, if possible, convert their idle assets into money. Therefore, we have a strong liquidity preference during depressions.

As incomes are lowered, on the other hand, the average worker is generally required to spend a larger portion, if not all, of his or her income to provide the basic necessities and conveniences of life. Thus, our propensity to consume increases while our propensity to save decreases accordingly. Keep in mind, however, that although we are spending a larger percentage of our income, the total amount of spending on consumption is lower than it was during the previous prosperity period.

Replacement Demand

When we are not producing at full capacity, there is less need to replace worn-out machinery and equipment. Instead of replacing depreciated machinery, a firm can merely use other machinery that has not been in use. Only when it is really necessary, or when production starts picking up, will the average firm replace its machinery and equipment as quickly as it depreciates. Although some individuals and firms claim that a depression is the ideal time to replace machinery and equipment because of the low prices, relatively few firms follow this policy. The lack of capital funds, the uncertainty of the future, and the fear of obsolescence discourage the pursuit of such a policy. Thus, the tendency of firms not to replace their worn machinery and equipment during a depression brings about sizable reductions in the production of such items.

Consumers, too, have a tendency to repair and to patch up their durable goods instead of replacing them. People are inclined to get a new set of tires and a tune-up and to keep the old car instead of trading it in for a new one. We are more inclined to get our shoes resoled rather than buy new ones, repair our appliances, put off buying a new home, and, in general, postpone our purchases of durable goods and other items that we can do without during a depression period.

Psychological Forces

All this, of course, has a tendency to keep the demand for capital goods and durable consumer goods low. Total production is low and results in idle capacity throughout the economy. With production, employment, income, prices, and profits low, a pessimistic attitude undoubtedly prevails. Businesspeople do not invest under such conditions, and their reluctance to invest has a deflationary or contracting effect on the economy. Only when the businessperson thinks that conditions are going to improve will investments be made. Thus, this pessimistic outlook has an adverse effect on the economy. Likewise, the consumer decreases spending. When workers are no longer receiving overtime pay, when some workers are put on a short workweek, or when layoffs begin to appear in the workplace, people are more cautious about spending money and cut down on installment buying. Thus, the actions of businesses and individuals during a depression have a tendency to hold down the total demand for goods and services and make the recovery to prosperity more difficult.

RECOVERY

Although corrective and expanding forces may be at work, their effect may be a bit slow as far as the unemployed individual and the unprofitable firm are concerned. Nevertheless, recovery always comes sooner or later.

Starters

What leads us from the road of depression to that of prosperity? It may be some exogenous force such as population increase, innovations, war, or the use of monetary or fiscal policy. Even without such external factors, however, the relationship of certain of the basic elements of the business cycle may eventually shift to a more favorable position and initiate an upward movement in the economy. Five changes that frequently occur may start the recovery.

Cost-Price Relationship.   After a depression has existed for a period of time, a better cost-price relationship develops. Statistical evidence shows that costs generally lag behind prices in their movements during the cycle. On a downturn, prices fall first and at a more rapid rate than costs. Prices also reach their low point before costs do, often while costs are still dropping. Eventually costs dip lower than prices, and it again becomes profitable for businesses to produce certain goods that may not have been yielding a profit. Prices frequently begin to rise sooner and faster than costs. Thus, on the upward swing of the cycle the margin between price and cost is widened, resulting in increased profits and additional investments.

In a freely competitive economy, during a depression unemployed workers bid against each other for jobs; firms with decreasing profits compete against each other for sales; and landholders compete against each other for rents. The total effect reduces the costs of products and gradually brings cost sufficiently below prices so that firms find it profitable to operate. Firms also look for new techniques and devices to reduce cost, increase productivity, and make profits. Thus, after we have been in a depression for some period of time, a more favorable price-cost relationship develops which tends to increase productivity and reduce costs.

Inventory Adjustment.   A second factor that tends to spur production is the method of handling inventories. After we remain in a depression for a period of time, inventories become depleted. Sales demand is filled out of inventories for several months, and companies finally come to the point where inventories get so low that they have to be replaced. When inventories stabilize at lower levels, most current sales have to be satisfied indirectly by ordering goods from the producer. This may result in production increases sufficient to stimulate the economy.

Borrowing.   The accumulation of excess reserves and the downward pressure on interest rates may encourage some borrowing by businesses. A business that can make a 15 percent return by investing money in machinery, equipment, and buildings necessary to produce goods or services may defer doing so if it is necessary to pay 12 percent interest on the money borrowed for investing. However, if the interest rate were to fall to 10 percent, or less, the business might be encouraged to invest either retained earnings or borrowed money. Such investment would increase production and employment.

Replacement Demand.   Another stimulant to production may come in the capital goods area. Although firms and individuals have a tendency to postpone replacement of capital goods and durable consumer goods during a depression, they cannot do so forever. The old machinery can take only a certain amount of repair, and equipment does wear out. Furthermore, improvements in new machinery that increase productivity may make it more economical to replace old machinery. So it is also with the consumer. The family car reaches such a condition that it needs more than new tires. It may be more economical to get a new car than to make major repairs. Spending by businesses and individuals for replacement of capital goods and durable consumer goods increases demand in those areas. This leads to increased production and gives a boost to the economy.

Psychological Outlook.   The general outlook may change. While it is true that businesspeople and consumers tend to be pessimistic during a depression, most individuals realize that depressions do not last forever. Thus, after being in a period of low business activity for a number of months, people begin to look for an upturn. In fact, many individuals may decide to spend on the presumption that an upswing is just around the corner. Businesspeople also figure that they should get ready for better things, or they may figure it is about time to look at the long-run view of the economy. In either case, a decision to invest in anticipation of future improvements may occur. Such action could start or help start the economy on a move upward.

A favorable change in any of these five areas—cost-price relationship, inventories, interest rates, replacement of capital assets and durable consumer goods, and the psychological outlook—may lead to an increase in production. Sometimes the increase is insufficient to bring the economy out of the depression. In fact, we may have a short spurt in business activity only to be followed by a slackening. The pickup may be substantial, however, especially if there is a concerted move of several of the forces.

Production, Employment, and Income

Regardless of what causes it, the force that leads us out of depression is the increase in production. If production increases, employment and income will naturally increase. With higher incomes, people increase their demand. Prices remain fairly constant during the early part of the recovery, since the increase in demand is met by an increase in the supply of goods and services. However, when demand increases sufficiently, prices begin to rise. Cost, too, remains relatively low, especially during the early part of the recovery, since competitive bidding for idle materials and labor is limited because of their abundance. Profits increase as sales increase. Larger inventories are held in the expectation of higher sales. Increased profits bring about increased investment, which in turn leads to greater demand for bank loans, and excess reserves theoretically decrease. Higher bank deposits, however, often forestall the decrease of excess reserves until late in the recovery period or well into the prosperity period. As a result, interest rates rise slowly.

As incomes increase, people spend more and there is a weakening of liquidity preferences. People are inclined to spend their increased incomes because they were probably forced to do without many things during the depression period. Idle capacity tends to diminish as output increases, and if the economy picks up to any extent, the general outlook becomes more favorable. If businesses are optimistic and think that business conditions are going to improve, they are inclined to invest in machinery, equipment, buildings, and materials. As they do this, production, employment, income, and demand increase. Likewise, consumers increase their spending. In fact, with a rosy outlook they will probably go into debt to obtain the goods and services they desire. Thus, the economy will get an added boost and the recovery is on its way.

PROSPERITY

Prosperity generally has favorable social and political consequences as well as a good economic effect on society, especially if it is high-level prosperity with full employment. Prosperity, however, is not all milk and honey. Certain ill effects, such as inflation, shortages of goods, and reckless spending, may develop.

Cost-Price Relationship

As production, employment, and incomes begin to rise, the interactions of the endogenous forces are such that they work congruously to augment the upswing. Although prices, for example, remain steady in the early part of the recovery, they rise if the upswing continues. With increased production the economy eventually reaches the "bottleneck" stage, a period in which some goods are relatively scarce and marginal and higher-cost facilities are pressed into service. This brings about an upward price movement. Such increases often trigger a general rise in prices. As explained previously, prices increase faster than do costs. During an upswing, this relationship results in higher profits since, in addition to greater sales, large profit margins exist. This brings about further incentives for investment. This investment is augmented by the multiplier-and-accelerator effect, and it can further activate the upswing.

Inventory Adjustment

The build-up of inventories also plays an important role in this phase of the business cycle. Most producers and merchants keep inventories at a certain ratio to sales. Therefore, when sales increase, the size of inventories increases. This means that production must increase not only to satisfy the greater demand by consumers but also to build up inventories.

In addition to the normal build-up to keep the inventory in proper ratio to sales, a second force, namely the price factor, accelerates inventory accumulation. Many businesspeople are very astute. They know how to make profits, and they know that if they build up inventories at low costs, profits are magnified as prices increase. Therefore, whenever price increases are anticipated, there is a normal reaction that induces the average merchant to build up inventories to the extent of increasing the ratio of inventory to sales.

When this action is multiplied by the hundreds of thousands of producers, wholesalers, and retailers who keep inventories, it can be seen how production would increase considerably beyond the actual consumer demand. This inventory build-up leads to a further increase in employment, income, and profits.

Replacement Demand

In addition to the inventory accumulation that augments the upswing, there is a tendency to replace worn-out assets at an accelerated pace and to add new assets to meet the expected expansion of business, especially as the economy begins to approach the stage of full capacity. This replacement becomes all the more feasible when interest rates are still low. Since the interest rates are "sticky," there is an inclination to borrow before interest rates begin to rise. This increased investment, through the multiplier and the accelerator effects, adds to total income, and the cumulative action of the endogenous factors can push the economy up to a level of full employment.

Liquidity Preference and Saving

During prosperity the levels of production, employment, and income are high, and high income means a large demand. As demand continues to increase, prices rise, especially when we reach the stage of full employment where we can no longer increase supply fast enough to satisfy demand. Costs continue upward because of the competitive bidding for labor, resources, and capacity. Inventories, investments, and the demand for loans reach new levels. The decrease in excess reserves and the shortage of loanable funds force the interest rates upward. Liquidity preference decreases as prices begin to rise, giving a further impetus to the upswing. As prices rise, the value of money begins to decrease. Thus, many individuals and firms endeavor to convert their money assets into property and other real goods. This, in turn, increases the total demand for goods and services and adds to the inflationary pressures of the economy.

An increase in the marginal propensity to save (decrease in the marginal propensity to consume) appears, but it is usually not sufficient to stem the tide of the upswing in the economy. When the general outlook is optimistic, as it usually is during the prosperity period, further encouragement is given to consumption and investment in the economy. The level of economic activity may increase until we reach the stage of full employment. At that time further increases in demand, investment, loans, and such can lead only to inflation.

RECESSION

Prosperity does not last forever. Downswings are certain to occur. Exactly when or to what extent is not easy to predict. Nevertheless, individuals and firms can prepare for such emergencies. Once a recession has commenced, it may lead to a mild or serious depression depending on the circumstances existing in the economy at that particular time.

Cost-Price Relationship

During prosperity periods, the relationships between the endogenous factors eventually change in such a manner that they bring about a downturn in the economy. While production, employment, and income are at their peak, some tapering off in consumer demand may appear. Sometimes the mere fact that demand begins to increase at a decreasing rate can cause difficulty. One element bringing about a slackening of demand is the fact that the marginal propensity to consume declines as incomes increase. Consumer resistance eventually brings a halt or slowdown to price increases, and the price level stabilizes at some point. Costs continue to increase even during prosperity as businesses attempt to increase output by bidding against each other for the relatively scarce labor, resources, and capacity. The rising costs gradually squeeze out some of the profits, which tends to make businesses a bit more cautious about investment.

Inventory Adjustment

When demand slackens and prices stabilize, producers, wholesalers, and retailers begin to reduce excess inventory. Just as we have an inventory build-up adding to the recovery, we can have the reverse situation during a recession.

Furthermore, if prices stabilize or begin to fall, the wholesaler attempts to deplete any excess inventory being carried. Therefore, goods are supplied out of inventory rather than being ordered from the producer. In fact, if the price level is dropping, the wholesaler not only reduces excess stock but undoubtedly reduces the ratio of inventory to sales. As merchants fill more and more orders out of inventory, an adverse effect on production takes place. This in turn decreases employment and income and can precipitate a downswing in our economy.

According to some economists, inventory accumulation and depletion play a major role in the cause of business cycles. Frequently cycles are characterized by this phenomenon. Inventory depletion, for example, contributed heavily to the slowdown in the economy in the 1974–1975 recession. It likewise contributed substantially to the recessions of 1980 and 1982.

Replacement Demand

Reduced employment and income during a recession bring about a further reduction in demand. Profits diminish and investment falls off, especially with high interest rates. Businesses find it unnecessary to replace capital assets that wear out if there is no use for such machinery and equipment. Idle capacity begins to appear as production schedules are cut back. Consumers, likewise, begin postponing the purchase of durable goods. The more difficult it becomes to repay, the more reluctant individuals are to extend or renew credit. Prices eventually begin to fall. This causes further postponement of purchases as consumers hold off in anticipation of further price cuts. Price declines bring a further reduction in profits, which means less investment. This in turn further reduces production, employment, and income.

Liquidity Preference and Saving

Falling prices strengthen the liquidity preference as the value of money increases. The attempt to convert goods into money increases the supply of assets offered at a time when demand is low. This has a deflationary effect. The propensity to save, however, declines with the decrease in incomes. Although individuals and families may desire to save even more than they had in the past, they may be unable to do so because of reduced income or unemployment.

Psychological Outlook

In general, the declining production, employment, income, profits, demand, and prices become cumulative. This results in a reduction in investment. The reduction in investment and consumer spending is accompanied by a reverse multiplier effect, and the accelerator may approach zero. Under such conditions, the general outlook may become pessimistic, and this has an adverse psychological effect on both investors and consumers.

As the recession gets under way, the changing relationships of the endogenous elements are such that they tend to further perpetuate the downswing. The recession continues until it reaches bottom. Somewhere along the way the stage of depression is reached. Whether the depression is severe or mild, the business cycle has been completed. The economy has moved through the four phases of the cycle: depression, recovery, prosperity, and recession. Once in the depression, it again requires a change in the relationships of the endogenous elements to bring about an upswing in business activity. The economy then moves through another cycle, maybe of greater or lesser intensity, maybe of shorter or longer duration. The pattern is similar in each cycle, although the characteristics of each may differ somewhat in regard to cause, amplitude, and duration.

FACTORS THAT MAY MODIFY THE BUSINESS CYCLE

The duration and the intensity of these fluctuations can be modified by the use of monetary, fiscal, and psychological measures, as we shall see later. In fact, it is because we know the pattern so well that action can be taken to avoid the two extremes of the cycle; widespread unemployment and runaway inflation.

External forces also affect the level of economic activity and often generate business fluctuations. For example, a war has a profound effect on the level of economic activity. The requirements for war and defense material necessitate increased production and employment. Additional attempts to increase production may lead to inflation unless definite measures such as material and wage and price controls are utilized to combat rising prices.

Similar impetus may come to the economy from population growth, changes in the money supply, or government deficit spending. On the other hand, the termination of a war can have a depressing effect on the economy as production is cut back, unless there is a substantial increase in consumer demand and private investment to offset the decrease in defense spending. Adverse effects can also result from serious catastrophes that force a reduction in production and income.

The typical pattern of the business cycle also is modified to the extent that we do not have perfect competition in the economy. For example, labor unions may be forceful enough to prevent wages from declining during a recessionary period. Oligopolies may push prices up sooner than expected or prevent them from falling in a recession. Government regulations may alter the normal movement of the interest rates.

The fact that all endogenous elements may not move or act in precisely the fashion described is no indication that the pattern is invalid. In any particular cycle one or more of the elements may act contrary to their usual movement. But generally a sufficient number of them react in the prescribed manner and with ample strength to overcome any countervailing force of a few maverick elements. This was the case in the recent recessions of 1980 and 1982, when, because of institutional factors, the general price level continued to rise instead of declining.

Some economists and government officials in the early 1960s suggested that business cycles were obsolete. They claimed that through the use of various monetary, fiscal, and other economic measures we were able to prevent wide oscillations in production, employment, and income. It is true that our measures and power to stabilize the level of economic activity and to keep it growing at a satisfactory rate of expansion have improved over the years. The underlying need for the use of these stabilizing measures, however, is the fact that in a free economy fluctuations do occur. Stabilization measures do not eliminate the business cycle but merely modify its impact or effects. Furthermore, the occurrence of recessions, nagging unemployment, full employment, inflation, sluggishness, and stagflation in the economy, all in the past 20 years, certainly indicate that business cycles are still with us.

BUSINESS CYCLE INDICATORS

Changes in business activity are reflected in different areas or sectors of the economy. In many cases we have statistics and indexes indicating the changes that are taking place. Although some indexes measure changes in particular activities in the economy, they are also representative of activity in the economy as a whole. In other cases we do have some measures of composite types of economic activity that pervade the economy. Therefore, they give a good reflection of the general status of the economy. Some business cycle analysts have combined a number of different indicators in an effort to develop a general indicator for the entire economy. For purposes of analyzing business cycles, statistical indicators are usually divided into three types: representative indicators, composite indicators, and general business indicators.

Representative Indicators

Although representative indicators are usually indexes that measure changes in a particular area of business activity, those that measure an essential area of business activity will reflect to some degree what is happening to the economy as a whole. The most reliable of these include the index of iron and steel production, bank clearings or bank debits, railway carloadings, and electric power output.

Other representative indicators include paperboard production, bituminous coal production, and the index of employment want ads. Many others have been used or suggested at various times, such as automobile production, agricultural output, and stock market prices, but these are frequently erratic.

Composite Indicators

Composite indicators are usually indexes that measure some type of activity that is widespread in the economy. Therefore, they are sure to give a good indication of the general level of business activity. Among the most widely used composite indicators are the index of factory employment, the index of payrolls, the Federal Reserve Board Index of Industrial Production, and the gross national product.

General Business Indicators

Most general business indicators combine a series of different indexes into one general index of business activity. Typical of these indexes are the following.

Index of American Business Activity.   This index, published by the Ameri-Trust Company, compiles several different indexes and measurements to cover the period from 1790 to the present. The data are expressed in deviations from the norm or trend line.

Business Week **Index.**   This index is compiled and published weekly in graphic and tabular form in *Business Week*. It reflects the combined movements of several individual series, including production of lumber, coal, paper, raw steel, automobiles, electric power, crude oil, paperboard, and railroad carloadings. The movements of the *Business Week* Index are shown in Figure 17-4. The recession of 1982 is readily observable from the data shown in Figure 17-5.

Statistical Indicators of Business Cycle Changes.   These indicators, published by the Statistical Indicator Associates, North Egremont, Massachusetts, comprise a total of 25 indicators. They include 3 separate groups: the **leading indicators**, which are composed of 12 indexes whose upward and downward turning points generally precede the peaks and troughs of general business activity; the **roughly coincident indicators**, a group of 6 other indexes whose turning points usually correspond to the peaks and troughs of general business activity; and the **lagging indicators**, made up of 7 indexes whose turning points occur after the turning points for the general level of business activity have been reached.

Data for each of the 25 indicators are shown in tables and graphs released weekly and/or monthly. The relationship of the leaders to the coincident and lagging indicators can be observed in Figure 17-5. Note that the leaders turn downward and upward before the coincident and lagging indicators. The leading indicators, as well as the coincident indicators, gave an early warning of the slowdowns that occurred in 1980 and 1982. The current status of these indicators together with their interpretation and forecast of business conditions is maintained and published by the Statistical Indicator Associates.

Business Conditions Digest.   This set of indicators published by the Department of Commerce contains graphs, charts, and tables for more than 100 National Bureau of Economic Research (NBER) business cycle indicator

Figure 17-4 *Business Week* Index

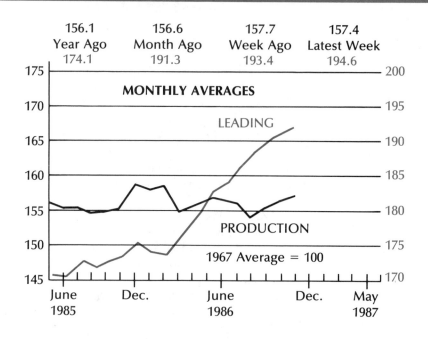

156.1	156.6	157.7	157.4
Year Ago	Month Ago	Week Ago	Latest Week
174.1	191.3	193.4	194.6

Source: Reprinted from the January 5, 1987 issue of *Business Week* by special permission, © 1986 by McGraw-Hill, Inc.

series, which are the source of those used by the Statistical Indicator Associates. The series are presented in convenient form for analysis and interpretation by specialists in business cycle analysis, but the Department of Commerce makes no attempt to interpret them or to make business forecasts.

By following the business cycle indicators closely a business cycle analyst or a business executive may be able to anticipate pending changes in the level of business activity. With this knowledge they may try to make proper adjustments in production schedules, employment, inventories, and financing to compensate for expected changes in business activity.

CAUSES OF THE BUSINESS CYCLE

Business cycles are rather complex phenomena, and many forces are active in changing the level of business activity. During the past 50 years there have been numerous theories offered for the explanation of business fluctuations. To date there is no one theory that completely and satisfacto-

Figure 17-5 Statistical Indicators

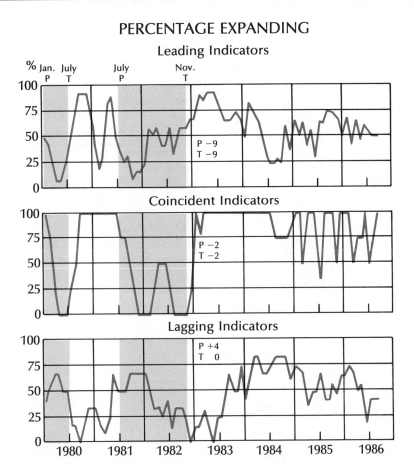

PERCENTAGE EXPANDING

Average leads (−) and lags (+) at peaks (P) and troughs (T) shown for recent cycles.

Source: *Statistical Indicator Reports* (October 22, 1986), North Egremont, MA.

rily explains the cause of business cycles. Nevertheless, a study of the various theories permits a better understanding of the possible causes of cycles and a clearer understanding of the complexities involved in their analysis. Although there are disagreements among the theories, frequently the differences are only a matter of emphasis. At other times it is obvious that one theory may be more applicable to a particular situation than is some other theory. At times a cycle may reflect some elements of several theories. For this reason it is worthwhile to be acquainted with the major theories. For the sake of simplicity we can classify these theories into four major catgories: real or physical causes, psychological causes, monetary causes, and spending and saving causes.

Real or Physical Causes

A traditional explanation of the cause of the cycle is the **innovation theory**. According to this theory, business cycles are caused by innovations in the form of new products, new methods, new machines, or new techniques.

Innovation leads to increased production, employment, and income in the economy. As businesspeople borrow to finance innovations, they set up new factories, buy raw materials, and hire workers. The increased income resulting from their spending, of course, increases the total demand in the economy. If their ventures are profitable, other investors will seek to imitate them. But as additional firms begin and continue to produce, a point of overexpansion is eventually reached. The reaction to this overexpansion brings about a contraction in the form of declining production, employment, and income. It is contended that the decline will be of a lesser degree than the expansion, and thus there will be a net gain in activity in the economy as a result of the innovation.

The intensity and duration of the cycle depend on the nature of the innovation. A simple innovation will result in a short, mild cycle. A series of innovations may occur in such an integrated manner, however, that the cycle could be more pronounced and continue over a longer period. Major innovations, such as the rise of the corporate form of business enterprise, the development of the steamboat, the perfection and use of electric power and the automobile, and the development of computers produced increased business activity on a larger scale.

Early in this century, **agricultural theories** of the business cycle were very popular. They tried to relate the general level of business activity to the weather, which affected the volume of agricultural output, which in turn had a definite effect on the level of business activity. Even though the proportion of agricultural production in the gross national product has declined dramatically, the volume of farm output today can influence the level of business activity to some extent. In short, a larger volume of agricultural output will require more labor and equipment to harvest and handle the crop, more transportation facilities, increased storage facilities, and an increased amount of credit to finance these operations. Such activity should give an impetus to the total economy.

A third important real cause of the business cycle is manifest in the **accelerator theory**. According to this theory, an increase in the demand for consumer goods may lead to a greater than proportional increase in the demand for capital goods. On the other hand, as consumer demand stabilizes or slackens, the firm will not require any additional machines. In such a case, its demand for machines will decrease in greater proportion than the change in consumer demand. (You will recall that we discussed the accelerator at length in Chapter 14.)

A similar phenomenon exists in the durable consumer goods industries and the handling of business inventories. It is for this reason that the fluctuations in the production of capital and durable consumer goods are of greater intensity than are the fluctuations for the economy as a whole.

Psychological Causes

Although the psychological theory is seldom offered as a complete or independent explanation of the cause of business cycles, it is incorporated in some way in nearly every other theory suggested. In brief, the psychological theory holds that when investors and consumers react according to some belief about future conditions, their actions tend to cause such a psychological outlook to become a reality. If investors think that conditions in the immediate future are going to be good, for example, they will increase their investment in machinery, equipment, and buildings in an effort to increase their total output and make more profit. Likewise, consumers who foresee good times ahead will spend money more readily and perhaps seek additional credit to increase their spending power. Such actions will tend to give a boost to the level of economic activity.

If the investors, on the other hand, expect sales and prices to be lower in the future, they will slacken their investments, and businesspeople will allow their inventories to dwindle and will be cautious about hiring additional workers. Also, if consumers observe that jobs are difficult to obtain, that overtime is no longer available, and that some workers in the plant are being laid off or are on a short workweek, they may be a bit pessimistic about the immediate future. In such a case consumers may limit spending, may be cautious about taking on new debt, and may even try to save for a possible layoff. The actions of both the investors and the consumers will tend to bring about a slowdown in the economy.

Furthermore, the psychological theory holds that the actions of some business leaders can influence other businesspeople and consumers to feel the same way. If our business leaders exude optimism and back it up with actual investments, this may influence the thinking of smaller businesses about the prospects of the economy. If these smaller businesses follow suit with increased investment, this will add a fillip to the economy.

Also, competition exerts a potent force on the economy in a psychological manner. Several firms competing for trade in a given area may misjudge their respective shares of the market. If they are optimistic, they may overestimate their individual shares. For a time there will be a substantial increase in business activity, but as the grim realities of the marketplace unfold, some or all firms may have to retrench on production. This, in turn, means a cutback in the demand for materials, labor, credit, and capital. In such a case a decline in the general level of business activity will set in.

In the 1970s the **theory of rational expectations** emerged as an explanation of changes taking place in the economy. It is based on the belief that businesses and individuals act, or react, according to what they perceive is going to happen in the economy based on past experience. The theory further contends that often expected results of federal government anticyclical policies and measures are discounted or offset by the actions of businesses and individuals. The theory of rational expectations will be considered more fully in Chapter 21.

Monetary Causes

Most monetary theories are based on the premise that the banking system in a typical industrial economy provides an elastic money supply through the use of bank credit. According to the monetary theory, the free and easy expansion of bank credit permits an overexpansion of investment. The use of bank credit modifies the forces exerting pressure on the interest rates. As a result, interest rates do not rise quickly, and frequently more investment takes place than would take place in the absence of bank credit. Eventually a position is reached in which the economy has excess productive capacity and abundant inventories. Readjustment comes about as businesspeople slacken their investment, prices begin to fall, production schedules are cut back, unemployment increases, and a recession commences. Retraction of credit by the banks during this period further augments the downswing.

Monetary theorists maintain that to eliminate the business cycle it is necessary to eliminate bank credit. The banks, on the other hand, maintain that they do not cause business cycles, since they do not force loans upon anyone, and that they merely service the business community when it needs money. Though complete elimination of bank credit might eliminate the cycle, it might also eliminate some of the healthy expansion and growth in the economy brought on by the use of bank credit.

Spending and Saving Causes

The spending and saving theories are of two broad categories. The first are the **underconsumption theories**. Some underconsumption theories hold that the economy does not distribute enough income among the factors of production to permit the purchase of the total goods and services produced by the economy. The more widely accepted theory, however, is that the economy does distribute enough purchasing power to buy the total goods and services produced but that all the income or purchasing power is not used. Hence, some goods will be produced and not sold. As a consequence, total production will be reduced, and this in turn reduces employment and income.

Some of the leading underconsumption theorists maintain that the basic problem is the unequal distribution of income in modern society.

The remedy suggested to eliminate or modify business cycles is the lessening of that inequality. This they say can be accomplished to some degree by the use of steeply progressive income taxes, more privately and federally sponsored income maintenance programs, the strengthening of labor unions, regulation of monopolistic pricing, and an increase of social ownership of certain industries. It is interesting to note that the first four of these suggestions particularly are to some extent present in our economy today.

The other important spending and saving theory is that of underinvestment. The **underinvestment theory** holds that income in the economy is equal to total production and that, to clear all goods off the market, spending equivalent to current income must take place. Since spending on consumption is less than the total income, however, the difference must be made up in the form of investment, or spending on machinery, equipment, and buildings. Whenever investment spending is equal to the gap between income and consumer spending, the economy will be in a stable position. But whenever investment spending is insufficient to fill the gap between consumer spending and total income, surpluses will exist in the markets. This will initiate a downswing in the economy. If for some reason investment spending is more than sufficient to fill the gap between consumer spending and total income, the total demand for goods and services will be greater than the total output, and it will tend to increase the level of business activity. Thus, business cycles are caused by variations in investment. The cycle can be modified or eliminated, therefore, by maintaining an adequate amount of investment. As we saw in Chapter 15, this is essentially the crux of the modern income-expenditure analysis.

SUMMARY

Unfortunately our economy cannot always be in a position of full employment and prosperity. There are many disturbing forces that cause changes in business activity. These forces include the trend, seasonal variations, irregular fluctuations, and the business cycle. The most dynamic of these is the business cycle.

Business cycles may be classified as either major or minor. The minor cycle occurs every 3 to 4 years and the major cycle approximately every 10 years. Business cycles are measured as fluctuations above and below the trend line. The cycle is the result of a complex series of interrelated, cumulative changes in business activity that sometimes lead to prosperity and sometimes to recession and depression. Recessions and depressions can be translated into millions of unemployed and a loss of billions of dollars in the nation's income.

Business cycles have a pattern, but the pattern is not uniform because of various forces both within and outside the cycle. This naturally makes forecasting business activity a bit precarious if not impossible. Certain relationships between or among these forces, such as cost-price relationships, interest rate changes, and inventory levels, act as upward or downward starters at the turning points of the business cycle.

Numerous indicators of business activity or business cycles are available. These can be categorized as representative indicators, composite indicators, and general business indicators. Among the most widely used are the lead-lag indicators of business cycle changes.

There are several causes of theories of the business cycle. No individual theory completely explains the cause of the cycle. Each theory, however, adds to the total understanding of the business cycle. Business cycles may occur due to real, psychological, monetary, or spending and saving causes, or a combination of these.

NEW TERMS AND CONCEPTS

Business cycle
Minor cycles
Major cycles
Prosperity
Recession
Depression
Recovery
Trend

Seasonal variations
Irregular or random fluctuations
Cyclical fluctuations
Endogenous forces
Exogenous forces
Leading indicators
Roughly coincident indicators

Lagging indicators
Innovation theory
Agricultural theories
Accelerator theory
Theory of rational expectations
Underconsumption theories
Underinvestment theory

DISCUSSION QUESTIONS

1. Distinguish between a cyclical fluctuation and a trend.
2. What are the four phases of the business cycle? How can you determine in which phase of the cycle the economy is at present?
3. What are the internal and external forces that influence the level of business activity?
4. During recovery and prosperity, what forces are building up that eventually will help bring about a downturn in the economy?
5. Differentiate between a representative and a composite business cycle indicator.
6. What indications of the innovation theory of the business cycle have you observed in recent years?
7. Do you think there is much validity to the underconsumption theory of the business cycle? Why or why not?
8. What kind of signals or indications are the various business indicators reflecting at the present time?

SUGGESTED READINGS

Bowers, David A. *An Introduction to Business Cycles and Forecasting.* Reading, MA: Addison-Wesley Publishing Co., 1985.

Kades, Eric. "New Classical and New Keynesian Models of Business Cycles." *Economic Review.* Federal Reserve Bank of Cleveland (Quarter IV, 1985).

Lackman, Conway L. "Short Range Economic Forecasting Methods." *Business Economics* (May, 1982).

"Long Swings II—Kuznets Explains History." *Monthly Economic Letter* (February, 1978).

Lucas, Robert E. *Studies in Business-Cycle*. Cambridge, MA: MIT Press, 1983.

Niemira, Michael. "Developing Industry Leading Economic Indicators." *Business Economics* (January, 1982).

Statistical Indicator Reports. North Egremont, MA: Statistical Indicator Associates, weekly.

U.S. Department of Commerce. *Business Conditions Digest*. Washington, DC: U.S. Government Printing Office, monthly.

Valentine, Lloyd M. *Business Cycles and Forecasting*, 8th ed. Cincinnati: South-Western Publishing Co., 1987. Chapters 1–4.

Walsh, Carl E. "New Views of the Business Cycle: Has the Past Emphasis on Money Been Misplaced?" *Business Review*. Federal Reserve Bank of Philadelphia (January–February, 1986).

18

EXPANSIONARY POLICIES

■

Since output and effective demand can come into equilibrium at a position of less than full employment, the economy can stabilize at an unemployment level and can remain there for some period of time in the absence of any artificial stimulus to the economy. Fortunately the income-expenditure analysis provides the basis for developing policies and measures, both intrinsic and extrinsic, designed to move the economy into equilibrium at high levels of employment. In effect, an endeavor is made to put handles on the economy, in the hope that pulling this lever or pushing that button will bring about a favorable expansion in the economy.

Today also various monetary and supply-side measures are being integrated and applied along with conventional demand management policies as a means of stabilizing economic activity and providing a foundation for long-run economic growth.

POLICIES TO ALLEVIATE UNEMPLOYMENT

Not only economists but also the general public are concerned with the problems that result from recessions and unemployment. The cost of a severe depression can be measured in billions of dollars. Important also are the hardships that accompany unemployment, such as bankruptcies, the waste of productive resources, plant idleness, and the resulting social deterioration.

These types of losses are exemplified in Figure 18-1, which shows the correlation between industrial production, unused capacity, and unemployment in past recessions. As noted in Chapter 17, the resulting GNP gap during the 1982 recession and its aftermath, for example, was equivalent to a $300 billion production loss.

When financial losses and serious social dislocations occur, economic policies and measures may be implemented to raise the level of economic activity. Even in the absence of a recession, economic measures may be used to stimulate growth and provide higher levels of production, employment, and income. These policies and measures should be consistent with the ideals of a democratic society; that is, in helping to create a greater

Figure 18-1 Production, Capacity Utilization,
and Unemployment, 1980–1986

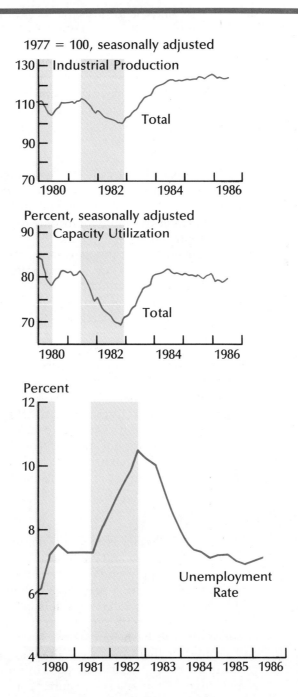

1977 = 100, seasonally adjusted

Percent, seasonally adjusted

Percent

Source: Board of Governors of the Federal Reserve System and U.S.
Department of Labor.

degree of stability or to raise the level of business activity, they should not weaken the spirit of free enterprise.

Three general policies can be developed to promote maximum income with full employment: (1) consumption may be stimulated by increasing the propensity to consume; (2) conditions favorable to a high level of investment may be encouraged; and (3) government spending may be used in an effort to bolster the level of business activity.

Built-In Stabilizers

Over the past few decades we have developed a number of economic institutions, or practices, that tend to serve as built-in stabilizers for the economy. An outstanding example is the Social Security System, devised to ensure greater continuity of income to elderly persons. Unemployment compensation and pension payments help to maintain consumption, even when recession occurs; they are shock absorbers that cushion the down-ward pressure of recession. The supplementary unemployment benefit plans and guaranteed annual income plans developed through labor-management negotiations are also helpful in this regard. In addition, economic stabilization features are cited as a major argument by advocates of federally sponsored income maintenance programs.

A progressive tax structure can serve as a further built-in stabilizer. When a period of prosperity occurs, high returns from a given tax rate can result in a budget surplus and thus exert a **fiscal drag** on the economy to help ward off inflation. On the other hand, during a recession the smaller revenue from taxes causes a deficit and leads to the necessity of government borrowing. This creates a **fiscal stimulus** for the economy.

Although they are not as noticeable, other government welfare programs have a similar stabilizing effect. In addition, corporate retained earnings and family savings can serve as built-in stabilizers.

Monetary Policy

Recall from Chapter 11 that the Federal Reserve can and does influence the amount of money and credit in the economy and that a liberalization of the money supply and/or lower interest rates can raise the level of economic activity during periods of unemployment.

Whenever a recession occurs, it is important that bank credit be easier to obtain, but only with proper safeguards. The Fed can help in making easier credit available by purchasing government bonds in the open market and paying for them by checks drawn against its own credit, which in turn will put the financial institutions in a position to expand their reserves. A reduction of the reserve requirements will produce the same result, for in either case the institutions are better able to make loans. A lowering of the discount rate serves as an additional inducement to borrow from the Federal Reserve Banks. Furthermore, liberalizing the money supply will lower interest rates. This should increase the gap between the marginal efficiency of capital and the rate of interest and encourage private investment. This, of course, raises effective demand and tends to reduce or eliminate the production gap.

Whether one or more of these methods will be used by the monetary authorities will depend on their judgment concerning the seriousness of the business recession or the need for expansion and the best way by which more liberal credit measures can be employed to stimulate the economy. Credit can be made more easily obtainable, but there is no certainty that business firms will increase their borrowings. If a recession has become serious and there is little prospect for improvement in business conditions, businesses may hesitate to borrow freely, even if credit is readily available at a low interest rate.

Economic stability and growth has become a primary objective of monetary policy. Because of its limitations, however, regulation of the money supply can only serve as a partial corrective to instability. The fiscal powers of the government are probably more effective for the task of raising the level of economic activity, especially during a period of serious unemployment.

Discretionary Fiscal Policy

The federal government has a powerful tool of stabilization in its fiscal policies and measures. Government revenues and expenditures may be adjusted in a manner that will bolster the economy during a recession, combat inflation when the economy is overheating, and promote economic growth in the long run. To understand the role of fiscal policy in maintaining economic stability, it is helpful to look at the government's sources of revenue and the direction of its spending. Three ways to finance government spending are available: taxation, borrowing, and printing money.

Taxation. If taxation is used to finance government spending, caution must be exercised not to tax funds that otherwise could be used for consumption or investment. It is of very little use to have the government spend more at the expense of consumption and private investment. The total effective demand remains constant, and no increase in employment results. On the other hand, if only idle funds are taxed, government taxation and spending lead to an increase in total effective demand via the balanced-budget multiplier effect. In fact, if the government could design a tax to absorb all those funds that are not spent on consumption or investment, government spending would always be sufficient to have total effective demand, including government spending, equal to total output. However, the practicality of designing and enforcing such a tax is rather remote. Furthermore, the equitableness of such a tax is questionable. Generally any tax structure absorbs consumer and investment funds to some significant degree.

Borrowing.   Borrowing is a more desirable method of raising funds for government spending when the purpose of spending the funds is to bolster the level of economic activity. The source of borrowing, however, will have a direct bearing on the effect. The government may borrow from individuals, businesses, or banks. In any case, the total effect will depend on whether or not it borrows idle funds. If, for example, it borrows funds through the sale of bonds to individuals and businesses who otherwise would use the funds for consumption and investment, the effect of government spending will be negated because the total effective demand will show no net increase. On the other hand, if the individuals and businesses use idle funds to purchase the government bonds, there will be a net increase in effective demand when the government spends the funds. This will bring about the desired effect by increasing production, employment, and income.

Since some individuals and businesses may give up otherwise spendable funds to buy government bonds, bank borrowing is usually recognized as the most feasible method to bring about an increase in the level of economic activity. It is not likely to have an adverse effect on the spending of current income by individuals and firms. It is true that banks may lend money that has been put into the bank by depositors. To this extent there is merely a transfer of funds from the depositors to the government. However, since savings deposits are usually considered idle funds by the depositors, that is, they do not intend to use them for consumption or investment immediately, government borrowing from the banks has a positive effect toward increasing the level of employment. Furthermore, the government can borrow funds in excess of the actual savings without hampering consumption or investment spending through the creation of bank credit. Usually when the government borrows by selling large amounts of bonds to the banks, the banks pay for the bonds by creating demand deposits for the government against which the Treasury can write checks. To this extent, there is an increase in the money supply as well as an increase in the total effective demand in the economy.

Printing Money.   Similar results can be accomplished by using printed money to increase government spending. This method has an additional advantage insofar as it eliminates the necessity of having the government go into debt. Increasing government spending by increasing the amount of currency, however, is often difficult unless the government can increase the basis of the money supply, such as gold, government bonds, or bank assets. Printing and engraving presses cannot be run at will without some regard to the valuation of the currency. To print money without regard to its backing can be disastrous. Furthermore, although U.S. citizens accept the creation of credit by the commercial banks, we seem to have an aversion to the printing of money by the government without proper backing. As a result, the use of printed money for government spending has not been a very acceptable method of bolstering the economy.

Some economists, though, suggest that the government use printed money. They reason that printed money is just as substantial as bank credit. Since the government has the right to coin money and to regulate its value, they think that it is wise to bypass the banks and print the money directly when needed for federal government expenditures to generate economic activity. These advocates cannot see why banks should be paid an interest rate for providing a service that is primarily a function of the government. If the government prints the money instead of relying on the sales of bonds to the banks, which pay for the bonds by the creation of credit, it can avoid the cost of paying interest. As an alternative, they suggest the use of interest-free financing. With this method, the Treasury sells non-interest-bearing notes to the Federal Reserve Banks, which in turn create deposits for the government.

Methods of Increasing Government Spending

Once it has been decided to use government spending as a means of raising effective demand to increase the level of employment, there remains the question of the exact method of accomplishing the objective. Three methods are suggested: increase spending and hold taxes, hold spending and decrease taxes, and increase both spending and taxes.

Increase Government Spending and Hold Taxes.   In this method, there is a positive increase in the amount of money spent by the government. For example, if the government has been spending $1,000 billion annually and taxing the same amount, it has a balanced budget. Now suppose that government increases spending to $1,050 billion annually. If taxes remain constant, the government is forced to borrow $50 billion for its additional expenditures. If the government borrows from the banks, individuals and business firms are not forced to give up spendable funds through higher taxation. As a result, the total spending should increase for the economy as a whole. Incomes increase not just by $50 billion but by some multiple thereof, depending on the size of the multiplier. This method is beneficial insofar as the government can easily maintain close control over the direction of additional government spending.

Hold Government Spending and Decrease Taxes.   This is often referred to as the "tax remission" plan. It also results in a deficit budget. For example, assume that the government is running a balanced budget of $1,000 billion annually, as stated in our first case. If the government decreases taxes $50 billion annually, it is $50 billion short of needed revenue. As a result, the government is forced to borrow $50 billion. If it borrows from the banks or borrows otherwise idle funds, it increases the total spending in the economy by $50 billion plus the multiplier effect. Although the government is not spending any more, it is assumed that the recipients of the tax remission will spend the money for either consumption or investment. To the extent that they may not, the effect of using this method to increase employment is lessened. The direction of their spending may also be less effective. This method is politically popular because both individuals and firms are usually happy about reduced taxes.

It is also possible to use a combination of the two methods mentioned above by increasing government spending and decreasing taxes.

Increase Government Spending and Increase Taxes Proportionately. This method maintains a balanced budget. The effectiveness of the method is limited by the fact that in raising taxes, the government may absorb funds that otherwise would be spent for consumption and investment. Therefore, the whole success of the program depends on the ability of tax measures to take in idle funds and, therefore, to increase the total effective demand in the economy. Since most tax measures force consumers and investors to give up their spendable funds to some degree, it usually requires a larger amount of government spending to raise the level of employment a given amount by this method than it does by the first two methods mentioned. By the previous methods, the government can raise total effective demand by $50 billion, exclusive of the multiplier effect, through borrowing. If it desires to raise effective demand by $50 billion through government spending financed strictly by taxation, however, more than $50 billion must be spent.

For example, if the marginal propensity to save is one-half, the government must tax and spend approximately $100 billion to raise effective demand $50 billion, exclusive of the multiplier. The first $50 billion of government expenditure merely offsets the decrease in consumption and private investment resulting from the tax. The second $50 billion adds to the total effective demand, since it in effect comes from savings that otherwise would not be spent. This is often referred to as the **balanced-budget multiplier effect**. If the marginal propensity to save is one-third for the economy as a whole, government taxation and spending must increase by $150 billion to effectuate a $50 billion net increase in effective demand, exclusive of the multiplier and accelerator effect. Thus, it is easy to recognize the limitations of this method as a means of raising effective demand to increase the level of employment. It would be practicable only for spending of small amounts or if the tax could be designed to tap primarily idle funds.

Direction of Emergency Government Spending

If a decision is made to utilize deficit spending as a means of raising the level of employment, a question naturally arises regarding the direction of such emergency government spending. Should the government increase its everyday services? Should it provide some new services? Should the spending be for consumption or investment purposes? Should it be used to create public service jobs? Should spending be concentrated or diversified? How much should it be and how long should it last? It is easy to see that the decision to use deficit financing is only the beginning of the issue. It is possible, for example, to alleviate the effects of unemployment by using direct monetary payments to the unemployed and the poor, or by spending for public works or public service job programs.

Direct Payments.   While the method of direct payments makes certain that those suffering most from the anguish of unemployment will receive direct aid, its total effect may be less than public spending in the form of public works. If the individual is given a direct payment, the bulk of the payment is spent for consumption. This increases the level of economic activity to some degree, provided the funds received do not come at the expense of consumption and investment elsewhere in the economy. Even if the individual is employed on a simple project such as leaf raking for the sake of dignity, the total effect is not much greater. The capital needed to put a group of individuals on such a job is limited to rakes, shovels, wheelbarrows, and perhaps a few trucks. Furthermore, the spending of a direct income payment primarily for consumer goods may have no greater effect than decreasing excess inventories of consumer goods.

Public Works.   On the other hand, a large public work, such as a bridge, a dam, a highway, or a building, necessitates the use of a large amount of capital goods and the production of a large amount of supplies, such as iron, cement, lumber, electric wiring, and glass plate. Furthermore, transportation is stimulated to some extent by the movement of goods. Not only are payments made to contractors, but contractors must pay subcontractors, suppliers, and transportation companies in addition to the workers directly on the job. These workers, in turn, spend on consumption. Consequently, workers are employed in the production of consumer goods that are purchased by these workers. All this tends to build up the multiplier effect and may even stimulate the accelerator principle. Thus, more secondary and tertiary employment is generated through public works than by a leaf-raking project or by direct payments.

As an attempt to alleviate unemployment, public works appear to serve the purpose better than other means. Not only is there a greater multiplier effect, but also there is always something to show for the spending and production efforts involved. In addition, workers have jobs and are able to purchase the consumer items they require.

The income-expenditure approach makes use of the employment multiplier, in addition to the investment multiplier, to show the net result of an increase in employment. The **employment multiplier**, k', is the ratio of the total increase in employment, N, to the original increase in employment, N_0. Therefore, $k' = N/N_0$, or $N = k' \times N_0$. This formula is used to measure the change in total employment compared with a primary increase in employment that results from any increase in effective demand. The employment multiplier may or may not be equal to the investment multiplier.

Once the employment multiplier is known, it can be determined rather easily what amount of employment on public works will be necessary to raise the total level of employment a desired amount. For example, assume an employment multiplier of 3 and a current level of 110 million employed. If it is desired to raise the level of employment to 116 million, the hiring of only 2 million workers in public works will be required to increase total employment by 6 million (3 × 2 million). If the employment multiplier were 4, it would require the hiring of only 1.5 million workers to raise employment by a total of 6 million (4 × 1.5 million). Thus, the higher the employment multiplier, the easier it is to bring about a desired level of employment through public works.

It is true that emergency spending can be used to fill the gap between output and effective demand whenever consumption and private investment are insufficient to bring about a high level of employment. But it may require sizable amounts of spending over extended periods of time. In the United States we did attempt to alleviate the serious unemployment of the 1930s through deficit spending on public works. Government deficit spending during that period seemed very high to most citizens, and we engaged in public investment for nearly a decade. Yet we were still a considerable distance away from full employment at the end of the decade. After World War II broke out, however, and we began to spend billions for defense and war purposes, we moved from a position of nearly 9 million unemployed in 1939 to full employment by 1942.

ANTIDEPRESSIONARY POLICIES OF THE 1930S

The economic, social, and political woes of unemployment emphasize the need for problem solving. In serious depressions unemployment imposes a hardship not only on individual employees and their families but also on the economy as a whole. Widespread and prolonged unemployment results in a loss of individual income and frequently brings about a deterioration of working skills. Furthermore, the loss of goods and services can be tremendous. Labor time lost today through idleness is gone forever. It is true that workers can work double time tomorrow to make up lost time today, but they could work the double time without having lost the original time.

Under the laissez-faire policy and the self-adjusting mechanisms of classical economic doctrine, there is little to do during a depression except to wait for full employment to return. However, with millions of workers unemployed, people going hungry, mortgages being foreclosed, values dropping, factories closing down, and members of Congress being plagued with complaints, it is difficult to stand by and wait for the economy to adjust to a high level of unemployment. Furthermore, many people, especially voters, have a tendency to blame adverse economic conditions on the political party in power. Therefore, in addition to the humanitarian motive (the promotion of public welfare) and economic justifications, political considerations usually enter the picture when a decision is being made about the use of antidepressionary or expansionary measures.

The GNP fell from a high of $103 billion in 1929 to a low of $56 billion in 1933 and averaged about $80 billion per year for the period 1929 through 1940. Since the GNP potential during the 1930s was over $100 billion per year, a further comparison reveals that the loss of production due to layoffs during this period was equivalent to a shutdown of the entire economy for a period of more than 3 years. Thus, it is easy to see that the loss through unemployment during a serious depression can be staggering. Such a situation certainly lends support to the adoption of at least certain income-expenditure policies for raising the level of employment. Therefore, it should come as no surprise to learn that our economic policies of the 1930s and subsequent years have paralleled, if not followed, the income-expenditure analysis in a great many respects.

New Deal Policies and Programs

At the time of the presidential elections in 1932 nearly 12 million persons were unemployed in the United States, not including millions more who were only partially employed. In short, one out of every four workers was idle, and many of the others were working only part-time. There seemed to be little doubt that the landslide vote for Franklin D. Roosevelt, who promised a New Deal for the people, manifested a minor political revolt brought on by adverse economic conditions and the excessive amount of unemployment in the economy.

Upon taking office, President Roosevelt pinpointed the primary objective of the administration: to halt the downward spiral of production, employment, income, and prices by bringing about an upward expansion of the economy through the use of monetary and fiscal policies. Like Keynes, he thought that it was the government's responsibility to take action that would help bolster the economy. The money supply was liberalized, even to the extent of devaluing the dollar, and fiscal policy became a tool to bolster the level of employment. Public works and deficit spending became the order of the day.

Roosevelt's objective was to improve the purchasing power of the masses, which would bring about increased demand and with it increased profits, production, and employment. Unlike the previous administration, which tried to work from the top down by extending aid to businesses to keep them operational, Roosevelt concentrated on working from the bottom up. Not only does this approach take advantage of the large propensity to consume among the lower income groups, but it is popular politically. Measures that provided financial aid to farmers, refinanced home mortgages, set up unemployment compensation and old-age insurance, and established minimum wage laws were all very popular with the people.

In addition, several billion dollars were expended on public works to provide employment for millions of workers. The Civilian Conservation Corps was established to give work and educational opportunities to millions of young men, and the National Youth Administration provided needed work for those in college.

Rate of Deficit Spending

While these various public works and other public-investment programs were being tried, the federal budget was running a deficit. After 11 years of surplus financing and of reducing the large debt incurred in World War I, the government went into debt each year from 1931 to 1940. Although tax revenues increased after the early Depression years, expenditures moved up at a faster rate and the federal government went deeper into debt. During this period, when government revenues ranged from $2 billion to $5 billion annually, federal deficits averaged over $3 billion annually. The national debt increased from $16 billion to $48 billion. In addition, state and local government debts were increased.

Lessons of the 1930s

Before the Depression, governmental units did their spending and building when everyone else did, that is, during prosperity. In the 1930s, however, public officials and others began to realize the value of public spending during depressions as a means of alleviating unemployment. They also became aware of the fact that much more could be accomplished through public works than through direct relief payments. Although the administration and Congress may not have been influenced by Keynes, certainly they had adopted policies that paralleled those of the income-expenditure analysis. Our experience in the United States between 1933 and 1945 with the public-spending program indicated the following: (1) our early attempts to alleviate unemployment repudiated the pump-priming theory; (2) it verified the multiplier theory; (3) although large, our spending during the 1930s was insufficient and indicated the need for a very large outlay of government spending during serious depression periods; (4) the war proved that a sufficiently large outlay of government spending could return an economy from a position of a considerable degree of unemployment to a full-employment stage within a relatively short period; and (5) better results are obtained through spending on public works than could be obtained through direct relief payments.

It is evident from the available data that there was some improvement in the level of employment as a result of the New Deal efforts. On the other hand, the results left much to be desired. Critics of government deficit spending, especially the advocates of laissez-faire and the balanced budget, point to the figures to demonstrate the lack of success of the spending program. How can a program be successful when after 8 years of spending we still had over 9 million unemployed? Although unemployment was still 9 million, we do not know what it might have been if the government programs had not been in effect. It might have been much higher. On the other hand, it might have been much lower, according to the critics, if the government had stayed out of the picture and let ordinary economic forces return us to full employment. As a result of not being able to determine what might have happened in the absence of our grand experiment, it is impossible to determine the success of the public-spending program.

Our experience of the 1930s leaves little doubt that our New Deal policies were similar to those advocated by the income-expenditure analysis, especially the idea of deficit spending and public works. Further evidence that we have accepted much of the income-expenditure theory can be found by analyzing the Employment Act of 1946 and the Full Employment and Balanced Growth Act of 1978.

EXPANSIONARY MEASURES OF THE 1960S

The Eisenhower administration, in addition to its strong reliance on monetary policies, did engage in some direct measures. Much more positive and direct action was undertaken by the Kennedy and Johnson administrations in the 1960s. During his first year in office, President Kennedy was instrumental in the passage of the Area Redevelopment Act of 1961. The Act endeavored to bring industry to depressed areas and jobs to displaced workers.

Since unemployment had consistently exceeded 5 percent since 1957 and because the economy was operating at less than 90 percent of its capacity, President Kennedy suggested in his 1962 *Economic Report* several depression-proof measures to bolster the economy and stimulate economic growth. As a result of his request, Congress enacted a bill providing a 7 percent tax credit allowance to stimulate new investment. It also permitted acceleration of depreciation cost as a way to encourage new investment. In addition, Congress enacted the Manpower Development and Training Act, passed the Emergency Public Works Act, and subsequently appropriated $900 million to be spent on various projects to help reduce unemployment.

The Historic Income Tax Cuts of 1964

In his 1963 *Economic Report*, President Kennedy pointed with pride to the economic accomplishments under his administration. But he stressed that in spite of the gains we still did not have maximum production, maximum employment, and maximum income as called for under the Employment Act of 1946. He indicated further that the economy was growing at only 3 percent annually compared with a potential growth of 4.5

percent. Consequently, as a means of bolstering the economy and accelerating economic growth, he presented a record-level budget and simultaneously requested a net tax reduction on personal and corporate incomes, which would result in an $11.8 billion deficit in the fiscal 1964 budget. After 13 months of intermittent hearings and debate on the merits of the tax cuts, Congress finally enacted a two-stage $11.5 billion personal and corporate income tax reduction bill in February, 1964. President Johnson immediately signed the bill into law with a word of encouragement to the general public to spend the increase in their disposable incomes that would result from the tax reduction.

In addition to the historic income tax reductions spread over a 2-year period in 1964 and 1965, Congress added to this stimulant by providing for excise tax reductions of $5 billion–$6 billion on a wide array of goods and services from automobiles to entertainment. These tax cuts were to serve as a means of raising the demand for goods and services and contributing to the improvement of production, employment, and income.

Deficit Spending in the 1960s

All these measures were accompanied by continuous deficit spending throughout the 1960s. In fact, President Kennedy knowingly used deficit spending as a means of bolstering the level of economic activity. To his critics who claimed that the deficits resulting from increased spending and decreased taxes would be inflationary, he pointed out on a nationally televised program that his proposal would not be inflationary. His proposal would result in an increase in production, employment, and income because at that time the economy was operating at less than full employment of labor, resources, and capacity. To President Kennedy and his Council of Economic Advisers, the deficits were to be down payments on future surpluses. A proposed deficit was labeled a "fiscal stimulus." In short, the stimulus (deficit) would lead to a higher level of employment and income.

At full employment the greater tax revenues would result in a surplus. Supposedly, when we reached the stage of full employment and budget surpluses, we could then declare a "fiscal dividend" in the form of increased government services or a further reduction in taxes. The payment of this fiscal dividend would then help avoid a "fiscal drag" on the economy that results from a surplus budget. Although we had a number of fiscal stimulants in the economy during the first half of the 1960s and eventually reached full employment by 1966, we never quite reached the surplus-budget stage. One part of the problem may have been that we were declaring fiscal dividends before reaching the full-employment and budget-surplus state. Another major difficulty in determining how well this policy of fiscal stimulants, fiscal dividends, and the avoidance of fiscal drags would work stemmed from the unforeseeable acceleration of spending that resulted from the escalation of the war in Vietnam. The deficits for the period involved are shown in Table 18-1.

Table 18-1 Revenues, Expenditures, and Gross Federal Debt (Billions)

Fiscal Year	Revenue	Expenditure	Surplus or Deficit	Total Debt
1960	$ 92.5	$ 92.2	+ 0.3	$ 290.9
1961	94.4	97.8	− 3.4	292.9
1962	99.7	106.8	− 7.1	303.3
1963	106.6	111.3	− 4.8	310.8
1964	112.7	118.6	− 5.9	316.8
1965	116.8	118.4	− 1.6	323.2
1966	130.6	134.7	− 3.8	329.5
1967	148.9	157.6	− 8.7	341.3
1968	153.0	178.1	− 25.2	369.8
1969	186.9	183.6	+ 3.2	367.1
1970	192.8	195.7	− 2.8	382.6
1971	187.1	210.2	− 23.0	409.5
1972	207.3	230.7	− 23.4	437.3
1973	230.8	245.6	− 14.8	468.4
1974	263.2	267.9	− 4.7	486.2
1975	279.1	324.2	− 45.2	544.1
1976	298.1	364.5	− 66.4	631.9
TQ[1]	81.2	94.2	− 13.0	646.4
1977	355.6	409.2	− 53.6	709.1
1978	399.6	458.7	− 57.2	780.4
1979	463.3	503.5	− 40.2	833.8
1980	517.1	590.9	− 73.8	914.3
1981	599.3	678.2	− 78.9	1,003.9
1982	617.8	745.7	− 127.9	1,147.0
1983	600.6	808.3	− 207.8	1,381.9
1984	666.5	851.8	− 185.3	1,576.7
1985	734.1	946.3	− 212.3	1,827.2
1986	769.1	989.8	− 220.7	2,132.9
1987 (est.)	842.4	1,015.6	− 173.2	2,372.4
1988 (est.)	916.6	1,024.3	− 107.8	2,585.5
1989 (est.)	976.2	1,069.0	− 98.2	2,684.3

1. The 3-month period from July 1, 1976, through September, 1976, is a separate period known as the transition quarter because the federal government shifted the beginning of the fiscal year from July 1 to October 1.
Source: *Economic Report of the President*, 1987.

Return to Full Employment

During the early 1960s socioeconomic measures, such as the introduction of the Medicare provisions of the Social Security Act, the increase in Social Security payments, and the hike in the minimum wage rate, were invoked in part with the idea that they would help reduce "nagging unemployment" and help stimulate economic growth. During this period, 1961–1965, the economy was continuously establishing new records of production, employment, and income; our real economic growth rate was exceeding 5 percent annually. In spite of all this, however, the economy did not reach full employment until early 1966. Unemployment, which had been near 7 percent of the labor force when the Kennedy administration took office, still totaled 5.5 percent of the labor force as late as June, 1965. During this time, moreover, the labor force was experiencing its most rapid growth in the history of the economy.

There was some discussion in the executive and legislative branches of the government about declaring another fiscal dividend in the form of a further income tax or excise tax reduction. By late 1965, however, the economy was approaching the stage of full employment. With record investment, high-level consumption, large outlays for Great Society programs, and especially accelerated spending resulting from the escalation of the war in Vietnam, we were at full employment by 1966 and beginning to experience noticeable upward pressures on the price level. Discussions then shifted to enactment of anti-inflationary measures, such as tighter money, reductions in government spending, and tax hikes.

FISCAL POLICIES OF THE 1970s AND 1980s

During the period 1966–1969, the economy was at full employment, and we were concerned primarily with measures to combat inflation. In 1969, unemployment averaged 3.5 percent. With the recession of 1970, in which the real GNP actually declined (but less than 1 percent), the rate of unemployment rose to 4.9 percent for the year and in some months reached 5.5 and 6 percent. Although there were still some inflationary pressures in the economy, primarily of a cost-push nature, the Nixon administration by late 1970 had shifted its emphasis from anti-inflationary policies to expansionary policies in order to reduce unemployment and generate an increase in production.

President Nixon and his Council of Economic Advisers did not abandon anti-inflationary measures. The administration engaged in more "jawboning" in an effort to hold the price line, and much more discussion arose regarding the reinstitution of wage-price guideposts or an incomes policy. President Nixon hoped that the rate of inflation would be reduced to 3.5 percent by the end of 1971 and that the unemployment rate would be down to 4.5 percent by that time. His economic game plan called for a return to full employment and stable prices by mid-1972.

It was evident by mid-1971, however, that progress toward his economic goals was minimal. Sizable wage and price increases were prevalent in spite of an unemployment rate of 5 to 6 percent in the summer of 1971. Consequently, in August, 1971, President Nixon made sweeping and drastic changes in the game plan. He imposed a 90-day freeze on all wages and prices, requested reinstitution of the tax credit to stimulate new investment, and asked Congress to reduce personal and corporate income taxes as a means of combating inflation, reducing unemployment, and expanding the economy.

During 1972, strict wage and price controls were enforced to suppress inflation. Although they were abandoned in favor of voluntary controls early in 1973, by the middle of the year price controls were reinstituted. But even this attempt to regulate prices went by the boards before the year was out. With continued expansion the economy reached the peak of the business boom by the fall of 1973. By that time the unemployment rate had declined to 4.6 percent. Most of the economic measures up to that time were designed to contain, or eliminate, inflationary pressures in the economy.

The Recession of 1974–1975

With the advent of the 1974–1975 recession, unemployment rose to over 5 percent by mid-1974. Inflation, however, was running at an annual rate of 12 to 13 percent. This put the economy back in a position of stagflation; that is, stagnation or sluggishness in the production sector of the economy and inflation in the price sector. By November, 1974, unemployment had risen to 6.5 percent. By April, 1975, it was 8.9 percent and rising. With a decline in the real GNP for five consecutive quarters, even a reluctant administration had to admit that the economy was in a state of recession and that conditions would likely get worse before they got better.

Toward the end of 1974 the prime rate on borrowed funds declined from 12 to 10 percent, the Fed eased the money supply, and the discount rate was finally lowered. Suggestions were made from many quarters that called for tax reductions, acceleration of the public employment program, and increase and extension of unemployment compensation, the establishment of a public works program, and the organization of a government agency to refinance financially troubled businesses. Faced with simultaneous recession and inflation, President Ford, in December, 1974, met with his economic advisers to determine the feasibility of shifting the emphasis of economic policy from fighting inflation to economic expansion and fighting unemployment.

In January, 1975, the President submitted a comprehensive economic program to Congress. This included a tax reduction and a proposed federal budget deficit of $51 billion. In the spring and early summer, income tax rebates of $23 billion were distributed to taxpayers. In addition, several other measures, such as expanded public employment programs and financial aid for home purchases, were discussed in Congress. On the monetary side, the Fed agreed to expand the money supply at a faster pace, and the prime rate fell to 7 percent by midyear.

With unemployment still above 7.0 percent, Congress enacted the Emergency Jobs Programs Extensions Act of 1976 to provide funds to sustain previous levels of public service employment and further to mandate that funds in excess of those needed for sustaining these levels be utilized to create new public service projects. This Act provided funding for an additional 415,000 public service jobs to be added to the 310,000 in existence at that time.

The Carter Package

Shortly after he took office in January, 1977, President Carter proposed a 2-year $31.2 billion economic stimulus program to encourage expansion of the U.S. economy. Although his proposed tax rebates did not materialize, Congress did enact the Economic Stimulus Appropriations Act in May, 1977, and the Youth Employment and Demonstration Projects Act in August of that year. These Acts provided approximately $20 billion to be used over the period of fiscal 1977 and 1978. Among other activities, the economic stimulus package provided funds for doubling public service employment and Job Corps enrollment. It was during this period also that the original Humphrey-Hawkins Bill, enacted as the Full Employment and Balanced Growth Act of 1978, put renewed emphasis on the reduction of unemployment.

The Recessions of 1980 and 1982

When the economy slid into a modest recession in 1980, limited measures were used to offset the downswing. Unemployment rose from 5.8 percent in 1979 to 7.1 percent in 1980 and reached a high of 7.6 percent in the latter part of the year. When President Reagan assumed office, the unemployment rate stood at 7.4 percent, but the inflation rate was near the double-digit level. It appeared that we had weathered the short 1980 recession. The prime rate of interest, however, was slightly over 20 percent, a record level. Productivity per labor-hour was also at a low ebb.

The President directed his main economic policy efforts toward reducing the rate of inflation, and implemented supply-side measures to encourage savings, stimulate investment, and motivate work effort. The administration supported the tight monetary policy of the Fed as a means of combating inflation. In spite of a tax reduction and other measures to expand production, recession reemerged in 1982.

The rate of unemployment exceeded 10 percent in the latter half of 1982 and the first half of 1983. Severe production cutbacks took place in the housing, auto, steel, machine tool, and other basic industries. With sluggish investment, large-scale layoffs, wage reductions, the piling up of inventories, and a record number of bankruptcies, President Reagan extended unemployment benefits, and provided funds for increased public works employment. The Federal Reserve increased the supply of money, and in a series of moves, the discount rate was cut from 14 percent in late 1981 to 8.5 percent by December, 1982. The prime rate tumbled from 16.5 percent to 11 percent in the same time period. The rate of inflation fell below 5 percent during this period.

During this recession unemployment peaked at 10.7 percent, the highest rate in more than 40 years. Moreover, Congress and the administration tolerated a federal deficit of $128 billion in fiscal 1982 and a deficit of $208 billion, the largest ever, in fiscal 1983. Although economic recovery began in early 1983, unemployment still averaged 9.5 percent for that year. It fell to 7.4 percent in 1984, and was still 7.1 percent for 1985, when both the discount and prime rates were cut again. With some sluggishness apparent in the economy in late 1985 and early 1986, the discount rate was lowered and the prime rate fell accordingly. By September, 1986, the discount rate had been reduced to 5.5 percent and the prime rate was at 7.5 percent. They were still at those levels in the spring of 1987.

SUMMARY

According to the income-expenditure approach, expansionary measures can be used to alleviate widespread unemployment. In addition to the internal forces in the private sector of the economy, the operation of built-in stabilizers, and the utilization of monetary measures by the Fed, fiscal measures can be used to stabilize the level of economic activity and the price level.

There are three sources of funds available for the government when it desires to increase total spending: taxation, borrowing, and printing money. Each has its advantages and disadvantages. If the government is going to use fiscal policy to bolster the level of business activity, however, more efficient results will be obtained if it is accompanied by a deficit budget.

The government can increase its spending and hold taxes constant, or it can hold spending constant and decrease taxes. In either case, the government will be forced to borrow the difference between what it spends and what it taxes. Some good may be accomplished by increasing both spending and taxes and thus maintaining a balanced budget. However, it will take more total government spending to obtain the same results by this method.

The direction of government spending is also important. For example, spending on public works can be more beneficial than using money for direct payments to the unemployed. Any increase in primary employment will bring about an increase in secondary employment through the employment multiplier effect.

Antidepressionary measures were tried during the serious depression of the 1930s. The grand experiment was that of the New Deal, with its various projects, programs, and agencies that attempted to put unemployed people to work. To what extent these antide-pressionary measures of the New Deal were successful is a debatable question. The programs, however, definitely did increase the level of employment, since they put millions of people to work directly on various projects.

The measures invoked during the Kennedy and Johnson administrations probably stimulated employment to some degree. Whether unemployment was serious enough, especially since in those years new employment records were being established, to warrant the adoption of such measures is still being argued. Nevertheless, high consumption, record levels of investment, continued spending on Great Society programs, escalation of the war in Vietnam, and continuous deficits led us back to full employment by 1966.

After 3 years of full employment and inflation, the economy entered a mild recession in 1970, and unemployment rose to 5 and even 6 percent. At that time President Nixon faced the difficult task of simultaneously combating unemployment and inflation. In the summer of 1971 he imposed a surprising 90-day freeze on wages and prices, requested a tax credit as a means of stimulating investment, and asked Congress to reduce personal and corporate income taxes as a means of expanding the economy.

As business activity expanded during the next 24 months, the economy was subjected to an off-again, on-again program of wage and price controls. By the fall of 1973 unemployment had dropped to 4.6 percent. With the advent of the 1974–1975 recession and the return of stagflation, a host of economic measures were recommended for expanding the economy in the hope of reducing unemployment without aggravating the current double-digit inflation.

With unemployment at still undesirable levels of 6 to 7 percent and higher, further stimulus, especially in the form of public service employment, was provided in 1977 and 1978 by the Carter administration's economic package. The Full Employment and Balanced Growth Act of 1978 also stressed the further reduction of unemployment as a national goal. By the end of 1978 unemployment dropped below 6 percent for the first time since the 1974–1975 recession. Unfortunately, by that time inflation had returned to a double-digit level.

Various demand management and supply-side measures were used to bolster economic activity during the 1980 and 1982 recessions. Measures such as extended unemployment benefits, public service employment, lower interest rates, money supply acceleration, tax reductions, and large federal deficits were employed.

NEW TERMS AND CONCEPTS

Fiscal drag Balanced-budget multiplier effect Employment multiplier
Fiscal stimulus

DISCUSSION QUESTIONS

1. How does unemployment compensation act as a built-in stabilizer for the economy? What do you think of the proposal

adopted in past recessions that extended unemployment compensation?

2. If the government decides to utilize deficit

spending as a means of bolstering the economy, is it better to borrow from the banks or from the general public? Why?

3. What are the merits of increased government spending versus a tax reduction, provided either is financed through borrowing?

4. What are the advantages of government spending on public works compared with direct payments as a means of alleviating a depression? Are there any disadvantages?

5. Do you think that employment on emergency public works should be limited only to those who are currently unemployed? Why?

6. Point out some of the problems involved in trying to stabilize the economy during a period of stagflation.

7. What do you think of a federally guaranteed annual income as an expansionary measure?

8. Do you see any apparent conflict in the simultaneous use of demand management and supply-side measures in an effort to offset the effects of a recession?

SUGGESTED READINGS

Boskin, Michael (ed.). *The Economy in the 1980s: A Program for Growth and Stability*. New Brunswick: Transaction Books, 1980. Chapter 4.

Carson, Robert B. *Economic Issues Today*. New York: St. Martin's Press, 1987.

Chandler, Lester V. *America's Greatest Depression, Nineteen Twenty Nine–Nineteen Forty-One*. New York: Harper & Row, Publishers, 1970.

Economic Report of the President. Washington, DC: U.S. Government Printing Office, annually.

Joines, Douglas H. "U.S. Fiscal Policy and the 70's Slowdown." *Economic Review*. Federal Reserve Bank of Atlanta (October, 1982).

Leftwich, Richard H., and Ansel M. Sharp. *Economics of Social Issues*, 7th ed. Dallas: Business Publications, Inc., 1986. Chapter 12.

Levy, Michael. *The Federal Budget: Its Impact on the Economy. Fiscal (year) Edition*. New York: The Conference Board, Inc., annually.

U.S. Department of Labor. *Employment and Training Report of the President*. Washington, DC: U.S. Government Printing Office, annually.

19
ANTI-INFLATIONARY POLICIES

∎

The income-expenditure analysis is often referred to as "depression economics." This stems from the fact that it originated, or at least crystallized, during the 1930s and, consequently, placed primary emphasis on the problem of unemployment. Concentrated efforts of the early advocates to determine the causes of and the remedies for equilibrium at unemployment levels caused people to think of the theory only in terms of depression policies. As a result, many people are inclined to lose sight of the fact that the income-expenditure approach can also be used to analyze inflation and formulate anti-inflationary policies. Although it did not originally stress the problem of inflation so much as the problem of depression, today much emphasis is placed on the analysis of inflation.

During periods of changing prices, some income recipients gain and others lose. The main hardships of inflation are the redistribution of income caused by rising prices and the deterioration of past savings. On the other hand, during depression there is not only a redistribution of income but also considerable unemployment. Probably due to the circumstances of the times in which the income-expenditure analysis was introduced, the inflationary problem did not appear as urgent as the problem of unemployment.

According to the income-expenditure approach, inflation will occur at the full-employment level if the effective demand exceeds total output. This will result when private investment and government spending are more than sufficient to fill the gap between consumption and total output. In short, investment will exceed savings. In such a case, current demand will exceed the value of the goods and services currently produced. Competitive bidding by spenders will pull prices upward. This is known as demand-pull inflation. In addition, there may exist separately or simultaneously cost-push inflation, structural inflation, and/or social inflation.[1]

The income-expenditure analysis provides an explanation of the causes and cures of unemployment and demand-pull inflation at full employment.

---

1. It is recommended that the reader review pages 65 to 67 of Chapter 4 for a refresher regarding the various types of inflation.

Unfortunately, the income-expenditure approach did not provide an adequate framework for analyzing the causes and cure of stagflation, which has plagued the U.S. and other economies during much of the 1970s and early 1980s.

Demand-pull inflation may occur due to an easy money situation, high levels of investment and consumption, and large government outlays and/or deficit spending. Since the effective demand is greater than the output of goods and services, two alternatives exist to combat such an inflationary situation. The first and best is to increase the total output of goods and services to satisfy the excess demand. But since this is not always feasible in a full-employment economy in the short run, at least not on a scale large enough to alleviate a serious inflationary situation, we must rely on the second alternative—reduce the total spending.

MEASURES TO REDUCE TOTAL SPENDING

A number of methods are available for reducing total spending in the economy. The reduction can be made in government spending, in private investment, and/or in consumption. In any case both the economic and the political effect of such actions must be considered. The method selected frequently depends on circumstances in the economy. Wartime inflation, for example, requires special measures.

Built-In Stabilizers

Our built-in, or automatic, stabilizers may not be strong enough to restrain inflation during the upswing of the economy. Nevertheless, the stabilizers are still there. With employment at a high level, for example, payroll taxes will be maximized and disbursements from the Social Security System minimized. This will help rake off excess spendable funds from the economy. Similarly, the flow into and out of private supplementary unemployment funds will have an anti-inflationary effect. Our personal and corporate income tax structure with given tax rates may yield a full-employment surplus, which will be anti-inflationary, and may even cause a fiscal drag on the economy. With rising incomes there will be a decrease in the marginal propensity to consume, and the rising rate of personal and corporate savings may act as a deterrent to inflation.

Monetary Policy

The government may also use monetary policy to combat inflation. Measures designed to tighten the money supply and/or increase the rate of interest tend to discourage investment. This, of course, lowers the total effective demand and tends to bring investment into line with savings. Investment could be reduced to a point where it just fills the gap between the combined effective demand of consumption plus government and total production at full employment. Here there is an advantage in having a central monetary authority that can easily raise, as well as lower, the interest rates for the purpose of raising or lowering the effective demand. The anti-inflationary effects of a rise in the interest rate, however, can be offset by a rise in the marginal efficiency of capital. Businesses will not hesitate to borrow and invest even at a higher interest rate if profits are rising. This frequently occurs when prices and, consequently, profits rise quickly during an inflationary period. According to the income-expenditure analysis there is little that can be done, in the absence of direct regulations, about controlling the marginal efficiency of capital. For this reason the government must rely heavily on tightening the money supply and manipulating the interest rates to combat inflation through its monetary policy.

Other Measures

The government may discourage investment and consumption by other means. It may impose credit restraint on both commercial and consumer loans. For example, it may limit borrowing for stock market purchases, it may tighten up restrictions on housing credit, and it may restrain consumer credit. The government may also rely on psychological measures to encourage individuals and firms to save instead of spend; and if absolutely necessary, it may impose voluntary or mandatory price and wage controls.

Government Surplus

Total spending may be reduced in the economy during an inflationary period by using policies opposite to those for increasing spending during a depression. First of all, the government can limit its spending to essentials. Furthermore, it can operate with a surplus budget to reduce consumption and investment. If the government taxes more than it spends, it will tend to reduce the total effective demand in the economy. In this case, unlike with expansionary policies, the government should endeavor to tax spendable funds, those that are going to be spent on consumption and investment, rather than idle funds.

The government can combat inflation by building up a surplus in two ways: hold taxes and decrease spending, or increase taxes and hold or decrease spending. It may also combat inflation to some extent by decreasing taxes and decreasing spending.

Hold Taxes and Decrease Spending.   If taxes are held constant and government spending is decreased for the purpose of combating inflation, it is more effective to decrease spending in those areas that tend to have the greatest multiplier effect. This method also has an advantage in that it is more palatable to the public than an increase in taxes. On the other hand, a reduction in government services necessitated by the decrease in spending may meet with some public resistance.

Increase Taxes and Hold or Decrease Spending. If higher taxes are to be used to combat inflation, taxes should be increased in such a manner that they absorb funds that otherwise would be spent on consumption or investment. Here again public sentiment may have to be weighed. If taxes are already high, as they are likely to be during an inflationary period, consumers and investors may not be receptive to the idea of still higher taxes. If this method is used to combat inflation, however, it is easy to see that a decrease in spending along with higher taxes gives a double effect.

Decrease Taxes and Decrease Spending. The combination of lower taxes and lower government spending can be deflationary if taxes are decreased in those areas where the money would otherwise be held idle. This will reduce total spending by the amount of the government spending, provided those who receive the tax reduction save more as a result. A major problem with this last procedure is the difficulty involved in designing a tax remission that will not release spendable funds. Even if such a plan could be designed, it would be difficult politically to rationalize a tax remission that is beneficial primarily to the higher income groups.

Regardless of the method used, the essential thing is to reduce effective demand. Thus, it is beneficial for government to build up a surplus. In this way, it can absorb the excessive spendable funds in the economy. Through taxation the government can reduce the total effective demand to a point where it will equal total output, and thus remove or lessen the demand-pull inflationary pressure. A reduction in government spending can be used to bring total investment plus government spending into equality with savings. It can reduce government spending to a point where the combination of government spending and investment will just equal the gap between consumption and output at full employment. On the other hand, an increase in taxes can be used to reduce the amount of consumption and investment to such a degree that government spending will fit into the gap between total private effective demand and total output, thus eliminating the inflationary gap.

If the government does use a surplus budget for the purpose of combating inflation, it is essential that the government maintain rather than spend the surplus. If it chooses to spend the surplus during the inflationary period, the desired anti-inflationary effects will be obliterated. In such an event government spending merely replaces the decreased spending on consumption and private investment, and thus inflationary pressures remain. The desired anti-inflationary effect of a surplus is negated also if the government uses the surplus to reduce the national debt. In such a case the recipients of debt repayment may spend the funds rather than save them.

Borrowing

Another method suggested to reduce the excessive spendable funds in the economy is government bond drives. This can be an effective method of reducing total effective demand, provided firms and individuals buy bonds with money they would otherwise spend on investment and consumption. Unlike bond drives during a depression, when an attempt is made to tap idle funds, the greatest anti-inflationary effect in this case comes from tapping spendable funds. A bond drive can be used in conjunction with or in lieu of an increase in taxes. Frequently it is easier to induce firms and individuals to give up spendable funds through bond purchases than it is to force them to give up funds through taxation.

THE TRADE-OFF BETWEEN UNEMPLOYMENT AND INFLATION

Once the economy is at full employment, it is difficult to ride the crest of the economy at the point where unemployment is minimized and the price level stabilized. The debate in recent years about the trade-off between increased unemployment and an increase in prices has renewed interest in the concept known as the **Phillips curve**. This curve was developed by a British economist, A. W. Phillips, who studied the relationship between the level of unemployment and wage increases in the United Kingdom for the years 1861 to 1913. From his studies he found that when unemployment was high, money wage increases were smaller, and that when a low level of unemployment existed, wage increases were larger. Phillips concluded that the money wage level would stabilize with a 5 percent unemployment rate.

In the 1960s U.S. economists began to apply the Phillips curve to changes in prices in relation to unemployment. This became feasible especially when the level of unemployment began to fall consistently below the 4 percent level. Subsequently a number of Phillips curves have been developed showing the relationship between price changes and the level of unemployment. Any interpretation of the curves must be made cautiously, since they are constructed with various assumptions. There is absolutely no certainty, for example, that because a given relationship occurred in the past, it will hold precisely in the future. Many conditions may change in the interim. Furthermore, several curves have been constructed from the same data, each showing a slightly different relationship depending on the time lag used.

Other curves, developed more recently, depict a rightward and upward shifting of the Phillips curve, indicating a higher-price-level–unemployment relationship in which both the price level and unemployment rates are higher as one is traded off against the other. Phillips curves for the years 1960 to 1982 would definitely move the price-unemployment line

Figure 19-1   Unemployment-Inflation Experience,
1960–1986

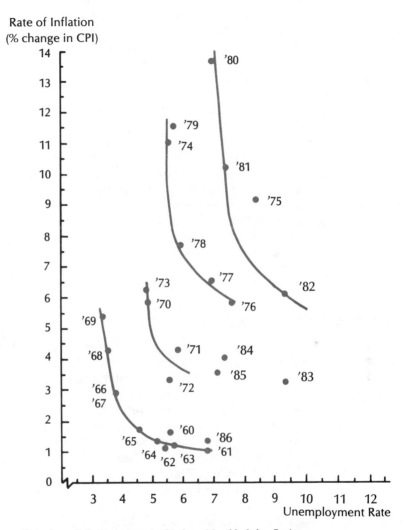

Source: Data from U.S. Department of Labor, *Monthly Labor Review*.

of best fit far to the right, as observable in Figure 19-1. This has led some analysts to challenge the Phillips curve and its relationship between unemployment and price-level changes. It should be remembered, however, that the Phillips curve was originally designed to measure the relationship between demand-pull inflation and unemployment, not cost-push, structural, or other varieties of inflation.

WARTIME INFLATION

Some of our strongest inflationary pressures occur during wartime periods. These are also times, however, when care must be exercised to utilize anti-inflationary measures in a fashion that will not hamper the war effort. Some of the methods that are suitable in peacetime would not be prudent in a war period and vice versa.

Causes of Wartime Inflation

The causes of wartime inflation are basically the same as the causes of demand-pull inflation in peacetime. In either case the inflation is caused primarily by an effective demand in excess of the productive capacity of a full-employment economy. This demand-pull inflation may or may not be augmented by cost-push, structural, or social inflation. In a peacetime economy the high effective demand usually results from high consumption and strong investment. In a wartime economy the effective demand exceeds the total output primarily because of the government's large demand for war materials. Since it is difficult to increase total output and since it would be folly to combat the inflation in wartime by reducing government spending on defense, it is essential to tackle the problem in a way different from that used in a peacetime economy.

Need for Reducing Consumption and Investment

In effect, it is necessary to reduce the effective demand for consumption and investment by an amount sufficient to permit government expenditure to fit into the gap between total output and the effective demand for consumption plus investment. Since much of the private investment will be converted into wartime production, the primary task is to reduce the demand for consumption. It becomes necessary to reduce not only the marginal propensity to consume but also the absolute amount of consumption. This is difficult to do because incomes rise substantially during a wartime economy. Thus, strong governmental measures may be required to adjust consumption to a proper level in a wartime economy.

Taxation.   The ideal measure to combat wartime inflation is heavy taxation. Through taxation, purchasing power can be transferred from individuals and firms to the government. This reduces the effective demand of the private sector of the economy and makes room for the necessary government spending on military goods and services. At the same time, it gives the government the means to make its purchases without going into debt. The most effective taxes are those that reduce consumption primarily, since a considerable amount of the private investment will still be essential. This means that taxes should hit hard at the middle and lower income groups, whose marginal propensity to consume is large. For example, very stiff income and sales taxes are beneficial. However, there may be considerable political and social opposition to such taxes.

Although heavier taxes on higher income groups may have a limited anti-inflationary effect through consumption reduction, they do provide much needed funds for the government. Furthermore, they tend to have a more popular social and political appeal.

Voluntary Savings.   A second method of combating wartime inflation is a program of voluntary savings, especially on the part of the consumer. The best method of accomplishing this is to encourage consumers to buy government bonds. In this way they not only will give up the purchase of consumer goods but also will transfer purchasing power to the government, which it can use to buy war materials.

Even though an appeal is made to the patriotism of consumers, its success in reducing consumption on a large scale is questionable. Frequently lower income groups will not readily reduce their consumption, especially since their incomes are increasing and they want to buy the goods and services that they were unable to purchase previously. Available evidence does not indicate that voluntary savings ever have been sufficient to arrest wartime inflation.

Compulsory Savings.   Since taxation plus voluntary savings are generally inadequate to finance a war, some advocate that more positive measures be exercised by the government. One of these is a program of compulsory savings. Compulsory savings may be justified on the basis of need and the common good. The government needs the money to finance the war, and it is in the common good to prevent inflation. No one individual or group of individuals can restrain the upward movement of prices. If all individuals are forced to save, however, the result can be a very strong restraining effect on inflationary pressures. A compulsory savings plan would require that a deduction, in addition to income taxes, be made from each individual's paycheck. This money would be credited to a special savings account that would remain blocked, except for emergencies, for the duration of the war or longer. Interest on these savings would be paid by the government.

Most proponents of compulsory savings suggest a progressive required savings rate. Since incomes would be increasing generally, this would permit those in the lowest income groups to maintain and perhaps to increase their normal consumption spending. Others with higher incomes would be required to save to such an extent that they would actually be forced to reduce consumption. Although the idea of permitting lower income groups to increase their consumption may not be anti-inflationary, it is consistent with the concept of social justice in our economy. Savings would be unblocked at, or some time after, the end of the war, depending on the extent of inflationary pressures in the economy. In total, such a plan could prove beneficial to consumers in the long run.

If compulsory savings are to be used, it is only equitable to hold the price level constant. It would be unfair to force individuals to save in order to reduce consumer demand and then let the value of their savings deteriorate by permitting prices to rise. Thus, if necessary, price and wage controls could be used to hold the price level.

In the absence of compulsory savings or some other method of holding the price line, a steeply progressive income tax and a stiff excess profits tax will limit the opportunity of profiteers to gain at the expense of consumers in a wartime economy. There is the possibility that the profiteers may lend their newly acquired income to the government through the purchase of bonds if it is not taxed. It may be more justifiable, however, to tax away any unearned increment rather than to permit the profiteers to hold claims against future resources by lending excess profits to the government.

A variation of compulsory savings in the form of a reimbursable income tax surcharge was recommended to combat inflation in late 1973.

Other Measures.   Other devices are sometimes used to reduce or to limit consumption and investment during a wartime period. For example, the rationing of goods and services may be used, especially when civilian products are in short supply compared with demand. Usually rationing via the allocation of coupons is used as a supplement or substitute for pricing as a rationing mechanism. Credit controls that increase the down payment and raise the size of installment payments by shortening the loan maturity on big-ticket items, such as autos, refrigerators, and furniture, can be instrumental in limiting the demand for goods and services. Credit restraints can also be used to restrict the purchase of homes. Higher interest rates and tighter money, of course, can limit private investment. Wage, price, material, and work force personnel controls may likewise be utilized during a wartime period.

HYPERINFLATION ABROAD

Inflation can be a serious malady and cause severe distortions in an economy. If left unchecked, it can run rampant, feed on itself, and develop into hyperinflation. Several European countries experienced inflation in the 1970s similar to that in the United States, but most of them had it in check by the mid-1980s, as shown in Table 19-1.

Unfortunately, in some other nations also shown in Table 19-1, especially in Latin America, inflation was not checked and took on characteristics of hyperinflation. Prices changed daily as printing presses ran off money much faster than the output of goods and services could grow. Finally by 1985–1986, fearing hyperinflation reminiscent of post–World War I Germany when prices changed hourly, workers were paid daily, and

Table 19-1 International Inflation Rates, 1980–1984

	1980–81	1983–84		1980–81	1983–84
Argentina	104.5%	626.7%	Italy	17.8%	10.8%
Belgium	7.6	6.3	Japan	4.9	2.3
Bolivia	32.1	1281.4	Mexico	27.9	65.5
Brazil	105.5	196.7	Peru	75.4	110.2
Canada	12.4	4.8	Switzerland	6.5	2.9
France	13.3	7.4	United Kingdom	11.9	5.0
W. Germany	5.9	2.4	United States	10.4	4.3
Israel	116.8	378.8			

Source: *Statistical Abstract of the United States*, 1986.

near-worthless money was used by some for wallpaper, certain of the Latin American nations took drastic steps to stop inflation.

In 1985 Argentina, for example, with its inflation rate soaring at a 2,000–3,000 percent annual rate, adopted a bold plan, hoping to remove the inflation mentality of its citizens. It created a new currency called the *austral* by lopping three zeros off the peso. It froze prices, wages, and official exchange rates. It promised to stop printing new money, reduce government spending, and balance the budget. The austral plan, as it is known, called for de-indexing wage and other contracts. In addition, it sought to privatize some of the 350 state-owned and/or -operated companies. Within a year the plan was successful in reducing inflation to a double-digit level.

In 1986 Brazil adopted a similar plan to combat its rapid inflation. It created a new currency, the *cruzado*, worth 1,000 cruzeiros; instituted wage and price controls; and abandoned automatic inflation adjustment measures. In 1987 the cruzado plan was acclaimed a success by the Brazilians.

In 1985 Bolivia's price index rose more than 8,000 percent. In the spring of 1986, with inflation running at an annual rate of 25,000 percent, it took a 2-inch stack of paper money to buy a chocolate bar. Unable to collect sufficient taxes to keep up with the rapid growth of government spending, Bolivia was running the money presses daily and printing 1 million, 5 million, and 10 million peso notes. Fearing the worst, Bolivia finally took drastic steps to stop its inflation. It devalued its currency by 93 percent, cut government spending, froze public sector wages, and eliminated many government jobs. By mid-1986 its currency had stabilized at 1.9 million pesos to the U.S. dollar. It had plans to replace the peso in early 1987 with the *condor*, worth 1 million pesos.

INFLATIONARY EXPERIENCE
IN THE UNITED STATES

The federal government did use many of the strong and broad measures mentioned above to attempt to control inflation during World War II and the Korean conflict. However, for our purposes, the past few decades provide a suitable period for a study, analysis, and evaluation of our attempts to use anti-inflationary measures. The strengths and weaknesses of measures used during this period are evident to some extent. During this span of time we experienced varying degrees of price stability, moderately rising prices, and strong inflationary pressures. Higher taxes, voluntary savings, budget surpluses, tight money, higher interest rates, wage and price controls, and credit controls were used to combat inflation.

Wage and Price Guideposts and Surtax of the 1960s

After several years of relative price stability during the 1950s, some price unrest became apparent in the economy in the latter half of 1961. President Kennedy, in his 1962 *Economic Report*, established a set of voluntary wage and price guideposts. If accepted by the major firms and unions in the economy, it would do much, according to the President, to restrain upward pressures on the price level. As a guide for noninflationary wage behavior, the rate of increase in wage rates (including fringe benefits) in each industry was to be equated with the national trend in overall productivity increase. Although general acceptance of the guideposts would maintain the stability of labor cost per unit of output for the economy as a whole, it would not stabilize labor cost per unit for individual firms or industries. The average productivity per worker in our economy increased about 3 percent annually, so the guideposts initially recommended that wage increases be held to 3 percent each year. This would allow the increase in wage cost to be absorbed out of rising productivity without necessitating a price increase. Subsequently, using a 5-year average, the guidepost figure was raised to 3.2 percent.

The guideposts, of course, stirred up considerable controversy in both wage and price circles. In many firms and industries where the rate of productivity was less than the national average, the guideposts were used by labor unions as a basis for a wage increase higher than the productivity rate increase within the firm or industry. In other firms or industries where the productivity rate exceeded the national average productivity increase, the firms often used the guideposts in an effort to limit the amount of a wage increase to 3 percent, even though they might have been able to afford higher wage increases. Another complaint was the fact that the guideposts tended to freeze labor's share of the national income.

The concept of price and wage guideposts seemed to be pushed out of the limelight by the emphasis on the tax cut in the 1963 *Economic Report* and by the poverty package in the 1964 *Report*. However, the guideposts were emphasized again by President Johnson and his economic advisers in the spring and summer of 1964. Subsequently, however, the AFL-CIO stated publicly that it did not intend to be limited by the wage guidepost in seeking wage increases during that year. The President of the United Auto Workers stated that since the productivity increase in the auto industry was much above the national average, the union was not going to limit its wage demands to the average of 3.2 percent. About the same time, steel companies were talking about the need for a price increase to offset some of their increasing costs. At that time President Johnson publicly warned that any increase in steel prices "would strongly conflict with our national interest in price stability."

With the return of stronger inflationary pressures in 1966, some delicate situations and open confrontations regarding the voluntary acceptance of the guideposts developed between the White House on the one hand and large industries and powerful unions on the other. Consequently, in 1967 the use of a specific guidepost figure was de-emphasized, although the guidepost concept was still retained. By 1968, however, the guideposts were virtually shattered as both labor unions and business firms posted wage and price increases substantially beyond the guidepost figures.

In his *Economic Report* of 1968 President Johnson called for the imposition of a 10 percent surcharge on personal and corporate income taxes as a means of combating inflation. The size of the proposed surcharge was increased from 6 percent to 10 percent because signs of an overheated economy were more in evidence, including the pending size of the federal deficit, in excess of $25 billion for fiscal 1968. The proposed bill to effectuate the tax became embroiled in a Congressional hassle about whether it was better to increase taxes or reduce federal spending. As a result of prolonged hearings and debate in Congress, final action on the tax bill was delayed until June, 1968. At that time Congress imposed a 10 percent surcharge on personal and corporate income taxes, making the surcharge retroactive to April 1 for individual income and January 1, 1968, on corporate income, effective until June, 1969.

The impact of the surtax fell more heavily on savings than expected, however, as consumers continued their outlays for goods and services, especially for new cars. The rate of savings fell sharply. Fixed investment for plant and equipment accelerated in the second half of 1968. Capital spending was no doubt spurred because investors thought that the 7 percent investment credit might again be suspended as an anti-inflationary measure. In spite of limited funds available for mortgages, there was no reduction in residential construction during the last half of 1968. There was some reduction in federal expenditures during this time, and the federal deficit was reduced from a rate of $9 billion in the first half of the year to $3 billion in the second half.

By mid-1968 a number of hefty national wage increases occurred within the economy, adding to the cost-push inflationary element. The shortage of skilled labor and even unskilled labor was evident in the economy.

Thus, labor unit costs rose sharply. Average hourly wage gains of 7 percent in manufacturing industries during the year plus a reduction in savings, however, offset the impact of the income tax surcharge.

All this, of course, caused prices to continue their upward movement through 1968. By the end of the year, the CPI had risen 4.7 percent. Thus, in spite of the addition of a strong fiscal measure to accompany somewhat restrictive monetary measures, little success was achieved in arresting the upward movement of prices in 1968.

Nixonomics

By the middle of 1969 prices were still rising. The CPI in the first half of 1969 rose at an annual rate of 6.3 percent. In 1969 price increases were especially noticeable in food costs, which were up at the rate of 9 percent annually, and services, which rose at a 7.5 percent annual rate in the first 6 months of the year.

Gradualism.   With the inauguration of the Nixon administration, inflation was cited as the nation's number one domestic issue. President Nixon adopted a policy of gradualism to bring inflation under control. In this regard, he wanted to return the economy to stable prices without seriously disrupting the growth in economic activity. Among other measures, he asked Congress to retain the 10 percent tax surcharge that was due to expire in June, 1969. The budget was balanced and, in fact, ran a slight surplus in fiscal 1970. Defense and other government spending was cut, and the Fed tightened the money supply. Although there was some discussion about the need for wage and price restrictions of some type, the President shied away from either formal or informal wage and price measures.

Wage and Price Controls of the 1970s

Economic pressures regarding prices, wages, and the balance of payments brought about a change of attitude on the part of the White House by mid-1971.

Phase I: The 90-Day Freeze.   With the knowledge that progress on his economic game plan was being stifled by substantial wage and price increases, President Nixon in August, 1971, made drastic and sweeping changes in domestic and international economic policies. Among other measures, he declared a 90-day freeze on all prices, wages, and rents; temporarily suspended convertibility of dollars into gold; imposed a 10 percent surcharge on imports; froze a scheduled pay increase for government employees; sought to reinstitute tax credits as a means of stimulating investment and jobs; and asked Congress to reduce personal income taxes and to repeal the 7 percent excise tax on automobiles.

Phase II. The 90-day freeze was followed by a Phase II control period. For the implementation of this phase the President established a Pay Board and a Price Commission. Each was to work out what it considered permissible noninflationary wage and price increases, respectively. The Commissions were composed of representatives of labor, management, and the general public.

The immediate effectiveness of the New Economic Policy in combating inflation can be gauged somewhat by the fact that during the 6 months before the freeze, prices increased at an annual rate of 4.5 percent; but in the 5 months subsequent to the freeze, they increased at an annual rate of 2.2 percent. The price level for 1972, during which price controls existed for the entire year, increased 3.3 percent, as shown in Table 19-2.

Phase III. In January, 1973, after commenting favorably on the results of Phase II in stabilizing prices and wages, President Nixon announced Phase III of his New Economic Policy, which in effect reestablished voluntary guideposts for price and wage increases. The guidepost figures used at that time were 2.5 percent and 5.5 percent annually for prices and wages, respectively.

Phase IV. The removal of compulsory Phase II controls proved to be premature, however. Consequently, on June 13, 1973, President Nixon declared a 60-day freeze on prices. Wages were not affected at this time. Instead of ending the freeze on all goods at the end of the 60-day period, prices were unfrozen selectively, and Phase IV controls were imposed on various categories of goods and services at different times before and after the 60-day period.

Slumpflation

In spite of an economic slowdown, prices soared in 1974. Unemployment moved above 5 percent and reached 6.5 percent by the end of the year, its highest level in more than a decade. President Ford then presented his anti-inflationary program, which advocated a tax surcharge, a decrease in federal spending, a balanced budget, several energy-saving measures, fuel conservation measures, tougher antitrust enforcement, a number of measures to encourage savings, exhortations to consumers to shop for bargains, establishment of a consumer committee, and an organization of inflation fighters, whose slogan was to be WIN (Whip Inflation Now). His proposals to alleviate unemployment included an expanded public service employment program, the injection of funds into the housing market, and tax credits for new investment. The major emphasis of President Ford's program at that time, however, was very definitely one of anti-inflation.

As the state of the economy deteriorated over the next few months

Table 19-2 Employment, Unemployment, and Inflation (Thousands)

Year	Total Employment	Unemployment	Rate of Unemployment	CPI (1967 = 100)	Rate of Inflation [1]
1960	65,778	3,852	5.5%	88.7	—
1961	65,746	4,714	6.7	89.6	1.0%
1962	66,702	3,911	5.5	90.6	1.1
1963	67,762	4,070	5.7	91.7	1.2
1964	69,305	3,786	5.2	92.9	1.3
1965	71,088	3,366	4.5	94.5	1.7
1966	72,895	2,875	3.8	97.2	2.9
1967	74,372	2,975	3.8	100.0	2.9
1968	75,920	2,817	3.6	104.2	4.2
1969	77,902	2,832	3.5	109.8	5.4
1970	78,678	4,093	4.9	116.3	5.9
1971	79,367	5,016	5.9	121.3	4.3
1972	82,153	4,882	5.6	125.3	3.3
1973	87,034	4,365	4.9	133.1	6.2
1974	85,064	5,156	5.6	147.1	11.0
1975	86,794	7,929	8.5	161.2	9.1
1976	88,752	7,406	7.7	170.5	5.8
1977	92,077	6,991	7.1	181.5	6.5
1978	96,048	6,202	6.1	195.4	7.7
1979	98,824	6,137	5.8	217.4	11.3
1980	99,303	7,637	7.1	246.8	13.5
1981	100,397	8,273	7.6	272.4	10.4
1982	99,526	10,678	9.5	289.1	6.1
1983	100,834	10,717	9.5	298.4	3.2
1984	105,005	8,539	7.4	311.1	4.3
1985	107,150	8,312	7.1	322.2	3.6
1986	109,597	8,237	7.0	328.4	1.9

1. Year-to-year changes.
Source: *Economic Report of the President*, 1987.

and it became evident that the economy actually was in a recession, the emphasis of economic policy began to shift toward expansionary measures. The real GNP had dropped for a third consecutive quarter, unemployment had reached 6.5 percent and was predicted to reach as high as 8 percent or more, the housing industry was still in the doldrums, inventories of such items as automobiles and appliances were piling up, investment plans were being trimmed, and economic conditions in Europe and Japan were likewise depressed. However, demand-pull price pressure had abated. But with a number of sizable wage settlements and administered prices being set, double-digit inflation still prevailed due to cost-push, structural, and social inflationary pressures.

It was apparent to all that the state of the economy had slipped downward from stagflation to **slumpflation**. Some analysts were talking in terms of a mini-depression.

This slumpflation, of course, threw economists into a new ball game. Previously they had figured they knew what measures to use to expand the economy during a recession and what measures to recommend to combat inflationary pressures. However, the simultaneous occurrence of recession and inflation, a condition with which we had very little experience before 1970, presented a real dilemma. Should the administration, for example, emphasize anti-inflationary measures and risk aggravating unemployment, or should it emphasize expansionary measures and risk higher prices? Not only is there an absence of foolproof economic measures to deal with slumpflation, but prudent decisions have to be made regarding which is a more serious problem—unemployment or inflation.

President Carter's Anti-Inflation Program

Unemployment remained at 7.7 percent in 1976, compared with 8.5 percent in the previous year. The CPI in 1976 rose only 5.8 percent, compared with a double-digit average for the previous 2 years. Thus, it appeared that the battle against inflation was meeting with some success. In 1977 inflationary pressures began to strengthen as the new Carter administration put more emphasis on reducing unemployment and as the economy continued to expand. Prices rose 6.5 percent in 1977, and in the spring of 1978 the CPI was again at the double-digit level.

Early in 1978 the President called for voluntary efforts on the part of management and labor to use moderation regarding price and wage increases. The President announced a policy of jawboning, in which a key member of the administration would meet "one on one" or in small groups with management and labor leaders to influence them on wage and price actions. However, this approach proved unsuccessful. In the meantime the Fed's continuing effort to combat inflation pushed the discount rate in a series of hikes from 5.5 percent in January, 1976, to 8 percent by September, 1978. The federal funds rate was still higher, and the prime rate on commercial loans exceeded 9 percent.

Finally, on October 2, 1978, President Carter announced a set of voluntary wage-price standards. These standards, which were noncompulsory, suggested that wage increases in the next 12 months should be held to 7 percent. Although the standards were voluntary, they did carry some clout insofar as the President authorized the withholding or cancellation of government contracts of $5 million or more to any firm not in compliance with the standards. The President's wage-price standards were greeted with mixed reaction in business, labor, and Congressional circles.

Reaganomics

At the time President Reagan took office, unemployment was running at a rate of 7.4 percent annually, the inflation rate was still close to the double-digit level, the discount rate was 14 percent, and the prime rate was a record 21.5 percent.

Within a few weeks after taking office President Reagan postponed, or canceled, numerous government regulations that were scheduled to take effect and eliminated the Council on Wage and Price Stability that had been administering the Carter wage-price standards. In addition, the President initiated a widespread program to cut federal spending in an effort to reduce the share of GNP going to the government.

He sought to implement a number of supply-side measures in an effort to encourage savings, stimulate investment, and motivate work effort for the purpose of expanding the economy and reducing inflation. Many of these measures were incorporated into the Economic Recovery Tax Act of 1981. The Tax Act included a 25 percent reduction in personal income taxes to be spread over a 3-year period, a reduction in the top marginal tax rate from 70 to 50 percent, reductions in corporate tax rates, tax credits on new investment, tax exemptions for interest earned on special all-savers accounts, and indexation of income tax rates starting in 1984.

A year later some of these measures were offset when the President and Congress found it necessary to rescind some tax reductions, impose some tax increases for fiscal 1983, and enact some new tax measures in order to keep the federal deficit for fiscal 1983 from becoming too large.

Another recession occurred in 1982, and unemployment reached an intolerable 10-plus percent. During the summer it was evident that the economy was in a classic state of stagflation. The Fed eased the money supply and helped lower interest rates. Between July and November, 1982, the discount rate was reduced from 14 percent to 9.5 percent in a series of moves. The prime rate fell from 16.5 to 13 at most large commercial banks. The inflation rate fell from the double-digit level to a rate of less than 5 percent annually by the end of President Reagan's second year in office.

Disinflation, a slowing down of the rate of inflation, continued during the economic recovery. The inflation rate hovered around 3 percent through mid-1986. A steep decline in oil prices, continued imports of large amounts of low-priced products, lower interest rates, moderation in wage increases, and declining food prices contributed to the lowering of the inflation rate. In fact, for a few months in early 1986, both the producer and consumer price indexes decreased, providing the first real taste of *deflation*, an actual drop in prices, in years. With some sluggishness apparent in the economy during 1986, the discount rate was lowered several times. It was set at 5.5 percent by September of that year.

SOME PROBLEMS OF DISINFLATION AND DEFLATION

Although disinflation and/or deflation is generally good for most members of society, it can cause hardship for certain individuals or segments of the economy. This is true especially for debtors who had anticipated paying off their debts with inflated dollars. Particularly hurt in the 1980s by the disinflation, or by deflation in some cases, were four broad segments of the U.S. economy: (1) commercial banks and government agencies that had loaned money to Third World nations, (2) the energy industry, (3) farmers, and (4) workers in certain industries. Although these are cited as problems associated with disinflation, it might be brought out that in large part they originated with overspending, overborrowing, and overconfidence associated with a prior inflationary period.

Third World countries borrowed heavily during the 1970s at high interest rates. They anticipated that their expanding economies would provide funds to pay off their loans. However, the softening of prices, along with lower sales, brought less income from their exports, especially from the United States. This meant less foreign exchange to meet payments on their debts, including interest. This forced them to borrow additional funds to meet interest payments. It also caused their creditors, including numerous U.S. commercial banks, to reschedule (postpone) principal repayments. Many commercial banks were hurt as a result of loan rescheduling, the need to allocate more funds for loan losses, and the actual write-off of some loans.

The dramatic drop (deflation) in oil prices, which contributed so much to the general disinflation, hurt the domestic energy sector of the U.S. economy. Many companies in the petroleum industry were forced out of business as oil prices declined. Widespread layoffs and wage reductions had a dampening effect on U.S. oil-producing areas, especially Texas, Oklahoma, and Louisiana. Numerous bankruptcies and the inability of oil producers to repay loans originating in the high oil price era of the 1970s had a deleterious effect on commercial banks and other creditors of energy companies. As a result, several bank failures occurred as banks wrote down or wrote off loans.

Another area hard hit by disinflation was the U.S. agriculture sector. Farmers, like oil producers and Third World nations, borrowed heavily at high interest rates to expand output and purchase new machinery and equipment in the 1970s and early 1980s. Decisions to borrow were based on strong domestic and foreign sales, high land values, and encouragement from creditors, such as commercial banks and farm banks. When sales slackened and farm prices dropped in the mid-1980s, many farmers found it difficult to meet interest and principal payments on their loans. Moreover, declining land values made creditors reluctant to extend or renew existing farm loans. As a result more farmers were forced out of business than at any time since the Great Depression of the 1930s. A large number of farm banks and commercial banks in farm areas, when unable to collect on farm loans, failed. Even the elaborate federal farm banking and credit system had to ask for special funding help from the federal government in 1986.

On a large scale, too, millions of U.S. workers experienced layoffs and wage reductions, in part because of disinflation. With lower prices, foreign competition, and the squeeze on profits in industries such as steel, autos, petroleum, shoes, and airlines, unions were forced into wage "give-backs" to protect jobs and help companies continue to operate. In spite of wage concessions by both managerial and hourly employees, however, widespread layoffs still took place in many of these industries.

SUMMARY

Demand-pull inflation occurs when the total monetary demand for goods and services exceeds the value of the current goods and services available. When such a situation arises, it can be alleviated either by increasing the output of goods and services or by reducing the demand. In a fully employed economy it is difficult to increase output; therefore, it is necessary to use the latter alternative. In this case, the effective demand of the government, consumers, and investors should be reduced.

The trade-off between unemployment and inflation is illustrated with a Phillips curve. Phillips found that when unemployment was high, money wage increases were smaller, and when unemployment was low, money wage increases were larger. In recent years, it appears that the Phillips curve may be shifting to the right, showing that both the price level and unemployment rates have become higher.

In a wartime economy it is difficult to reduce government expenditures without impairing the war effort. Therefore, measures must be used that tend to reduce consumption and private investment. Heavy taxation; voluntary savings; compulsory savings; rationing; and wage, price, and other controls can be used. It should also be remembered that inflation can be of a demand-pull, cost-push, structural, or social type.

Even with all our knowledge and experience about combating inflation, a lukewarm approach to the problem during the early years of the war in Vietnam caused the price level to increase noticeably in 1966 and 1967 after a period of substantial price stability. More serious measures, such as an income tax surcharge, tight money, and a balanced budget, were somewhat effective in moderating demand-pull inflation. But they were ineffective against cost-push inflationary pressures. In spite of the efforts made to contain inflation, the price level rose 25 percent during the 5-year period 1966–1971. In August, 1971, President Nixon imposed a 90-day freeze on all prices and wages. With the removal of controls in January, 1973, prices rose substantially, and controls were reinstituted by midyear. The effect was limited, however, and controls were subsequently removed. During 1974 the price level rose at an annual rate of 11 percent. By that time the economy was in a recession, and the emphasis was shifted from anti-inflationary to expansionary measures.

With the resurgence of double-digit inflation in 1978, President Carter introduced a set of voluntary wage-price standards calling for a 7 percent limitation on wage increases and a limit on price increases of one-half of one percentage point below each firm's average annual increase during the period 1976–1977. The effectiveness of the President's anti-inflation program was minimal during his term in office.

President Reagan's application of supply-side economic measures was more successful in lowering the interest rates and the rate of inflation. As the economy expanded slowly in 1986, the rate of inflation was between 1 and 2 percent, the discount rate was down to 5.5 percent, and unemployment was 7.0 percent.

NEW TERMS AND CONCEPTS

Phillips curve

Slumpflation

DISCUSSION QUESTIONS

1. How does a progressive income tax rate serve as a built-in stabilizer to offset inflation?

2. To combat inflation do you think it is better to decrease government spending and hold taxes constant, or to hold government spending constant and increase taxes?

3. Should we tax sufficiently to pay the full cost of a war, instead of borrowing, as a means of avoiding inflation? Why or why not?

4. Explain why measures that may diminish or eliminate demand-pull inflation may not work successfully against cost-push inflation.

5. Do you think President Nixon was wise in imposing a 90-day freeze on wages and prices in August, 1971? Explain.

6. Why is inflation difficult to combat if it occurs during a recession, as it did in 1974 and 1980?

7. Do you think voluntary wage and price standards such as those suggested by President Carter will ever work in our economy? Why?

8. Discuss the administration's current program to deal with unemployment and inflation.

9. Is disinflation always good for an economy? Why or why not?

SUGGESTED READINGS

"Disinflation Here or Gone." *NABE NEWS* (May, 1983).

Eastburn, David P. "Voluntary Inflation Restraint and Corporate Social Responsibility." *Business Review*. Federal Reserve Bank of Philadelphia (January–February, 1979).

Economic Report of the President. Washington, DC: U.S. Government Printing Office, annually.

Fischer, Stanley. *Indexing, Inflation, and Economic Policy*. Cambridge, MA: MIT Press, 1986.

Francis, Darryl R. "Inflation, Recession—What's a Policymaker to Do?" *Review*. Federal Reserve Bank of St. Louis (November, 1974).

Hailstones, Thomas J., and Frank V. Mastrianna. *Contemporary Economic Problems and Issues*, 8th ed. Cincinnati: South-Western Publishing Co., 1988.

Hein, Scott E. "Deficits and Inflation." *Review*. Federal Reserve Bank of St. Louis (March, 1981).

Santomero, A. M., and J. J. Seater. *The Inflation-Unemployment Trade-Off: A Critique of the Literature*, Research Paper No. 21. Federal Reserve Bank of Philadelphia (March, 1977).

Seidman, Laurence. "Fighting Inflation with a Tax-Based Incomes Policy." *Business Review*. Federal Reserve Bank of Philadelphia (January–February, 1980).

20

TAXATION, BUDGETARY POLICY, AND THE NATIONAL DEBT

■

We expect certain goods and services from our government. The institutional arrangement for financing government expenditures for those goods and services is taxation. For decades the primary purpose of taxation was to raise sufficient revenue to cover the cost of services expected from the various levels of government—federal, state, and local. Therefore, a balanced budget was a perennial target.

Over the years, certain services have become associated with a particular level of government. For instance, national defense and income security are associated with the federal government, and education and highway construction with state and local governments. Today all three levels of government participate in providing some services, such as education and public welfare.

TAXATION

Certain sources of taxes have become associated with specific levels of government. For many years personal and corporate income taxes were levied by the federal government only, as were tariffs and excise taxes. The general property tax and sales tax were used principally by state and local governments. Now, however, many sources of revenue are being taxed by more than one level of government. Income, for example, is commonly taxed by federal, state, and local governments. Figure 20-1 summarizes the sources and uses of federal revenues. With fiscal 1987 receipts and outlays of Social Security OASI and DI trust funds became off-budget items and exempt from any general budget limitation imposed by statute.

Characteristics of a Good Tax

In order to merit the mark of good taxation, the following characteristics must be met:

1. There must be a *justifiable* reason for the tax.

2. The tax must be *equitably* applied to taxpayers.

3. There must be *certitude* regarding the amount of the tax and the obligation of the taxpayer.

4. The tax must be *convenient* to levy and collect.

5. The tax must be *economical* insofar as the cost of collection is small compared with the revenue generated by the tax.

Figure 20-1   Federal Income and Spending, Fiscal Year 1988

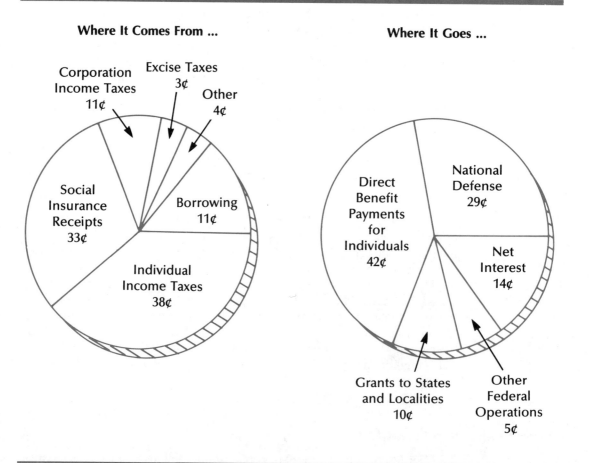

Source: *The United States Budget in Brief,* Fiscal Year 1988.

Equity or Fairness in Taxation

What is a fair or equitable tax? Various attempts have been made to establish principles that would be of practical value in apportioning the tax burden fairly. Among the proposals that have been advanced are the theories of cost of service, benefit received, and ability to pay.

Cost of Service. The cost-of-service theory suggests that individuals should contribute toward the cost of general government in proportion to the cost of the governmental services that they receive. The services implied here include those general services for health, sanitation, protection of person, and all others performed specifically for the individual. Other kinds of services, such as the construction and maintenance of highways and schools, should, it is argued, be paid directly through user fees.

Except for a few minor government services, the cost-of-service theory is untenable. First, it would be impossible to calculate the costs of the services to each individual. How, for example, would the costs of protection for persons and property be allocated among individuals? In the second place, the adoption of such a principle would mean the denial of any responsibility of the state for those not able to pay for public services.

Benefit Received. The benefit-received theory in taxation holds that individuals should contribute in proportion to the benefits received from the services of government. It is closely related to the cost-of-service theory; in fact, it might be said that the two theories are merely different aspects of the same general idea. For example, a person with $100,000 worth of real estate should pay 10 times as much in taxes as a person with only $10,000 worth. This is the principle that is followed in levying taxes on real estate. This argument implies that the person who owns more property or wealth receives more protection from government, and it costs government more to render these protective services.

While the benefit-received theory contains some validity, an attempt to apply it to all taxes would be difficult. To begin with, how could the value of a service be calculated? How should the costs of public education be allocated? Certainly the value of a public education may be different for the children of the poor than for those of the rich, who may prefer private education. Although the benefit-received theory in not practicable as a guide for the formulation of taxes in general, it is in operation in certain cases. Gasoline and liquor taxes as well as marriage and automobile license fees are based upon the benefit-received theory to a certain extent.

Ability to Pay. The theory of taxation often accepted with minimal argument is that of ability to pay. But how should the ability to pay taxes be determined? Should proportional standards be used by basing the tax on something such as real estate or income? Or should the tax be designed to produce an equality of sacrifice on the part of those who are taxed?

Proportional Standard. It is sometimes held that all taxes should be proportional. For example, if the tax base is real estate, then the total amount of the taxes to be paid by property owners should vary with the value of their property. If the tax base is income, the amount of the tax should be proportional to the income received. Of course, many of those who support this proportional concept have seldom given serious thought to the relative sacrifices involved in the payment of taxes by individuals with varying amounts of income or wealth. However, the fact that the proportional idea is widely accepted makes it a matter of importance. In recent years a number of proposals have been submitted in Congress to change our progressive income tax to a proportional tax, or *flat-rate tax.*

Equality-of-Sacrifice Doctrine. The equality-of-sacrifice doctrine of taxation is based upon the law of diminishing marginal utility of income: When income is small, the marginal satisfaction of a dollar is much higher than when income is large. A family with an income of $5,000 is much less "able" to pay $500 in taxes than a family with an income of $50,000 is able to pay $5,000. A majority of persons would probably agree that a proportional tax of 10 percent on incomes would "hurt" the family with the lower income much more than the one with the larger income, since the former would already be living closer to the subsistence level.

On the other hand, some contend that a 10 percent tax would call for equal sacrifice by both families. They argue that people adjust their scale of living to their income. Households with large incomes develop levels of living in accordance with their ability to maintain them. When they are forced to adjust their level of living downward, it entails proportionally as much sacrifice as does a proportional loss by a household on a lower level of living. For example, the feeling of sacrifice experienced by a wealthy person who is forced to give up a club membership as a result of a tax increase may be as great as the sacrifice of a worker who is compelled to forgo attendance at ball games as a result of the payment of a tax.

THE TAX-RATE STRUCTURE

The allocation of the tax burden is expressed in the tax-rate structure, which determines the amounts that individual taxpayers are called upon to pay. The amount of a tax is determined by applying the tax rate to the tax base. The **tax rate** is a percentage; the **tax base** is the value of the object upon which the tax is levied. For example, if the rate is 20 percent of one's gross income, the percentage indicated is the rate, and the gross income stated in terms of dollars is the base. In the case of taxes on real estate, the rate is usually given as so many mills or cents per dollar, or as a percentage of the assessed valuation. Thus, the rate might be stated as 5 cents per dollar or 5 percent of the assessed value of the property.

The relationship of rates to changes in the base is indicated by the terms "proportional," "progressive," "degressive," and "regressive."

Proportional Rates

A **proportional tax rate** is one that remains the same, regardless of the size of the base. For example, a 5 percent proportional tax on an income of $10,000 would amount to $500, and on $100,000, to $5,000. A strong argument in favor of a proportional rate is that, after payment, the taxpayers are left in the same relative position as they were before the tax. Many who advocate proportional taxes admit that the application of the rate structure may not result in imposing equal sacrifice upon taxpayers; however, they defend their position by denying that any satisfactory criterion for sacrifice has yet been demonstrated. Moreover, they argue that proportional, or flat-rate, taxes are simple to administer.

Progressive Rates

Because of a rather general acceptance that ability to pay should be used as a criterion for taxation, some taxes are applied at a progressive rate. A **progressive tax rate** is one in which the rate increases as the base increases. Thus, a tax of 1 percent on the first $1,000 of taxable income, 2 percent on the second $1,000, and so on, is a progressive tax. Of course, if this rate of progression were continued, the tax would absorb all income beyond $100,000 or more.

Opponents argue that progressive rates are unfair because they penalize the possession of wealth, the earning of income, and the exercise of hard work. Many of the United States' great fortunes were amassed through either an inheritance, a special skill or talent, or a personal characteristic, rather than through industriousness. As a result, and perhaps because there are few persons with exceptionally high incomes, there is a tendency in the United States to sanction steeply progressive income taxes. What constitutes a reasonable progressive rate, however, is a debatable question.

Opponents also suggest that progressive taxes tend to relieve the poor from the payment of direct taxes, which in turn causes a diminution of their sense of responsibility to support the government. Furthermore, if the poor are not taxed at rates as high as those for the rich, they will enjoy the services of government at the expense of others. They will then demand more and more, since the services will appear to cost them little or nothing.

Degressive Rates

A **degressive tax rate** calls for the payment of a larger amount of tax as the size of the base increases, but the payments are not progressively larger. In other words, a degressive tax is a progressive tax for which the rate increases at a decreasing rate. For example, a tax of 1 percent on a $1,000 base; 2.5 percent on $10,000; and 3.5 percent on $100,000 would be degressive.

Critics of progressive taxation point out that the determination of progressive rates rests upon the judgment of the individuals who establish them. Since there is no objective guide for the steepness of the rates, it is argued that once a progressive rate structure is adopted, the logical stopping place tends to approach 100 percent. Practically speaking, this would mean confiscation of the value of the base (property or income) at that point.

A degressive tax avoids confiscation. Thus, income taxes are usually progressive up to a certain level of income, then degressive for an additional level of income, after which they remain proportional.

Regressive Rates

A **regressive tax rate** is one that decreases as the size of the base increases. For example, assume that the rate on an income of $1,000 is 5 percent; on an income of $2,000, 4 percent; $3,000, 3 percent; $4,000, 2 percent; and $5,000, 1 percent. In such a case, the rate decreases as the base increases.

Although a sales tax is proportional, its opponents take delight in pointing out that, in effect, a retail sales tax is regressive. They argue that the share of smaller incomes spent for taxable goods is higher than that of larger incomes. With a 4 percent sales tax, for example, a family with a $24,000 annual income may purchase $20,000 worth of taxable commodities and pay sales taxes of $800. On the other hand, a family with an $80,000 income may purchase $40,000 worth of taxable commodities. They will pay sales taxes of $1,600. Consequently, it is argued that the lower income family is paying a higher rate of 3.3 percent ($600 ÷ $24,000) on the basis of its income, whereas the higher income family is paying a tax rate of only 2 percent ($1,600 ÷ $80,000) of its income. However, it is incorrect to call the sales tax regressive, since the base of the tax is sales (purchases), not income. Both families are paying a proportional tax rate, 4 percent, compared with its proper base. Anyone who claims that the sales tax is regressive should be careful to emphasize that it is regressive in relation to income, not in relation to its true base, purchases.

To recapitulate, a proportional tax is one in which the rate remains the same as the base increases; a progressive tax is one in which the rate increase keeps pace with the rate of increase in the base; a degressive tax is one in which the rate increases as the base increases, but the rate increases at a decreasing rate; and a regressive tax is one in which the rate decreases as the base increases. Some taxes have elements of one or more different rates in their structure.

THE TAX BURDEN

The burden of a tax does not always rest on the person or the firm paying the tax. For example, taxes on cigarettes, wines, liquors, and other consumer goods are paid by the manufacturer or distributor, who usually adds the amount of the tax to the selling price of the commodity and passes the burden of the tax along to the final consumer. Many taxes can be shifted, but it is not possible to shift the burden of a tax on personal income. The fact that it is possible to shift the burden of some taxes more easily than that of others is one reason for the continuing debate over what taxes should be levied.

Three stages or aspects of passing the burden from one taxpayer to another, or **shifting of taxes**, are recognizable. The **impact of a tax** is the financial burden entailed by the payment of the tax. For example, when an importer of Scottish tartan cloth pays the import duty, the impact of the tax is on the importer; but the importer adds the amount of the tax to the price of the materials. A tailor who then buys the cloth in effect reimburses the importer for the amount of the duty paid and adds that amount to the prices of garments made for customers. Therefore, the burden of the duty is actually on the final customers, not on the person who initially paid the tax to the government. The same thing is true of sales taxes when the amount of the tax is added to the selling price of the commodity and is passed on in this way to the final purchaser.

The **incidence of a tax** is the point at which the burden of the tax ultimately rests. For example, the incidence of a cigarette tax is on the consumer. The **effect of a tax** is an economic consequence of the payment of the tax. For example, the increase in the price of a good resulting from the payment of a tax on it is an effect. Also, if the increase in price results in a decrease in the quantity of the good that is purchased, this result is also an effect of the tax.

The burden of many taxes tends to be shifted forward to the ultimate purchaser. Occasionally the effect is shifted backward, as when an increase in price by the amount of the tax results in a reduction in sales and, consequently, a decrease in the demand for materials and labor for the production of the good. In such a case, part of the effect of the tax is shifted backward to the suppliers of the materials and labor involved.

By definition a **direct tax** is one, such as an income tax, that cannot be shifted; an **indirect tax**, such as a liquor tax, is one that can be shifted. The distinction between the two is clear, according to definition. However, when individual taxes are considered, it is not always certain whether they are direct or indirect.

PURPOSES OF TAXATION

Taxation has been used for a variety of purposes. Three major purposes or objectives are discussed in the following paragraphs.

Cover the Costs of Government

For decades the primary purpose of taxation was to raise sufficient revenue to cover the cost of services expected from various levels of government. Accordingly, a balanced budget was a perennial target. In seeking a balanced budget, the government could take certain measures to ensure its objective. If prosperity abounded and tax revenues were pointing toward a surplus, the government could either reduce taxes, expand its services to the people, or repay some of the government debt. On the other hand, during a period of economic slack when falling tax revenues would threaten a deficit, the government was expected to tighten its economic belt and reduce spending.

Redistribute Income and Wealth

In the past few decades more and more use has been made of taxation as a means of redistributing income and wealth in the U.S. economy. Relying on the ability-to-pay concept, individuals and business firms in higher income levels have been taxed at higher rates to provide revenues for services that are shared in greater proportion by those in lower income levels. Higher corporate and personal federal income tax revenues which go into the general fund, for example, may be used indirectly to provide public service employment for the unemployed, aid to families with dependent children, or food stamps for the poor. In other instances, tax credits or rebates may be given in larger proportion to lower income taxpayers. It is interesting to note that government transfer payments now provide about 13 cents out of each dollar of personal income compared with less than 5 cents two decades ago. The use of taxation for the avowed purpose of redistributing income has become a very controversial issue in recent years. The total of all government expenditures for social welfare programs, for example, increased from 10.5 percent of the GNP in 1960 to nearly 20 percent by 1986.

Stabilize Economic Activity

Over the past 40 years we have established a policy of using taxation and government spending for the purpose of stabilizing economic activity. During that time we have developed a set of fiscal measures to combat recessions and inflation and to stimulate the rate of economic growth. The use of these fiscal measures involves the federal budget and has an effect on economic activity and on the price level. Some modification of this policy occurred in the early 1980s when President Reagan recommended the reduction of federal spending as a percentage of the GNP.

BUDGETARY POLICY

The size, growth, and nature of the federal budget, whether it is balanced or unbalanced, affects our national debt. Interrelated are monetary measures involved in financing any deficit. These measures may have an influence on the structure and maturity of the national debt. Management of the national debt can have a stabilizing or a destabilizing effect. We now turn to an analysis of budgetary policy.

Types of Budgets

The types of budget we have will affect the level of economic activity to some degree. There are three types: a balanced budget, a deficit budget, and a surplus budget.

Balanced Budget. In general, a balanced budget is usually thought to have a neutral effect on the economy. Since government expenditures equal taxation with a balanced budget, total spending in the economy remains unchanged. What individuals and business firms give up in spendable funds to pay their taxes is counterbalanced by the government spending of the tax receipts. At times, however, it is possible for a balanced budget to bring about an expansionary effect in the economy. This occurs if the government taxes idle funds that will not otherwise be spent by individuals and businesses. Effective demand would then increase.

The expansion of effective demand through the balanced budget multiplier effect will depend on the propensity to consume or save. Assume that the average propensity to consume is 100 percent. In such a situation there would be no balanced-budget multiplier effect, since the adverse effect of taxation on the private sector resulting from the tax would be offset by the government spending the tax receipts through the public sector.

However, if the propensity to save were one-fifth, and the federal budget were balanced at $1,000 billion, theoretically the government would be taxing $200 billion of funds that were going to be saved. When the government spent these funds, it would have an expansionary or inflationary effect depending on the status of the economy. This effect would be lessened, of course, to the extent that any of the savings would have been used for private investment.

Deficit Budget. A deficit budget will generally increase the level of economic activity or will be inflationary, depending upon the status of employment in the economy. Remember that with a deficit budget the government spends more than it taxes. To take care of this excess of spending over taxation, the government will be required to borrow funds. If it borrows idle funds or money created by banks, the total effective demand of the economy will be increased. The increase occurs because the total spending by the government is greater than the amount of spendable funds given up by firms and individuals through taxation. Therefore, the level of economic activity will increase if the economy is at less than full employment, and inflation will occur if the economy is at full employment. It is for this reason that a deficit budget is frequently referred to as a fiscal stimulus. The fiscal stimulus, however, will be offset to some extent if the government borrows funds that individuals and businesses might otherwise spend on consumption and investment.

Surplus Budget. A surplus budget means that government spending is insufficient to offset the decline in spendable funds given up by individuals and businesses in the form of taxes. As a result, there is a net decrease in effective demand. Consequently, a surplus budget is often considered by some as a fiscal drag on the economy. This drag effect, of course, would be modified to the extent that the government might tax idle funds that would not be spent otherwise. It could also be offset if the government were to use the surplus to retire the debt. At times a surplus budget may be used as an anti-inflationary measure to slow down the rate of inflation.

Budget as a Stabilizer

If used properly, a budgetary policy can help to stabilize the economy and modify business cycles. A surplus budget helps prevent inflation during a prosperity period, and a deficit budget helps offset the widespread unemployment during a depressionary period. The use of budgetary policy is shown in Figure 20-2.

When the budget is used as a tool for economic stabilization, it is desirable to balance the budget over the period of the cycle instead of trying to do it on an annual basis. To accomplish this, it would be necessary for the surplus of prosperity to equal the deficit of the recession. However, this would be difficult to accomplish. A question might arise about whether we should start such a stabilizing practice by building up a surplus during prosperity and then spending it during the next recession, or whether we should incur the deficit during the recession and then repay the debt with the surplus obtained during the subsequent period of prosperity.

Assuming that the first method is utilized, a second problem arises. How much surplus needs to be accumulated during the prosperity period? This depends not only upon the inflationary pressures of prosperity but also upon the estimated deficit during the subsequent recession in the economy. It is practically impossible, however, to determine what the duration and the intensity of the prosperity will be, let alone the duration and the severity of the subsequent recession. Therefore, it is usually more feasible to run the deficit first. This also has its weaknesses. How can we be assured that the subsequent prosperity will be long enough or

Figure 20-2 The Budget Used as an Anticyclical Device

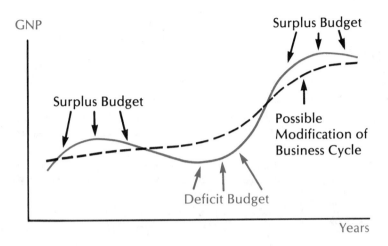

strong enough to permit an accumulation of a surplus sufficient to pay off the deficit incurred in the previous recessionary period?

Another weakness of the deficit-first method is that most legislators are willing to use deficit spending during a recessionary period to help alleviate unemployment, but many of them are reluctant to institute measures required to build up the necessary surplus during prosperity years. In short, deficit spending, insofar as it can be used to bolster the level of economic activity, can be very popular with the public during a recession, but increased taxes to combat inflation during a prosperity period are seldom popular.

It should be remembered also that a surplus acquired during a prosperity period should be held in cash reserve for best results. It should not be used to pay off the debt until the level of economic activity begins to stabilize or decline. If the surplus is used immediately to pay off the debt incurred during the recession, it will merely result in putting back into the economy an amount of money equivalent to the surplus. Thus, the reduction of spendable incomes through taxation will be offset by government expenditures plus debt repayment. This means that if the recipients of debt repayment spend or invest the money received from the government, the total spending in the economy will remain the same. In such a case, the surplus budget will have a neutral effect instead of being anti-inflationary. The better practice would be to hold the surplus funds until economic activity begins to decline. Repayment of the debt at such time could give a boost to the economy if the recipients of debt repayment were to spend or invest these funds.

The process of using the budget as a stabilizer is further complicated when stagflation occurs and inflation exists during a recession or general slowdown in economic activity. A surplus budget at such a time would aggravate unemployment and have unpopular economic and political effects.

The Full-Employment Budget

In recent years there has been a tendency to look at the so-called **full-employment budget** instead of the actual budget for the purpose of analyzing the fiscal effects of the budget. Regardless of the state of the actual budget, the full-employment budget is a measure of the potential revenue and expenditure that would result if full employment existed. Some think that the actual budget may be misleading. Let us say, for example, that the existing budget shows a deficit (or fiscal stimulus) of $25 billion and that the rate of unemployment is 6 percent. Projection may indicate that if the economy were at full employment (5 percent unemployment or less), the budget would show a surplus of $10 billion. Thus, if the economy expands toward the full-employment level, it will encounter a fiscal drag, which would impede the attainment of a full-employment objective.

Proponents of "functional finance," who look at the budget as a tool of stabilization and growth rather than as something to be balanced annually or even periodically, would contend that the inherent drag of the full-employment surplus should be eliminated if the economy is to attain its goal of full employment. This, of course, could be accomplished by increasing the size of the current deficit (fiscal stimulus) through reducing taxes or by increasing government spending.

Carrying the analysis one step further, proponents of this theory claim that once full employment and a balanced budget have been reached, care must be taken to prevent the development of a subsequent budget surplus on the economy. It is pointed out that with a given tax rate, total revenues will increase by $20–$25 billion annually as a result of the normal forces of growth in our economy. To prevent this surplus from occurring, a fiscal dividend may be declared in the form of either a tax reduction or an increase in federal spending. Little emphasis is given to the notion that surpluses should be accumulated during prosperity to offset the deficits of previous periods.

Of course, if the federal budget is used as a fiscal tool to stabilize economic activity, and deficits occur over an extended period of time, the national debt will grow. The growth of a national debt creates other problems. Moreover, the actual management of the national debt can have a stabilizing or destabilizing effect on the level of economic activity.

PROBLEMS OF THE NATIONAL DEBT

Our experience with budgetary policy as a means of stabilizing business activity is rather limited. It is difficult, therefore, to determine whether we can time our deficits and surpluses accurately and have them of proper size to act as stabilizers of the economy. Furthermore, we have not had sufficient experience in the past 50 years to determine whether, in the absence of emergencies, the deficits and the surpluses can offset each other sufficiently to prevent a growing debt. We incurred a sizable debt during the Depression of the 1930s as a result of our deficit-spending program. Without having had a chance to diminish this debt, we entered World War II, which pushed the debt up to about $285 billion. Our opportunity to reduce the debt was further hampered by the outbreak of the Korean conflict in 1950. The escalation of the war in Vietnam in the mid-1960s interfered with our experiments to use fiscal stimuli and fiscal dividends and to avoid fiscal drags on the economy. In the interim years, however, we made very little headway in reducing the debt. In fact, the federal debt, now over $2 trillion, has grown to such proportions that it presents several problems. A few of these problems are treated in the following paragraphs.

Bankruptcy

Many people think that the debt may become so large that it will bankrupt the nation. It is commonly believed that the federal government may get into a situation where it will be unable to pay off the debt. This misunderstanding arises from the failure to distinguish clearly the true nature of government financing and the power of the federal government to raise tax revenues. When the government borrows and repays funds, it is more like the financial transactions taking place within a family than the type of financing practiced by private enterprises.

Comparison with Business Debt.   In accounting we learn that whenever a business has total current liabilities in excess of current assets, it lacks solvency. In short, it does not have sufficient cash or current assets to pay its current debts in the immediate future. When debtors press for payment, the company may voluntarily and legally have itself declared bankrupt, or the debtors may force the company into bankruptcy. In either case, the court will decide whether the business should continue under receivership, that is, under a court-appointed manager, or whether the assets of the company should be liquidated to pay off the creditors.

This basic difficulty arises in connection with a business debt because whenever the firm pays off its debt, it decreases the total assets of the company. Money paid out actually leaves the firm, thereby reducing the assets. If debt payments are so large that the company is forced to suspend payment, the creditors may force liquidation of the firm through bankruptcy proceedings to recover payment on the debt.

Comparison with Family Debt.   The national debt is more like an internal family debt than a business debt. Consider the family as a spending unit and suppose that a son borrows $900 from his parents for such things as dates, ball games, and school supplies over the period of the school year and that he intends to repay it from the money he earns from summer employment. When he borrows, he does so within the family unit. Likewise, when he repays the $900 in the summer, the money remains within the family.

When the son pays his debt, his individual assets are decreased by $900 but his parents' assets are increased by $900. Therefore, the net assets of the family remain the same. Unlike the debt repayment of the firm, in the family situation no money leaves the family as a result of the debt repayment. There is merely a transfer of cash from one member of the family to another. Therefore, there is no net reduction of assets, nor is there any money leaving the family.

The Federal Debt.   When the federal government borrows money, it borrows primarily from individuals, businesses, and banks within the economy. When it makes repayments on the debt, the money stays within the economy. There is no reduction in total assets when the government makes repayment on the debt. Furthermore, the government's ability to repay is governed only by the total assets of the economy or, more immediately, by the total income of the economy and the government's ability to tax. For example, the national debt in 1986 was $2,133 billion. Considering that the GNP was $4,209 billion and that the total national income was $3,387 billion, it is easy to see that the total income of the nation was sufficient to take care of debt repayment if the government decided to raise taxes sufficiently to obtain funds required to pay it off.

Theoretically, but unrealistically, the government could tax a sufficient amount to pay the debt off in the course of 1 year. If the government were to do this, it would not in any way reduce the total income or assets of the nation as a whole. The taxation and repayment of the debt would merely cause a redistribution of income, or cash assets, inside the economy. The income given up by individuals and firms in the form of taxes would be offset by payment of those holding the debt. Thus, the total income or assets of the economy would be the same after payment of the debt as before. The major difference is that income and cash assets held by various individuals and firms would be changed. It must be pointed out, however, that foreigners now hold about 11 percent of the national debt, compared with less than 5 percent in 1970.

Although a tax rate sufficient to pay off the debt in 1 year would be prohibitive, certainly over a long period, say 30 or 40 years, the government could operate at a surplus sufficient to pay off the debt. Surpluses obtained during prosperous periods could be used to pay the debt during periods of contraction in the economy.

Effect on Redistribution of Income

The question naturally arises: Why doesn't the government take more positive steps to pay off the debt? Reluctance to reduce the debt by sizable amounts stems not only from the fact that the large tax necessary to do so would be politically unpopular, but also from the fact that it would cause disruptive economic repercussions. One important problem involved would be the redistribution of income brought about by repayment of the debt.

If the debt were to be paid off on a large-scale basis, heavy taxes would reduce total effective demand, especially among the lower and middle income groups. Whether such a reduction in effective demand would be offset when the government used tax money to pay off the debt would depend on what the recipients of debt repayments would do with the money they received. Since it is quite possible that the total propensity to consume or to invest of the debt holders who receive repayment would be less than that of the taxpayers in total, the net effective demand of the economy could easily be reduced by repayment of the debt. The possibility of this occurring becomes evident when we look at the ownership of the debt. It is generally agreed that the lower income groups do not hold much of the federal debt. It is held primarily by banks, businesses, government agencies, and individuals in the higher income groups. This is shown in Table 20-1.

Of course, if the debt holders would spend the income they received at the time the debts were repaid, it would not have an adverse effect on the economy. This would tend to be the case if the debt were repaid during a full-employment period. It would be best, however, to pay off the debt during periods of less than full employment with money obtained

Table 20-1 Percentage Ownership of the U.S. National Debt, 1986

U.S. government agencies and trust funds		17.9%
Federal Reserve Banks		9.0
Private investors		73.1
Commercial banks	9.7%	
Money market funds	1.3	
Insurance companies	4.8	
Other companies	3.2	
State and local governments	11.2	
Individuals	8.0	
Foreign and international	11.0	
Miscellaneous [1]	23.9	
Total		100.0%

1. Includes savings and loan associations, nonprofit institutions, credit unions, corporate pension funds, and certain U.S. government deposit accounts.

Source: *Federal Reserve Bulletin* (February, 1987).

through taxation during a prosperous or inflationary period. In this way the debt could be used as a tool for economic stabilization.

Burden of the Debt

It is often thought that when the debt is not paid during the period in which it is incurred, the burden of paying the debt is passed on to future generations. The extent to which this may be true depends upon whether we are considering the effect on the total economy or on individuals and firms.

Effect on Total Economy.   If we are considering the total economy, it is impossible to pass the real cost of the debt on to future generations. The real cost of the debt to the total economy can only be measured by the loss of goods and services that individuals and firms must forgo when they give up their purchasing power to buy government bonds. When consumers and investors purchase such bonds, they not only buy fewer goods and services for themselves but also give the government revenue to make its purchases. World War II was a prime example of this. The decrease in consumer production was in effect the real cost of the debt. The people in the economy at the time the debt was incurred shouldered the real burden of the debt through the loss of goods and services.

For the economy as a whole the debt repayment, whether repaid immediately or postponed until future generations, will not cost anything in terms of goods and services. As a result of the redistribution of income that takes place at the time the debt is repaid, some individuals and firms may suffer a loss of purchasing power; but this will be offset by gains to others, and no net decrease in purchasing power in the economy will take place. For example, if the debt were to be paid even in a period of 1 year, the total tax necessary to pay off the current debt would be over $2 trillion. This would have a tendency to decrease the total purchasing power of the economy. It would reduce effective demand and result in decreased production. When the government paid out the $2 trillion to debt holders, however, it would tend to offset the adverse effect of the tax. Total purchasing power in the economy would remain the same. The effective demand, and therefore production, would remain the same, provided the propensity of the debt holders to consume and to invest was the same as that of the general taxpayers. There would be no loss of total goods and services at the time the debt was repaid. Thus, since there is no cost for the economy as a whole when the debt is repaid, it is impossible to pass the cost of the debt on to future generations.

Effect on Individuals.   Although the cost of the debt cannot be passed on to future generations from the viewpoint of the total economy, the burden for individuals and firms can be passed on to future generations. If the government were to pay off the debt in a relatively short period, say within the generation in which the debt occurred, the particular individuals taxed to pay the debt would have to give up purchasing power. Thus, they would be burdened with individual cost of the debt to the extent that each is taxed. If payment of the debt is postponed for a generation or two, however, the tax will fall to a large extent on the descendants of those individuals and businesses in the economy at the time the debt was incurred. Thus, even though the net cost or burden of the debt cannot be passed on to future generations, the individual burden can be passed on to them.

The Money Supply and the Debt

Another problem involved in the repayment of the debt, which tends to strengthen our reluctance to pay it off, is the effect of the repayment on the money supply. We know that when an individual or a business loans the government money, there is no increase in the money supply. For example, if Mr. Sanchez buys a bond for $1,000, he generally will pay cash for it. There is merely a transfer of cash from the individual to the government, with no change in the total money supply. If a bank loans the government money, however, it can pay for the bonds in cash or through the creation of a demand deposit against which the government writes checks. In Chapter 10 we learned that the demand deposits brought about by the creation of credit increased the money supply. Therefore, if a bank were to buy $5 million worth of bonds and pay for them with a demand deposit, it would increase the money supply accordingly. This process is referred to as **monetizing the debt**.

When the government goes into debt by borrowing from the banks, it increases the money supply and thus increases the level of economic activity, or it adds inflationary pressures to the economy. In 1986 the money supply was approximately $676 billion. Of this amount, $288 billion was in the form of demand deposits. A substantial portion of these demand deposits came into existence as a result of the sale of government bonds to Federal Reserve and commercial banks. Therefore, the national debt was supporting a sizable part of the total money supply.

We know that a decrease in the money supply will have a tendency to decrease our level of economic activity and/or decrease the price level, unless offset by some other force such as an increase in the velocity of money. Just as the debt was monetized when the government borrowed from the banks, the money supply will be decreased when the debt is paid off. This is known as **demonetizing the debt**. Thus, if the government were to reduce the federal debt by sizable amounts over a relatively short period of time, it could reduce the money supply to such an extent that it would have an adverse effect on the level of economic activity. Payment of the debt supported by bank credit would be beneficial during a period of full employment insofar as it could reduce inflationary pressures. During periods of less than full employment, however, such debt repayment could be harmful to the economy as a whole, unless offsetting measures were invoked.

Size of the Debt

The mammoth size of the current debt, now over $2 trillion, is in itself sufficient to discourage many people regarding its repayment. It might be pointed out that although we have not reduced the debt absolutely, increased productivity and higher income have reduced the size of the debt relative to our annual income.

In effect, through our increased productivity and higher price level, the monetary income of the nation increased more than twice as fast as the national debt during the period 1950–1980. As a result, the national debt relative to GNP was reduced from 88 percent to 33 percent. However, during the 1980s the debt has increased faster than production and income. By 1986, the debt had climbed back to 50 percent of GNP. Nevertheless, some analysts still think that we have less to worry about today than we did 20 or 30 years ago. It should be remembered, however, that decreasing income resulting from either a falling price level or a drop in production or employment would increase the size of the debt relative to income and make repayment more burdensome.

The suggestion has occasionally been made that we should postpone payment on the debt, since it becomes less burdensome as the years go on. To the extent that we increase income as a result of increased productivity, this suggestion has some merit. But if the higher GNP and, therefore, the greater income is brought about primarily by higher prices, the suggestion is a poor one, since greater problems than that of debt retirement will result from rising prices. Furthermore, if the purchasing power of a $100 bond at the maturity date is of less value than the $50 price of the bond at the purchase date due to continuous inflation, the purchase of bonds by individuals and firms could be discouraged at a time when the government needed money in the future.

Refunding the Debt

Since government debt obligations may reach maturity at a time when the U.S. Treasury does not have the money to pay them, the problem of refunding the debt arises. At such a time, the federal government generally will issue and sell new bonds to raise money to pay off the matured obligations. This, however, may not be accomplished easily, especially when billions of dollars' worth of securities may be maturing within a short period of time. Furthermore, at times the government may be forced to pay a higher interest rate when it borrows funds for this purpose.

There is a long-standing Congressionally imposed 4.25 percent ceiling on the interest rate that the Treasury can pay on long-term government securities (those maturing in more than 5 years). There is, however, no interest rate ceiling on short-term government obligations. Congress over the years has denied the Treasury's request to totally remove the interest rate ceiling, but it has exempted as much as $250 billion in long-term securities from the interest rate ceiling. With the rise in market interest rates it has been impossible for the Treasury to sell long-term securities at the 4.25 percent interest rate ceiling. In the early 1980s, for example, it was possible for an investor to buy existing long-term government bonds at discounts yielding over 14 percent. In addition, high-grade corporate bonds were yielding 10 to 12 percent. Thus, the Treasury was forced to sell short-term obligations on which there was no interest rate ceiling in order to refund the debt or raise new debt money. It was paying interest rates of 14 to 16 percent for money borrowed in the short-term market. Fortunately, by 1986 interest rates in general had dropped well below 10 percent, which made it easier for the government to refund the debt. Refunding is quite a problem because over $400 billion of the national debt becomes due and payable annually.

Burden of Interest Payments

Included each year in our national budget is $200 billion or more for payment of interest on the debt. Although taxation for the payment of this interest does not impose a net burden or cost on the economy as a whole, it does cause an annual redistribution of income and, therefore, a burden to individuals and firms in the economy. If the government had originally increased taxes instead of going into debt, or if the government had paid off the debt shortly after it had been incurred, it would have imposed a smaller total burden on the individuals than it does when the debt repayment is postponed. With postponement of the debt the redistribution of income necessary to retire the debt is not only in excess of $2 trillion, the amount of the principal, but also over $200 billion annually for interest on the debt. This interest continues only as a result of postponement of debt repayment. Furthermore, as interest rates rise, the cost of carrying the debt rises. Whereas the federal debt increased fourfold between 1970 and 1986, the cost of carrying the debt rose ninefold. It is a matter of judgment whether individuals and firms would prefer the hardship of paying off the debt in a relatively short period of time or of giving up more of total income but spreading the hardship or inconvenience in smaller doses over a longer period of time. Because of the higher amount of interest paid relative to income, interest payments were equal to 6.0 percent of national income in 1986 compared with 1.7 percent in 1970.

Productivity of the Debt

If a business firm borrows money to erect a new building, buy machinery and material, or hire additional labor to produce goods, it can increase its total production. The loan it receives is said to be productive, since it can increase the total output of the company and enhance its profits. In fact, firms borrow billions of dollars annually for this very purpose.

Individuals may also borrow to enhance their purchasing power. They may be prompted to do this especially if the purchase of certain commodities has greater utility to them at the time of borrowing than the purchase of these commodities would have in the future. Evidently we do prefer present utility in many cases, since consumers borrow billions each year to buy automobiles, appliances, homes, furniture, and the like.

Government borrowing and the consequent debt may be productive, or it may increase the total utility of the economy, in much the same manner as do business and consumer loans. Financing government dams, reforestation projects, highways and roads, aircraft developments, educational facilities, labor retraining, the elimination of poverty, medical research, space explorations, pollution control, and urban renewal through debt can be very productive. In some cases consumers' satisfaction may be increased as a result of the improvement of roads, the development of recreation facilities, and the like. Similar to the individual or the firm, the nation or its administrators must decide whether increased productivity and the utilization of current consumption are of greater value than the disutility of paying off the debt.

DEBT CEILING

The statutory limit or ceiling on the national debt was first established in 1917 when Congress passed the Second Liberty Bond Act. Before World War II, Congress set individual ceilings on the various types of government debt. But in 1941 Congress abolished the individual debt ceilings and created one ceiling on the total debt outstanding. Since the debt ceiling has been raised dozens of times in the past years, increasing from $275 billion in 1954 to more than $2 trillion in 1986, the statutory limit on the national debt has been a topic of controversy in recent years.

A federal deficit accompanied by a rise in the debt ceiling will generally provoke more opposition than a deficit that does not involve a hike in the debt ceiling. Furthermore, the cause of the debt plays an important role in its acceptance. Large debt ceiling increases brought about as a result of emergency government spending have traditionally incurred less Congressional opposition than smaller increases related to nonemergency spending.

Many arguments can be marshaled for and against the debt ceiling. Opponents of the ceiling maintain that it may at times limit needed expenditures on important government programs, such as defense or recession spending, whenever tax revenues are not up to expectations or the government has failed to increase taxes sufficiently to take care of its spending obligations.

It is also claimed that a debt ceiling results in fiscal subterfuge by the

Treasury. The statutory limit is on a defined portion of the total federal debt that is usually associated with the annual federal budget. The federal government, however, has many nonbudgetary financial obligations. Many federal agencies, which normally borrow funds from the Treasury, may be empowered to sell their own securities to private financial institutions and investors if they desire. Frequently when the Treasury is pinched for funds and is approaching the debt limit, it will request a particular agency to sell its own securities in the market rather than to borrow from the Treasury.

Critics of the debt ceiling contend further that it restricts the freedom of the Treasury to manage the debt efficiently, especially when the debt is close to the ceiling. In such a circumstance, the Treasury may have to wait until old securities mature before issuing new ones for fear of going over the debt ceiling. Critics of the ceiling argue that it would be better for the Treasury to experiment with new issues sometimes before the expiration of the old in order to try out the interest rate and to have time to make any necessary adjustments to obtain the best price. Otherwise the Treasury will be at the mercy of the market if it must wait until the time that various issues expire before issuing new securities to replace them. President Nixon endeavored to get around the debt ceiling in 1969 by proposing a restructuring of the debt in such a manner that it would have excluded $100 billion of the current debt from the statutory limit. This would have permitted the administration to add debt without requesting an increase in the ceiling. His proposal, however, did not receive favorable treatment by Congress.

Proponents of the statutory limit, of course, stress the fact that the debt ceiling is needed to restrain government spending and that it prevents the national debt from getting dangerously high. Although the debt ceiling seems to have been raised liberally by Congress in the past several years, the presence of the debt ceiling does tend to make Congress look more closely at the budget and decide whether it really wants to approve any appropriations that will necessitate borrowing and raising the debt ceiling. It might also be argued that insofar as the ceiling limits deficits in the annual budget, it makes the taxpayers more conscious of the total cost of government services. Many taxpayers may not balk at expenditures of $1,075 billion with a tax bill scheduled to be only $1,000 billion. But if they were taxed $1,075 billion to cover the total cost of the federal spending, they may very well decide to do without some of the government services. In short, deficits and a rising national debt can deceive the taxpayers about the true cost of government services.

In the early 1980s a movement developed, with the support of President Reagan, for the adoption of a Constitutional amendment that would require the federal government to balance its budget each year. The amendment would have required Congress to balance the federal budget annually unless an exception was approved by a vote of three-fifths of the Congress. In a 1982 vote, however, Congress rejected the balanced-budget amendment.

Subsequently, in order to limit debt accumulation, Congress enacted the Balanced Budget and Emergency Deficit Control Act of 1985 (Gramm-Rudman-Hollings Act). It calls for Congress to reduce the federal deficit each year and finally produce a balanced budget by 1991. According to the Act the deficit is to be no more than $144 billion in fiscal 1987 and reach zero by 1991.

SUMMARY

Taxation is the institutional arrangement to finance government expenditures. Consequently, we have various kinds of taxes associated with specific levels of government. A good tax is one that is justifiable, equitable, certain, convenient, and economical. Various theories have been proposed for apportioning the tax burden fairly, such as the cost-of-service, benefits-received, and the ability-to-pay theory. How much a particular tax costs an individual taxpayer depends on the tax rate structure, which involves the tax base and the tax rate. A tax rate may be proportional, progressive, degressive, or regressive. The taxpayer upon whom the tax is levied does not necessarily bear the burden of the tax, since the impact of many taxes can be shifted in such a manner that the incidence of the tax falls elsewhere.

Taxes may be used to cover the cost of government services, to redistribute income and wealth, or (as a fiscal tool) to stabilize the level of economic activity. When used in this last respect, deficits incurred during a recession can be offset by surpluses accumulated during prosperity periods. Instead of endeavoring to balance the budget annually, it can be balanced over the length of the business cycle. However, certain difficulties are involved when this is attempted. The most pronounced is the problem of making sure that the surpluses are sufficient to offset the deficits.

As a result of our inability to balance the budget, either annually or over the period of the cycle, we have incurred considerable debt in the past few decades. The present national debt is over $2 trillion.

Contrary to common belief, it would be exceedingly difficult to bankrupt the nation as a result of the large debt, since most of the debt is held domestically. The problem of redistribution of income that accompanies debt repayment is more realistic than the bankruptcy problem. Although we have the ability to pay off the debt, redistribution of income could occur in such a manner as to decrease the total effective demand in the economy.

Although the burden of the debt for the total economy cannot be passed on to future generations, it is possible to pass the burden of the debt on to particular individuals and business firms in those future generations.

Payment of that portion of the debt supported by bank credit could result in a decrease in the money supply. Such demonetization of the debt could have an adverse effect on the level of economic activity just as the monetization of the debt can have an expansionary or an inflationary effect on the economy.

Just as private consumer or business debt can be productive, likewise the federal debt may be productive and may even create consumer satisfaction.

Our continuous federal debt has caused a burden of over $200 billion annually in the form of interest payments. In order to restrain national debt accumulation, Congress enacted the Gramm-Rudman-Hollings Deficit Reduction Act in 1985.

NEW TERMS AND CONCEPTS

Tax rate	Regressive tax rate	Direct tax
Tax base	Shifting of taxes	Indirect tax
Proportional tax rate	Impact of a tax	Full-employment budget
Progressive tax rate	Incidence of a tax	Monetizing the debt
Degressive tax rate	Effect of a tax	Demonetizing the debt

DISCUSSION QUESTIONS

1. Do you think that the ability to pay should be the primary basis of taxation? Why or why not?
2. Is our current progressive federal income tax equitable? Why or why not?
3. How is our taxing system used to redistribute income and wealth? Do you think it should be used for this purpose?
4. Is it feasible to balance the federal budget over the period of a cycle? Give reasons.
5. If you owned a $5,000 government bond, would you be willing to relieve the government of its obligation to pay you in the interest of eliminating our national debt? Why or why not?
6. How would the concept of interest-free financing for federal borrowing alleviate the interest burden of the federal debt?
7. Should the ceiling on the national debt be removed? Why or why not?
8. Do you think the U.S. government ought to be required to balance the budget annually? Why or why not?

SUGGESTED READINGS

Bennett, James T., and Thomas J. Dilorenzo. "Off-Budget: Federal Spending Booms." *Economic Review*. Federal Reserve Bank of Atlanta (April, 1983).

Cunningham, Thomas J. "The Long-Run Outcome of the Permanent Deficit." *Economic Review*. Federal Reserve Bank of Atlanta (May, 1986).

———, and Rosemary T. Cunningham. "Projecting Federal Deficits and the Impact of the Gramm-Rudman-Hollings Budget Cuts." *Economic Review*. Federal Reserve Bank of Atlanta (May, 1986).

"The Deficit Puzzle: Fitting the Pieces Together." *Economic Report*. Federal Reserve Bank of Atlanta (August, 1982).

Hailstones, Thomas J., and Frank V. Mastrianna. *Contemporary Economic Problems and Issues*, 8th ed. Cincinnati: South-Western Publishing Co., 1988.

Herber, Bernard P. *Modern Public Finance: The Study of Public Sector Economics*, 3d ed. Homewood, IL: Richard D. Irwin, Inc., 1975.

Pechman, Joseph A. (ed.). *Setting National Priorities: The 1984 Budget*. Washington, DC: The Brookings Institution, 1983.

Schultze, Charles L. "The Administration's Goals: Steady Growth, High Employment, and a Balanced Budget by 1981." *Improving the Long-Term Performance of the U.S. Economy*. Washington, DC: U.S. Government Printing Office, 1977.

Tucker, James F. "Growth of Interest Payments on the Federal Debt." *Cross Sections*. Federal Reserve Bank of Richmond (Spring, 1986).

The United States Budget in Brief, Fiscal Year ———. Washington, DC: U.S. Government Printing Office, annually.

21
THE CHANGING ECONOMIC ENVIRONMENT

■

A review of the economic role of our government over the past several decades shows clearly that our overall economic policies and many of the measures used to implement these policies were based on the principles of the Keynesian income-expenditure analysis. A close reading of the Employment Act of 1946 and the Full Employment and Balanced Growth Act of 1978 will reveal the definite steps we have taken in the direction of income-expenditure policies. Furthermore, a study of the recommendations of the President's Council of Economic Advisers and of the Joint Economic Committee of Congress will reveal that these groups were setting goals and suggesting anticyclical measures based upon income-expenditure analysis.

The objectives of full employment, stable prices, and a healthy rate of economic growth are accepted by both major political parties. The use of monetary, fiscal, and psychological policies to attain these goals also has bipartisan support. Although the first major acceptance of government intervention to alleviate unemployment is to be found in New Deal policies, the Republican administration made some attempts in this direction in 1932. The idea of using monetary and fiscal policies to combat depression was new in the 1930s. Therefore, the attempts of the Republicans and the early New Deal programs meant a struggle for Congressional, business, and public acceptance of the principle of government intervention as a means of stabilizing the level of economic activity.

RECENT U.S. ECONOMIC POLICY

In the next few decades, this principle became more widely accepted, not only by economists but also by members of Congress, public administrators, businesses, and the general public. The possibility of and the desire for blending free enterprise and government cooperation for the purposes of stabilizing the economy were recognized repeatedly. By the mid-1950s, it appeared that the greater role of government in the economy was here to stay. It was not a question of whether or not the government should play a positive role in helping to maintain a high level of economic activity, but a question of the extent and the nature of government action.

Most economists and political leaders agree that we have tended to follow a middle course. We have not engaged in undue government intervention, but on the other hand, we took positive action when needed. We have not gone so far as Keynes suggested in socializing investment, and we have not yet used compulsory saving on a national scale to combat inflation. However, in the early 1970s the administration did reluctantly impose compulsory wage and price controls as a last resort, and President Carter invoked voluntary wage-price standards in 1978 and 1979. Perhaps we have found a happy medium in the application of the policies and measures based upon the income-expenditure analysis. The extent of government intervention in the economy, however, was destined to be a major economic and political issue.

In spite of the evidence to the contrary, many people today still think of the income-expenditure approach as depression economics and, therefore, as out of fashion in a period of relative prosperity. It cannot be denied that the great amount of government spending in the last 40 years has been a big factor in helping to maintain a high level of employment. Even in the nonwar years, government spending has been responsible for 14 to 22 percent of the GNP, as shown in Table 21-1.

Whether we would have maintained our high levels of employment during the nonwar years in the absence of a high rate of government spending for defense and other purposes is something about which we can only speculate. It can always be argued that reduced spending would have permitted reduced taxes, and that, therefore, increased consumption and investment would have made up for any decrease in government

Table 21-1 Government Spending and the GNP (Billions)

Year	GNP	Government Spending	Government Spending as a % of GNP
1945	$ 212	$ 75	35%
1950	287	39	14
1955	400	75	19
1960	507	100	20
1965	691	138	21
1970	993	220	20
1975	1,549	340	21
1980	2,633	588	22
1985	3,989	815	20
1986	4,209	865	21

Source: *Economic Report of the President*, 1987.

spending. Although this was true in the immediate post-World War II period, it may not have been true for the post-Korean war period. There would have been a good possibility that, in the absence of any pent-up demand for consumer goods, businesses and individuals may have been inclined to save a certain portion of any substantial tax cuts they might have received. A similar impact occurred at the end of the Vietnam war.

What would happen in our economy today with its approximately $300 billion military defense spending program if suddenly we were to enter into a major disarmament agreement with other nations throughout the world? Certainly in the short run there would be considerable disruption, displacement, and unemployment in the economy. Even in a period of 3 or 5 years, private spending might not increase sufficiently to offset such a drop in government spending. Usually the suggestion is made that if peace and disarmament were negotiated, it would be wise to make the reductions in military spending gradually. It is also suggested that it would be beneficial to increase government spending in other areas, such as pollution control, urban redevelopment, mass transportation, highway construction, education, medical care, and other public activities, in order to offset the adverse economic effects of sizable reductions in military spending. All this, of course, could make one wonder if military spending is not serving as a built-in crutch for the economy and camouflaging the fact that we might be more susceptible to Keynes' prognostication of chronic unemployment than we like to believe. On the other hand, there is no assurance that the economy could not have done as well as it has in the past 30 years or more in the absence of huge outlays for defense purposes.

It should be remembered that the income-expenditure approach can be used to analyze an inflationary economy just as well as a depressionary economy. As pointed out in Chapter 19, anti-inflationary policies can be developed as readily as expansionary policies.

One difficulty with the application of policies based on the income-expenditure approach is that it is easier to obtain public acceptance for expansionary measures than it is for anti-inflationary measures. Most members of Congress will support the idea of government spending, decreased taxes, public works, easy money, public service employment, and the like to raise the level of economic activity during slowdowns and recessions. But during prosperity it takes a bold political leader to advocate higher taxes (especially for the lower and middle income groups), a surplus budget, credit restriction, tight money, and other measures distasteful to the general voting public. The reluctance of federal administrators and legislators to adopt anti-inflationary policies, for example, was very evident in the middle and late 1960s and throughout the 1970s. Of course, the opposition to these measures is strongest in election years. As a result, wise economic policy is often sacrificed for political expediency.

Whether we like it or not, the income-expenditure approach has become an integral part of our economic analysis and serves as a guide for governmental economic policy. A person is free to accept or reject policies based on this analysis. A dislike for such policies, however, or disagreement with some of the principles, should not blind one to the fact that the income-expenditure framework is an excellent tool of analysis for the study of economics.

During the past few decades considerable emphasis has been placed on the achievement of our primary domestic economic goals of full employment, stable prices, healthy economic growth, and balance-of-payments equilibrium. The desire for steady jobs, good wages, economic security, stable prices, and an abundance of goods and services was quite natural. By and large, during the 1950s and 1960s the economy proved capable of attaining these goals.

In fact, for a while these primary goals were largely taken for granted. Consequently, citizens of our society, although not ignoring these goals, began placing more emphasis on new or supplementary goals for the economy. These included elimination of poverty, income stability, preservation of the environment, equal employment opportunity, and improvement in the quality of life. The higher rates of unemployment, double-digit inflation, and negative economic growth that characterized the recession-inflation periods of 1970 and 1974–1975, however, renewed emphasis on the primary goals. Even so, people have still become embroiled in a general movement to seek fresh solutions to existing economic and social problems, while learning how to handle new problems that are arising and adopting policies to prevent the problems that may arise in the future.

THE CHANGING ECONOMIC ENVIRONMENT

Important changes in the economic environment of the United States and, in fact, the rest of the world have occurred in the past 25 years. Among these changes were the blackouts of the late 1960s and the concern about the shortage of strategic materials as reflected in books such as *The Limits of Growth* and *Mankind at the Turning Point*.[1] The OPEC embargo and the political problems in Iran had a drastic effect on oil prices, the U.S. economy, and the world economy. The flood of imports, especially autos, steel, and textiles, into the U.S. was a trade reversal. The outflow of gold, creation of SDRs, demise of the gold standard, and rise of the European Monetary System revealed changes on the international scene.

In addition, there was a substantial growth in government transfer payments and a decline in the rate of growth of productivity in the U.S. compared with other nations. The introduction of many socioeconomic regulations impacted cost and productivity. Attempts at wage and price

---

1. Donella H. Meadows, et al., *The Limits of Growth: A Report for the Club of Rome on the Predicament of Mankind* (New York: Universe Books, 1972); Mihajlo Mesarovic and Edward Pestel, *Mankind at the Turning Point* (New York: New American Library, 1976).

controls in peacetime challenged both management and labor. Double-digit inflation and high and volatile interest rates were new to the U.S. economy. The decline of workers' real income and stagflation, particularly in the 1974–1975, 1980, and 1982 recessions, were changes unforeseen in earlier decades.

Slowdown in Growth Rate and Productivity

The U.S. economic growth rate slackened substantially in the 1970s, as shown in Figure 21-1. From the mid-1970s the average annual increase in productivity per labor-hour declined as indicated in Table 21-2, and by 1979 it was a negative value. The structure of the labor force was

Figure 21-1 Output per Hour in the Private Business Sector (1947–1985 Actual Levels and 1947–1967 Trend Extrapolated)

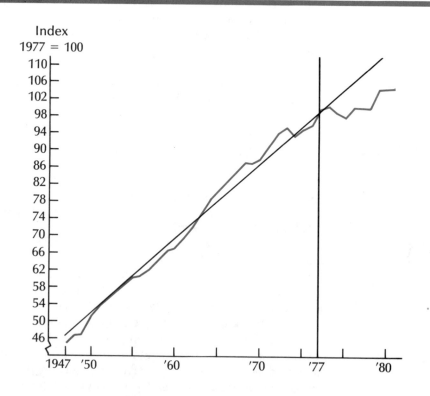

Source: Adapted from *Economic Review*, Federal Reserve Bank of Kansas City (November, 1979), and updated from the *Economic Report of the President*, 1986.

Table 21-2 Changes in U.S. Nonfarm Labor Productivity, 1971–1986

1971	3.2%	1979	− 1.2%
1972	3.2	1980	− 0.3
1973	2.0	1981	1.4
1974	−2.1	1982	−0.4
1975	2.0	1983	2.7
1976	2.8	1984	2.3
1977	1.7	1985	1.0
1978	0.8	1986	1.4

Source: *Economic Report of the President*, 1987.

changing, also, as women were joining the labor force in ever-increasing numbers and minorities constituted a larger portion of the labor force.

Increased regulation in some areas such as pollution control (EPA), occupational safety and health (OSHA), equal employment opportunity (EEOC), and consumer product safety (CPSA) added to the cost of doing business. Manufacturers, for example, were spending $6 billion to $8 billion annually on pollution controls. One study indicates that regulations were costing American industry more than $100 billion annually. On the other hand, deregulation of the airlines, the trucking industry, and banking paved the way for increased competition in those industries.

Total business investment as a share of U.S. GNP over the last 20 years has been the lowest of any major industrialized nation, as shown in Table 21-3. An important reason for our limited investment is found in the very large percentages of our GNP that are in the form of consumer goods and services or government services, which do not add measurably to our productive capacity. In fact, in earlier years political leaders in the U.S. were guilty of bragging about the large amount of the GNP that was in consumer goods and services compared with other nations. The important relationship between investment and productivity can be seen in Figure 21-2. Here it can be seen that nations with higher percentages of GNP invested in fixed capital tend to have larger annual increases in productivity.

Higher investment rates abroad caused the gap in the growth rate between the United States and other leading nations in terms of per capita output to diminish. Comparisons of per capita GNP, given in Table 21-4, show that several nations are clustered near the United States. The growth lag in U.S. manufacturing labor productivity in recent years is clearly shown in Figure 21-3.

The problem of stagflation that occurred in the 1970s was aggravated by high wage settlements in spite of the decline in productivity. The rise

Table 21-3 International Investment Patterns

	Gross Fixed Capital Formation as a Percent of GNP [1]			
	1984	1980	1975	1970–1975
United States	15.8%	15.6%	16.3%	17.6%
Italy	18.0	19.7	20.6	21.0
United Kingdom	17.1	17.3	20.1	19.3
Canada	19.0	22.9	24.2	22.7
West Germany	20.2	22.7	20.7	23.9
France	20.8	21.5	23.2	23.7
Japan	28.2	31.8	32.2	34.0

1. Fixed capital formation consists of residential structures, nonresidential structures, and producers' durable equipment.

Source: International Monetary Fund, *International Financial Statistics* (June, 1986).

in the "discomfort index," which is the combination of unemployment and inflation, can be observed in Table 21-5.

Decline in Real Income

Added to the decline in productivity, there was an actual decline in real income in terms of the average weekly wage of workers during the 1970s. While the average worker's weekly money wages increased from $136.90 in 1972 to $267.26 (an increase of $130.36) in 1982, the worker's real wage, or purchasing power, declined by $30.26. (See Table 21-5.) In spite of having more in his or her paycheck, the worker was unable to purchase any more goods or services. Also, the increase in money wages moved the worker into a higher income tax bracket. Consequently, the worker was paying higher taxes on less real income. By 1986 the worker's real wage had not improved very much.

Indexation of wages to the Consumer Price Index (CPI) became prevalent as organized workers negotiated COLA (cost of living adjustment) clauses into their collective bargaining agreements. Military pensions and Social Security benefits were also tied to the CPI. In 1986, it was estimated that over 50 million people had some form of income tied to the price index.

Antitax and Antispending Movement

During the late 1970s, a rebellious attitude against high taxes developed and manifested itself with the passage of Proposition 13 in California.

Figure 21-2 Investment and Productivity, 1980–1984

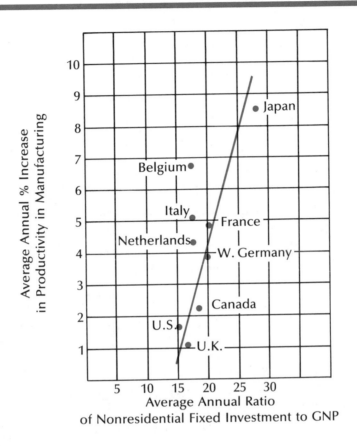

Source: International Monetary Fund, *International Financial Statistics* (June, 1986).

This 1978 referendum mandated a reduction of about 50 percent in local property taxes, or about a one-fourth cut in local tax revenue. A wave of taxpayer sentiment for tax reductions followed the successful passage of Proposition 13. By 1980 several states had proposals on their ballots that would require substantial limitations on or reductions in local government spending and taxing. Not only were property taxes being affected, but personal income taxes as well. At the federal level, major tax reductions occurred with the Tax Equity and Fiscal Responsibility Act of 1982 and again in the tax revision act of 1986.

The antitax sentiment was also behind the movement to amend the U.S. Constitution to require the federal government to operate within a

Table 21-4 International Comparisons of Per Capita GNP, 1983

Switzerland	$15,633
United States	14,093
Norway	12,930
Canada	12,662
Sweden	10,744
Denmark	10,684
W. Germany	10,672
Australia	9,727
Japan	9,697
France	9,473

Source: *Statistical Abstract of the United States*, 1986.

Figure 21-3 Growth in Manufacturing Labor Productivity, 1975–1984

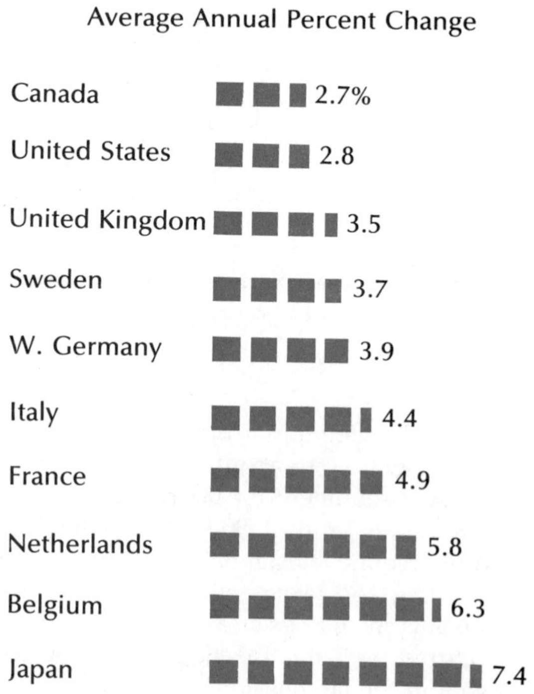

Average Annual Percent Change

Canada	2.7%
United States	2.8
United Kingdom	3.5
Sweden	3.7
W. Germany	3.9
Italy	4.4
France	4.9
Netherlands	5.8
Belgium	6.3
Japan	7.4

Source: *Statistical Abstract of the United States*, 1986.

Table 21-5 Economic Activity in the United States

Year	Annual Real GNP Growth	Capacity Utiliza- tion	Change in Produc- tivity	Unemploy- ment Rate	Inflation Rate	Discomfort Index	Real Wages (1977 dollars)
1971	3.3	91.9%	3.2%	5.9%	3.4%	9.3%	$190.58
1972	5.6	83.5	3.2	5.6	3.4	9.0	198.41
1973	5.5	87.6	2.0	4.9	8.8	13.7	198.35
1974	− 0.7	83.8	− 2.1	5.6	12.2	17.8	190.12
1975	− 0.9	72.9	2.0	8.5	7.0	15.5	184.16
1976	5.3	79.5	2.8	7.7	4.8	12.5	186.85
1977	5.4	81.9	1.7	7.1	6.8	13.9	189.00
1978	4.6	84.4	0.8	6.1	9.0	15.1	189.31
1979	2.8	85.7	− 1.2	5.8	13.3	19.1	183.41
1980	− 0.2	79.1	− 0.3	7.1	12.4	19.5	172.74
1981	1.9	78.3	1.4	7.6	8.9	16.5	170.13
1982	− 2.5	70.3	− 0.4	9.7	3.9	13.6	168.09
1983	3.6	74.0	2.7	9.6	3.8	13.4	171.26
1984	6.4	80.8	2.3	7.5	4.0	11.5	172.78
1985	2.7	80.3	1.0	7.2	3.8	11.0	170.42
1986	2.5	79.4	1.4	7.0	1.1	8.1	171.07

Source: *Economic Report of the President*, 1987.

balanced budget. Of course, if such a proposal were adopted, it would drastically change the usefulness of federal government spending as a tool of economic stabilization. The balanced-budget proposal, however, was defeated by Congress in 1981. But it was still being proposed by President Reagan in 1987.

THE THEORY OF RATIONAL EXPECTATIONS

The changing economic conditions of the 1970s brought a change in economic thinking. It became apparent that Keynesian-type economic policies and measures had not been effective in our attempt to achieve and maintain full employment, stable prices, and a healthy rate of real economic growth. It appeared to some economic analysts and political leaders that these policies and measures contained inherent weaknesses. Some thought that the conventional economic wisdom of the previous few decades did not work in the changing economic environment of the 1970s. Others suggested that we erred in not applying stabilization measures properly.

It was under these circumstances that we began seeing and hearing the terms "rational expectations" and "supply-side economics" creep into our economic literature and political oratory. A supposedly new theory called rational expectations emerged. In large part, it is a modification of the psychological theory of the business cycle.

The psychological theory is based on the premise that people react according to what is in their minds. If they think that economic conditions are going to be favorable, they will react accordingly. In doing so, their actions will tend to improve the level of economic activity. Thus, if business leaders think that sales are going to be good in the future, they will invest in machinery, equipment, and buildings. They will stock raw materials and hire additional workers. They will borrow to finance this expansion. These actions result in increased investment as well as additional payments for labor and raw materials. Income and investment are increased further via the multiplier and accelerator.

When a consumer is working, perhaps with some overtime, and expects the situation to continue for some time, he or she will be inclined to spend liberally and even increase purchasing power through the use of credit. These actions on the part of the investors and consumers tend to increase the level of business activity.

On the other hand, if sales are sluggish, inventory high, and profits low, business leaders may have a dim outlook on the immediate future. They will hold back on their expansion programs, endeavor to reduce inventories, lay off excess labor, and adopt a wait-and-see attitude about investing. These actions tend to slow down, or depress, the level of economic activity. Likewise if a worker begins to lose overtime, if she observes layoffs taking place within the plant and perhaps is cut back to 4 days per week, she will be less optimistic about the future. In fact, she may become pessimistic. In such a case, she will become more cautious about her spending and be reluctant to take on additional credit, or even renew existing credit, as she makes repayments on current debts. This action, of course, will tend to soften the economy.

To summarize, according to the psychological theory of the business cycle, when business investors and consumers think that economic conditions are going to be good, their actions will be such that they will tend to bolster the economy. When their outlook is pessimistic, their actions will be such that they will tend to depress the economy. In short, their actions are procyclical since they tend to augment upward and downward movements of business activity.

While agreeing with the psychological theory, the theory of **rational expectations** goes a step or two further. First, it suggests that individuals and businesses not only respond to specific stimuli connected with past or current events, but also react according to their expectation about the future. Secondly, the theory, sometimes referred to as the rational expectations hypothesis, states that while acting on the basis of rational judgment, investors and consumers through their actions or deeds may at times neutralize the impact of government economic stabilization measures.

This is especially so in turbulent economic times, such as the past few decades.

There is now a better understanding by businesses and the general public regarding the operation of our economy and the application of monetary and fiscal measures to stabilize the level of economic activity. Today, for example, business investors viewing an expanding economy with rising prices may expect the Fed to respond with tighter money and higher interest rates. Anticipating the Fed action may induce investors to borrow and invest even more than originally planned, thus aggravating the inflationary situation. In another case, anticipating the implementation of an incomes policy (voluntary guideposts or outright wage and price controls) may lead a firm to seek immediate price increases and grant wage concessions it would not otherwise grant. This would diminish the intended impact of the incomes policy.

Likewise, consumers in an expanding economy with upward price pressures may anticipate the imposition of credit restrictions or an increase in home mortgage rates. Consumers may accelerate their spending for consumer goods, especially big-ticket items, or hasten to purchase homes in spite of high prices and high interest rates in order to avoid still higher prices and interest rates later on. This, of course, offsets the desired effects of the pending anti-inflation measures.

On the other hand, during the early stages of a recession, business leaders, on the basis of past experience and rational expectations, may anticipate a lowering of the discount and prime interest rates. Another expectation might be the adoption of tax credits or accelerated depreciation on new investment as economic stimuli for the economy. Instead of spending currently, investors may decide to postpone the purchase of equipment or the construction of new buildings until the expansionary economic measures are in place. This again will diminish the effect of the government's anticyclical measures.

In other cases, the government action to combat inflation may be mollified if investors, workers, and consumers rationally expect inflation to continue unabated. In the late 1970s, for example, inflationary expectations of the general public in large part were based on statements by government economists that the embedded rate of inflation for the U.S. economy was 8–10 percent and that it was going to take several years to wring inflation out of the economy. Inflationary expectations were reinforced by observations that multiyear wage contracts still had time to run, minimum wage rates were scheduled to increase, and many forms of income were indexed to the CPI. There was also a loss of confidence in government programs to stem the tide of inflation.

In this atmosphere, consumers continued to buy in spite of higher commodity prices and higher interest payments. Businesses invested more regardless of declining bond prices, higher interest rates, and escalating wage rates. Workers demanded higher wages to offset the impact of inflation on their purchasing power, and lenders required higher nominal interest rates to avoid a decline in real interest rates. Again, this tended to aggravate inflation and offset government measures to combat inflation.

SUPPLY-SIDE ECONOMICS

Our inability in the late 1960s and throughout most of the 1970s to maintain high levels of employment, stable prices, and healthy economic growth rates led some economists and political leaders to question our conventional income-expenditure theory and demand management policies based on that theory. Possibly the policies had been mismanaged, or perhaps they were no longer appropriate in our changing economic environment. Others suggested that we had overtaxed and overregulated the economy to such an extent that the incentives to save, to invest, and even to work were diminished. The result was the slowdown in economic growth. In the search for a better explanation of what was happening to the economy and for a remedy to our economic problems, the concept of supply-side economics emerged. Much has been heard about supply-side economics in recent years, and it has become the basis for a new and different set of economic policies and measures.

A suitable place for a study of supply-side economics to begin is with a definition. Although supply-side economics means different things to different people, the following definition will serve our purpose. **Supply-side economics** is an approach to analyzing the economy that focuses on the impact on the total supply of goods and services of policies that affect saving, investment, entrepreneurship, and work effort. Supply-side policies are a combination of budgetary, tax, monetary, and regulatory measures designed to encourage saving, investment, and work effort to bring about high employment, stable prices, and a healthy economic growth rate, via their effect on total supply.

Tax Rate and Output

Supply-side advocates blamed many of the current problems of the economy on high tax rates and burdensome regulations. Figure 21-4 depicts one way the supply-siders look at the economy. It shows tax rates as the independent variable and output (GNP) as the dependent variable. It indicates that at a zero tax rate and a 100 percent tax rate there will be very little, if anything, produced. At a tax rate of 100 percent, individuals are not going to work and/or operate businesses if all their income is going to be confiscated through taxation. Thus, there will be no production and no government revenue.

On the other hand, if the tax rate is zero, people will work and operate businesses but the government will collect no revenue. In fact, according to supply-siders, a zero tax rate will result in zero production as well

Figure 21-4   Tax Rate–Output Curve

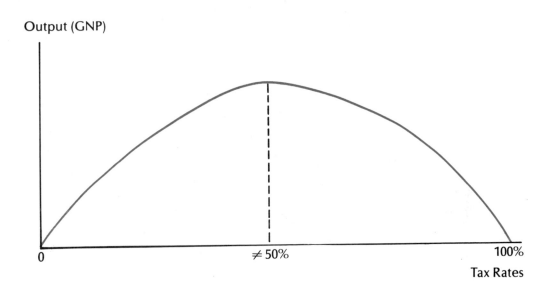

because the government would not have the means to provide many of the basic essentials necessary for production, such as roads and bridges, protection of property, a judicial system, and education. It should be kept in mind that the optimum tax rate that maximizes output is not necessarily a 50 percent rate. Moreover, no one knows for certain what the optimum tax rate is or the exact shape of the output line.

Nevertheless, supply-siders claim that we were at tax levels in excess of the optimum rate. As we raised taxes in past years, total output and employment were restrained. They suggested that a reduction in tax rates was necessary to increase production and employment.

Labor Tax Wedge.   Taxes, particularly payroll taxes, also affect the supply of labor utilized. Figure 21-5 shows the demand for labor by employers, D_L, and the supply of labor, S_L. At a particular wage rate, W_0, Q_0 amount of labor will be offered where the supply and demand are equal. Assuming no payroll tax, the wage received by workers is equal to the cost of hiring the workers. As payroll taxes, t, are imposed, however, the cost of employing workers is actually more than the wage payments to the workers. Consequently, the quantity of labor demanded will be less. At the same time the workers' take-home pay will be less because of payroll taxes they must pay, and the supply of labor offered will be less. As shown in

Figure 21-5   Labor Tax Wedge

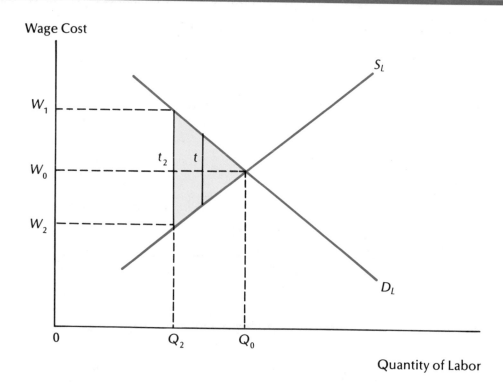

Quantity of Labor

Figure 21-5, for example, as payroll taxes increase to t_2, the cost of employing workers will rise from W_0 to W_1 and the after-tax wage received by workers will decline from W_0 to W_2. As a result, the amount of labor demanded and the supply offered will both decline from Q_0 to Q_2. In short, payroll taxes act as a **labor tax wedge** between what it costs to employ a worker and the income received by the worker. According to many supply-side advocates, a decrease in tax rates was necessary to bring about an increase in the quantity of labor demanded and the supply offered in order to increase employment or reduce unemployment.

Investment Tax Wedge.   A similar **investment tax wedge** exists, according to some supply-siders, between the quantity demanded and the supply offered in the market for loanable funds. This is so because the lender has to pay tax on interest income received and the borrower has to pay tax on investment income received from the productive use of the funds borrowed. This decreases the quantity of loanable funds demanded and reduces the supply offered. Supply-side advocates suggested that a lowering of tax rates would stimulate investment by providing a greater after-tax return to both the lender and the borrower.

A reduction in tax rates, according to the supply-siders, would also encourage savings by increasing the after-tax return on savings. The savings could be used for investment, which would increase output and income.

Supply-siders also believed that because of high marginal tax rates, many funds were being diverted into tax-sheltered investment. They felt that tax-sheltered investments were less productive than investments that produced taxable returns. Therefore, they maintained that lower tax rates would encourage more productive investment, which, in turn, would increase output, employment, and tax receipts.

The Laffer Curve.   The graph most often associated with supply-side economics is the **Laffer curve**. Supply-side advocates claim that much of the benefit from tax reductions, as explained in the preceding paragraphs, could be obtained without substantially affecting tax revenues. Taking a leaf from the pages of classical writings, the Laffer curve depicts the relationship between tax rates and tax revenues, as shown in Figure 21-6.

Figure 21-6   The Laffer Curve

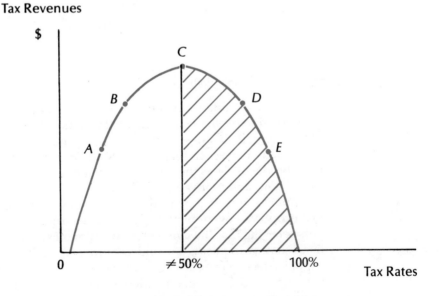

With tax rates on the horizontal axis and tax revenues on the vertical axis (or the reverse, as some prefer), the figure shows two points at which tax revenues are zero: at the 100 percent tax rate and at the zero tax rate. It is axiomatic that if the tax rate is 100 percent, the tax base will soon erode and disappear and tax revenues will fall. On the other hand, if the tax rate is zero percent, there may be much economic activity and a large tax base but no revenue. It is doubtful, of course, that either extreme would be reached.

Nevertheless, the Laffer curve shows that at some optimum tax rate revenues will be maximized. This is point C on the curve, but again it is not necessarily a 50 percent tax rate. As tax rates exceed the optimum rate, tax revenues decline. This is referred to as the *prohibitive range*. If the tax rates move from C to D or D to E, it can be seen readily that tax revenues will decline. Claiming that we were in the prohibitive range, Laffer and other supply-siders inferred that tax rates could be reduced without reducing current tax revenues.

The problem is, however, that we do not know the optimum tax rate that will maximize tax revenues, or even if we were, or are today, in the prohibitive range for certain. But assuming we are in the prohibitive range, we do not know the exact shape of the Laffer curve or whether it is skewed toward the 100 percent or zero percent tax rate. Moreover, presuming we are in the prohibitive range, how close are we to the optimum rate? A decrease in tax rates from E to D or C will increase tax revenues, but a decrease in rates from D to B will not increase revenues. Moreover, a tax cut from C to B or A will reduce tax revenues, as will any downward movement in tax rates on the left half of the curve. Another complexity, of course, is the fact that we have varying tax rates and numerous tax bases, each with different tax rate elasticities.

Government Spending and Regulation

Another important belief of supply-siders is that government spending is less productive than spending by the private sector. Consequently, they suggest a reduction in government spending to permit tax reduction. The consequent increase in real income to the private sector will then be spent more productively as the increased income encourages savings, stimulates investment, and motivates work effort.

Supply-siders also point out, as did many of the classical economists, that excessive government regulation may stifle production and total output. Believing that the amount of government social and economic regulation today is imposing an undue burden on producers and employers, supply-siders recommend deregulation, the removal of unnecessary government regulation, in order to increase productivity, total output, employment, and income.

Need for a Stable Money Supply

A final proposal of supply-side economics is the need for a stable money supply in order to provide high employment, stable prices, and a steady and healthy rate of economic growth. The need for a stable money supply is so strong that many supply-siders recommend a return to a gold standard in light of past inflation rates and the seeming inability of U.S. monetary authorities to prevent wide fluctuations in the growth of the money supply and the cost of money.

Criticisms of Supply-Side Proposals

Some strong criticisms have been made of certain supply-side propositions. One criticism concerns the effect of a tax cut on interest income, investment income, and wage and salary income. The supply-side viewpoint is that an increase in the after-tax return on savings, investment, and worker effort may induce more savings, generate additional investment, and encourage more worker effort. Lower tax rates, for example, may change the opportunity cost of various alternatives and induce a shift in choices made by individuals. Lower tax rates, which provide higher returns for work, increase the opportunity cost of leisure. Higher after-tax returns for savings increase the opportunity cost of consumption. The higher opportunity cost, according to supply-side proponents, induces individuals to choose more savings over more consumption, and to opt for more work instead of more leisure. The choice of more savings or more work in response to a tax cut is known as the **substitution effect.**

Critics of the tax cut proposal note that some individuals have a target income that they desire to obtain from their savings or work effort. If the after-tax income on savings and work effort is increased, the individual may decide that fewer savings and/or less work is needed to maintain the target level of income. The choice of fewer savings or less work in response to a tax cut is called the **income effect**. At the present time, there is no strong empirical evidence that shows to what extent the substitution effect is greater than or less than the income effect.

Another criticism concerns the growth of the tax base illustrated in the Laffer curve. (We have already discussed the problems concerning the optimum tax rate and the shape of the curve on page 410.) Some supply-siders claim that tax reductions could generate sufficient increases in economic activity, and therefore the tax base, to make up for the loss of revenue resulting from the decrease in tax rates. Critics point out that while it may be true that a decrease in the tax rate may increase the size of the base, there is no assurance that the increase in tax revenue from the increase in the tax base will offset the revenue lost from the decrease in the tax rate. In fact, much of the evidence is to the contrary.

The supply-side viewpoint that government spending is less productive than spending by the private sector is also open to much debate. Critics still argue strongly that the multiplier effect of government spending is greater than that of the private sector because the marginal propensity to consume of the private sector is less than 1. The issue is further complicated when the social benefits of government spending are compared with those of private sector spending.

Reaganomics: An Application of Supply-side Measures

It should have been evident to the average follower of economics that once Ronald Reagan was elected President we would get a dose of supply-side economics. His campaign speeches and preelection association with Arthur Laffer and other supply-side theorists gave evidence of his supply-side leanings. The direction that economic policy would take was reinforced after the election by the appointments of several supply-side advocates to cabinet-level positions. Their advice, along with the input of other close associates of the administration, assured that supply-side economics was in store.

Reaganomics can be defined as the application of certain supply-side measures in the attempt to achieve long-run, high-level employment, price stability, and a steady rate of economic growth. President Reagan's economic proposals included:

1. Reduction in government spending as a percentage of the GNP.

2. Reductions in personal and corporate income tax rates.

3. Tax credits and accelerated depreciation to stimulate investment.

4. Reduction in the highest marginal personal tax rate from 70 percent to 50 percent.

5. All Savers Certificates, Individual Retirement Accounts (IRAs), and Keogh Accounts to encourage tax-sheltered savings.

6. Removal of regulations that restrict or impair productivity and production.

7. New Federalism, which will return or shift many economic and social welfare functions from the federal government to state and local governments.

8. Eventual balancing of the federal budget.

9. Possible return to the gold standard to stabilize the growth of the money supply.

Within President Reagan's first two years in office, Congress had implemented many of the President's supply-side proposals.

We have seen, however, that supply-side proposals are not designed as short-run remedies to cure recession or stagflation. Rather, they are long-run proposals designed to bring about high employment, stable prices, and a healthy rate of economic growth.

Conflicting conclusions from various studies add to the uncertainty about the effectiveness of supply-side measures regarding savings, production, work effort, and tax revenues. But it appears that the investment tax credits, accelerated depreciation schedules, and lower marginal tax rates did contribute to the 1983–1986 economic expansion following the recession in 1982.

In all probability, supply-side economics will not replace income-expenditure or demand-management analysis. Rather it seems destined to be integrated with demand management, and in the future, we will consider both the supply-side and the demand-side effects before implementing many of our economic policies and measures. President Reagan was doing just that by the end of his second year in office. Moreover, during the first year of his second term he pushed a second major supply-side type of income tax rate reduction through Congress.

SUMMARY

The major economic policies of our nation for the past 40 years or more have been an outgrowth of the income-expenditure analysis. Fundamentals of this analysis are evident in our monetary, fiscal, and psychological policies, and they are spelled out in the annual *Economic Report of the President*. The objectives of full employment, stable prices, a healthy rate of economic growth, and the use of government intervention to stabilize the level of economic activity are stated clearly in these *Reports*. We have taken a middle course regarding the use of government intervention as a means of stabilizing the level of business activity. In most instances we use indirect measures before resorting to direct government action.

The failure to reach and maintain these goals in the 1960s and 1970s led to questions about the adequacy of our conventional economic policies and measures to deal with existing problems. Had we mismanaged our policies, or were they no longer appropriate in the new economic environment?

The theory of rational expectations suggests that the public is better informed today about the economy. Moreover, consumers and businesspeople react not only on the basis of what has happened in the past or is currently happening. Their actions are guided primarily by what they believe is going to happen in the near future. For example, an anticipated decrease in the discount rate or decrease in taxes may cause businesses to delay investment. On the other hand, an expected rise in the discount rate or higher taxes may cause them to accelerate investment. Consequently, their actions often are procyclical in nature and sometimes discount or abort government economic policies and measures designed to stabilize economic activity and the price level.

The slowdown in growth and productivity and the stagflation in the 1960s and 1970s led also to the emergence of supply-side economics. Supply-side economics consists of a set of policies and measures to encourage savings, stimulate investment, and motivate workers in an effort to increase the supply of goods and services. This in turn would bring about high-level employment, stable prices, and sustained growth of economic activity.

The supply-side proposals are demonstrated by use of the tax-output curve, the labor tax wedge, and the Laffer curve. Although supply-side economics is not a complete replacement for demand-management policies, it is not going to fade away. In all probability, it will be melded with demand management and monetary measures. In the future, we will no doubt take into consideration the supply-side as well as the demand-side effects before implementing economic policies or measures.

NEW TERMS AND CONCEPTS

Supply-side economics
Labor tax wedge
Investment tax wedge

Laffer curve
Substitution effect

Income effect
Reaganomics

DISCUSSION QUESTIONS

1. Why does it seem easier to get expansionary measures passed by Congress than it does to have anti-inflationary bills enacted?
2. Do you think we should have some definite guides for the institution of anticyclical measures, such as lowering the discount rate at one level of unemployment or inflation, engaging in deficit spending at another level, and so forth? Explain.
3. Do you see any substantial difference in the final goals of the advocates of demand-management and the advocates of supply-side policies?
4. How important is the relationship between business investment and economic growth?
5. Do you see any contradiction between the theories of rational expectations and supply-side policies?
6. What criticisms are expressed about supply-side propositions?
7. Distinguish between the substitution effect and the income effect of a decrease in payroll taxes.
8. Indicate some ways in which supply-side measures were incorporated into President Reagan's economic policies.

SUGGESTED READINGS

Barlett, Bruce. *Reaganomics: Supply-Side Economics in Action.* Westport, CT: Arlington House Publishers, 1982.

Begg, David K. H. *The Rational Expectation Revolution in Economics.* Baltimore: The Johns Hopkins University Press, 1983.

Drucker, Peter F. *Toward the Next Economics.* New York: Harper & Row, Publishers, 1981.

Evans, Michael K. *The Truth about Supply-Side Economics.* New York: Basic Books, Inc., 1983.

Gilder, George. *Wealth and Poverty.* New York: Basic Books, Inc., 1981.

Hailstones, Thomas J. *A Guide to Supply-Side Economics.* Reston, VA: Reston Publishing Company, 1982.

————. *Viewpoints on Supply-Side Economics*. Reston, VA: Reston Publishing Company, 1982.

McComas, M. "Did Supply-Side Incentives Work?" *Fortune* (November, 1984).

The New American Boom: Exciting Changes in Life and Business between Now and the Year 2000. Washington, DC: Kiplinger, 1986

Reynolds, A. "How Supply-Side Triumphed." *Challenge* (November/December, 1984).

Roberts, P. C. "The Supply Siders Were Right after All." *Business Week* (May 12, 1986).

Supply-Side Economics in the 1980s. Federal Reserve Bank of Atlanta, 1982.

PART 6

INTERNATIONAL ECONOMICS

22
INTERNATIONAL TRADE AND AID

■

Just as trade between various sections of a nation can improve the welfare of all people involved, so too can trade between nations benefit both the exporter and the importer. Different languages, habits, or customs are no more justifiable reasons for not carrying on trade than are imaginary boundary lines between states or regions a valid reason for stifling trade within a nation.

In some nations the amount of international trade is minimal, but in others it constitutes a substantial portion of the nation's total production and trade. In many countries, such as Australia, Belgium, Canada, Denmark, Great Britain, Norway, and Switzerland, the values of either exports or imports amount to more than 20 percent of their respective national incomes. Although the United States has a much larger total value of foreign trade than any other nation in the world—indeed the value of its exports alone exceeds the total production of many nations—the value of its exports is only about 5.2 percent of its gross national product, while the value of its imports approximates 8.7 percent of gross national product. In 1986, for example, United States total merchandise exports were about $220 billion and imports $338 billion compared with a U.S. GNP of over $4 trillion.

International trade, nevertheless, is important to our economy. In 1986 we engaged in trade with some 150 nations, possessions, or territories throughout the world. Our biggest customer was Canada, to which we exported over $54 billion in merchandise. During the same year we sent $31 billion worth of goods to Latin American countries. A total of $60 billion was shipped to various countries in western Europe, where Great Britain and West Germany, respectively, accounted for $11 billion and $10 billion worth of our exports. Another $57 billion went to Asia. Our big customers in Asia were Japan with $26 billion and Taiwan and Korea with $4 billion and $7 billion, respectively. Over $7 billion of our exports found their way to Australia, New Zealand, and South Africa. In broad categories some of our leading imports and exports of merchandise are shown on Table 22-1.

The amount of merchandise trade activity fluctuates with changing

Table 22-1 Selected U.S. Exports and Imports, 1986 (Millions)

Exports

Capital goods (except automotive)	$79,184
Industrial supplies and materials	63,404
Food, feeds, and beverages	22,584
Automotive vehicles, parts, and engines	23,898
Consumer goods (nonfoods) except automotive	14,533

Imports

Automotive vehicles, parts, and engines	$78,100
Consumer goods (nonfoods) except automotive	77,963
Capital goods except automotive	75,724
Petroleum and related products	33,892
Food, feeds, and beverages	24,020

Source: *Survey of Current Business* (March, 1987).

economic conditions throughout the world. The dependence on foreign oil by the United States is a case in point. In 1973, for example, petroleum imports amounted to $8.4 billion and constituted 12 percent of the total value of U.S. merchandise imports. Following the OPEC embargo in 1973–1974, oil prices quadrupled and petroleum imports rose in 1974 to $26.5 billion, or 26 percent of the value of our imports. By 1981, we were importing $61.9 billion in oil, which still accounted for 24 percent of the U.S. merchandise imports. Since 1981, the world market for oil has changed drastically. Oil-exporting nations suddenly were faced with excess supply and falling prices, a situation that benefits those nations dependent on imported petroleum. By 1986, the United States was importing $33.8 billion in oil, and as a percentage of total U.S. imports, oil had diminished to approximately 9 percent.

All this trade, of course, takes place as nations seek to improve their economic standards and to take advantage of the laws of absolute and comparative advantage, explained in Chapter 2. The law of absolute advantage is manifest readily in the exchange of coffee from abroad in return for United States machinery. The law of comparative advantage may help explain historically why the United States exported large-sized automobiles while at the same time it imported sport-type and smaller cars. Much is gained by all the countries involved in the international flow of goods and services. Unfortunately, most of the trade is carried on among developed nations since most other nations have very little to trade.

BARRIERS TO FREE TRADE

Nevertheless, most nations of the world are reluctant to adopt a free-trade policy, and numerous restrictions are still invoked in the area of international trade. Although economic arguments strongly favor free trade, most decisions affecting international trade are made in the political arena. Unfortunately the pressures of apparent short-run economic advantages and political expediency usually overshadow the less obvious and long-run advantages of free trade. Consequently, a myriad of restrictions still prevail in trade markets throughout the world today. One of the most common forms of restriction is the tariff.

The Tariff

A **tariff** is a duty or tax levied on foreign imports. It may be a **specific tariff** in absolute terms, such as 25 cents per pound or per unit of a commodity. It may be an **ad valorem tariff** in relative or percentage terms, such as 15 percent of the value of the imported commodity.

Purpose of a Tariff.   A tariff may be levied either for revenue or for protective purposes. In the early days of the United States, the primary purpose of import duties was to raise revenue to help defray the expenses of operating the new federal government. Later, however, we shifted in large part to a protectionist tariff policy to protect our new industries.

To be effective, a tariff must serve one purpose or the other, since the two objectives are to a large extent incompatible. If a tariff is designed to obtain revenue, it must be high enough to yield a revenue. But if it is too high, it will discourage the importation of goods and services, and consequently there will be very little revenue flow from the tariff. On the other hand, if protection is desired, the tariff must be high enough to keep out foreign products. If it keeps out foreign products, however, there will be very little tariff yield for revenue purposes. Although there may be an optimal tariff, which will serve both purposes, it cannot serve either purpose as well as a tariff designed with only one objective in mind.

Arguments for Free Trade.   Since there are many other sources of government revenue and at present a relatively small amount of income is derived from import duties, it is difficult to support any argument that a tariff is essential to raise revenue.

The gain or advantage of trade between regions or nations is obvious. The fundamental argument for free trade, and against protective tariffs, is that tariffs deny individuals and nations the benefits of greater productivity and the higher standard of living which results from the exercise of the laws of absolute and comparative advantage. Tariffs disturb and restrict the free movement of goods and services, eliminate the advantages of specialization and exchange, and prevent the optimum use of scarce resources. From an economic point of view, the argument for free trade is so basic that it is easy to refute most arguments against free trade and for tariffs. As a result, the trade restrictionists must use several offensives to make a dent in the free-trade defense. Even at that, restrictionists must move outside the area of economics to find their most reasonable arguments against free trade.

Regardless of what type of argument is put forth, it should be remembered that ultimately the consumer pays the tariff. Although the actual customs duty is levied on the importer, it generally is passed on to the consumer in the form of higher prices. The main beneficiary of the tariff is the relatively inefficient producer and perhaps in the short run the employees, whose jobs are more secure because of the tariff.

Arguments for Tariffs.   Numerous arguments in favor of tariffs have been offered. They touch upon the military, social, and political as well as upon the economic aspects of international trade. Although a few of the arguments have some validity and merit, by and large tariffs are difficult to justify from a long-run economic point of view.

Protect Infant Industries.   The protection of infant industries is one of the oldest and most valid of the tariff arguments. It was instrumental in promoting the shift in our tariff policy from one of revenue to one of protectionism in the early part of the 19th century. In its simplest form it states that new or infant industries, especially in developing nations, are frequently at a cost disadvantage compared with mature firms in the same industry in the more developed nations. It follows then that if this cost disadvantage is removed by applying a tariff to industry imports from the foreign countries, the domestic firms will be given an opportunity to compete with foreign producers. This supposedly gives the infant industry an opportunity to grow and develop. The true infant-industry protectionist maintains that the tariff should be continued only until the firms in the domestic industry have reached a state of maturity. At that point the tariff should be removed and the domestic industry be forced to compete with the foreign imports or go out of business.

Equalize Costs.   A similar argument is made for the so-called scientific tariff that is designed to equalize the cost of production between domestic and foreign producers. Advocates of this tariff argue that it would remove any advantage to foreign producers arising from availability of raw materials, differences in efficiency, lower wages, and the like. It would make the cost (including tariff) or the price of both the foreign and domestic products equal. Consequently, this would remove the fundamental benefit and reasons—increased productivity, lower costs, and a higher standard of living—for international trade.

Protect U.S. Jobs.   It is often suggested that the use of tariffs creates or protects domestic jobs. Arguments of this type tend to be shortsighted and take into account only one side of international trade. They propose that if tariffs are imposed, foreign products will be kept out of the United States. As a result, consumers will shift to the purchase of domestically produced goods and services, which in turn will result in increased domestic production and employment.

The protectionists forget, however, that international trade is a two-way street. We not only import goods and services but also export them. Foreigners cannot continue to buy from us unless they have U.S. dollars, and the primary way they obtain these dollars is by selling goods to the United States. If we impose tariffs and cut down imports, foreigners will have fewer U.S. dollars to buy our goods. The net result will be that any immediate increase in employment generated by tariffs will be offset by a decrease in production and employment in our export-producing industries. A tariff also brings about a transfer of income from the purchasers of the domestic product protected by the tariff to the domestic producers (and employees) of that product.

Protect High U.S. Wages.   It is frequently argued that tariffs are necessary to protect our high U.S. wage rates. It is pointed out that most foreigners have lower wage rates than do U.S. workers, and, therefore, foreign exporters have an unfair advantage over domestic producers. It is contended further that, if lower-priced foreign goods are admitted into our nation, competition will force U.S. producers to cut costs, particularly wages, in an effort to stay in business.

There would be some element of truth in this argument were it not for the fact that the wage cost per unit of a good is more important in determining cost than is the wage rate itself. Productivity per worker varies among different countries. It is possible that nations with high wage rates may have lower unit labor costs because of higher levels of productivity per work-hour. This is not only possible but also probable, since many studies show a high correlation between wage rates and productivity throughout the world. Consequently, a nation with a high wage rate may very well have a lower unit cost of production, in which case there should be no need for tariffs to protect the high wage rates.

Even if it is granted that the wage cost per unit may be lower in some foreign industries, it is still a disservice to the U.S. consumer in the long run to subsidize the less efficient domestic producer with a tariff. It would be far better to force the domestic producer to improve efficiency and to lower costs or go out of business. In that way, as mentioned previously, our labor force, resources, and capital would be channeled into more productive uses.

Retain Money at Home.   One of the weakest arguments for tariffs is the proposal that it keeps our money at home instead of sending it abroad. It is often stated that if we buy a car from Japan, we have the car but Japan has the money; whereas if we buy domestically produced automobiles, we have both the cars and the money in the United States. This argument, of course, completely loses sight of the fact that Japan probably would use the dollars received from the sale of their automobiles to purchase U.S. goods and services, and the dollars would return to the United States.

Develop and Protect Defense Industries.   One of the strongest and most valid of the protectionist arguments for tariffs is that tariffs will help develop and protect defense industries. This is an especially poignant argument when one remembers that the Japanese invasion of Southeast Asia cut us off from our rubber supply in Malaya in the early stages of World War II. Thus, a strong argument can be made from a military point of view that we should establish and maintain tariffs for industries producing strategic defense materials. It can be reasoned that without tariff protection some of these industries may have to close down as a result of foreign competition. In such a case our labor force, resources, and capital formerly used in these industries will be dispersed elsewhere. Consequently, if a war breaks out we will be at a distinct disadvantage in the production of military goods and armaments if we are unable to secure needed imports. At the present time many producers of strategic military goods and services are protected by tariffs, subsidies, or other measures.

Diversify Industry.   A similar argument is put forth regarding the use of tariffs to diversify the industrial structure of a nation. When a country specializes in the production of one or a few commodities, its economy is very vulnerable to wide fluctuations resulting from variations in demand for its product(s). Many times a softening of world demand and prices can bring economic disaster. Therefore, tariffs can be used to keep out imports and to encourage the development of certain industries in the domestic economy. With a broader industrial structure, the economy will become more stable and be less affected by fluctuations in the world demand for certain products. Although this argument has some degree of validity, it has relatively little application to more developed economies which are known for their widely diversified industries.

Effect of Tariffs on Trade.   The impact of tariffs on trade can be illustrated through the use of supply and demand curves. Assume in the absence of foreign trade that the equilibrium price and quantity of television sets in the United States are P_e and Q_e as depicted in Figure 22-1a. In this case, domestic demand is totally satisfied by domestic supply.

Now assume that the United States becomes an open market for television sets with no tariffs applied on foreign imports. In Figure 22-1b, the domestic supply and demand for television sets are again represented by D and S. However, if foreign producers can produce and ship television sets to the United States for a delivered price of P_1, then the new supply curve becomes S_1. This supply curve is perfectly elastic and indicates that with free trade there is an unlimited quantity of imports available at that price. The marketshare for domestic producers at the price of P_1 has shrunk

Figure 22-1   Effect of Tariffs on Trade in Televisions

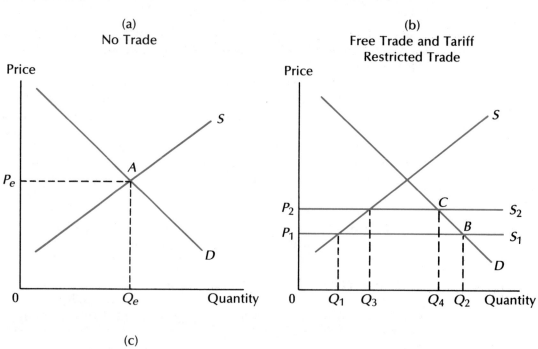

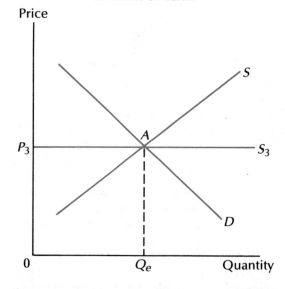

to $0Q_1$, while the marketshare now held by foreign producers is Q_1Q_2. The total number of television sets supplied by both domestic and foreign producers amounts to $0Q_2$, with the resulting new equilibrium position occurring at point B.

If a tariff is applied to imported television sets in order to protect American producers, the perfectly elastic supply curve shifts upward to S_2, reflecting the higher price brought about by the tariff. The new equilibrium is at point C in Figure 22-1b. With tariff protection, domestic producers can increase their marketshare from $0Q_1$ to $0Q_3$, while at the same time foreign producers experience a decline in their marketshare from Q_1Q_2 to Q_3Q_4. The cost of the tariff is a higher price to consumers for television sets and fewer units purchased at the higher price. Domestic producers are better off, whereas foreign producers are worse off. The tariff results in a misallocation of resources, not only in the television industry but throughout the economies of the United States and the exporting nations.

As the tariff increases, these effects become more pronounced. For example, in Figure 22-1c if the tariff were raised so that the new market price is P_3, domestic demand is once again satisfied entirely by domestic supply, and the tariff has the effect of acting as an embargo on foreign imports. As can be seen at the equilibrium position at point A, zero units are supplied by foreign producers at that price.

Quotas, Embargoes, Subsidies, and Exchange Controls

In addition to tariffs, several other devices, often referred to as **nontariff barriers**, are used to grant an advantage to domestic producers. Each has an effect similar to the tariff in that it restricts imports, grants aid to domestic producers to compete with foreign imports, or encourages the export of commodities. The most frequently used measures are import quotas, embargoes, export subsidies, and exchange controls.

Import Quotas.   An **import quota** is simply setting a maximum absolute amount of a particular commodity that may be imported. Setting definite limits on the amount that may be imported serves to protect the domestic producer and industry against the full effect of foreign competition. Consequently, it is similar in effect to, but more restrictive than, a tariff. Sometimes both a tariff and a quota are used, in which case the limited amount that is imported is subject to a customs duty.

Another form of the quota is the **tariff quota**, which does not set absolute limits on imports but places a financial restriction against excessive imports. The tariff quota permits a certain amount of an imported commodity to come in at one tariff rate, but charges a higher tariff rate for imports over and above the so-called optimum amount.

Embargoes.   An **embargo** involves the complete cessation of trade between nations or in particular products and is usually implemented for noneconomic reasons. An embargo may be applied to imports, exports, or both. When applied, the embargo has the same effect as an export or import quota equal to zero.

The United States has had an embargo on trade with Cuba since Fidel Castro's rise to power in 1959. In 1973, the United States found itself cut off from oil exports from Arab oil-producing states. In this case, an embargo was placed on oil exports to the United States because of our support for Israel. In 1975, because of fear of possible domestic shortage, the United States placed an embargo on grain exports to the Soviet Union and again in 1980 because of the Soviet Union's invasion of Afghanistan.

Over the years, the United States has also placed embargoes on the export of specific military hardware to several Middle Eastern countries and on the import of illegal drug substances such as cocaine and marijuana. In 1986, pressure was placed on the United States government to embargo trade with South Africa because of that nation's apartheid policies. The United States reacted by enacting both sanctions and restrictions on trade with South Africa.

Export Subsidies.   The **export subsidy** is designed to encourage exportation of certain goods or to prevent discrimination against exporters who may have to sell their product at a world price that is below the domestic price. Not only have direct cash payments been made for the exportation of some commodities, but also the large-scale sale of a number of surplus farm products has been promoted through the use of subsidies. In the United States, for example, the government has purchased surplus crops, such as wheat and cotton, from U.S. farmers at government-supported prices, which have often been above the domestic market price. These crops have subsequently been sold to foreign nations at world prices below the United States domestic price. In this way the government, or we should say the U.S. consumer, has paid a subsidy to have goods exported.

Exchange Controls.   The flow of international trade can be affected greatly by the use of **exchange controls**. Controls may take the form of rationing a nation's scarce foreign exchange, which would limit the overall imports into the nation. More specific regulation of imports is possible through the use of multiple exchange rates. In this case different exchange rates are set for various commodities. In this manner the importation of some commodities can be encouraged while others are discouraged. Since exchange rates can be set arbitrarily by the government, they can be applied readily to restrict the free flow of goods and services in a fashion similar to tariffs and quotas.

UNITED STATES TRADE POLICY

In its early history the United States endeavored to be a leader in the promotion of world trade, but its attitude has changed from time to time. Initially the new nation used the tariff primarily for revenue purposes.

Tariffs were necessarily low to encourage the importation of goods so that more tariff revenues could be collected. In fact, in the first few decades, 90 percent or more of the revenue obtained by the federal government came from tariffs.

Although protection became more important in United States tariff policy thereafter, the tariff continued to be a major source of federal revenue until the Civil War. As protection became more predominant with the growth of U.S. industry, tariff rates continued to climb. After World War I, tariff rates were at their highest level in history, but they were pushed still higher by the Hawley-Smoot Tariff Act of 1930. Shortly thereafter there was hardly an import commodity that did not have a tariff, and some rates exceeded 100 percent of the original value of the commodity. The average tariff as a percentage of the value of all imports was about 33 percent.

Reciprocal Trade Agreements

The Great Depression of the thirties and the inauguration of the New Deal political program by the newly elected Democratic administration ushered in a new policy of lower tariffs. Under the Reciprocal Trade Agreements Act of 1934, the President was given authority to lower tariffs by as much as 50 percent, without further Congressional approval, provided other nations would make reciprocal concessions. As a result of this Act, more than 30 separate agreements were made with foreign nations.

Included in the Act was the famous "most-favored-nation clause" by which concessions made in bilateral agreements were generalized to all nations. When we lowered our tariff on wool imports from Australia, for example, it was required that this lower rate must apply also to imported wool from any other nation that did not discriminate against the United States. In short, we had to extend to all nations the same tariff benefits we gave to most-favored nations. On the other hand, we did not enter into any trade agreement with a foreign nation unless it extended to us the same tariff concessions on various commodities that it gave to its most-favored nation(s).

Although tariffs were reduced substantially under the Reciprocal Trade Agreements Act in the next two decades, the reductions and coverage permitted by the Act were weakened by various amendments and revisions. In 1951 the "escape clause" became a part of the Act. This clause permitted the raising of tariff rates if the Tariff Commission found that existing tariffs were causing harm or seriously threatening domestic producers. A 1954 amendment prohibited any tariff reduction that might threaten national security. These reservations were carried through in both the Trade Expansion Act of 1962 and the Trade Act of 1974.

The Export-Import Bank

In the past few decades, the United States has tried to promote freer trade by direct internal legislation and by cooperation through international organizations and agreements. It has also given substantial financial assistance in an effort to promote world trade. In addition to membership in the World Bank, the International Monetary Fund, and other financial organizations, which we shall examine in greater detail later, the United States has its own bank for financing world trade. As a financial aid to the development of world trade, in 1934 the federal government established a government instrumentality known as the Export-Import Bank.

The Export-Import Bank was inaugurated during the Depression for a number of purposes, primarily for financing exports from the United States. It was anticipated that the Export-Import Bank would aid in the financing of expected increases in trade with the Soviet Union, officially recognized by the United States in 1933, and with various Latin American countries. The Bank has been a source of aid in trade with numerous nations. The Bank under certain conditions guarantees U.S. exporters that they will be paid for the sale of their goods to foreign nations. Sometimes the Bank makes loans to foreign importers to buy U.S. goods. The Bank mainly finances private exports and imports between the United States and other nations that cannot be financed at reasonable rates through regular international financial channels.

In recent years, however, as a result of growing financial resources, the Bank has been making loans for private and government development projects in underdeveloped nations. In this regard it does not attempt to compete with national and international finance agencies, such as the World Bank and the International Finance Corporation.

General Agreement of Tariffs and Trade

After World War II several of the Allied nations, exclusive of the Soviet Union, met for the purpose of promoting free trade among nations of the world. The outcome was the formulation of the General Agreement on Tariffs and Trade (GATT), which was drawn up at Geneva in 1947 and signed by 23 nations, including the United States. GATT called for equal and nondiscriminatory treatment for all nations in international trade, the reduction of tariffs through reciprocal trade agreements, and the easing or elimination of import quotas. One of the main provisions of the Act was that of extending the most-favored-nation principle to all signers. At the present time more than 80 nations have adopted the General Agreement on Tariffs and Trade. Since GATT is an informal agreement, a nation is not compelled to eliminate or reduce any of its trade restrictions.

Trade Expansion Act of 1962

The policy toward lower tariffs was reinforced in the United States by the passage of the Trade Expansion Act of 1962. This Act was designed for three purposes: (1) to stimulate the economic growth of the United States and to enlarge foreign markets for its products; (2) to strengthen economic relations with foreign countries through the development of open and nondiscriminatory trading in the free world; and (3) to prevent Communist economic penetration. The Act contained special provisions for dealings and agreements with the Common Market.

To ease any hardship that may have resulted from liberalizing trade restrictions, the Act provided relief for import-injured industries. Individual firms could under certain conditions be eligible for adjustment assistance. Workers who were laid off or displaced because of increased foreign imports resulting from implementation of the Act were also eligible for assistance. Such assistance was extended to some autoworkers and steelworkers in the early 1980s.

On the basis of the authority given to the President under the Trade Expansion Act of 1962, the United States entered negotiations with other nations in an effort to bring about substantial reductions in world tariffs. After 3 years of difficult negotiations in the Kennedy Round, one of the most massive assaults on tariffs in history was agreed upon by the 53 nations participating in the talks under the auspices of the General Agreement on Tariffs and Trade. The United States, for example, granted tariff concessions on thousands of items ranging from automobiles, steel, and chemicals to nuts, cameras, and toupees. These tariff reductions were a great inducement to world trade and helped bring many of the nations closer together economically as well as politically.

U.S. Trade with Communist Countries

A cold war atmosphere prevailed between the East and the West during much of the 1950s and the 1960s, and restrictive trade policies were imposed by both the United States and the Soviet Union. In the late 1960s and early 1970s political antagonisms abated somewhat, and relations between the United States and the communist nations began to mellow. As the communist economies grew, the advantages of trade with the United States and other free nations became more and more apparent to both sides. The United States Department of Commerce in the late 1960s began to encourage U.S. businesses to carry on trade with the Soviet satellite nations of Eastern Europe.

In spite of ideological and political differences as well as dissimilarities in economic structures, trade between the United States and communist countries grew rapidly in the early 1970s. Large commercial transactions developed in certain specialized areas, such as equipment and technology for the automobile, chemical, petroleum, and agricultural industries. U.S. exports to the communist countries (U.S.S.R., People's Republic of China, Bulgaria, Czechoslovakia, East Germany, Hungary, Poland, and Rumania) increased dramatically from $354 million in 1970 to $7.2 billion by 1985.

Both the United States and the communist nations are making adjustments to remove trade barriers and to pave the way for smoother exchanges of goods and services. In addition, many U.S. manufacturers, banks, and other types of businesses have established contacts or offices in communist countries. Since the population, area, and resources of the communist nations are substantial and these nations are in need of many goods and services that the United States and other western nations can supply, there is a strong indication that East-West trade will grow during the forthcoming years. Such trade will be economically beneficial to all nations involved. Whether it is a wise move on the part of the United States from a political or military viewpoint may be another question.

Trade Act of 1974

In December, 1974, Congress passed the Trade Act of 1974 as a successor to the Trade Expansion Act of 1962. Provisions of the Act cleared the way for the United States to play a major role when 105 nations met in Geneva to draw up new rules of international trade and commerce in the spring of 1975. The Act provides the President with a wide range of measures designed to open trade doors around the world. The President may (1) reduce or raise U.S. tariffs during negotiations; (2) impose an import surcharge up to 15 percent; (3) reduce or eliminate nontariff barriers, such as export subsidies, import quotas, investment restrictions, health and safety codes, and pollution standards, subject to Congressional approval; and (4) retaliate against unreasonable foreign restrictions on U.S. trade. The Act also permits the President to extend most-favored-nation treatment to communist nations. Like its predecessor Act, the Trade Act of 1974 provides various types of assistance to import-injured firms and workers.

Multinational Trade Negotiations and the Tokyo Round, 1978

Much progress toward the development of freer trade occurred in the 1950s and 1960s. This promotion of international trade was instrumental in overall economic growth and the improvement in the standard of living in the world's three major industrial sectors—North America, western Europe, and Japan. In the 1970s, however, the movement toward free trade slowed. Increased competition from newly industrialized nations, the OPEC oil embargo and price increases, worldwide inflation and disruption in financial markets, and unemployment associated with the international recession of 1974–1975 discouraged the move toward freer trade. Several nations, including the United States, adopted safeguards against imports, implemented export subsidies, and filed antidumping claims against exporters who were selling below their domestic prices. These restrictive activities were concentrated in textiles, automobiles, steel, shoes, agriculture, and shipbuilding.

As a result of the slowdown in the free trade movement, the United States, other leading GATT nations, and some developing nations entered into multilateral trade negotiations in 1978. Later in the year, the Tokyo

Round of these negotiations led to agreement on a trade package to relax tariff and nontariff barriers, the formulation of rules for trades and codes of fair conduct, and the design of effective mechanisms for settling disputes. The package included tariff cuts that averaged 30 percent by the United States with reciprocal reductions by its trading partners.

The negotiators also agreed to remove burdensome industrial and agricultural nontariff barriers. Moreover, they agreed on measures to improve the GATT framework for dealing with agricultural issues and handling trade with developing nations, balance-of-payments problems, and export restrictions. The package also provided a code on safeguards for protecting import-injured businesses and employees.

The severity of the worldwide recession in 1982 and the resulting high unemployment led many nations to impose restrictive measures against imports. At the GATT meeting in December, 1982, certain members expressed a strong concern about the wave of protectionism sweeping the world. They warned of the possible development of a trade war. As a result, the GATT members recommended that import restrictions be limited in the hope of maintaining freer trade.

TRADE POLICY TODAY

Whenever economic conditions are unfavorable, protectionism tends to become a strong political force. Despite several years of economic expansion, many industries throughout the United States continue to suffer from the flow of foreign imports. Examples of hard-hit industries include shoes, textiles, autos, machine tools, steel, and agriculture. Although the Reagan administration is strongly committed to the principle of free trade, huge, record-setting trade deficits are producing pressures on the administration to adopt a highly protectionist trade policy.

The trade deficits of the mid-1980s were largely the result of an overvalued dollar. Although the dollar's value in world financial markets has declined markedly since its peak in 1985, chronic trade deficits persist. Consequently, Congress has introduced hundreds of bills that seek to protect American industries. Legislation has been introduced to impose both general and country-specific surcharges to reduce the deficit. President Reagan stood firm against these strong protectionist measures, but occasionally departed from free-trade doctrine by embracing temporary "voluntary" quotas on Japanese cars or heavy duties on such imported items as motorcycles. However, Japan's resistance to dropping barriers to American goods and services, the steady decline in manufacturing employment, and a plunge in U.S. agricultural exports resulted in additional protectionist concessions from the administration.

In 1985, the administration offered a series of actions in an attempt to reduce pressures for more extreme forms of protective barriers to trade. Remedies include government initiated complaints against unfair trade practices; quicker processing of injury claims by domestic industries; tighter rules against copyrighting and counterfeiting; a $300 million allocation to permit the Export-Import Bank to counter foreign subsidies, and a push to convene additional rounds of trade talks with GATT. These measures reflected an attempt to prevent another 1930s-style trade war from erupting. But as trade deficits with Japan continued to mount, in 1987 the United States enacted import duties of 100 percent on nearly $300 million worth of Japanese products. These measures were the first U.S. trade sanctions against Japan since World War II. They reflect the serious concern caused by an annual trade deficit with Japan in excess of $58 billion. The U.S. position on free trade is crucial, for any movement to protectionism is likely to produce retaliatory trade barriers against the U.S.

EUROPEAN ECONOMIC INTEGRATION

Since the end of World War II, many dramatic developments have taken place in the sphere of international economics. One major development has been the voluntary efforts by a number of nations to integrate certain of their economic activities for mutual benefit. Another development has been the effort of some of the more affluent nations to extend economic and technical assistance to the developing nations. Both of these movements are having a pronounced influence on the economic, social, political, and military relations of the family of nations throughout the world.

The most significant economic integration effort has been that made in Europe. This has come in a series of steps involving coordination, cooperation, and eventually economic integration.

Organization for Economic Cooperation and Development

In 1948, 18 European nations joined together to form the Organization for European Economic Cooperation (OEEC). One important function of the organization was to administer aid under the Marshall Plan. But its general purpose was the joining together of European nations to use their individual capacities and potentialities in order to increase their production, to develop and modernize their industries, and to expand trade among themselves by reducing tariff barriers.

The OEEC was replaced in 1960 when the United States and Canada joined the 18 European nations of the OEEC to sign a pact setting up a new agency known as the Organization for Economic Cooperation and Development (OECD). The stated objectives of this new organization were to promote prosperity, to maximize economic growth, and to establish financial stability in the nations of the industrial west. Also, the OECD would help underdeveloped nations obtain sound economic growth and contribute toward the expansion of world trade.

European Common Market

In 1952 a more definite step was taken with the formation of the European Coal and Steel Community for the purpose of pooling the coal and steel resources of six nations and eliminating trade barriers on coal, iron ore, iron, and steel. The six nations that joined in the agreement were France, West Germany, Italy, Belgium, the Netherlands, and Luxembourg.

The success of the European Coal and Steel Community led to the formation of the European Economic Community (EEC), promoted in part by the United States, by the same six nations in 1958. The goals established by the Common Market, as it is usually called, were (1) to abolish tariff and import quotas among the six nations within 10 to 12 years, (2) to establish within a similar period a common tariff applicable to all imports from outside the Common Market area, (3) to attain eventually the free movement of capital and labor within the Common Market nations, and (4) to adopt a common policy regarding monopolies and agriculture.

By 1968, all tariff barriers among the six nations were removed, 2 years ahead of schedule. The common external tariff was achieved a few years later. Some progress has been made toward common internal policies regarding monopoly control, transportation, and social security systems. Furthermore, labor force training and mobility have received increased coordination. By 1982 the member nations had formed the European Monetary System (EMS). It established the European Currency Unit (ECU) as a common monetary unit of account. The existence of the Common Market has contributed greatly toward economic growth and prosperity in western Europe.

Although many of the economic concessions made within the Common Market have been extended to outside countries, some nonmember nations consider the Common Market to be a threat to their trade. This could be true if the promotion of trade within the member nations resulting from reduction of the internal tariffs comes at the expense of imports from outside the Common Market. In fact, the common external tariff could be used, if desired, to form a strong trading bloc. In this regard, with the enactment of the Trade Expansion Act of 1962 and the Trade Act of 1974, the Congress of the United States gave the President special powers of negotiation in dealing with the Common Market nations.

Great Britain did not join the Common Market when it was formed because of its reluctance to abandon its preferential treatment of other members of the British Commonwealth. Twice during the 1960s Great Britain made an attempt to join the Common Market. These requests for admission were denied, however, on the basis of conditions Britain established for entry into the Common Market. By 1973, however, these differences were reconciled, and along with Denmark and Ireland, Britain became a member of the Common Market.

In 1981 the third enlargement of the Common Market occurred with the accession of Greece, and in 1986 the membership of the Common Market expanded again with the addition of Spain and Portugal. The population of the 12-member Common Market now stands at 320 million, with Spain and Portugal increasing the land area size of the Market by one-third. As a result of these expansions, a shift in policy emphasis away from the wealthier northern countries of Europe to the less developed area of the south is likely. The Common Market's outlook on the world is also likely to change. With Spain and Portugal as members, there is a strong incentive to improve and expand political and economic ties with South and Central America as well as with certain parts of Africa.

From the point of view of the United States, the 12-nation Common Market is likely to impact trade mainly in agriculture. The United States exports approximately $2 billion in agricultural products annually to Spain and Portugal. Membership of these nations in the Common Market will undoubtedly diminish imports of American agricultural products. The shift in trade from the United States to other Common Market members is somewhat typical. After Greece joined the Common Market, its imports from member nations increased while those from the United States decreased.

The importance of carrying on trade with the Common Market is reflected in the fact that, outside of the United States, the Common Market is the largest free trade area in the world. The Common Market accounts for over a fifth of world trade and is a leading economic partner for most countries. Over 20 percent of the Common Market's exports are received by the United States, and the Common Market, in turn, receives almost 22 percent of the value of American exports. The total value of visible trade between the U.S. and the Common Market is now in excess of $100 billion. Compared with the United States, the Common Market has a larger population, a greater gross national product, a higher value of international trade, and a larger total civilian labor force.

Over the years, the success of the Common Market arrangement encouraged the formation of similar organizations in Central and South America, in the Caribbean, in Southeast Asia, and among communist nations. None of these, however, have been as successful as the European Common Market.

UNITED STATES FOREIGN AID

In addition to its endeavor to promote world trade, the United States has extended a considerable amount of direct economic aid to other countries. In early post-World War II years, funds were utilized especially for reconstruction purposes, but in more recent years much aid has been given to developing nations. Here again aid has been both direct and indirect through international financial institutions.

Bilateral Aid

During World War II we exported nearly $40 billion in military and nonmilitary goods under the Lend-Lease program. Nearly two-thirds of this amount went to Great Britain. The Soviet Union received nearly $10 billion, and France received about $2.5 billion. Smaller amounts were shipped to other nations. Since that time, other forms of aid have been granted to many foreign nations.

Economic Cooperation Administration.   In 1948 the United States Economic Cooperation Administration (ECA) program, otherwise known as the famous Marshall Plan, went into effect to aid the nations of western Europe. In addition to receiving financial aid from the United States, the various nations agreed to take domestic steps necessary to improve their respective economies and to participate and cooperate with one another in seeking solutions to their common economic problems. The name of the ECA was changed a number of times; however, the objective remained the same, and aid continued to pour into western Europe during the 1950s.

Technical Assistance.   In his inaugural address in 1949, President Truman laid the foundation for a new type of foreign aid program designed to encourage the advancement of underdeveloped nations through the extension of technical assistance from the United States. Most previous aid had gone to developed nations in need of reconstruction. The new program was put into effect in 1950 when Congress approved the Act for International Development. Billions of dollars have since been appropriated for technical assistance, and today there are thousands of U.S. technical experts throughout the world giving advice and assistance to foreign nations endeavoring to improve their agricultural and industrial production.

Development Loan Funds.   As a further indication of the increased emphasis on economic development as the principal goal of our foreign aid program, in 1957 Congress established the Development Loan Fund and appropriated nearly $1.5 billion for its operation. The Fund was empowered to guarantee or make loans to persons, businesses, and governments in foreign nations for various industrial, financial, and commercial development projects. All projects and loans must have the approval of the foreign government. The Development Loan Fund was combined with the International Cooperation Administration as part of the Agency for International Development in 1961.

From the end of World War II until 1986, the United States distributed $277 billion in foreign assistance to more than 120 nations. Of this total,

$14 billion was contributed to seven separate international financial institutions (exclusive of the International Monetary Fund).

AID THROUGH THE WORLD BANK

Since World War II the United States has been a large contributor to foreign aid through various international institutions. The World Bank is one such institution. Established in 1945, the World Bank is composed of the International Bank for Reconstruction and Development (IBRD) and its affiliate, the International Development Association (IDA). The IBRD has a second affiliate, the International Finance Corporation (IFC).

The International Bank for Reconstruction and Development

The IBRD was created in 1945 and is now owned by the governments of 148 countries. The Bank makes and guarantees loans for productive reconstruction and development projects, both from its own capital, which is provided by its member governments, and through the mobilization of private capital. The Bank's capital is so structured that risks are shared by all member governments roughly in proportion to their economic strength. Bank loans are made for the purpose of raising living standards in developing countries.

The present subscription of member nations exceeds $58 billion, with the United States accounting for approximately one-fifth of this amount. Loans generally have a grace period of 5 years and are repayable over 20 years. In fiscal 1985, the World Bank, through its IBRD affiliate, approved loans worth $11 billion to some 44 member countries.

The IBRD has traditionally financed all kinds of capital infrastructure such as roads, railways, ports, power facilities, and telecommunications. However, its development strategy also places emphasis on investments that can directly affect the well-being of poor people in developing countries by making them more productive and by integrating them as active partners in the development process. Despite a shift to lending for poverty relief and human development, loans approved by the IBRD for population, health, and nutrition projects for fiscal 1985 amounted to little more than one-twentieth the value of those approved for energy or agriculture and less than a quarter of those approved for education.

In response to the debt crisis of developing nations, the IBRD inaugurated a program of structural-adjustment lending in 1980. Loans are granted to support programs of specific policy changes and institutional reforms designed to achieve a more efficient use of resources. It is anticipated that structural-adjustment lending will ease balance-of-payment problems for developing countries and also provide the foundation and incentive for future growth.

The International Development Association.   This institution was established as an affiliate of the World Bank in 1960 largely at the initiative of the United States. The IDA seeks to provide assistance to very poor countries and on financial terms that impose a lighter burden on their balance of payments than other World Bank loans. To be eligible for IDA assistance, a country must have an annual per capita gross national product of less than $791, in 1983 U.S. dollars. More than 50 countries are eligible under this criterion, but about 90 percent of the loans go to countries with a per capita GNP below $400.

Membership in IDA is open to all members of the IBRD, and 133 were members in 1986. The funds used by IDA, called credits to distinguish them from IBRD loans, come mostly in the form of subscriptions, general replenishments from the more industrialized and developed nations, and transfers from the net earnings of IBRD. IDA credits are made only to governments and have 50-year maturities at no interest. After a 10-year grace period, 1 percent of the credit is to be repaid annually for 10 years, while in the remaining 30 years, 3 percent is to be repaid annually.

In fiscal 1985 the IDA disbursed over $2.4 billion to some 45 nations. Recent emphasis of the IDA has been in Africa, for which a special fund has been established and over $1 billion contributed.

The International Finance Corporation.   The IFC is the affiliate of the World Bank that was established in 1956 to promote and provide support for the private sector in developing member countries. Membership in the IBRD is a prerequisite for membership in the IFC, which totals 127 countries. During 1985, the IFC approved 75 loans and investments in 38 developing countries totaling $937 million. Legally and financially, the IFC and IBRD are separate entities. The IFC has its own operating and legal staff, but draws on the IBRD for administrative services.

The IFC has an ambitious 5-year plan for 1985–1989 during which it hopes to invest $7.4 billion of its own money in projects and to act as a catalyst for over $25 billion from other investors and lenders. In addition to its traditional function of promoting private direct investment, preferably in the form of joint ventures between local and foreign investors, the IFC has become very active in promoting the flow of indirect (or portfolio) foreign investment to the Third World. Also, the IFC has expanded its activities to include assistance such as providing insurance, underwriting Eurodollar bond issues, and setting up new investment banks.

In addition to the World Bank and its affiliates, a number of regional development banks exist. These include the Inter-American Development Bank, the African Development Bank, and the Asian Development Bank. In a smaller perspective, their aims and purposes are similar to those of the World Bank.

SUMMARY

Although international trade can enhance the welfare of all nations concerned, there are still many restrictions to the free flow of goods and services among nations. Probably the most widespread restriction is the tariff, which may be levied for either revenue or protectionist purposes.

Supporters of the tariff present many arguments, including the fact that tariffs are needed to protect infant industries, to equalize costs of production, to protect U.S. jobs, to protect high U.S. wages, to help retain money at home, to help develop and protect defense industries, and to diversify industry. Most of the arguments in favor of the tariff are based on short-run disadvantages that would arise in the move toward freer trade. They tend to neglect, however, the long-run economic advantages that would accrue to U.S. consumers if tariffs were reduced or eliminated. Other devices used to restrict trade are import quotas, embargoes, export subsidies, and exchange controls.

During the 19th century and the early 20th century, tariff rates rose intermittently. Record rates after World War I were pushed still higher by the Hawley-Smoot Tariff Act of 1930. But in the mid-1930s a new policy of lower tariffs was inaugurated in the United States. Under the Reciprocal Trade Agreements Act of 1934, the President was given authority to lower tariffs by as much as 50 percent. The Export-Import Bank, established in 1934, helps promote international trade by rendering financial assistance to U.S. exporters and foreign importers.

In 1947 we entered the General Agreement on Tariffs and Trade (GATT) with several other nations of the world. In 1962 the Trade Expansion Act gave the President further powers to reduce tariffs. This Act also provided relief for import-injured firms and workers. Substantial progress in tariff reductions was made under this Act as a result of the Kennedy-Round negotiations with other GATT nations. U.S. trade with communist countries greatly expanded in the 1970s, and the Trade Act of 1974 paved the way for the U.S. to play an even greater role in international trade and commerce. In 1978 the Tokyo Round of Multinational Trade Negotiations provided a boost in the trend toward freer trade. In 1986, as a result of record trade deficits along with a loss of employment and income in manufacturing, the United States faced strong domestic pressure to implement protectionist trade barriers.

One of the most significant economic developments since the end of World War II has been the trend toward European economic integration. This has been promoted through a series of organizations. The success of these organizations, especially the Common Market with its goals to eliminate international trade barriers among the member nations and to establish a common external tariff, has stimulated the formation of similar organizations in other parts of the world.

In addition to promoting international trade, the United States has given $277 billion in foreign aid since 1945. Much of this aid has been given directly under such programs as the Marshall Plan, the Economic Cooperation Administration, and the Development Loan Fund. Technical assistance, as well as direct loans and grants, is a part of the United States foreign aid policy.

Another sizable portion of our foreign aid has been given through international organizations. The United States, for example, is the largest single contributor to the World Bank. In fact, our capital subscription amounts to about one-fifth of the total World Bank subscription.

NEW TERMS AND CONCEPTS

Tariff

Specific tariff

Ad valorem tariff

Nontariff barriers

Import quota

Tariff quota

Embargo

Export subsidy

Exchange controls

DISCUSSION QUESTIONS

1. How does the law of comparative advantage, demonstrated in Chapter 2, promote world trade?
2. What is the relative importance of international trade for the United States as compared with foreign nations?
3. It is frequently said that a revenue tariff and a protective tariff are incompatible. Explain.
4. Explain how international trade can raise the standard of living of any two countries involved.
5. Is the argument that a tariff protects infant industries valid? Why or why not?
6. Under what conditions is technical assistance more valuable to a developing nation than a loan?
7. Does the growth of major trading organizations promote free trade? Explain.
8. Should United States aid to developing nations be given directly or through international organizations? Why?

SUGGESTED READINGS

Annual Report. Washington, DC: International Monetary Fund, annually.

Annual Report. Washington, DC: World Bank, annually.

Dreyer, Peter H. "E.C. Enlargement Seen Hurting U.S. Exports." *Europe* (September/October, 1985).

International Financial Statistics. Washington, DC: International Monetary Fund, monthly.

Lindert, Peter, and Charles P. Kindlebeger. *International Economics*, 7th ed. Homewood, IL: Richard D. Irwin, Inc., 1982.

Labreque, Thomas G. "The Case for Lending to Developing Nations." *Enterprise* (March, 1983).

Root, Franklin R. *International Trade and Investment*, 6th ed. Cincinnati: South-Western Publishing Co., 1988.

23

THE BALANCE OF
INTERNATIONAL PAYMENTS

∎

It should be apparent by now that the economic actions of the United States and many other nations frequently have international repercussions. There are over 5 billion people in the world living in more than 150 countries. The disparity between the productivity, natural resources, population, and types of goods produced in different countries helps encourage trade between them. Businesses seek to expand trade beyond domestic boundaries. All this, plus a general lack of domestic self-sufficiency, naturally promotes world trade among various nations. This in turn means that payment must be made for goods and services exchanged and that we must deal in the complexities of providing payment.

BALANCE OF TRADE

As nations engage in world trade, some tend to export more than they import from other specific nations, and vice versa. In many cases of multilateral trade, however, a surplus against one nation may be offset by a deficit against another nation. Country *A*, for example, may export $100 million in commodities to Country *B*, but import $100 million from Countries *C* and *D* combined. At the same time Country *B* may be exporting $100 million in goods to Countries *C* and *D*. In such a case, not only would world exports be equal to world imports, as they necessarily must be, but all nations would have an even balance of exports and imports.

This will not happen often, however, and some nations end up with a so-called **favorable balance of trade**, in which exports exceed imports, or an **unfavorable balance**, in which imports exceed exports. The term "favorable balance" is a misnomer, however. It is a holdover from the 18th and 19th centuries, when it was stressed that a nation with an excess of exports over imports was in a favorable position because it could force its debtor nations to pay the differences in gold and silver. We shall see later, however, that a nation with a continuous "favorable balance" eventually will find itself at a disadvantage when foreigners experience a shortage of the favored nation's currency and are unable to continue to purchase from it. It is common knowledge today that a nation which sells abroad must also buy from foreign nations to give them its currency with which they can purchase its goods.

History also reveals a correlation between the economic development of a nation and the status of the balance of trade. Emerging or developing nations are generally heavy importers, especially of machinery, equipment, and various types of finished goods. Exports in the early stages of economic growth will generally consist largely of raw materials from the nation's natural resources. A developing nation, lacking aid and investment capital, must finance imports by diverting natural resources and agricultural commodities in sufficient quantities from domestic to foreign (export) uses. As a country develops and is able to produce more of its own capital and finished goods, there will be less need for imports and an even balance of trade may come about. Finally, its debts liquidated, a fully developed industrial nation tends to be a large exporter of capital. Consequently, a nation may shift from a longtime debtor position to a creditor position as its balance of trade shifts from one side to another. For nearly a century prior to 1971, the United States usually had an annual excess of exports over imports of merchandise, as reflected in Table 23-1.

Table 23-1   Exports and Imports of Merchandise for the United States (Millions)

	Exports	Imports	Excess of Exports (+) or Imports (−)
1970	$ 42,649	$ 39,866	+$ 2,603
1975	107,088	98,041	+ 9,047
1976	114,745	124,051	− 9,306
1977	120,816	151,689	− 30,873
1978	142,054	175,813	− 33,759
1979	184,436	211,819	− 27,346
1980	224,237	249,574	− 25,388
1981	236,254	264,143	− 27,889
1982	211,013	247,344	− 36,331
1983	201,712	268,928	− 67,216
1984	219,916	334,023	− 114,107
1985	213,990	338,279	− 124,289
1986	221,753	369,461	− 147,708

Source: *Economic Report of the President*, 1987, and *Survey of Current Business* (March, 1987).

United States Trade Items

In 1986 the United States had a merchandise import balance of $147.7 billion. In addition to the export and import of merchandise, income from services performed by one country for another enters into the balance of trade. These services may include such items as shipping charges, insurance, banking services, and tourist transportation services. On this latter point, not only do travel charges enter the balance of trade, but likewise tourist spending on commodities and services in foreign nations is an import into the tourist's homeland. When a tourist from the United States, for example, buys a bottle of perfume in Paris, it has about the same effect on the balance of trade as the importation of French perfume for consumption in the United States. Tourist spending is an item of notable magnitude in our balance of trade. U.S. tourists in 1986 generated a net

Table 23-2 United States Balance of Payments, 1986
(Billions of Dollars)

Merchandise trade balance		−$147.7
Exports	+221.7	
Imports	−369.4	
Military transactions, net		− 2.4
Net investment income		+ 22.9
Receipts	+ 90.6	
Payments	− 67.7	
Net travel and transportation expenditures		− 10.1
Other services		+ 11.9
Balance of trade on goods and services		− 125.4
Remittances, pensions, and other unilateral transfers		− 15.1
Balance on current accounts		− 140.5

Changes in U.S. and Foreign Assets

U.S. assets abroad, net	(−)	− 99.8
U.S. official reserve	+ 1.3	
U.S. government assets	− 2.0	
U.S. private assets	− 99.1	
Foreign assets in U.S., net	(+)	+ 213.3
Foreign official assets	+ 33.4	
Other foreign assets	+179.9	
Statistical discrepancy		+ 27.0
		+140.5

Source: *Survey of Current Business* (March, 1987).

debit balance (outflow) of $10.1 billion as a result of spending on travel abroad compared with foreign spending in the United States.

The balance of trade is also affected by the receipt of income from investments in other countries. The receipt of interest and dividends by U.S. corporations and individuals for their investments in Germany, Canada, France, and other countries constitutes a flow of funds into the United States. Likewise interest and other payments to the United States government from abroad are inflows. On the other hand, the payment of interest and dividends to foreigners on their investments in the United States constitutes an outflow of funds. In 1986 the United States had a net investment balance of $22.9 billion from foreign investment.

Another item that must be considered in the balance of trade is expenditures for military purposes. The sale of military goods by the United States to other countries is a part of the total exports of our nation. Conversely, our overseas military expenditures for various purposes constitute an outflow of income and have the same effect as tourist spending abroad or importing foreign goods. United States government spending to maintain U.S. troops and installations in West Germany, Japan, South Korea, and elsewhere has been sizable. In addition to military expenditures for our own armed forces abroad, billions more are spent in the form of grants of military supplies and equipment for the armed services of other nations. Offsetting this is the inflow of funds from the direct sale of military equipment and munitions to foreign nations. In 1986 this resulted in a net outflow of $2.4 billion in the United States balance of trade.

When the various items mentioned above were added to the export and import of merchandise, the balance on current accounts for 1986 showed a deficit of $140.5 billion, as indicated in Table 23-2 and Figure 23-1. This deficit was settled by changes in U.S. and foreign assets, as shown in the bottom section of Table 23-2.

Debits and Credits

International trade items are recorded as debits or credits on the international balance of accounts. A *debit entry* is made for transactions that give rise to a claim for payment by foreigners from any U.S. resident, business, or the government. The largest debit category arises from the importation of goods and services. In addition to commodities, this debit includes charges for shipping on foreign vessels, insurance, banking and brokerage charges, and the like.

In addition to imported goods and services, another important debit category is our capital outflow. Any time U.S. residents purchase foreign securities or open a foreign bank account, a debit entry is registered in our balance of payments. When a U.S. resident purchases a foreign bond, for example, or builds up a bank account in a foreign nation, a debit arises in the United States balance of payments. Direct investment abroad arising from the acquisition or construction of a building or factory is

Figure 23-1   U.S. International Transaction Balances: 1970 to 1985

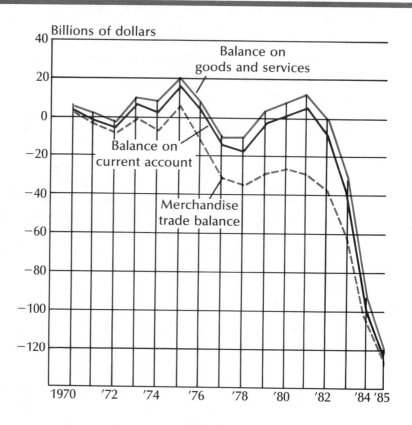

Source: *Statistical Abstract of the United States,* 1986.

treated as a debit item, even though there is no claim by foreigners to payment from the U.S. owner.

Debit entries are also made for unilateral transfers abroad, which arise as a result of gifts and grants, personal remittances, pensions, and other similar one-way transactions. These transfers may be made by individuals, institutions, or the government. Large expenditures for foreign aid by our government are included in this debit category. Movements of gold are also entered as debits or credits. An inflow of gold from abroad, like an import of goods or services, is a debit transaction in the balance of payments.

Credit transactions are the opposite of debit transactions and give rise to U.S. claims against persons, firms, institutions, and governments of foreign nations. Major credit items in the United States balance of payments include exports of goods and services, inflow of capital into this country, increases in foreign-held U.S. bank deposits or decreases in U.S. bank balances held abroad, increases in foreign investment in U.S. securities and physical assets, unilateral transfers from abroad, and, in the past, gold exports from the United States.

In total, debits must equal credits, and they do. To make them balance, however, changes in the ownership of securities, buildup or depletion of bank deposits, or an inflow or outflow of gold may take place. In Table 23-2 credits are designated with a (+) and debits with a (−) sign.

BALANCE OF PAYMENTS

More important than the balance of trade on goods and services in international economics is the balance of payments. It is the latter that designates whether or not a nation is going to have an inflow or outflow of currency or the purchase or sale of short-term securities.

Although the flow of goods and services is the largest category of international transactions, it is by no means the only segment that must be considered. Whether or not a particular nation will have a positive or deficit balance of payments will depend on many other transactions. Even though a nation may have an excess of exports over imports, it does not assure a favorable balance of payments. In spite of its very favorable export balances in the 1960s, the United States, for example, had sizable deficits in its balance of payments during that decade.

In looking at the balance of payments, not only must one consider the dollar claims of the rest of the world against the United States that result from sending imports into the United States, but one must also look at the dollar claims of foreigners arising from other sources. These claims arise in large part from the flow of funds and capital among nations.

A typical balance of payments is shown in Table 23-2. This balance of payments shows a deficit in the balance on current accounts. First, it is obvious that our imports exceeded our exports by a sizable amount, and on that basis we owed foreigners $147.7 billion. Added to that deficit must be a net deficit of $10.1 billion for U.S. travel expenditures abroad. Also, our military transactions abroad exceeded our sales of military goods to foreigners by $2.4 billion.

On the credit side, our investment income exceeded that of foreigners by $22.9 billion, and the value of other services totaled $11.9 billion. Combining the debits and credits leaves a debit or deficit balance on goods and services of $125.4 billion. To this, however, we must also add $15.1 billion for remittances, pension payments to U.S. citizens living abroad, and unilateral transfers. This results in a balance in the current account that is a deficit of $140.5 billion.

This deficit had to be paid for in some way. Before August, 1971, the United States settled its deficit balance of payments in part through the sale of gold in exchange for dollars held by foreign central banks and governments. Today deficits and surpluses are settled through changes and adjustments in U.S. and foreign assets, both government and private. This includes the purchase and sale of U.S. government and corporate bonds; and adjustments in U.S. and foreign bank accounts, both in the U.S. and abroad. Also included are changes in official U.S. reserve assets, such as gold, convertible currencies, Special Drawing Rights, and the U.S. reserve position with the International Monetary Fund. The lower part of Table 23-2 reveals how the $140.5 billion deficit in the U.S. balance of payments for 1986 was settled.

Since apparent deficits, such as that for 1986, are usually settled or eliminated by changes in U.S. and foreign liquid assets and occasionally by the flow of gold, some international trade analysts object to the use of the term **deficit balance of payments**. They contend that both sides of the balance-of-payments account must be equal, just as does any balance sheet based on the double-entry method of accounting. Although this is technically correct, the terms "deficit" and "surplus" are commonly used today by most economists, financiers, and government officials in reference to the balance of payments. Also, the balance of payments is considered to be more nearly equivalent to a statement of income, showing income or loss, rather than a balance sheet that shows changes in assets, liabilities, and stockholders' equity.

It should be remembered that the surplus or deficit is not nearly so important as is the means of settlement. Whether the means is a temporary stopgap measure, whether it is remedial or preventive, and how permanent or enduring it is will all have an important effect in determining whether an imbalance in trade will be corrected.

FOREIGN EXCHANGE RATES

As trade takes place among different countries, goods and services are exchanged, international investments are made, and money and asset flows settle differences between debtor and creditor nations. Since most of the international exchange of goods and services is carried on by individual persons and business firms, the question naturally arises regarding the manner in which payment is made for the purchase of foreign goods and services.

To start with, it should be mentioned that international sales are similar to domestic sales except that the international sellers usually desire to be paid in their domestic currency for the goods they sell, rather than in the domestic currency of the buyers. Consequently, a conversion must be made from the buyer's currency to the seller's currency to complete the transaction. The method of settlement for the purchase of a foreign good or service can be hypothetically demonstrated by assuming that a U.S. retail clothing store desires to purchase six tweed suits at a total cost of £1,000. Let's assume the rate of exchange between British pounds and U.S. dollars is £1 = $1.80; the U.S. retailer will go to a bank such as the Chase Manhattan and purchase a bank draft for £1,000 by paying $1,800, plus a small service charge. The retailer will then mail this draft on a British bank to the British tailor, who will present it to a bank in London, let us say Barclay's Bank, for payment of the £1,000 or for deposit to an account. Since the Chase Manhattan and other U.S. banks dealing in foreign exchange maintain deposits in foreign banks such as Barclay's Bank of London, Barclay's Bank will honor the draft and reduce by £1,000 the deposit account of the Chase Manhattan Bank in Barclay's Bank.

On the other hand, if a British manufacturer purchased $1,800 worth of tools and equipment from a U.S. machine tool shop, the British manufacturer would go to a bank, again let us say to Barclay's Bank in London, and purchase a bank draft for $1,800, paying £1,000 for it plus the service charge. In this case, when the British manufacturer sent the draft to the U.S. tool company, the tool company would present the draft for payment at the Chase Manhattan Bank. After paying the U.S. exporter $1,800, the bank would debit the London bank's dollar deposit account on its record.

In that way the $1,800 paid to the Chase Manhattan Bank by the U.S. importer for the £1,000 foreign exchange draft can be used to pay the U.S. export company which presents the $1,800 draft sent to it by the British importer. In London the £1,000 paid by the British importer for the $1,800 bank draft can be used to pay the £1,000 draft presented by the British exporter. In this simplified case, as depicted in Figure 23-2, the foreign deposits of the respective banks would remain the same. It is easy to see that many of our foreign trade transactions can be paid by offsetting charges without necessarily involving a large currency flow among nations. But as simple as it is, the example demonstrates how funds are converted from one currency into another. It should be remembered, however, that imbalances often exist between nations that must be settled in one way or another.

Currency exchange rates between countries play an important role in international economics. A particular exchange rate may make it more expensive or less expensive to buy foreign goods and services. If a U.S. importer, for example, can purchase a British pound for $1.80, he may find it profitable to purchase a £10 British camera that would cost him $18. But if the exchange rate were $2.00, he might not find the £10 camera such a bargain. Since a change in the exchange rate may actually reverse the flow of goods and currencies between different countries, it is essential to understand how exchange rates are determined. Exchange rates may be flexible, they may be fixed, or they may be controlled, depending on what system is in force.

Flexible Exchange Rates

Exchange rates, which are the prices of foreign moneys or claims thereto, may be determined by the free forces of supply and demand. In

Figure 23-2 Purchase and Redemption of Foreign Exchange Drafts

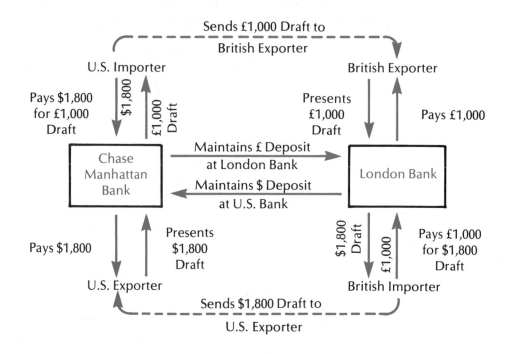

such a case the exchange rate will fluctuate with changes in exports and imports and the consequent changes in all factors affecting the supply of and the demand for foreign exchange. In international exchange, the term **floating rate** is commonly used to refer to an exchange rate that is not fixed.

If we assume that the exchange rate between the Canadian and U.S. currencies, for example, is one Canadian dollar to one U.S. dollar and that a certain balance of trade exists, it can be demonstrated how exchange rates fluctuate in the absence of controls. Figure 23-3 indicates the price at which U.S. dollars can be exchanged for Canadian dollars. The American demand curve for Canadian dollars (D_1) slopes downward and to the right, indicating that as Canadian dollars become less expensive, Canadian goods will become cheaper as well and more Canadian dollars will be demanded. The supply curve of Canadian dollars (S) slopes upward and to the right, indicating that as the Canadian dollar becomes more expensive in terms of the American dollar, Canadians will increase their purchases of American goods. As Canadians increase their expenditures on American goods, they increase the quantity of Canadian dollars available to Ameri-

Figure 23-3 Restoring Equilibrium with Flexible Exchange Rates

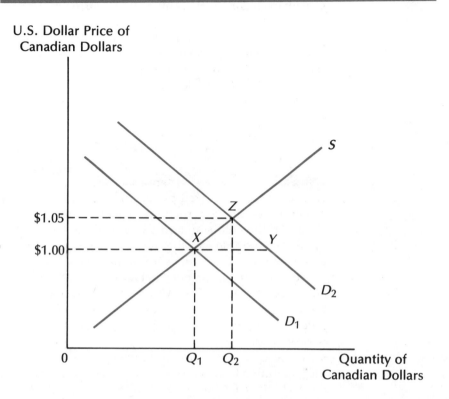

cans. The intersection of the supply and demand curves determines the equilibrium U.S. dollar price of a Canadian dollar.

If Americans increase their purchases of Canadian goods and services and spend more as tourists while visiting Canada, the demand for Canadian dollars would increase. This would make Canadian dollars relatively scarce. The increase in demand for Canadian dollars by Americans is shown by the shift in the demand curve from D_1 to D_2, and the resulting shortage of Canadian dollars at the exchange rate of $1 Canadian = $1 U.S. is shown by the amount XY.

With the increase in demand for the Canadian dollar relative to the U.S. dollar, the Canadian dollar will appreciate in value. Let's assume that the new equilibrium is Z; the price of the Canadian dollar rises to $1.05 in U.S. currency and the U.S. dollar is discounted to 95 cents in Canadian currency when used to purchase Canadian goods and services. An item that formerly cost the American importers $10 U.S. will now cost $10.50 U.S.

In the mid-1950s, for example, the price of the Canadian dollar in U.S. currency was $1.04. In the early 1960s, however, we could obtain a Canadian dollar for 93 cents in U.S. currency. In late 1986, it took $0.72 in U.S. currency to purchase a Canadian dollar.

Flexible exchange rates serve as a means of correcting a disequilibrium in the balance of payments. As such, they keep international commercial relations from becoming one-sided and keep alive comparative advantage as the principle of world trade.

Gold Standard

A common method of establishing exchange rates in the earlier part of this century was the gold standard. Under the gold standard, nations defined their currency in terms of gold. Also, the unrestricted purchase and sale of gold as well as the freedom to import and export gold as a means of settling international balances of payment was permitted. A nation on the gold standard stood ready to convert its currency into gold upon demand. Hence, the amount of gold each nation held affected its money supply and the level of domestic economic activity.

The U.S. dollar at one time was defined as approximately 1/20th of an ounce of gold and the British pound as 1/4th of an ounce of gold. At these approximate values, the British pound exchanged for 5 times as much as a dollar, and the exchange rate between dollars and pounds was set at £1 = $5.

These exchange rates were fixed, since whenever they diverged from the determined values, they would automatically be restored. Assume, for example, that the price of a pound rose in terms of a dollar to £1 = $6. At this exchange rate, American importers would find it cheaper to purchase gold with dollars than to exchange their dollars directly for pounds. On the other hand, British importers would find it less costly to convert their pounds into gold and ship gold as payment for U.S. imports when the price of a pound fell below $5. Consequently, the dollar price of a pound remained at $5 because Americans would refuse to pay more than $5 for a pound and the British would refuse to accept less.

Under this system, adjustments in the balance of trade or in the flow of gold came through changes in the price levels in individual countries. If the United States experienced a trade deficit with Great Britain, the dollar price of pounds would rise above $5 and gold would flow from the U.S. to Great Britain as a means of settling the deficit. However, since the United States tied its money supply to its gold holdings, the outflow of gold would automatically diminish the U.S. money supply and depress prices. Great Britain would be the recipient of an increased inflow of gold, and assuming full employment, the result would be higher prices brought about by an increased money supply. Higher prices in Great Britain accompanied by lower prices in the United States would deter U.S. imports from Great Britain, while Great Britain's imports from the United States would increase. The initial trade deficit would be corrected, and the decrease in demand for British pounds and the increase in demand for U.S. dollars would restore the exchange rate to its fixed level.

Controlled or Fixed Exchange Rates

With the abandonment of the gold standard in the 1930s by most major nations throughout the world, including Great Britain and the United States, many nations adopted exchange controls or restricted convertibility immediately. Although some nations did allow their exchange rate to fluctuate freely, most imposed controls when World War II erupted. As a result, between 1945 and 1971 most nations adopted some type of a fixed or controlled exchange rate, rather than relying on a freely fluctuating exchange rate. By controlling the exchange rate, a nation hopes to avoid the severe effects on domestic employment, income, and prices sometimes brought about by exchange rate corrections in a freely fluctuating market.

Fixed or controlled exchange rates usually involve an agreement among governments to maintain a particular exchange rate for their currencies. For example, in 1962 the Canadian government agreed to establish an official exchange rate of $1 Canadian equal to 92.5 U.S. cents. To maintain that rate of exchange, the Canadian government agreed to buy and sell foreign exchange as the market price deviated up and down. Thus, if there were a strong demand for Canadian dollars that might increase the market rate of exchange to $1, the Canadian government would purchase U.S. dollars in sufficient quantity to drive the price up to the official exchange rate. A nation with a managed currency usually established an "exchange stabilization" fund composed of its own currency, foreign currencies, and gold that was used for buying and selling foreign exchange.

Restoring exchange rates to their agreed-upon level can be depicted graphically with supply and demand curves. In Figure 23-4a the demand curve for Canadian dollars on the part of Americans is represented by D_1 and the supply of Canadian dollars available to Americans is represented by S_1. Assume the exchange rate is fixed at $1 Canadian = $0.925 U.S. and there is an increase in demand for Canadian dollars by Americans. The demand curve shifts to the right (D_2), and because the exchange rate is fixed, the result is an excess demand for Canadian dollars, as indicated by the quantity AB. Left alone, market forces will tend to drive the price of Canadian dollars upward to 94 U.S. cents, as indicated by point X.

Under a fixed exchange rate system the Canadian government would intervene by buying American dollars with Canadian dollars. As a result, the supply curve of Canadian dollars shifts to the right in Figure 23-4b. Because of government intervention, the price of Canadian dollars has

Figure 23-4   Restoring Equilibrium with Fixed Exchange Rates

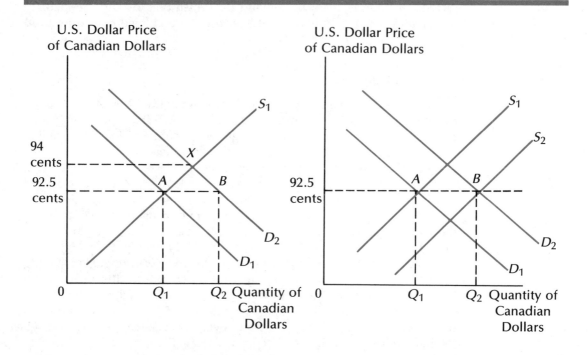

declined to 92.5 U.S. cents, with the new equilibrium occurring at point *B*. Although the American dollar price of a Canadian dollar remains the same, the quantity of Canadian dollars has increased.

If for some reason there were a strong demand for the American dollar and the market rate of exchange declined to $1 Canadian equals 90 U.S. cents, the Canadian government would purchase U.S. dollars for $1.10 in Canadian money and sell the dollars to Canadian importers for $1.075 Canadian ($1 Canadian = $0.925 U.S.). In short, the Canadian government would simply make more U.S. dollars available in Canadian exchange markets.

On June 1, 1970, the Canadian government announced that Canada would not maintain the exchange rate of the Canadian dollar within the margins required by International Monetary Fund rules. Canada decided to let the exchange rate float to seek its own level. By the end of the year, 98.3 Canadian cents were exchanging for a U.S. dollar, and by September, 1986 it took $1.39 Canadian to obtain a U.S. dollar.

Exchange controls may be unilateral; one nation may determine the level at which it desires to stabilize the exchange rate between itself and other nations. The rate, however, may be detrimental to other nations, in which case exchange rate competition or retaliation may ensue and give rise to a "currency rate war." To avert this possibility, exchange controls have been established by many nations. Two or more nations agree on the exchange rates to be established, and all make an effort to maintain such agreed-upon rates. Exchange rates may be managed to an even greater degree by any nation through rationing the supply of exchange that is available for particular uses. This, in turn, limits the total demand for foreign exchange and influences the market rate.

INTERNATIONAL MONETARY FUND

With the demise of the gold standard in the 1930s and the outbreak of World War II, an unstable exchange situation developed as more and more nations moved to exchange controls. It became evident to nations throughout the world that more stability in exchange rates was desirable, but by some method less rigid than the gold standard. An international conference was held in Bretton Woods, New Hampshire, in 1944. As a result, the **International Monetary Fund (IMF)** was established in an attempt to stabilize exchange rates and to provide temporary assistance to nations with deficit balances of payments.

Establishing Exchange Rates

To fulfill the objectives of the Fund, each of the 30 original signatory members was asked to establish a par value for its currency in terms of gold or U.S. dollars, which were redeemable in gold. Once these values were established, the IMF then established international exchange rates. Members were charged with an obligation to maintain their respective exchange rates within 1 percent. In the case of Great Britain, for example, the exchange rate of the pound at one time was set at a par value of $2.40 with permissible fluctuation from $2.424 to $2.376. If the rate exceeded either limit, however, Great Britain was expected to use its stabilization fund to buy or sell pounds in an effort to bring the rate within the limits set by the IMF.

Assistance to Members

Each member nation was assigned a quota or subscription of funds, which it had to contribute to the IMF in the form of gold or its own currency. Member nation quotas were established on the basis of a number of factors, but primarily on the basis of national income, population, and the flow of foreign exchange transactions. At least 25 percent of the subscription had to be paid in gold (or 10 percent of the nations's gold holdings, whichever was less) and the remainder in domestic currency.

With the existence of the IMF, any particular nation that has a deficit balance of payments or a shortage of foreign exchange should not be required to alter its domestic prices, as was the case under the gold standard, or to change its exchange rates, as experienced under the individually controlled exchange rate system, to obtain relief. Furthermore, the mechanism of the IMF was originally designed to prevent wide fluctuations that could come about under a system of freely fluctuating exchange rates. Any member nation that has a shortage of a particular type of foreign exchange can obtain temporary relief by borrowing exchange, gold, or **Special Drawing Rights (SDRs)** from the Fund.

One of the main functions of the IMF is the administration of Special Drawing Rights, introduced in 1970. SDRs are a collectively managed asset of the Fund, sometimes referred to as "paper gold." They are now a principal source of international reserves. A country with a balance-of-payments deficit can draw upon these reserves to settle its indebtedness to others rather than transferring ownership of gold or currencies. In effect, a nation buys the needed exchange with its own currency. It is intended that ordinary transactions between nations will continue to involve private agencies. Only when a nation has a shortage of foreign exchange is it expected to resort to this form of borrowing from the IMF. Similarly, nations with balance-of-payments surpluses may accumulate these drawing rights much as they would accumulate gold reserves.

Nations that continuously experience a deficit balance of payments or shortage of exchange and whose difficulty cannot be corrected by temporary borrowings from the IMF may have to seek other remedies. All member nations have agreed that they will consult through the IMF on all such major international problems. Any nation may, however, change its exchange rate by 10 percent merely by notifying the IMF; but any further devaluation must have the Fund's prior approval.

Experience of the IMF

Although the establishment of the IMF was heralded with great expectations, it has met with only modest success in its years of operation. Since its primary function is to offer relief from temporary disequilibrium in the balance-of-payments problems, it would necessarily function better in a more stable international situation than in one replete with serious monetary crises.

The recent international debt crisis of developing countries is a case in point. Many of these countries were forced to increase their borrowing in the 1970s and early 1980s as a result of several shocks to the global economy. These shocks included sharp changes in the world price of oil, a recession in developed countries, a significant appreciation of the U.S. dollar, and historically high interest rates. Compounding the problem, many developing nations had pursued monetary and fiscal policies that were counterproductive. Combined, these factors resulted in a loss of confidence on the part of creditors. Developing countries were unable to roll over maturing debts and finance current account deficits.

As doubts about their solvency arose, developing nations turned to the IMF for assistance. Requests were made for debt relief, postponement of interest payments, and rescheduling or cancellation of regular loan payments. Because its resources are limited, the IMF's capacity to expand the supply of credit depends on its ability to persuade other creditors that policies undertaken by debtor countries offer reasonable hope of restoring creditworthiness. Thus, the IMF's response to these requests required austere domestic programs directed at improving the capacity of developing countries to meet their external obligations. Usually, these restrictive policies involved a tight monetary and fiscal approach to the domestic economy.

Opposition to such painful austerity programs hardened in some countries. Mexico fell out of compliance and threatened not to pay off its debts unless it continued to receive funds from international banks. Brazil and Peru both balked at having to implement IMF's austerity programs, while Argentina designed its own stabilization program with IMF approval. Concern over the solvency of developing nations resulted in a decline in net lending to these countries by private creditors from $57 billion in 1981 to virtually zero in 1983. By 1985, net lending by the IMF also slowed to a trickle, and, given the current schedule of repayments of debtor nations, the IMF may soon become a net recipient rather than a net supplier of funds to Third World countries.

Progress among debtor nations has been uneven. Although some countries, including Mexico and Peru, have made substantial progress, others have not. The IMF is being criticized for using a short-term balance-of-payments approach to lending rather than promoting long-term growth. The critical issue for the IMF is how to resolve the economic problem of debtor nations in a mutually advantageous manner.

UNITED STATES BALANCE OF PAYMENTS

The history of the United States balance of international payments reflects events of the world, such as the Depression of the 1930s, the flight of capital from Europe before World War II, the postwar dollar shortage, the rebuilding of foreign economies, the gold outflow, and the worldwide energy and resource crises.

Dollar Shortage

The United States was the only major nation in the world whose industrial structure was unscathed by World War II; consequently, many of the war-torn countries, especially in Europe, turned to the United States to purchase essential goods and services. Since they had little in the way of imports to offer in exchange for our exports during World War II, the United States developed large surpluses in its balance of payments. Therefore, there was an extreme "dollar shortage" in international exchange markets throughout the world in the late 1940s to mid-1950s, as foreigners clamored for U.S. dollars.

In the late 1950s a dramatic shift in the demand for U.S. dollars occurred. By that time many of the war-torn countries had rebuilt their economies with new and modern industrial structures that increased their productive capacity considerably. They were no longer as dependent on the United States for goods and services. In fact, many of them by that time were competing successfully with the United States in world markets. Although we retained a favorable balance of trade, the size of our export-import gap dwindled in some years. We continued to increase our outlays for military operations overseas, to extend large grants and loans to foreign nations, to increase our direct investments abroad, and to purchase short- and long-term foreign securities. As a result, many nations began to accumulate dollar reserves. As foreign nations became less inclined to hold dollars, the situation was reversed, and instead of a "dollar shortage," foreign nations began to build up large claims against U.S. dollars.

Gold Outflow

Since these dollar claims were not needed to buy additional U.S. goods and services, some nations used them to purchase short-term U.S. government obligations on which they received interest income. Many nations, however, requested gold payment in exchange for their dollar claims. There was a continuous drain or outflow of gold from the United States. Some authorities viewed the gold drain with alarm and employed numerous steps in an effort to arrest the outflow of gold. Measures included the reduction of overseas military spending, decreases in foreign aid, reduction of U.S. tourism, the adoption of more tying clauses to our aid, accelerated export promotion, and taxes on U.S. investments abroad.

By 1965 the bulk of our $10.7 billion gold supply was serving as a reserve behind our money supply. Although it was not felt that we would need much, if any, of our reserve supply to make gold payments in exchange for dollars, it was suggested that there would be a great psychological advantage in letting the rest of the world know that we stood ready to use all our gold to support the dollar. Furthermore, it was becoming evident that with continued increases in our money supply over the next few years the current gold holding would be inadequate to maintain the required 25 percent gold reserve ratio behind U.S. dollars. Thus, in March, 1968, a bill eliminating the 25 percent gold cover (reserve) behind Federal Reserve notes was passed in Congress.

Some monetary authorities suggested a devaluation of the dollar to correct our deficit balance-of-payments position and reverse the drain of gold. Other monetary authorities looked upon the gold drain from the

United States simply as a normal reaction in international economics. They suggested that any nation would inevitably gain and lose gold at various times and under certain conditions. Authorities also suggested that the better distribution of gold and the improved convertibility of several of the foreign currencies resulting from our gold drain would promote and facilitate world trade.

To ease the gold drain from the United States, the Gold Pool nations of the world in 1968 agreed to the adoption of a two-tier gold price, one price for monetary purposes and one price for the free gold market.[1] In short, instead of trying to keep both prices at $35 per ounce, it was decided to let the market price of gold fluctuate. The Gold Pool nations also agreed to stop buying gold for monetary purposes in an effort to divert gold into the free market. By increasing the supply relative to demand, they hoped to keep the market price of gold in line with the monetary price of $35 per ounce.

In 1969 the shortage of international liquidity was eased when the major financial nations of the world, through the IMF, agreed to the creation of $9.5 billion in Special Drawing Rights, which were formally introduced in 1970. Since SDRs can be used for the settlement of international payments, this move took some of the pressure off the demand for dollars and gold. This, along with the two-tier gold price and other measures, helped to reduce the speculation in gold and bring the free market price of gold, which had reached $42.50 per ounce, down to the monetary price of $35 per ounce by December, 1969.

The stable price of gold was temporary, however, as further disquieting forces sounded. A near crisis of the French franc resulted in a devaluation of the franc and a revaluation of the German deutsche mark. In 1971 the United States experienced a substantial deterioration in its trade position and faced a deficit balance of trade for the first time in nearly a century. Consequently, the price of gold began to rise substantially.

In the spring of 1971 many dollars were being sold in exchange for other currencies, particularly German deutsche marks. On speculation that the deutsche mark would be revalued again and thus worth more dollars, the sale of dollars became so heavy that major foreign exchange markets were temporarily closed. When the markets reopened, the Austrian schilling was revalued. The German deutsche mark was allowed to "float" (that is, the rate of exchange was unpegged) to permit the market to seek and establish new exchange rates between the deutsche mark and other currencies. At the same time, the Netherlands guilder also was floated and the Swiss franc was revalued. Within a short time the average appreciation of the major world currencies vis-à-vis the dollar was 10 to 12 percent.

---

1. The Gold Pool members included the United States, Great Britain, Belgium, West Germany, France, Italy, the Netherlands, and Switzerland.

It was under these circumstances that President Nixon, on August 15, 1971, among other sweeping changes in domestic and foreign economic measures, established a 10 percent surcharge on imports and suspended the convertibility of dollars for gold.

Devaluation of the Dollar

It was evident that the U.S. dollar was overvalued in world markets and that currencies of several other nations, especially those with substantial surplus balances of payments, such as Japan and West Germany, were undervalued. It was also evident that the United States could not continue forever as a major supplier of international liquidity for the entire world. In spite of this, the action of President Nixon startled the international financial world and brought about serious repercussions.

The United States subsequently used the 10 percent surcharge as a club to encourage various nations to adjust their currencies and to take other steps to improve world trade. In December, 1971, after numerous meetings, the Group of Ten in cooperation with the IMF agreed to the so-called Smithsonian Accord, by which they pledged to work for an "effective" realignment of important world currencies.[2] In early 1972 the U.S. import surcharge was modified and the dollar was devalued by 8.57 percent when Congress officially raised the price of gold to $38 per ounce. As a part of the international accord, the Japanese agreed to revalue the yen, and the deutsche mark and the guilder would continue to float before new exchange values were set for them. In addition, to provide greater flexibility in official exchange rates, the official "band" within which exchange rates were permitted to fluctuate was widened from 1 percent to 2.25 percent.

The United States balance of payments failed to improve substantially in 1972. Moreover, the international monetary authorities failed to come up with any further solutions to the world monetary problems, and the relationship of the U.S. dollar vis-à-vis foreign currency, especially the deutsche mark and the yen, continued to deteriorate. Consequently, in February, 1973, the United States again devalued the dollar. This time the value of the dollar was decreased by 10 percent and the price of gold raised to $42.22 per ounce.

Increased reliance on high-priced oil imports and surging inflation aggravated the U.S. deficit balance of trade, which reached record deficits of more than $30 billion in 1977 and 1978. This further weakened the U.S. dollar in foreign exchange markets. In the meantime, speculators

---

2. The Group of Ten included Canada, Belgium, France, Italy, Japan, the Netherlands, Sweden, West Germany, Great Britain, and the United States.

bid the price of gold to more than $600 per ounce. By the fall of 1978, for example, it took 54 cents to buy a deutsche mark, compared with 27 cents in 1970. The deterioration of the dollar prompted U.S. monetary authorities to intervene to stabilize the dollar and prevent its further decline in value. Their actions consisted of selling Treasury gold, borrowing from the IMF, borrowing from foreign central banks, selling U.S. government bonds in foreign currency denominations, raising the discount rate, and taking other measures such as voluntary wage-price standards in an attempt to slow down the rate of U.S. inflation.

The dollar improved markedly from 1980 to 1984 in relation to other currencies. In fact, the dollar's value soared by about 65 percent against other major currencies, and by the beginning of 1985 it was at its highest level since flexible exchange rates were adopted in 1973. As the dollar's value appreciated in financial markets, however, U.S. current account deficits continued to worsen. Deficits in the current account increased to $40 billion in 1983, $107 billion in 1984, and $117 billion in 1985. During this period, the United States experienced an economic growth rate that exceeded most of its trading partners. With increased national income, our demand for foreign imports also increased. A relatively rapid growth rate, combined with low inflation rates, increased after-tax business profits, and higher real interest rates stimulated an unprecedented foreign demand for dollar-denominated assets. As a result, despite huge trade deficits, the dollar continued to strengthen.

After four consecutive years of strong appreciation, the U.S. dollar began to depreciate in March, 1985. By March, 1986, the dollar had depreciated approximately 30 percent against major currencies. Several factors prompted the dollar's depreciation. As real interest rates in the United States fell, foreign demand for dollar-denominated assets declined. In addition, the decline in world oil prices decreased foreign demand for dollars, since oil payments are denominated in U.S. dollars. Another important factor was the continued increase in the supply of dollars resulting from the growing deficit in the U.S. current account. Thus, the supply of dollars increased as the demand for dollars decreased.

A further impetus to dollar depreciation resulted from the September, 1985, meeting of Finance Ministers and Central Bank Governors of the Group of Five Countries in New York. The countries (Japan, France, West Germany, Great Britain, and the United States) agreed that further appreciation of the nondollar currencies was desirable. To this end, they resolved to adopt coordinated policies to promote real economic growth and to intervene, whenever necessary, in foreign exchange markets to stabilize the dollar.

As the United States confronts many of its international problems, it becomes apparent that we do not control our economic destiny as we once did some 30 years ago. Becoming a full-fledged international economy requires continuing adjustments.

SUMMARY

Nations of the world are not completely independent. Consequently, they engage in trade with one another, and numerous commodities are transferred among them. Some nations at certain times export more goods and services than they import, and as a result they have a favorable balance of trade. The United States had a favorable trade balance for 30 years or more prior to 1971. More important than the balance of trade, however, is a nation's balance of payments, which takes into account the spending of money abroad and foreign spending in the domestic nation. When a nation has a surplus or deficit balance of payments, settlement is made by paying the difference in foreign currencies, gold, or SDRs or by selling securities.

The United States' deficit balance of payments in 1985 was $117.7 billion. This deficit was settled primarily by changes in U.S. and foreign assets. In previous years deficits were settled in part by the sale of gold to the creditor nations.

Since payment for imports is made by the purchase of foreign exchange, international exchange rates play an important role in the trade between nations. A decrease or increase in exchange rates can make the purchase of foreign goods more attractive or less attractive and affect the balance of payments. Exchange rates can be established in various ways. They may be fixed as they were under the gold standard, they may be flexible and be determined at any time by the supply and demand for different currencies, or they may be managed or controlled by the government or by an international organization.

The United States, after having sizable surplus balances of payments during World War II, has been in a deficit-balance position during the past 25 years or more. Although there was a dollar shortage during the early postwar days and during the mid-1950s, the situation has reversed considerably since then. In the 1950s and the 1960s foreign claims against U.S. dollars resulted in a heavy outflow of gold. Then a number of corrective measures, including the creation of SDRs and the adoption of a two-tier gold price, were instrumental in arresting the U.S. gold outflow, at least temporarily. But continued deficits of payment caused the gold drain to resume. Dramatic action by President Nixon in August, 1971, which stopped the redemption of dollars for gold by the U.S. Treasury and imposed a 10 percent surcharge on most U.S. imports, had a worldwide impact.

Subsequently a number of adjustments were made in various exchange rates as a result of devaluations and revaluations of currencies. The United States, for example, devalued the dollar in 1972 and again in early 1973. Continued large deficits in the U.S. balances of payments during the 1970s weakened the dollar vis-à-vis other major currencies. During the 1980s, however, the dollar rebounded and appreciated 65 percent against major currencies. The dollar reached its peak in early 1985 before declining sharply. Record-setting deficits in the current account continued to be of concern.

NEW TERMS AND CONCEPTS

Favorable balance of trade	Deficit balance of payments	International Monetary Fund
Unfavorable balance	Floating rate	(IMF)
Balance on current account	Gold standard	Special Drawing Rights (SDRS)

DISCUSSION QUESTIONS

1. Explain how a nation can have a favorable balance of trade but still have a deficit balance of payments.
2. How does U.S. direct private investment abroad affect the balance of payments?
3. If interest rates in foreign nations rise substantially compared with interest rates for borrowed or invested funds in the United States, what effect do you think this has on our balance of payments?
4. If a U.S. merchant were to purchase a dozen Viking sewing machines from Sweden, explain the process involved in making payment for the machines.
5. Explain the difference between a flexible exchange rate and a managed exchange rate.

6. When exchange rates were pegged to the gold standard, how did the flow of gold from a debtor nation to a creditor nation eventually tend to reverse the balance of payments?
7. Should the United States devalue the dollar further in an effort to improve its balance of payments?
8. Assume a speculator purchased a million dollars' worth of West German deutsche marks and the United States subsequently devalued the dollar by 20 percent. How much in dollars would the speculator gain or lose by converting the deutsche marks back to dollars after the devaluation?

SUGGESTED READINGS

Caves, Richard E., and Ronald W. Jones. *World Trade and Payments, An Introduction*, 4th ed. Boston, MA: Little, Brown and Company, 1985.

Eiteman, David K., and Arthur I. Stonehill. *Multinational Business Finance*, 4th ed. Reading, MA: Addison-Wesley Publishing Company, 1986.

Ingram, James C. *International Economics*, 2d ed. New York: John Wiley & Sons, 1986.

Report to the Congress of the Commission on the Role of Gold in the Domestic and International Monetary System. Washington, DC: U.S. Government Printing Office, 1982.

Sobol, Dorothy M. "The SDR in Private International Finance." *Quarterly Review*. Federal Reserve Bank of New York (Winter, 1981/82).

Wallich, Henry C. "Evolution of the International Monetary System." *Challenge* (January/February, 1979).

World Economic Outlook. Washington, DC: International Monetary Fund, April, 1986.

GLOSSARY

Accelerator effect The relationship between the secondary, or induced, investment brought about by the spending of the increased income resulting from the multiplier on the original investment.

Accelerator theory According to this theory, an increase in the demand for consumer goods may lead to a greater than proportional increase in the demand for capital goods.

Administered price A predetermined price set by the seller rather than a price determined solely by demand and supply in the marketplace.

Adminstered pricing A situation in which a seller can exert an undue influence on the price charged for a product because of the absence of competition.

Ad valorem tariff A tax or duty in relative or percentage terms, such as 15 percent of the value of the imported commodity.

Advances A method by which a member bank may borrow from the Fed.

Adverse clearing balance A situation that occurs when the bank has more withdrawals than new deposits.

Agricultural theories Theories of the business cycle which endeavor to relate the general level of business activity to the weather.

Average fixed cost The total fixed cost divided by the number of units produced.

Average product The output per unit of input.

Average propensity to consume (APC) The percentage of total income spent on consumption out of any given level of income.

Average revenue Revenue per unit of output.

Average total cost Total cost divided by the number of units produced. Also, the average fixed plus the average variable costs.

Average variable cost Unit variable cost, which is the total variable cost divided by the number of units produced.

Balance on current account Balance on current exports, imports, and unilateral transfers.

Balanced-budget multiplier effect The net increase in economic activity that may result from the transfer of funds from private spending to government spending.

Bilateral monopoly A situation in which a monopsonist faces a monopolist.

Break-even point The point at which total revenue equals total cost.

Business cycle A process of cumulative change in the total economy over a time span longer than a year.

Capital Those goods used to produce other goods.

Capital consumption allowance The amount of depreciation and obsolescence in the GNP.

Capital goods Economic goods used to produce other goods.

Cash balance approach The analysis of the quantity theory of money that puts emphasis on what individuals and firms do with their money—spend it or save it—and the length of time they may hold onto their money.

Circular flow of economic activity The continuous operation of demand, production, income, and new demand.

Civilian labor force Consists of all persons in

463

the total labor force except members of the armed services.

Command economy An economy in which most decisions regarding what and how much to produce are made by a central authority.

Commodity money A type of money in which some commodity, such as wheat, tobacco, or stone, actually serves as money.

Compensatory spending The use of government spending sufficient to make up, or compensate, for the lack of adequate consumption and investment during periods of unemployment.

Competition Rivalry among individuals and firms that makes the free enterprise system work.

Concentration ratio The percentage of total shipments in a given industry that is accounted for by the four leading firms in that industry.

Constant returns to scale A production situation in which output changes in equal proportion to a change in the scale of inputs.

Consumer goods Economic goods that are directly utilized by the consuming public.

Consumer Price Index (CPI) An index that compares the price of a group of 400 basic commodities and services used by an average family of four.

Consumption The use of a good or service.

Cooperative A type of business enterprise owned primarily by the people who use it or buy from it.

Corporation A separate legal entity apart from its owners or shareholders.

Cost-push inflation Inflation characterized by a spiral of wage cost increases and price increases.

Credit money Money in which the intrinsic value of the material content is less than the monetary value.

Cross elasticity of demand The relationship between the quantity demanded of one product compared with the change in price of some other product.

Cyclical fluctuations Changes in the level of business activity that come about regardless of the trend, seasonal, or irregular forces.

Decreasing returns to scale A production situation in which output changes less than proportionately to a change in the scale of inputs.

Deficit balance of payments A balance in which payments to foreigners exceed payments from foreigners.

Degressive tax rate A tax rate that increases at a decreasing rate as the size of the base increases.

Demand A schedule of the quantities of a good that purchasers will buy at different prices at a given time.

Demand curve A curve that indicates the number of units of a good or service that consumers will buy at various prices at a given time.

Demand deposits Bank checking deposits.

Demand-pull inflation (excess-demand inflation) Inflation that occurs when the total demand for goods and services exceeds the available supply of goods and services in the short run.

Demonetizing the debt A decrease in the money supply that could result when federal debt is paid off.

Depression The period in which the level of business activity has dropped as far as it is going to drop in a particular cycle.

Derivative deposit A loan in the form of a bank deposit.

Derived demand The demand for a good or service that grows out of the desire to satisfy the demand for some other good or service.

Direct tax A tax, such as an income tax, that cannot be shifted.

Discount rate The interest rate at which banks may borrow funds from the Federal Reserve Banks.

Discounts A method by which a bank may borrow from the Fed by rediscounting its customers' notes or other eligible commercial paper.

Discretionary income Income remaining after required and necessary spending takes place. Income over which one has a choice to spend or not to spend.

Diseconomies of scale Scale of operations beyond the optimum scale, causing the long-run *ATC* to rise.

Disposable personal income (DPI) Personal income minus personal taxes.

Distribution The allocation of the total product among the factors of production.

Division of labor The breakdown and simplification of jobs.

Double coincidence of wants In a barter economy, the need to find someone who wants something that a trader has in exchange for something that person has that the trader wants.

Economic good An object that is material, useful, scarce, and transferable.

Economic policy Guide for action taken under a given set of circumstances.

Economic services Nonmaterial activities that are useful, scarce, and transferable.

Economic theory Rules and principles of economics that serve as a guide for action under a given set of circumstances.

Economics A science that is concerned with the production, distribution, and consumption of goods and services.

Economies of scale Any scale of operations up to and including the optimum scale, or any scale or size of operations that results in a lower average cost curve.

Economizing The process of applying scarce resources in an endeavor to satisfy unlimited wants.

Effect of a tax An economic consequence of the payment of the tax.

Effective demand The actual demand for goods and services by both consumers and businesses.

Elastic demand When the price changes, the quantity sold changes by a greater percentage than the price changed and so the elasticity is numerically greater than 1. Also, if price changes and total revenue moves in the opposite direction from the price change.

Embargo A complete cessation of trade between nations or in particular products.

Employed civilian labor force The difference between the civilian labor force and the unemployed.

Employment multiplier The ratio of the total increase in employment to a primary increase in employment that results from any increase in effective demand.

Endogenous forces Those elements within the very sphere of business activity itself.

Entrepreneur A person who organizes a business enterprise and assumes the risk.

Entrepreneurship The act of organizing and assuming the risk of a business enterprise.

Equilibrium A stable flow of economic activity.

Equilibrium price The price at which the quantity demanded equals the quantity supplied.

Excess reserve Any reserve that a bank may have over and above the legal required reserve.

Exchange The process of trading the excess of specialized commodities over and above the needs of the individuals who produce them to others for goods required or desired.

Exchange controls The establishment, usually by government, of monetary exchange rates between two national currencies.

Exogenous forces Those elements usually considered as being outside the normal scope of business activity.

Explicit costs Expenditures for production that result from agreements or contracts.

Export subsidy The payment of money or some other benefit to encourage the exports of certain goods.

Factors of production Labor, land, capital, and entrepreneurship.

Family A group of two or more persons living in the same dwelling who are related by birth, marriage, or adoption.

Favorable balance of trade A trade balance in which exports exceed imports.

Federal Funds Market A fairly well-organized market where interbank borrowing takes place.

Fiat money Money backed up by the promise of the government to redeem it or to exchange it for other types of money.

Fiscal drag A budget surplus that may have a dampening effect on the economy.

Fiscal stimulus A deficit budget that stimulates economic activity.

Fixed costs Those costs that remain constant as output varies.

Floating rate An exchange rate that is not fixed.

Flow-of-funds system of national accounts A system that measures payment of all transactions in the economy that occurred as a result of cash payments or extensions of credit.

Form utility The improvement or increase in the usefulness of a commodity by changing its form or shape.

Franchise A government-granted monopoly given to a firm to supply a particular type of service.

Free enterprise capitalistic system (market economy) An economy in which the decisions about what and how much to produce, and the manner in which goods and services are to be allocated, are made primarily by individuals and firms in the economy.

Free good A good that lacks the element of scarcity and, therefore, has no price.

Frictional unemployment Unemployment because of job terminations by employees, discharges, or relocation.

Full-bodied money Money in which the intrinsic value of the material content is equal to the monetary value (face value).

Full-employment budget A measure of the potential revenue and expenditure that would result if full employment existed.

Full-employment unemployment rate The rate of unemployment that can be expected from normal frictional unemployment in the labor force.

General controls Instruments or measures through which the Fed can control bank credit. General controls affect the overall supply of money.

Gold standard A monetary system in which a nation's money supply is backed by holdings of gold.

Gross national product (GNP) The current market value of the total goods and services produced by our nation's economy over a given period of time.

GNP implicit price deflators An index used for converting GNP and related data from current dollar figures to constant dollar figures.

Household A unit that includes all persons living in the same dwelling who are related by blood, marriage, or adoption.

Impact of a tax The initial money burden entailed by the payment of the tax.

Implicit or imputed costs Expenditures that are attributable to the use of one's own factors in the production process.

Import quota A maximum amount of a particular good that may be imported.

Incidence of a tax The point at which the burden of the tax ultimately rests.

Income A flow concept; the total value of the goods and services produced over a period of time.

Income effect The substitution of leisure for work when after-tax income is raised because the individual is able to reach his or her target income with less work.

Income elasticity of demand The relationship between changing income and changes in demand for a particular good or service.

Increasing returns to scale A production situation in which output changes more than proportionately to a change in the scale of inputs.

Indirect tax A tax that can be shifted.

Individual supply The quantities of the good that an individual or firm stands ready to sell at various prices.

Inelastic demand A relative change in price results in a smaller relative change in quantity sold. Also, if price changes and total revenue moves in the same direction as the price change.

Inflation A persistent increase in the price level.

Innovation theory According to this theory, business cycles are caused by innovations in the form of new products, new methods, new machines, or new techniques.

Input-output tables A table showing the value of inputs and outputs of various industries in the economy.

International monetary fund (IMF) An organization that attempts to stabilize exchange rates by providing temporary assistance to nations with deficit balances-of-payments problems.

Investment Spending on capital goods.

Investment tax wedge A tax that causes a gap between the amount paid by a borrower for funds and the income received by the lender.

Irregular or random fluctuations Changes in economic activity occurring from some unexpected or unusual event.

Labor The time and the effort of human beings involved in the production process.

Labor force participation rate The percentage of the total population in the labor force.

Labor tax wedge A tax, usually a payroll tax, that causes a gap between the cost to hire a worker and the actual wage received by the worker.

Laffer curve A graph showing the relationship between tax rates and tax revenues.

Lagging indicators A group of 7 indexes whose turning points occur after the turning points for the general level of business activity have been reached.

Laissez-faire A policy of nongovernment intervention. A policy of government "hands off" in the economic activities of the individuals and businesses.

Land A term that includes not only real estate but also all the resources of the land, sea, and air.

Law of diminishing marginal productivity, or diminishing returns As additional units of a factor of production are combined with fixed quantities of other factors, a point will be reached where the increase in output resulting from the use of an additional unit of that factor becomes smaller.

Leading indicators A group of 12 indexes whose upward and downward turning points generally precede the peaks and troughs of general business activity.

Liquid assets Assets that include United States savings bonds, savings accounts, and checking accounts, but exclude currency.

Liquidity preference The desire to hold assets in the form of cash.

Long run A period of time in which all factors of production, including machinery, buildings, and other capital items, are variable.

Macroeconomics The part of the study of economics that deals with the aggregates of economics, such as total production, total employment, and the general price level.

Major cycles Changes in total economic activity that show a wide and deep fluctuation in business activity.

Marginal cost The increase (decrease) in the total cost resulting from the production of one more (less) unit of output.

Marginal efficiency of capital (MEC) The expected rate of return on investment, or the expected profit from a given investment.

Marginal product The increase in total output resulting from an additional unit of input.

Marginal propensity to consume (MPC) The relationship between the last increment of income received by individuals and businesses and the amount of that income spent on consumption.

Marginal revenue The increase (decrease) in total revenue that results from the sale of one more (less) unit of output.

Market demand The total quantity of a good that would be bought in the aggregate by individuals and firms at each of several prices at a given time.

Market supply The total quantities of the good that sellers stand ready to sell at different prices at a given time.

Member banks Commercial banks that belong to the Federal Reserve System.

Mesoeconomics Study of economics as a set of dynamically interrelated sectors and industries.

Metallic money A special type of commodity money in which some metal, such as gold, silver, or copper, is used.

Microeconomics The part of the study of economics that deals with the economic problems of the individual, the firms, and the industry.

Minor cycles Changes in total economic activity of relatively mild intensity in which the fluctuations are noticeable but not severe.

Mixed economy An economy that contains a mixture of perfect and imperfect competition and both regulated and nonregulated enterprise.

Monetizing the debt An increase in the money supply that results when banks purchase new government securities by creating credit.

Money Anything that is commonly accepted in exchange for other goods and services.

Money income Income derived from the production of goods and services.

Monopolistic competition A market condition in which there are a relatively large number of firms supplying a similar but differentiated product, with each firm having a limited degree of control over price.

Monopsonistic competition A condition in which there are many purchasers who offer differentiated conditions to sellers.

Monopsony A condition in which there is only one buyer for a good or service.

Moral suasion A host of different measures that the Federal Reserve uses to influence the activities of member banks.

Multiple expansion of bank credit The process of expanding the money supply by making loans in the form of demand deposits.

Multiplier The description of the increase in total income resulting from an increase in investment or government spending.

Multiplier effect The spending and respending of income that generates more income.

National income (NI) The total factor costs of the goods and the services produced by the nation's economy. Also it is equivalent to the earnings or income of the owners of the factors of production that were used in producing the GNP.

Net national product (NNP) GNP minus capital consumption allowance and indirect business taxes.

New Federalism A program designed to transfer, or return, numerous social and economic functions from the federal level to the state and local government level.

Nominal profit That amount of profit that is neither excessive nor minimal but is the amount necessary to induce the entrepreneur to stay in business.

Nontariff barriers Nontax measures, such as import quotas, embargoes, export subsidies, and exchange controls.

Normative economics That area of economics dealing with what ought to be.

Oligopoly A market condition in which relatively few firms produce identical or similar products.

Oligopsony A situation in which a few consumers dominate the market.

Open-market operations The purchase and sale of securities by the Fed in the open market.

Opportunity cost The amount of payment or cost necessary to attract a given factor of production away from a similar or the next best opportunity for employment.

Optimum scale of operation Scale or size of operation at which the lowest point on the average cost curve is attained.

Overhead The aggregate of the items of fixed cost.

Paper money Money in the form of bills and notes.

Partnership An association of two or more persons to carry on as co-owners of a business for profit.

Perfect competition A market condition in which there is perfect information about markets and prices on the part of all buyers and sellers, perfect mobility of the various factors of production, and perfectly free entry into and exit from an industry.

Personal income (PI) The current income received by persons from all sources.

Phillips curve A curve showing the relationship between unemployment and inflation.

Place utility The increased utility that occurs when a good or service has more usefulness in one location than another.

Positive economics That area of economics dealing with what is.

Possession utility The utility that results when the ownership of a good or service is transferred from one person to another.

Price elasticity of demand A measure of the responsiveness of quantity purchased to a change in price.

Price index An index that compares the average of a group of prices in one period of time with the average of the prices of the same group of goods and services in another period.

Primary deposit A deposit that arises when you put money into your checking account.

Prime loan rate The rate at which the individuals and firms with the best collateral can borrow.

Principle of comparative advantage One producer produces that commodity in which that producer has the greater comparative advantage and the other producer produces that commodity in which it has the lesser comparative disadvantage.

Principle of subsidiarity A principle that implies that each higher unit in the economy exists to give assistance to, or to benefit, lesser units.

Privatization The process of shifting or returning economic functions or services performed by the government to the private sector of the economy.

Production The creation or addition of utility.

Production function The relationship between factor inputs and product output.

Profit The incentive for obtaining and using capital goods to produce goods and services that satisfy consumer needs. Also, the excess of revenue over all costs of production.

Progressive tax rate A tax rate that increases as the base increases.

Propensity to consume The percentage of total income spent on consumption.

Proportional tax rate A tax rate that remains the same, regardless of the size of the base.

Prosperity An overall high level of economic activity.

Prudential judgment A judgment based to a large extent upon the knowledge and the experience of the individual.

Public good An economic good to the supplier but a free good to the user.

Pump priming The use of government spending to increase and maintain the flow of goods and services at a higher level.

Pure competition An ideal set of market conditions that assumes that there are many sellers of an identical product, all consumers and sellers are informed about the market and prices, there is free entry into and exit from the market, and no individual seller or consumer can influence price.

Pure monopoly A market condition in which there is only one producer or seller of a commodity.

Pure profit Any amount over and above nominal profit.

Quantity theory of money An attempt to explain the relationship between the quantity of money and the price level.

Rational expectations (Theory of) An economic theory suggesting that individuals and business react according to what they think is going to happen in the future.

Reaganomics The name given to President Reagan's application of supply-side economic policies.

Real GNP GNP divided by implicit price deflators.

Real income The constant dollar value of the goods and services produced. Also, the purchasing power of money income.

Real per capita disposable income Per capita disposable income adjusted for changes in the price level.

Recession A noticeable drop in the level of business activity.

Recovery A rising level of business activity.

Regressive tax rate A tax rate that decreases as the size of the base increases.

Representative money Money, usually paper, that serves in place of metallic money.

Required reserve The amount of reserves that banks must hold against demand deposits.

Roughly coincident indicators A group of six indexes whose turning points usually correspond to the peaks and troughs of general business activity.

Science An organized body of truth, arranged and systematized with reference to general laws or principles.

Seasonal variations Recurring fluctuations in business activity during a given period, usually 1 year.

Selective controls Controls that affect the use of credit for specific purposes such as the purchase of stocks.

Shifting of taxes Passing of the tax burden from one taxpayer to another.

Short run A period of time in which some factors of production are fixed.

Short-run equilibrium price That price which

results from the interaction of demand and supply over a short period of time.

Simple multiplier A ratio of the total increase in income resulting from an increase in total investment or the initial increase in income compared with the initial increase in investment.

Single proprietorship One-person ownership of a firm.

Slumpflation A combination of inflation and a slumping economy.

Social inflation Inflation that results from the increasing demand for government-provided social services.

Special Drawing Rights (SDRs) A form of credit issued by the International Monetary Fund.

Specialization The process by which an individual, a firm, a geographic area, or a nation limits the scope of its productive efforts instead of trying to produce everything that is needed by that unit in the economy.

Specific tariff A tariff in absolute terms, such as 25 cents per pound or per unit of a commodity.

Stagflation Simultaneous recession and inflation.

Structural inflation Inflation that results from the upward mobility and downward rigidity of prices and wages.

Submarginal producers Producers whose costs are greater than their revenue.

Substitution effect When one firm lowers its price and gains an increase in sales at the expense of other firms that did not lower their prices.

Substitution effect The substitution of work for leisure when after-tax income is increased because the value of work relative to leisure is increased.

Supermultiplier A ratio of the total income resulting from the interaction of the multiplier and accelerator to the original increase in investment.

Supply curve A line or curve indicating the number of units of a good or service that will be offered for sale at different prices.

Supply-side economics An economic theory that suggests the need to encourage savings, stimulate investment, and motivate workers

to bring about high employment, stable prices, and economic growth.

Supramarginal producers Producers who have revenue greater than costs and are making a profit.

Tariff A duty or tax levied on foreign imports.

Tariff quota A quota that does not set absolute limits on imports but that places a tax on imports above a certain level.

Tax base The value of the object upon which the tax is levied.

Tax rate The percentage that is multiplied times the tax base to get the total tax that must be paid.

Time utility The utility that occurs when a commodity or service is more useful at one time than at another.

Token money Credit money is frequently referred to as token money. Most coin money in the United States is token money.

Total cost The sum of total fixed and total variable costs at a particular level of production.

Total labor force A measure of all those in the noninstitutional population who are working or are seeking work.

Total revenue The amount of revenue or income received from the sale of a given quantity of goods or services.

Transactions approach The analysis of the quantity theory of money that assumes that any money received generally will be spent directly or indirectly to buy goods and services.

Transfer payment A payment of money for which no current goods or services are produced.

Trend The directional movement of the economy over an extended period of time such as 30 to 50 years.

Underconsumption theories Theories which say that business cycles are caused when, for any number of reasons, all national income is not spent and some goods remain unsold. Total production will be reduced, which in turn reduces employment and income.

Underemployment A condition that occurs when a worker is employed but is not working to full capacity.

Underground, or subterranean, economy The value of goods and services produced for which no monetary transactions take place.

Underinvestment theory A theory that holds that recessions occur because of inadequate investment in the economy.

Unemployed labor force All persons in the labor force seeking work.

Unemployment The number of workers in the labor force who are not currently working, but are seeking work.

Unfavorable balance A trade balance in which imports exceed exports.

Unitary elasticity A given percentage change in price resulting in an equal percentage change in the quantity sold. Also, if price changes and total revenue remains constant.

Utility The ability of a good or service to satisfy a want.

Variable costs Costs of production other than fixed cost, such as labor and materials.

Wage-price spiral Another name for cost-push inflation.

Wealth Things of value owned.

Workable competition A theory that implies that it is not necessary to have all the conditions of pure competition to serve the best interest of the consumer.

INDEX